JOURNEY THROUGH
FRANCE

W·W·NORTON

NEW YORK · LONDON

This edition published by W. W. Norton & Company,
Inc., 500 5th Avenue, New York, New York 10110
http://www.wwnorton.com

ISBN 0-393-32067-7

Produced by AA Publishing, a trading name of
Automobile Association Developments Limited,
whose registered office is Norfolk House, Priestley
Road, Basingstoke, Hampshire RG24 9NY.
Registered number 1878835.

The contents of this book are believed correct at
the time of printing. Nevertheless, the publishers
cannot be held responsible for any errors or
omissions or for changes in the details given in this
book or for the reliance on the information
provided by the same. Assessments of attractions
and locations are based on the authors' own
experience and, therefore, descriptions given in
this guide necessarily contain an element of
subjective opinion which may not reflect the
publisher's opinion or dictate a reader's experience
on another occasion. We have tried to ensure
accuracy in this book, but things do change and we
would be grateful if readers would advise us of any
inaccuracies they may encounter.

Contributors: Janet Beart-Albrecht, Elizabeth
Cruwys, Lisa Davidson, Heidi Ellison, Jed English,
Geoffrey Finch, Teresa Fisher, Cynthia Guttman,
Patricia Kessler Caffrey, Beau Riffenburgh,
Michael Taylor.

Copy editors: Sarah Hudson, Barbara Mellor,
Joan Miller, Pam Stagg

Colour separation by L C Repro & Sons Ltd,
Aldermaston, England
Printed and bound in Italy by G Canale & C SpA

CONTENTS

C O N T E N T S

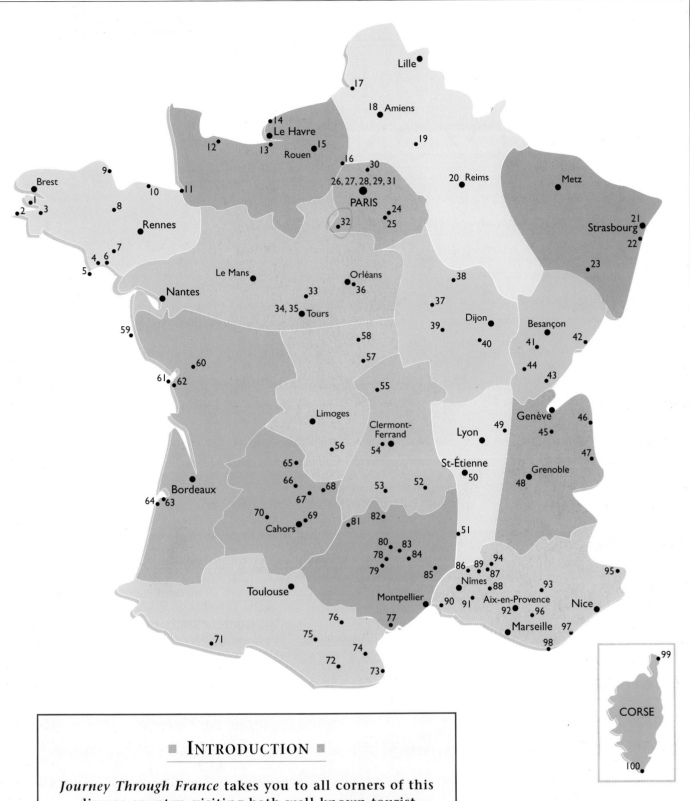

Map labels

Lille
17
18 Amiens
14
Le Havre
19
12
13 Rouen
15
16 30
20 Reims
Metz
9
Brest
26, 27, 28, 29, 31
10 11
PARIS
21
Strasbourg
2
1
3
8
24
22
Rennes
32
25
23
4 6 7
5
Le Mans
Orléans
38
Nantes
33
36
37
34, 35 Tours
39 Dijon
Besançon
59
58
41 42
60
57
44
43
61 62
55
Limoges
Genève 46
49
45
56
Clermont-
Lyon
47
Ferrand
65
54
St-Étienne
Grenoble
66
50
48
68
53 52
Bordeaux
67
64 63
70 69
81 82
51
Cahors
80 83
78 84
94
86 89 87
95
79
85
Nîmes 88
93
Toulouse
Montpellier
90 91 Aix-en-Provence
76
77
92 96 Nice
75
Marseille 97
74
98
72
73
99

CORSE

100

INTRODUCTION

Journey Through France takes you to all corners of this diverse country, visiting both well-known tourist locations and hidden gems. And at every location you can enjoy a tour by car or on foot, and even a canal trip. Use the numbers on the locator map above and the contents pages to find your location.

The symbols on the right are plotted on extracts from IGN sheet maps for general guidance, but plan your routes in advance and check access and opening times of attractions with the tourist office before setting out. Where not shown, map scales are approximately 4cm to 1km for Top 25 maps and 4cm to 10km for the Top 250.

 Start point of walk

 Start point of tour

Route of walk/tour

 Direction of walk/tour

③ Walk/tour point of interest

PRESQU'ÎLE DE CROZON

***N**o one can claim to know Brittany until they have explored this remote and spellbinding peninsula reaching into the Atlantic, with its rolling hills, giddy barren clifftops, sleepy fishing villages and breathtaking coastal views.*

The Presqu'île de Crozon (Crozon peninsula) in Finistère – one of the more traditional corners of Brittany, rich in folklore and Celtic tradition – forms part of the Parc Régional d'Armorique, a 1,100sq km area of protected land, noted for its remarkable beauty and diversity. It is also sufficiently remote to avoid the excesses of tourism.

FROM THE 'MOUNTAINS' TO THE SEA

Taking in the Montagnes d'Arrée (the highest hills in Brittany), with the moors and marshes and the unspoilt forests around Huelgoat, the Parc Régional d'Armorique extends westwards along the Presqu'île de Crozon to embrace the islands of Ouessant and Molène and some of Finistère's most exciting coastal scenery. From the summit of Mènez-Hom – one of the finest viewpoints in this area – all these features can be seen in one immense panorama.

At the northern approach to the peninsula, the pretty harbour town of le Faou basks contentedly in the Faou estuary. To the west, the

attractive village of Landévennec occupies a peaceful promontory on the Aulne estuary, believed to be the site of Brittany's oldest abbey, founded here in about 485 by the Welsh missionary St Gwennolé, then left to decay after the French Revolution.

From the small port of le Fret a regular boat service crosses the Rade de Brest channel to the naval city of Brest, with its harsh, postwar architecture. At the top of the peninsula lies the simple seaside resort and old lobster-fishing port of Camaret-sur-Mer, where the excellent seafood restaurants lining the weatherbeaten quayside make an ideal spot for lunch.

The chapel and naval museum, housed in the Château Vauban, and perched on a natural breakwater protecting the harbour, are well worth a visit.

CAP DE LA CHÈVRE

The town of Crozon, on the south coast, is the gateway to the atmospheric resorts and charming little villages of Cap de la Chèvre at the southwestern point of the peninsula. The seaside town of Morgat once specialised in sardine fishing, but is now a popular family resort with pretty, pastel-coloured houses, a sheltered crescent of silvery-white sand and a bustling yacht marina. From Morgat to the cape, the road runs through the bleakest part of the entire peninsula – an austere landscape of rocks, pine woods and heathland, blasted by the ocean winds and dotted with hamlets huddled together in the sheltered valleys.

ABOVE LEFT: the sheltered harbour of Camaret
BELOW: the isolated headland and beach at Pointe de Dinan

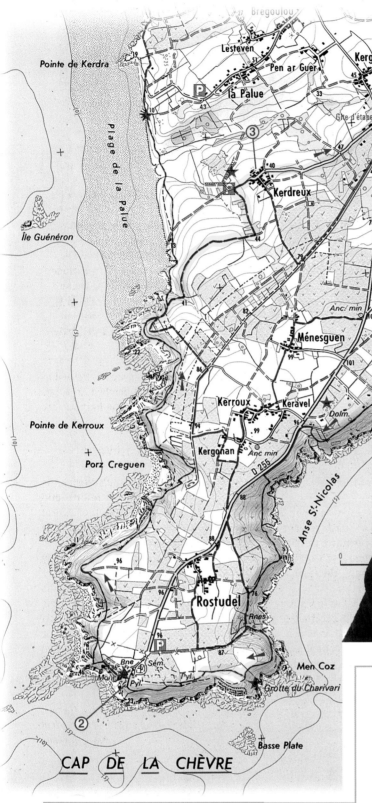

BELOW LEFT: a typical granite gargoyle grimaces from the church at le Faou

Crozon's seafood

While it may not be one of France's greatest gastronomic regions, Brittany is one of the country's foremost fishing regions, which is reflected in the countless cheap, cheerful harbourside bistros of the Crozon peninsula. With the gigantic piles of prawns, crabs and oysters displayed on fishmongers' trays, brought to the early morning *criée* (fish auction) by weathered fishermen dressed in Breton red, you are unlikely to find fresher or more succulent seafood anywhere in France!

W A L K

length of walk: 10km
time: half a day
IGN Top 25: sheet 0418ET

The only way to experience the full, breathtaking power of the Breton coastline's wild beauty is on foot. This dramatic clifftop walk requires steady nerves and dependable, non-slip footwear.

❶ Start in the village of **St-Hernot**, 3km south of Morgat, where the old school houses the Maison des Minéraux, a collection of over 500 mineral specimens taken from the region, showing its great geological wealth and beauty. There is also a delightful medieval church, and opposite is the village store which sells bread, cheese, tomatoes and other picnic fare. Turn left off the D 255 as you enter the village, up a long dirt track in front of the Maison des Minéraux. After about 800m you will reach a T-junction signposted right to Cap de la Chèvre or left to Morgat. Turn left, through some trees. After a few minutes, just as you emerge from the woodland, you will notice a small, wooden sign to the right, marked 'sentier côtier' (coastal path). This leads through gorse and scrub to the cliff edge and the craggy **Pointe de St-Hernot**, which is fringed by a small, sandy beach.

Turn right at the cliffs along a narrow, single-file path towards the cape. The coastal path, clearly way-marked by yellow circles painted on strategic boulders all the way to the cape, follows one of the most spectacular stretches of the Breton seaboard, with its deeply indented coastline sheltering tiny coves and white, sandy beaches. The path itself is sometimes very steep, passing through pinewoods, along the very edge of the cliffs (not for those who suffer from vertigo) and across barren heathland, brambles and bracken, flecked with bright yellow gorse and mauve heather.

❷ The **Cap de la Chèvre**, marked by a French Navy signal station, offers a sweeping panorama which takes in the most westerly points of Finistère. To the south are **Pointe du Van** and **Pointe du Raz**, while to the north are **Pointe de Penhir**, **Pointe de St-Mathieu** and the **Tas de Pois** (Pile of Peas), a dramatic stack of rocks off Camaret-sur-Mer, teeming with gulls, fulmars, cormorants, guillemots and stormy petrels. Also at the Cap is a monument, representing the wing of an aircraft, which commemorates those aircrew of *Aéronautique Navale* killed or missing in active service in the Atlantic.

Stay on the *sentier côtier* and make your way round the cape on to the bleaker, more exposed Atlantic seaboard, with its towering clifftops of stunted heathland and massive ocean rollers pounding the jagged rocks far below.

❸ After about 1.5km, look out for a signpost inland to the village of **Kerdreux**, a charming hotch-potch of flower-decked stone cottages. From here, a winding country lane returns to St-Hernot.

BRETAGNE

POINTE DU RAZ

Who has never dreamed of journeying to the end of the earth, of gazing out to sea from a deserted clifftop knowing that, beyond the few islands on the horizon, lies nothing but the vastness of the ocean? Such a magical place really does exist – at Pointe du Raz, France's finis terrae.

Heroes of the sea

The islanders of the Île-de-Sein are a proud, resilient people, with a brave history of rescuing sailors from shipwrecks. Their most recent moment of glory dates from 18 June 1940, when the entire male population set sail for England, in response to General de Gaulle's rallying broadcast from London, inviting the French nation to support him. After the war, de Gaulle honoured four great centres of resistance – Paris, Nantes, Grenoble and this tiny Breton island.

The Cap Sizun, France's most westerly region – wild and remote, rich in folklore and Celtic tradition, and once known as *finis terrae* (land's end) – was for many centuries independent from France. This part of the country still retains a strong personality of its own, especially in Cornouaille, the area of southern Finistère whose name recalls the Cornish origins of the early Celts who sailed from Britain to settle here. Breton is still a living language, more festivals and processions flourish here than in any other region, and it is not unusual to see older citizens dressed in regional costume, the women often wearing their distinctive lacy *coiffé* head-dresses.

Cornouaille also boasts some of Brittany's most dramatic coastal scenery, with barren, splintered rocky promontories and sheer, rugged cliffs which are home to great colonies of seabirds. The further west you travel, the bleaker and more austere the seascapes become. At the westernmost tip of mainland France, the Pointe du Raz, it really does feel like the end of the earth.

There are excellent views along this rocky stretch of coastline at Pointe du Raz

▪ ÎLE-DE-SEIN ▪

The views out to sea from the Pointe du Raz are dazzling. The Île-de-Sein, France's final outpost, lies 9km offshore

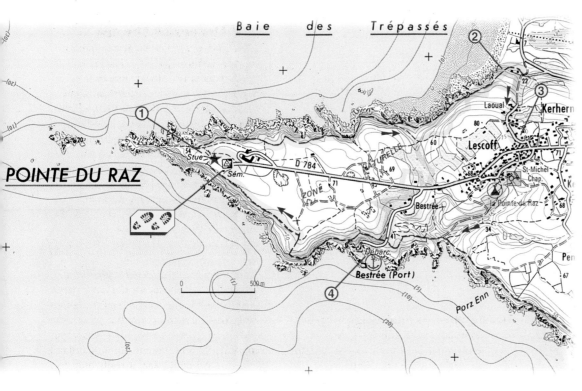

POINTE DU RAZ

Baie des Trépassés

BELOW RIGHT: wood carvings at Pointe du Raz's museum

ABOVE: walking the cliffs of Cap Sizun

across a notoriously dangerous strait which, according to an old saying, 'no one passes without fear or sorrow'. This island – a flat, treeless sliver of land 2km long and in places just 100m wide – is believed to have been the last refuge of the Druids in Brittany.

▪ RESTORING NATURE ▪

Nearly one million visitors from all over Europe come each year to marvel at the breathtaking views of the cape. This intense pressure has inevitably trampled the vegetation and eroded the landscape, so a massive rehabilitation programme has recently been launched, moving the shops, cafés and car park away from the promontory, opening a new tourist office and heritage centre, realigning footpaths and restoring damaged vegetation, in a successful attempt to restore the heathland and return the cape to its former natural splendour.

The lighthouse on Pointe de Raz rises above a sea of gorse bushes, which set the cliffs ablaze with colour in the spring

WALK

length of walk: 6km
time: half a day
IGN Top 25: sheet 04190

The thin, rocky finger of Pointe du Raz reaches out to sea like the prow of a ship. This walk takes you along the edge of its towering clifftops, a dizzy vantage point from which the plunging, foaming and crashing of the sea on the rocks far below is an unforgettable sight, especially on a windy day. Wear sturdy, non-slip shoes or, preferably, walking boots.

❶ Set out from the car park, past a chain of gift shops, cafés and the tourist office, towards **Pointe du Raz**, where the gulls swooping and swirling overhead escort you along well-marked paths towards this famous 'land's end'. The site is marked by two lighthouses, la Plate and la Vieille, on a distant jagged rock offshore, marking the tip of the point. There is also a sad statue of **Notre-Dame des Naufragés** (Our Lady of the Shipwrecked), with a sailor at her feet. Walk round the point and head eastwards along the northern coast of **Cap Sizun**. The route follows a narrow, waymarked coastal path on the jagged cliff edge, through a bleak seascape of coarse grass and scrub, relieved occasionally by a splash of bright golden gorse or a clump of purple heather. After a while, the path skirts the edge of a series of deep chasms, including the terrifying **Enfer de Plogoff** (Plogoff Inferno), where the waves crash deafeningly against the sheer walls.

❷ Before long, the vegetation becomes more lush, leading to a huge expanse of flat sand – the **Baie des Trépassés** (Bay of Dead Souls), renowned for the many legends that have grown up around its sinister name. It is believed that dead bodies were once loaded onto boats here, bound for the Île-de-Sein, a former Druidic burial site. Another tradition, backed up by countless tales of ghostly riders emerging from the sea, and the sound of hymns and church bells ringing out from the deep on feast days, is that the submerged 5th-century city of **Ys** stands in this bay. However, the most likely – and equally melancholy – explanation is that, because of the prevailing winds, the bodies of ship-wrecked sailors from Pointe du Raz tend to be washed ashore here.

❸ Carry on up a steep path into the village of Lescoff, a huddle of typical low stone cottages with steep, grey slate roofs and wind-blown gardens. Cross the mainroad, following signs to the village chapel, and continue down a rough track back onto the well-trodden coastal path.

❹ Head back towards the cape until you reach the tiny fishing port of Bestrée. From here, take a lane which leads back to the car park.

LOCRONAN

Visiting Locronan, one of the prettiest villages in France, is like winding the clock back to the Renaissance, when it was one of the most successful weaving towns in Brittany. Today, its marvellously preserved buildings remain imbued with the history of the rich merchants who created them.

Of all Breton weaving towns, Locronan has retained the most evidence of its former wealth, derived mainly from the manufacture of sailcloth. In its main square, flanked by a large church and a magnificent assembly of Renaissance houses built by rich clothiers, the 18th-century cloth hall, the low houses on rue Moal where the weavers lived, and the ancient loom on display in the town museum all testify to the importance of the cloth trade.

■ GOLDEN AGE ■

During the 15th and 16th centuries, Brittany became rich by manufacturing and selling cloth made from flax and hemp. Locronan's weavers were the first to make *Olonne*, a kind of hempen cloth which rapidly became much sought after as sailcloth. Before long the town was supplying sails to the French, English and Spanish navies. However, when Louis XIV abolished Locronan's monopoly on sailcloth, Vitré, Rennes and Fougères took up the

Locronon's Troménie

No other region of France can boast such a profusion of crosses, crucifixes and chapels as Brittany, all annually respected in the religious processions unique to the region, called *pardons*. Although these provide an excellent opportunity to admire the traditional costumes, they are by no means intended as a tourist attraction, but rather as solemn expressions of a deep religious faith. They take place all over Brittany, especially between May and September. Best-known is the Troménie in Locronan, but equally spectacular are the *pardon* of St Anne at St-Anne-d'Auray, the *pardon* of St Yves in Tréguier, the *pardon* of the Sea in Dinard and the torch-lit processions across the sand dunes at Ste-Anne-la-Palud.

trade and the town's economy collapsed. As a direct consequence, time stood still in Locronan, leaving as a legacy of its heyday a remarkable collection of ancient buildings which have now been occupied as high-quality craft and antiques shops.

A lace stall displays its wares at Quimper

The cobbled main square of well-preserved Locronan

Quimper and *crêpes*

Brittany's great gastronomic speciality is undoubtedly the pancake – either delicious *galettes*, made with buckwheat flour and salted butter and filled with ham, cheese and other wholesome savoury delights, or sweet *crêpes*, made with wheat flour and filled with sugar, honey or melted chocolate. In Quimper, every street smells of pancakes, for this is the *crêpe*-making capital of the world, and home of France's top *crêpier*. There is even a museum devoted to the history of *crêpes* near the aptly-named Place au Beurre (Butter Square).

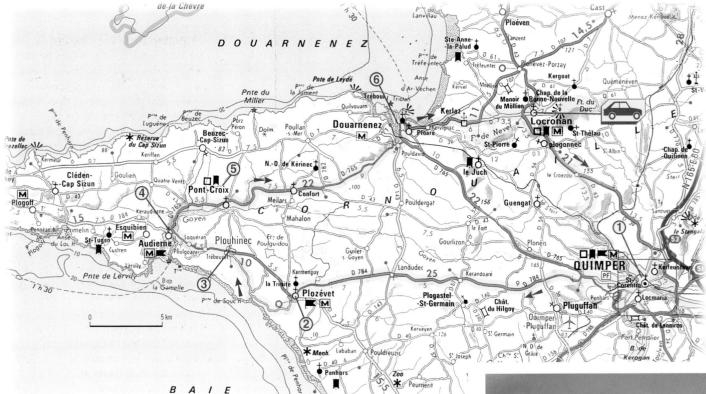

▪ THE TROMÉNIES ▪

The village's most striking feature is the 15th-century church of St-Ronan in the main square and the adjoining Chapelle de Penity, where the patron saint is entombed. St Ronan was a 5th-century Irish bishop and miracle-working hermit who reputedly suffered considerable harassment from local Druids. After his death, Locronan became an important place of pilgrimage. The tradition still continues. On the second Sunday in July the town hosts a *pardon* – known as the *petite Troménie* – when a spectacular procession of villagers in Breton costume, bearing crosses, statues and banners, ascends the hill, re-enacting a time-hallowed walk that, according to tradition, the saint took daily, barefoot.

Every sixth year (2001, 2007 etc), this procession culminates in a week-long festival, the *grande Troménie*, when pilgrims circle the hill stopping at 12 points representing the Stations of the Cross, where each parish exhibits its saints and reliquaries. The route follows the boundary of a long-vanished Benedictine priory, built on the site of a forest sacred to the Druids, and founded in the 11th century as a retreat, hence the name of the *pardon* – *Tro Minihy* (tour of the monastery or retreat) or *Troménie*. The town museum is devoted to *pardons*, together with ancient crafts, costumes and paintings by local artists.

The harbour at Douarnenez, where fish is the raison d'être

T O U R

length of tour: 124km
time: one day
IGN Top 250: sheet 105

The ancient duchy of Cornouaille and the Pays Bigourden capture all that is most picturesque and traditional in this historic region. From the old capital of Quimper to the quaint fishing villages and colourful ports of the coast, this drive takes you through the heart of traditional Brittany.

❶ Setting out from **Locronan**, turn left at the roundabout just outside the village onto the D 63. Continue through lush, rolling countryside to **Quimper**, capital of the ancient duchy of Cornouaille, the oldest city in Brittany, with a rich historical and cultural heritage. Quimper is world-renowned for its pancakes and its distinctive, traditional hand-painted pottery. Leave Quimper on the D 765, heading to Audierne. After about 5km turn left on to the D 784 signposted to Plozévet, Plouhinec and Audierne.

❷ Pass through the village of Landudec and on to **Plozévet**, where the church has a notable 15th-century porch and a sacred fountain.

❸ Turn left in Plozévet, along the **Chemin de la Corniche par Pors Poulhan** (coastal route via Pors Poulhan). The lane, edged with drystone walls, drops down to the water's edge as it runs through this small maritime community. There are delightful whitewashed cottages dotted about on the hillside, all facing the sea and quaint fishing harbour, which is full of brightly coloured traditional craft and guarded by a small lighthouse. From here, the road climbs up to the village of **Plouhinec**, with its oversized church and spiky spire.

❹ Back on the main road, it is a further 5km to **Audierne**, at the mouth of the River Goyen, known for its abundant bird population. Audierne is a splendid town – half-resort, half-port – with houses ranged round a bay and boats moored outside its shops and restaurants. This region, the Pays Bigourden, stretching inland from the bay of Audierne, is one of the most traditional parts of Brittany, where *crêpes* and cider, Breton costumes and Celtic music are still very much a part of daily life.

❺ Leave Audierne on the D 765 signposted to Douarnenez. The road winds steeply above the river until it reaches Pont-Croix. This is a delightful small town where medieval houses cluster round a tall-spired church and spacious main square on the hill and also tumble down to an old river crossing, once a small port.

❻ Continue on the D 765 to **Douarnenez**, a characterful old fishing town with a wonderful bay (the largest stretch of sheltered water in France) and a rich maritime heritage. This is vividly illustrated in an excellent maritime museum, housed in a series of boat-sheds on the quayside, with floating exhibits moored alongside. The D 7 from Douarnenez to Locronan provides dazzling views looking back over the waterfront of Douarnenez, before touching on the water's edge, then climbs once more through the village of Kerlaz and on through the picturesque countryside returning to Locronan.

CARNAC

*N*owhere else boasts as many prehistoric monuments as Brittany. Even the words used internationally to describe them – dolmens (table stones), menhirs (long stones) and cromlechs (curved stones) – are Breton. The majority are clustered in and around Carnac, making it the world's premier megalithic site.

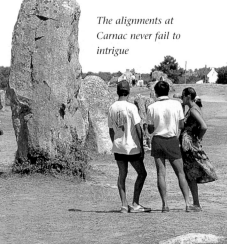

A statue of St-Cornély stands in a niche between two paintings of farm animals on a wall of Carnac's church

Carnac is thought to have been continuously inhabited longer than anywhere else in the world – since at least 5700 BC. Its several thousand remaining megaliths long pre-date Stonehenge, the Pyramids, Knossos and the great Egyptian temples of a similar name at Karnak. Their most intriguing constructions – the alignments – take visitors to the heart of Brittany's mysteries and legends: over 3,000 standing

Unsolved mystery

The astounding alignments of Carnac defy explanation. Most experts agree that they originally had religious, astronomical or ritual purpose – or perhaps all three – but still the mystery remains unsolved. Local legend has it that they were Roman soldiers, miraculously turned to stone by Carnac's patron saint, Cornély, as he fled for his life from Rome in the 3rd century. US marines in World War II allegedly believed them to be German anti-tank devices. As Gustave Flaubert remarked, 'Carnac has had more nonsense written about it than it has standing stones.' But the fact that their origins have been lost in the mists of time greatly adds to their mystery.

stones dating from 5000 BC to 2000 BC, laid out in precisely spaced rows and stretching almost endlessly, punctuated by great burial tumuli. Their sheer size raises the question of how and where they were quarried, and how they were transported and erected in such regular order by people who had only the most rudimentary implements. Even more intriguing – what was their ancient significance?

■ ASTERIX AND OBELISKS ■

Countless other monuments lie dotted around the countryside, including the Tumulus de Kercado, the burial place of a Neolithic chieftain and one of the most complete surviving barrows, used by insurgent Breton royalists during the French Revolution

The alignments at Carnac never fail to intrigue

The panelled vaulting of the parish church at Carnac is decorated with paintings

as a hiding place. North of the tumulus stands the mighty Géant de Manïo, a huge dolmen between two sets of alignments that apparently points the way to the Quadrilatère, a strange square-shaped group of menhirs. Visit the sites at dusk or dawn, when the visitors have gone: shrouded with mist in the half-light, these mysterious stones still seem to retain a little of their ancient power.

■ SHOPPING, SAINTS AND SANDS ■

Just south of the megaliths, the town of Carnac is one of the liveliest resorts in the popular Morbihan holiday region. It is divided into two distinctive sections – the smart seaside district, Carnac-Plage, and the attractive old town, Carnac-Ville, centred on the 17th-century church of St-Cornély, whose statue can be seen on the façade between two oxen. St-Cornély is the patron saint of farm animals, and the ancient

tradition of bringing diseased cattle here to be cured, dating back to Roman times, is still honoured at the saint's *pardon* on the second Sunday in September.

The Romans enjoyed heated seawater baths at Carnac; now an ultra-modern Thalassotherapy Centre flanks the salt-water lake near the town centre.

Carnac-Plage lies a short distance south of Carnac-Ville and – in contrast to the standing stones – the lines here are more horizontal as row upon row of people lie tanning themselves on the golden sands of Morbihan Bay. Carnac-Plage boasts a total of six beaches, the best being the lengthy Grande Plage with its safe swimming and sailing marina, or the quieter and smaller Men Du to the east. Fringing the beaches are neat rows of smart villas and small, seaside hotels, a plethora of tourist shops, crowded bars and restaurants, and several lively night spots, making Carnac one of the most popular resorts in Brittany and the ideal choice for a family holiday.

A wide expanse of golden sand at Carnac-Plage

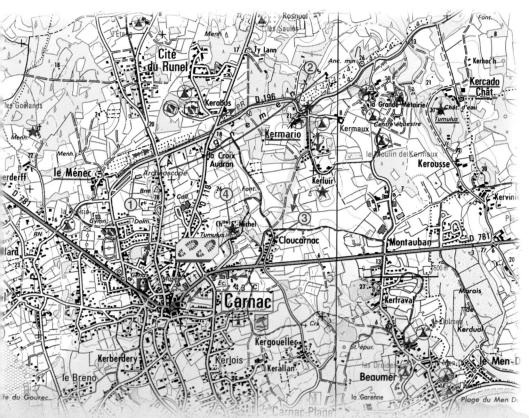

WALK

length of walk: 5km
time: half a day with visits
IGN Top 25: sheet 0821OT

The best way to visit the alignments is on foot or by bicycle (for hire from Carnac-Plage). Go early or late in the day, and allow ample time if you can for a visit to the fascinating prehistory museum in Carnac-Ville, which helps to set the stones in context and establish the enormous time-scale involved.

❶ Start at **place de la Chapelle** in the town centre, by the **Musée de Prehistoire James Miln-Zacharie le Rouzic**. This, the world's most important museum devoted to the megalithic era, is named after the Scot James Miln, who began excavations in Carnac, and local Zacharie Le Rouzic, who supported his work. Not only does the museum attempt to unravel the mysteries surrounding these extraordinary monuments, but it also contains a treasure trove of megalithic artefacts, including weapons, tools, jewellery, reconstructed burial places, decorated pottery and engraved stones.

❷ Head southwards past the tourist office, leaving the church on your right. Take the first right, then right again almost immediately into rue du Courdiec. Continue straight across rue de Bellevue (signposted to les Alignements). After a short distance, on the left is a menhir marked by a cross, and to the right, distant views of **Chapelle de St-Michel** which crowns a vast tumulus covering several ancient burial chambers. Turn left at the next crossroads and walk alongside the **Alignements du Ménec** (Place of Remembrance) to the **Archeoscope**, a 25-minute audio-visual show which magically winds the clocks back to Neolithic times by means of special effects.

❸ Turn right out of the Archeoscope and return to the crossroads. Continue straight over, following the line of the megaliths. At the traffic lights, turn left then immediately right. A little further on reach the **Alignements de Kermario** (Place of the Dead), the second of four sets of alignments which are all displayed in a scale model of the area in the information centre. The Kermario alignments alone are 1,200m long, with 1,029 menhirs in ten rows.

❹ Continue along the road for a couple of minutes, looping round the monuments, and take the second turning to the right, clearly marked Chemin du Kerluir. Turn right down a dusty, narrow lane to the right, the Chemin de Groux er Gwen, which soon becomes a grassy track. Follow the path towards la chapelle de St-Michel, on top of a small hill, until you reach the hamlet of **Cloucarnac** on the outskirts of town. Turn right on to the D 781 (route de la Trinité sur Mer). A steep lane to the right curves up to **la Chapelle de St-Michel**, offering fine views over the town and many of its megaliths. Return to the main road. Continue straight across at the traffic lights, following signs to Centre du Bourg, to return to place de la Chapelle.

BELLE-ÎLE

***T**he aptly named Belle-Île is not only the largest of Brittany's myriad islands and the one with the richest and most turbulent history, but it is also the most picturesque, celebrated for its quaint, pastel-coloured resorts and its surprisingly diverse scenery.*

The island's history is long and varied: its first settlers were Celts from the western fringes of Europe, followed by Romans from the south (who called it Vindilis). Later, Saxons settled there, then Normans. During the centuries that followed, the English repeatedly invaded, frequently holding the island for lengthy periods of time.

■ A TURBULENT PAST ■

One of Belle-Île's most interesting historical phases was during the mid-17th century, when it was held by Nicolas Fouquet, Louis XIV's sly Superintendent of Finance, who fortified the island and even had a private navy stationed here, ready to strike against the 'Sun King' should he defraud the state. Fouquet was eventually imprisoned by the jealous king for rashly building a private palace at Vaux-le-Vicomte, near Paris, more lavish than Louis's

ABOVE: lobster ports line the quayside in the sheltered port of Sauzon

Island celebrities

From the mid-19th century, Belle-Île has been popular as a working retreat for artists and writers. Dumas, Flaubert, Proust, Gide and Colette all visited on occasions, as did composer Albert Roussel; for a while it was home of Belle Epoque actress Sarah Bernhardt. Former president François Mitterrand was a frequent visitor. The island was also a source of inspiration for artists including Matisse, Derain and Monet who, during a lengthy stay in Bangor in 1886, painted Cosquet and the famous offshore Aiguilles (needles) at Port Coton (above) over 30 times, declaring of the island, 'The more time I spend here, the more I am filled with wonder.'

BELOW: The dark and rugged coastline of Belle-Île

T O U R

length of tour: 33km
time: half a day
IGN Top 250: sheet 105

Everywhere on Belle-Ile there is something of interest, from tremendous fortificaptions and lighthouses to quaint fishing villages, from sheltered sandy coves to the seething maelstrom of the Côte Sauvage. This leisurely but hilly car tour (or bicycle ride) takes in the southern part of this remarkable world apart.

❶ From place de la République on the waterfront at **le Palais**, avenue Carnot leads straight out of town on the D 190 to Bangor. As you leave Le Palais, you pass through two ancient gateways, Porte Vauban and Porte Bangor. Turn off almost immediately to the left on to the D 30a, which winds through the lush landscapes and picturesque hamlets of Borthélo and Port Salio, until you reach **Bordardoué**. Here a small lane takes you to the shore, where a door in the former fortificaptions leads to a beautiful, sheltered, sandy beach.

❷ Return to Bordardoué and turn left, back on to the D 30a. The road descends towards Port-Yorc'h, another delightful beach, hidden between two craggy points. The road runs beside Les Grands Sables, the island's biggest beach, then up to **Pointe de Kerdonis**, with its fine views of the Morbihan coast, Rade du Palais and the neighbouring islands of Houat and Hoëdic (the names mean 'duck' and 'duckling' in Breton). A lighthouse here commands the narrow passage between Hoëdic and Belle-Île.

❸ Continue on the coast road to Bordehouat, passing Port An-Dro, a sandy beach off a small valley where English forces landed in 1761, prior to the Treaty of Paris. Turn left in the village, then take the second left again to the town of **Locmaria**. The church of Notre-Dame-de-Boistord here is built on the spot where a massive elm tree once grew. According to legend, when the tree was felled to replace a broken mast, it made a fearsome cracking noise, striking terror into the hearts of those who were cutting it. The town still has a reputation among islanders as a place of sorcery. A downhill road to the right of the church leads to Port-Maria, a deep cleft in the rocks which shelter a small sandy beach.

❹ Return to Locmaria and take the main road (D 25) signposted to Sauzon, le Palais and Bangor. After 1.6km, turn left at a crossroads known as les Quatre Chemins (the Four Paths) onto the D 190a to **Bangor**, an attractive town which takes its name from the religious settlement or *bangor* founded by the first Celtic monks to settled here. From Bangor, cut across country to Cosquet, then left to rejoin the D 190 to Kervilahouen, from where you take the road to the **Grand Phare**, Belle-Île's massive lighthouse, built in 1835. Its light is one of the most powerful in Europe, visible far out to sea, and its viewing platform offers an unforgettable view of the entire island.

❺ Return to Kervilahouen and continue straight up the D 190 towards le Palais. Turn right onto the D 25 just after the aerodrome as far as les Quatre Chemins. Turn left to rejoin the D 190 back to le Palais.

own at Versailles. Following Fouquet's departure, Belle-Île passed to the French Crown and the great military architect Vauban was sent to make it impregnable.

Another notable event took place in 1763 when the island, then in the hands of the English, was exchanged for Menorca in the Treaty of Paris, and thus transferred once and for all back to the French.

■ THE ISLAND TODAY ■

Today the tranquil 84sq km island is home to 4,300 year-round residents, known as the Bellilois, with fishing, farming and tourism as their main sources of income. In summer, the population swells to 35,000 but, despite this massive influx of visitors, Belle-Île never feels crowded. Its main attraction is its exhilarating variety of scenery.

The island's interior is a schist plateau of windswept moorland, ablaze with the colours of gorse and heather, jostles with lush green valleys, small settlements of whitewashed cottages and golden fields of wheat. The well-protected landward coast is bounded by calm waters, soft dunes, sprawling sandy beaches and creeks that are ideal for bathing. The Côte Sauvage, facing the ocean, is rugged and wild, as its name suggests – its craggy cliffs are riddled with caves and battered relentlessly by the Atlantic swell.

Belle-Île's two main towns – le Palais and Sauzon – are both delightful seaside resorts and fishing harbours. The port at le Palais is protected by Vauban's striking star-shaped Citadelle (fortress), which now contains the Musée Historique, recording the island's past. At the Pointe des Poulains, the northernmost tip of the island, the views across the Quiberon peninsula to the mainland are breathtaking. The island's most dramatic seascapes are best viewed from Port Coton and Port de Donnant, where the cliffs are at their highest and the sea lashes against the needle-shaped rocks below. On the road from Port de Donnant there are two menhirs standing side by side. They are known as Jean and Jeanne – two young lovers who, unable to wait for their wedding night, came here for a secret meeting but were turned to stone for their sin.

BELOW: restaurants and cafés overlook the harbour at le Palais

GOLFE DU MORBIHAN

Its name means 'Little Sea' in Breton. The great Golfe du Morbihan, a vast, circular, land-locked lagoon, virtually cut off from the sea, is studded with safe beaches and peppered with tiny islands that are fun to explore by pleasure cruiser.

The moated 13th-century Château de Suscinio

The surrounding countryside – with traditional-style fishing villages, megalithic monuments and historic castles and churches – is a source of almost endless delight.

ISLAND OF BIRDS

The Golfe du Morbihan is one of France's finest centres for bird-watching. Its prime position, on Brittany's western seaboard, makes it the first port of call for many migrating birds. In the winter it hosts the largest concentration of seabirds and wildfowl on the French Atlantic coast, making it a bird sanctuary of international importance. Its numerous protected reserves include marshy Séné, the

A sweeping aerial view of the land-locked lagoon of the Golfe du Morbihan

Rhuys peninsula and the aptly named Île-aux-Oiseaux (Island of Birds). These sanctuaries are home to egrets, stilts, avocets and other waders, along with herons, cormorants and migratory Brent geese, mallards and red-breasted merganser, spoonbills, sandpipers, oyster-catchers, curlews and kittiwakes.

GATEWAY TO THE GULF

Set in southern Brittany, where the climate is appreciably warmer than in the north, the city of Vannes boasts a stirringly patriotic

past. Formerly a Gallo-Roman centre, in the 9th century it became capital of Brittany under the Breton chief, Nominoé, Count of Vannes and the first Duke of Brittany.

A historic capital city, Vannes was the seat of the Breton Parliament in the final years of Brittany's independence, and was the venue for the declaration of unity between France and Brittany in 1532. It is one of the few towns in the region to have escaped serious damage during World War II, sheltering an impressive collection of ancient buildings behind its medieval ramparts.

Vannes' small, yacht-filled port lies at the tip of a long, canal-like waterway a couple of kilometres from the sea. Blending perfectly into the townscape, its waters reflecting the sails, trees and medieval houses. In fact, but for the salty sea air, you would hardly know that Vannes was on the coast, let alone that it was the gateway to the great Gulf of Morbihan.

SPANISH CONNECTION

Vannes' medieval centre is largely pedestrianised. At its heart, la Cathédrale de St-Pierre (St Peter's Cathedral) is an eclectic blend of architectural styles from the 13th to the 18th centuries, embracing Romanesque, flamboyant Gothic and even Italian Renaissance in a rotunda chapel housing the tomb of the town's patron saint, St-Vincent Ferrier. This Spanish missionary monk achieved considerable fame here in the 15th century as a preacher, performing many miraculous cures, some of which are depicted on the ancient tapestry in the chapel.

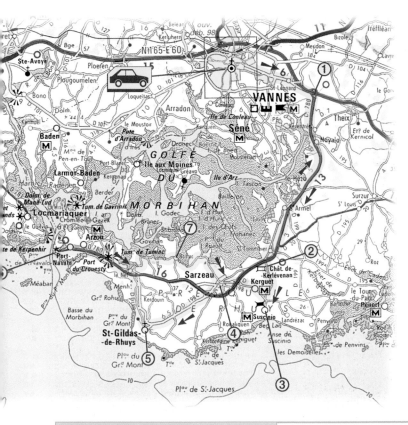

Forest of masts in the harbour of the historic capital city of Vannes, an ideal centre for boat excursions

T O U R

length of tour: 82km
time: half a day
IGN Top 250: sheet 105

The Presqu'île de Rhuys, reaching out to protect the Golfe du Morbihan from the south, basks in a sub-tropical micro-climate (Brittany's only vineyards are here) and offers delightful fishing villages, impressive historic sites and magnificent ocean beaches. This easy drive takes you from Vannes to the very tip of the peninsula and back again.

❶ Leaving the port in **Vannes** and heading eastwards out of town, follow the signs to Nantes, via the suburbs of Séné and St Léonard to touch on the main N 165 dual carriageway for 400m. Then turn off on to the D 780 to Noyalo. Bypass Noyalo, and continue down towards the Presqu'île de Rhuys, the name given to the southerly arm of land enclosing the gulf. Leave the main road at St Colombier and pass through the village.

❷ Join the D 780 again briefly, turning left almost immediately onto the C 4 by the classical **Château de Kerlévenan**. From here, follow signs to the **Château**

de Suscinio, a massive 13th-century castle, formerly the summer residence of the Dukes of Brittany, and surrounded by a sea-filled moat. Today it houses a museum of Breton history. Just beyond, a tiny hamlet of quaint fishermen's cottages leads to an expanse of golden, sandy beach.

❸ Return past the castle to the D 198 and follow signs, through Kerguet, to Sarzeau, an attractive town wrapped around a spacious market square. A sculpture here commemorates Alain-René Lesage, one of France's best known 18th-century satirists, who was born in the town.

❹ Leave Sarzeau, following signs to **St-Gildas de Rhuys**, a popular family resort centred on an ancient monastery founded here in 530 by a Celtic monk called Gildas. In the early 12th century, the monks developed unorthodox behaviour, so the famous theologian Abélard (Héloïse's former lover) was sent here to reform them. The monks tried to poison him but Abélard managed to escape via a secret underground passage. Behind the town is a charming little fishing harbour, Port aux Moines, framed by two small, sandy coves.

❺ From St-Gildas de Rhuys, follow the signs to Arzon and

Port Navalo, hugging the coastline until you rejoin the N 780, passing, on the left, **Port de Crouesty**, a recently developed smart marina (with capacity for over 1,000 boats) and holiday centre. **Port Navalo** is another small port and popular tourist resort, which takes full advantage of its splendid setting at the tip of the Rhuys peninsula, and offers pleasure-boat tours of the gulf.

❻ Head back to Vannes on the D 780. After 3km, turn left through le Net and on to **Port du Logeo**, a delightful fishing village of blue-shuttered, whitewashed cottages gathered round a tiny harbour, where the local catch is sold daily on the waterfront. Continue on to **Brillac (❼)** then follow the coast road (signposted Sarzeau par la Golfe) to return to Sarzeau. From here, you rejoin the D 780 and in due course arrive back at Vannes.

Sunset over the marina of Port Navalo

Virtually opposite the cathedral is the medieval market hall, La Cohue, which now houses the Galerie des Beaux-Arts, with modern works by local artists, and the Musée du Golfe et de la Mer, which covers the history of the Gulf and its local fishing industry.

From the market hall, a web of narrow cobbled streets, lined with half-timbered houses, small museums, boutiques and antiques shops, leads to a section of the old town walls. Across a small bridge, the allée des Frères-Jolivel in promenade de la Garenne provides a memorable panorama of old Vannes.

ℱorêt de Brocéliande

It is almost impossible not to be seduced by the ancient Forêt de Brocéliande, a magical and mysterious region at the heart of Brittany, steeped in myth and magic, and the legendary setting for tales of King Arthur, the Round Table and Merlin the magician.

The great Forêt de Paimpont (also known by its Arthurian name of Brocéliande) is all that remains of a vast primeval forest that once covered most of eastern Brittany. The largest area of woodland in Brittany, it comprises 7,000ha of conifers, beech and oak, interspersed with mystical clearings, rocky outcrops, eerie lakes, deserted moors, haunted castles and other places of enchantment. There can be no denying it: the forest has a definite magic about it.

■ THE FOREST CASTS ITS SPELL ■

At the heart of the forest is the attractive village of Paimpont. Its purplish-grey terraced houses cluster around a 12th-century abbey church, which conceals within its plain interior a silver reliquary of St Judicaël, an ivory crucifix and some fine woodwork and statues. The walls of the old abbey are lapped by a boating lake. Paimpont makes an ideal base for exploring such wonders of the forest as the

Fountain of Youth, with its supposedly magical powers and, near by, Merlin's tomb, a simple shrine to King Arthur's great wizard.

■ MERLIN'S MAGIC ■

The main focus of the Arthurian legends is la Fontaine de Barenton, an enchanting – and enchanted – spring set in mossy stones among the gnarled roots of an ancient tree. This is

Magic and myth

Legends abound throughout Brittany, and nowhere more than in the Forêt de Brocéliande, with its magicians, spirits, fairies and demons. According to songs of the Middle Ages, after the death of Christ, Joseph of Arimathea, one of his disciples, left Palestine and settled here, bringing with him the Holy Grail, the cup from which Jesus drank at the Last Supper. In the 6th century, King Arthur and the Knights of the Round Table came to the forest in search of the Holy Grail. It was here that the young king received the sword Excalibur from the fairy Viviane, the mysterious Lady of the Lake who later beguiled Merlin.

The 15th-century Château de Trecesson in the forest has a turreted gatehouse and a moat

where Merlin first saw the beautiful fairy Viviane, who cast upon him a spell that he himself had taught her. He fell in love with her and, once in her thrall, was to remain eternally under her spell, willingly imprisoned inside a large flat stone, the Perron de Merlin, near the spring. According to tradition, if water from the magic spring is sprinkled on the stone Merlin will conjure up thunder and rain. Apparently, even during the 20th century, Merlin's help was successfully invoked to end severe droughts.

Another incorrigibly romantic spot is the Val sans retour (Valley of No Return), a steep footpath with all exits barred by thickets of gorse and giant furze. Viviane, betrayed by one of her lovers, is said to have turned him to stone and cast a spell over the valley so that

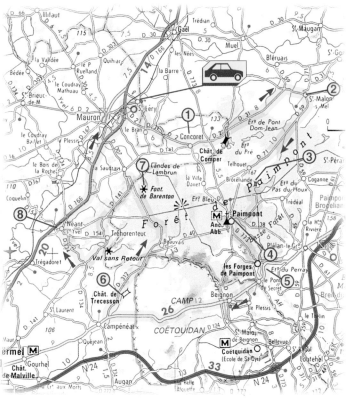

Merlin is spellbound by his lover, the beautiful enchantress Viviane

Trees form a canopy over one of the many trails in the forest

only faithful lovers could pass through without risk, while unfaithful ones would be trapped there by a magic wall of air.

In the church of the nearby village of Tréhorenteuc mosaics and paintings illustrate this and other local legends, while the stained-glass windows illustrate Arthur's search for the Holy Grail. The forest is criss-crossed with nature trails and footpaths, so take care take care not to get lost if exploring on foot. Periodically, groups claiming Druidic beliefs remove the signposts that direct visitors to the wonders of Paimpont, in an attempt to keep the sites secret and preserve the mysteries of the forest.

The mossy spring known as la Fontaine de Barenton is one of the sites connected with Arthurian legend

T O U R

length of tour: 85km
time: half a day
IGN Top 250: sheet 105

Moated castles and half-timbered châteaux, the Fountain of Eternal Youth and Merlin's Tomb are all included in this intriguing car tour of a mysterious and little-visited region.

❶ From the village of **St-Léry**, with its beautiful 14th-century church, take the winding D 167 signposted to Concoret. After 3km, turn left at an unmarked crossroads along the D 2 to **Concoret**, a picturesque village with a striking creeper-clad church, which, according to legend, once had the Devil as its rector!

❷ Leave the village on the D 2. Continue straight on at the D 773 crossroads, past the old, fortified **Château de Comper**, where the fairy Viviane was supposedly born

and where she brought up Lancelot, the gallant Knight of the Round Table. About 10km later, turn right into the peaceful village of **St Malon-sur-Mel**, with its lovely squat church. From here, take the D 59 towards Telhouët. The first turning to the right leads to the **Tombeau de Merlin** (Merlin's Tomb) and the **Fontaine de Jouvence** (Fountain of Youth).

❸ Back on the D 59, fork right onto the D 71 to Telhouët. Turn left in the village to the beautiful, half-timbered **Château de Brocéliande** on the shores of the Étang de Pas-du-Houx, the largest lake in the forest. The road briefly skirts the lake, then swings sharply to the right, leading to a T-junction. Turn right onto the D 40 towards Paimpont, then right again at the next junction to **Paimpont**, where signs to *Centre Bourg* will lead you straight to the abbey church on the edge of a lake.

❹ Leave Paimpont on the D 773 towards the pretty lakeside hamlet of **les Forges de Paimpont**, named after

the iron forges which operated here in the 16th century, using local iron ore and charcoal from the forest.

❺ Turn right at the main road then, after 11km, turn right onto the D 312 past the 15th-century **Château de Trécesson** — a haunted, fairy-tale castle of towers and turrets, appropriately encircled by a moat — then fork off to the left to Beauvais.

❻ Go straight across a small crossroads and fork right soon afterwards (signposted to Tréhorentruc). Continue straight on until the hamlet of Folle Pensée. Branch off here to the right to the **Fontaine de Barenton**.

❼ Return to Folle Pensée and on to the next T-junction. Turn left through Tréhorenteuc, past the entrance to the Val sans retour (Valley of No Return).

❽ At the next crossroads turn right onto the D 134 to **Néant-sur-Yval**. A right turn beside the church leads to the D 776bis link-road to the D 776. Turn right at the main road, bypassing the rambling market town of Mauron, then right onto the C 2, to return to St-Léry.

CHAPELLE NOTRE-DAME-du-HAUT

The medieval town of Moncontour, with its steep cobbled streets, stepped alleys and beautiful granite houses within its ancient ramparts, commands an imposing site on the spur of a rocky ridge, standing guard over two valleys. Outside the town is the little chapel of Notre-Dame-du-Haut, home to a collection of colourful statues.

At first glance, Moncontour appears to be a typical, sleepy hilltop town centred on a triangular main square, with a delightful Renaissance church that boasts some of the finest stained glass in Brittany. A huddle of half-timbered houses surround the church, decorated with carved doorways, statues and traditional wrought-iron picture signs to identify the local butcher, baker and other trades. However these picturesque façades mask a history of violent turmoil.

■ FROM CONFLICT TO COMMERCE ■

Following its fortificaption in the 11th century, the town became the object of numerous attacks by rival Breton families. It was later bitterly disputed during the Wars of Religion, after which, in 1626, Cardinal Richelieu had its castle and most of its ramparts destroyed.

During the late Middle Ages, Moncontour became one of the most prosperous towns of the region, thanks to its flourishing trade in leather and linen. The Moncontourais relive their golden age by hosting a lively, atmospheric medieval fair each summer, in August.

The town's annual Celtic music festival – *the Nuits d'Armor* – in mid-July is equally spectacular, famed throughout Brittany for the virtuosity of its musicians, the agility and grace of its dancers and the colour and complexity of their regional costumes.

■ A CURE FOR ALL ILLS ■

Just a short distance outside Moncontour, hidden amidst lush, rolling countryside, is a small, robust chapel, simply decorated with

The tiny, stone Chapelle Notre-Dame-du-Haut contains seven wooden statues of local healing saints

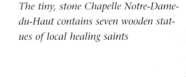

Moncontour is strategically positioned on a rocky ridge

WALK

length of walk: 6km
time: 2–3 hours
IGN Top 25: sheet 0917E

A ramble through the hilly lanes to the south-east provides a leisurely opportunity to admire the lovely countryside and the old stone cottages so typical of the region, as well as the magnificent views of medieval Moncontour.

❶ Start in place de Penthièvre, the main square of **Moncontour**. Take rue du Temple, to the left of the church. This road bends round to the right past the Hôtel de Ville, then drops down to a T-junction opposite an antiques shop. Turn left along the ramparts and carry on until you reach a crossroads at the foot of the town.

❷ Turn right on to the D 768, signposted to **Lamballe**. A few minutes later turn right at another cross-roads, just past the police station, on to the D 6.

❸ This road climbs steeply up to the village of **Trédaniel**. At the next junction, turn right again on to the D 6a, signed to Chapelle Notre-Dame-du-Haut. Continue up past the pretty stone houses of Trédaniel, skirting its ancient church, until you reach another crossroads, marked by a crucifix on the left-hand side. Go straight ahead and after about 800m you will glimpse the steep slate roof of the tiny, stone **Chapelle Notre-Dame-du-Haut**, nestling in lush meadowland. There are sweeping views across the gently undulating, fertile country-side. Behind the church, note the ancient wind-worn stone cross with its naïvely carved figure of Christ.

❹ Return to the previous crossroads and turn left along one of Trédaniel's back streets, rue des Châtaigniers, lined on both sides by quaint cottages and farm buildings. The lane drops steeply, but not without giving the most magnificent views looking down towards Moncontour. A little further on it is possible to catch a glimpse of the towers and turrets of **Château des Granges**, a privately owned castle, originally medieval but rebuilt in the early 19th century, crowning a wooded hill to the north of the town.

❺ At the end of the lane, turn left at the T-junction, and into the outskirts of Moncontour. At the foot of the hill, a narrow flight of steps leads up through the Jardins de l'Europe Jean Monnet – small gardens laid out on the old ramparts, in the shade of plane trees. Continue up a second set of steps, the Marches de la Porte d'en Bas, beside the Hôtel de Ville, to return to the main square.

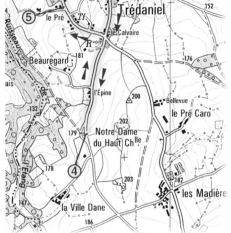

Celtic music

Moncontour's annual Celtic music festival – *the Nuits d'Armor* – in mid-July is a spectacular affair, famed throughout Brittany for the virtuosity of its musicians, the agility and grace of its dancers and the colour and complexity of their regional costumes.

wooden pews, an uneven stone floor and walls and an arched wooden ceiling, painted with Celtic symbols. Looking inside, you will find the painted wooden statues of seven Breton healing saints, believed to date from the 16th century.

St Yvertin is depicted holding his head – he cures headaches and migraines; St Mamert holds out his neatly coiled intestines – he cures colic and other digestive difficulties; Ste Eugénie, the only female saint, helps women with the pains of childbirth; St Lubin cures rheumatism and eye ailments; St Hubert assists with sores and dog bites; St Méen soothes madness and nervous disorders while St Houarniaule calms irrational fears. A splendid *pardon* in honour of these great healers takes place every year on 15 August. Note also how huge clumps of mistletoe – a plant deeply embedded in Celtic folklore and much esteemed by the Druids as a cure-all – have sprouted in the trees surrounding the church.

Inland pleasures

Away from the wild romance of the coast, there is another Brittany waiting to be discovered. Inland there is countryside of rich pastures and bleak moors broken by little rivers and scattered with forests. The granite fishermen's cottages of the coast give way to picturesque, whitewashed farmsteads, hidden flower-decked villages and medieval market towns. In this great region rich in history and heritage, the locals always seem to have time to chat, to welcome you into their farm kitchens for a *galette* (buckwheat pancake) and a glass of *cidre*, the traditional tipple, or to challenge you to a game of *palet*, Brittany's answer to boules.

ABOVE LEFT: picturesque old houses line the narrow rue de Dames in Moncontour
RIGHT: medieval fête in Moncontour's main square

ÎLE DE BRÉHAT

The Île de Bréhat is, without doubt, one of the most beautiful corners of northern Brittany – a lush paradise of subtropical flowers in the south and a wilderness of windswept, pink granite reefs in the north, with a surprising number of historic sites; and all just 15 minutes by boat from the mainland.

Bréhat is actually two islands, joined by a narrow causeway, and surrounded by a multitude of tiny islets, some accessible at low tide, but most just rugged, pinky-orange rocks jutting out from the deep turquoise sea.

Although inhabited as early as prehistoric times, and later occupied by the Romans, Bréhat only really entered the history books in the 5th century, when a monk called Budoc founded the first monastery in the region on neighbouring island of Lavrec. The monastery was destroyed during the Norman invasions of the 9th and 10th centuries. The island was well known for its hardy seamen: legend has it that one medieval Bréhatin fisherman visited the New World before Columbus, later advising the great Genoese explorer which course to follow on his Atlantic crossing.

▪ COMPARE AND CONTRAST ▪

The two main islands of Bréhat together cover an area of less than 5sq km, yet they offer their many visitors a variety of landscapes. The northern island is comparatively wild and deserted, with windswept meadows of hemlock and yarrow, and scrublands of ferns, pines and heathers. The Paon lighthouse marks the northernmost tip of the island, where dramatic red cliffs drop sheer into the perilous sea, studded with reefs and swept by strong currents.

The southern island, by contrast, is more welcoming and rural, with narrow country lanes bisecting tiny hamlets with neatly walled gardens brimming with flowers. With its palm trees and lush vegetation, and the heady scent of pine and eucalyptus filling the air, there is an almost Mediterranean atmosphere.

Both islands are car-free, like the Channel Island of Sark. The islanders

The Pink Granite Coast

The whole of the northernmost stretch of the Breton coast, from Bréhat to Trégastel, is known as the Côte de Granit Rose, because of its richly coloured landscape of rose-red rocks, its myriad pinky-orange islands which pepper the sea, and its quaint villages, constructed from this pink granite.

The most remarkable stretch of coastline lies between Perros-Guirec and Ploumanac'h, where the Sentier des Douaniers (Path of the Excisemen) winds round the clifftops past a spectacular display of russet-coloured, water-sculpted rocks, with such fanciful names as 'the Pancake', 'the Turtle', 'Napoleon's Hat' and 'the Torpedo'. Viewed at sunset, they make an unforgettable sight.

ABOVE: Port-Clos on Île de Bréhat is the ideal starting point for walks, bicycle rides and boat trips

BELOW: the rocky shores of Île de Brehat

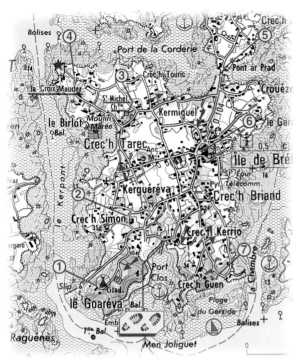

Bréhat's *fruits de mer*

A platter of *'fruits de mer'* is one of the highlights of Breton cuisine – a medley of shellfish and crustaceans, beautifully arranged on a bed of seaweed and served as an appetiser, generous main dish or even an entire meal. On the Île de Bréhat you will notice fishermen scouring the rocks and pools of the reefs for spider crabs, prawns, *praires* and *palourdes* (types of clam), winkles, whelks and oysters – 'queens of the sea' – to appear on your plate at dinnertime.

W A L K

length of walk: 5km
time: half a day
IGN Top 25: sheet 081450T

What better way to explore this car-free paradise than on foot or by bicycle? A frequent ferry service leaves the mainland from the Pointe de l'Arcouest just north of Paimpol, taking 10–15 minutes for the crossing. From Port-Clos, waymarked paths and narrow lanes criss-cross the island, leading to all the main sights.

❶ From **Port-Clos**, follow rue Principale until you reach the main square. Turn left here, following the clear ground-level arrows indicating Kerniquel and the Chapelle St-Michel. After a few minutes, branch left down to the pine-clad slopes of the **Bois de la Citadelle** (Forest of the Citadel), with its 19th-century fortress and lifeboat shelter buried in dense woodland at the south-westernmost tip of the island.

❷ Return towards Port-Clos, then branch left to the village of **Crec'h Simon** with its traditional steep-roofed pink granite houses and their tiny, flower-filled gardens.

❸ Continue northwards (still following signs to Chapelle St-Michel) past the hamlet of Crec'h Tarec, Bréhat's execution site during the 16th-century Wars of Religion. A flight of 39 steps leads up to the chapel, sitting on a small hill which offers panoramic views of the entire island and its surroundings. There are 86 islets and reefs in the archipelago. To the north, between the north and south islands and bounded by the Ar Prat bridge, stretches the expansive, circular Baie de la Corderie – Bréhat's main anchorage, flanked by beautiful villas and holiday homes.

❹ Return to the foot of the hill and continue along a narrow lane to **la Croix Maudez**, the most ancient crucifix of the archipelago. It was erected in 1788 in memory of a monk called Maudez who founded a monastery on the neighbouring Île Maudez in the 6th century.

❺ From Croix de Maudez follow signs through the hamlet of Kermiquel, with its many tiny floral gardens. Turn left at the T-junction of the D 104 to **Pont ar Prad**, constructed by Vauban, Louis XIV's great military architect, in the 18th century.

❻ Return southwards along the D 104 to **le Bourg**, the picturesque capital of the island, dominated by the unusual pink granite belltower of its 16th-century church. The quaint houses are grouped around the main square, shaded by plane trees. On most days there is a small market selling everything you could possibly require for a picnic.

❼ From le Bourg, head southwards (signposted Port-Cros), and bear left down a winding path to enjoy your picnic at the **Plage du Gerzido**, the island's best beach, where you can enjoy safe swimming at low tide. From here, it is just a short distance back to Port-Clos.

use tractors as transport, and bikes can be hired in Port-Clos.

▪ ISLAND OF FLOWERS – A SUBTROPICAL PARADISE ▪

The best time to visit is in late spring and summer when the island is ablaze with an abundance of flowers. Tradition has it that, many centuries ago, early Bréhatin mariners returning from far distant shores brought back with them seeds of the agapanthus, aloe, hortensia and mulberries that today grace the southern island.

Thanks to the influence of the Gulf Stream, Bréhat enjoys an exceptionally mild climate, enabling exotics such as eucalyptus, figs and dazzling yellow mimosa to flourish, while, deep blue hydrangeas and brilliant red geraniums flower well into October and even November, harmonising with the pink granite rocks and the cool blues and greens of the seascape.

ABOVE: Bastille Beach a Ploumanac'h on the mainland, where the water-worn rocks have inspiring names

St-Malo

The bustling walled town and one-time pirate base of St-Malo is perhaps the most attractive of the Channel ports, set between the wide, shallow bay of le Mont-St-Michel and the Côte d'Emeraude of Brittany, with its grassy clifftops, magnificent sandy beaches and old-fashioned holiday towns.

There are magnificent views from Quic-en-Groigne tower, St-Malo castle

St-Malo took its name from a 6th-century Welsh monk, Maclow, who converted the inhabitants of the fishing village of Aleth (now St Servan) to Christianity and became their bishop. The villagers later moved to a more strategic position on the bay and the new city of St-Malo emerged, a walled fortress founded by a proud and patriotic folk, who defiantly declaimed '*Ni Français, ni Breton, Malouin suis!*' (Not French, not Breton, but Malouin). The town has always been fiercely self-sufficient. Even the 15th-century castle, with its great keep and watchtowers com-manding impressive views of the harbour, was constructed to maintain the independence of the people from the Duke of Brittany. Today it houses the historical Musée de la Ville, which recounts the citadel's eventful history.

■ PIRATES, PATRIOTS AND PIONEERS ■

St-Malo's extensive harbour area continues the long maritime tradition of a town famed for its privateers, its slave-traders and its explorers. With the development of ship-building and navigation in the 16th century, Breton sailors began their voyages of discovery. Local explorer Jacques Cartier was the first to sight Canada and it was sailors from St-

A statue commemorates the navigator Jacques Cartier (1491–1557), who was born in St Malo

Malo who first discovered a group of islands, in the South Atlantic, known to the British as the Falklands, the Spanish as Las Malvinas and the French as Les Malouines. St-Malo was also home-port to privateers – pirates licensed by the French Crown to prey on foreign ships on condition they returned them to port and handed over a proportion of the spoils to the State. Not surprisingly, however, most ships were looted and their crews disposed of at sea, causing grave losses to the English, Spanish

Rance valley cider

In a country famed for its wines, the more authentic Breton tipple is cider, still considered a standard accompaniment to *crêpes Bretonnes*. The best cider comes from the Rance valley to the southwest of St-Malo – dry *cidre brut* or sweet *cidre doux*. A small *lambig* (cider brandy) or *chouchen* (sweet, honey-based mead) provides the perfect end to a traditional Breton meal.

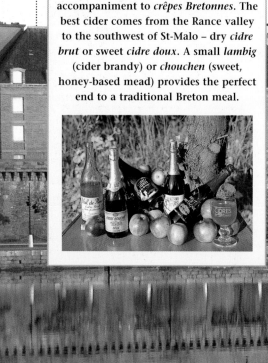

TOUR

length of tour: 101km
time: at least half a day
IGN Top 250: sheet 105

The tiny backroads of the Rance estuary, threading and twisting through flower-filled hamlets, waterside villages and a labyrinth of hidden inlets, provide a unique insight to this maritime region. The elegant resort of Dinard and the beautifully preserved citadel of Dinan combine to make this a tour of exceptional variety and interest.

❶ From **St-Malo** follow signs for Dinard, to cross the Barrage de la Rance, a dam and innovative, pollution-free hydro-electric generating station which uses only tidal power. A right turn at the crossroads leads to **Dinard**, the most elegant resort on the Côte Emeraude (Emerald Coast), with luxurious hotels, exotic gardens and princely villas in a picture-postcard setting on the Rance estuary.

❷ Return to the dam, turning right just before you reach it, and continue straight ahead to La Richardais and the sensational country house of **Montmarin**, home of a former shipmaster, rich from his trade with distant lands. Its sumptuous gardens teeter on the banks of the Rance, heavy with the scent of agapanthus – its balustrades, terracotta statues and fine staircases fanning out towards the landing stage, as access to Montmarin was then from the sea.

❸ Continue on the D 114 towards Dinan, through several attractive villages, including **Landriais-sur-Rance** with its pleasant beach and landing-stage. Beyond Landriais, continue to Dinan on the D 12, take the third exit at the roundabout, bypass Plouer-sur-Rance and continue to the village of **La Hisse**. Cross the traffic lights and a mini-roundabout, and head straight for the port of Dinan.

❹ The road drops steeply to the valley floor and runs alongside the port – a thin finger of river flanked by yachts and a clutter of restaurants, crêperies and bars, guarded by **Dinan** and its dramatic viaduct overhead. Continue up the hill into Dinan, one of Brittany's most beautifully preserved medieval towns, famous for its traditional crafts of woodcarving, glass-blowing, weaving and engraving.

❺ Leave Dinan over the viaduct to Lanvallay on the N 176, following signs to St-Malo. Leave the hamlet of St Piat, then after 800m take the D 29 to the left, signposted to La Vicomté. After La Vicomté turn left again to **Mordreuc**, a picturesque clutter of old stone cottages, on the water's edge and smothered in flowers. There are impressive views downstream to the **Pont St Hubert** suspension bridge.

❻ Head towards **Pleudihen-sur-Rance** on the D 48, with its interesting Musée du Cidre, located in an old farmhouse outside town. Leave Pleudihen on the D 29, signposted to St-Malo. After Le Buet, take the second turning on the left (directed to La Chapelle St Magloire) until you reach La Ville es Nonais. At the crossroads take the D 7 to **St Suliac**, a pretty village with a robust-looking church, several appealing places to eat, a tiny beach, a promenade shaded by plane trees, and boat club. From here, follow the winding D 117 to St Jouans de Guérets, then join the main D 137. The first exit returns you to the centre of St-Malo.

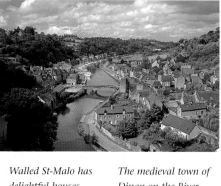

Walled St-Malo has delightful houses built in 18th-century style

The medieval town of Dinan on the River Rance

and Dutch navies. Two of St-Malo's most notorious corsairs – René Dugay-Trouin and Robert Surcouf – are remembered in statues on the city walls.

■ INTRA MUROS ■

The 1.6km-long coastal walls of St-Malo have stood firm against attack since the 12th century. But the town itself has proved less resistant and was almost destroyed in a tough two-week battle during World War II. The granite-built old town – the heart of St-Malo – known today as Intra Muros (within the walls), is almost entirely a masterful reconstruction from wartime rubble. Its main sights include the ancient Cathédrale St-Vincent, noted for its medieval stained glass and modern Celtic bronze altar, the largest salt-water aquarium in Europe and a museum of dolls and toys, plus tempting shops and restaurants.

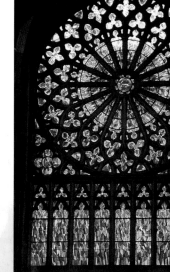

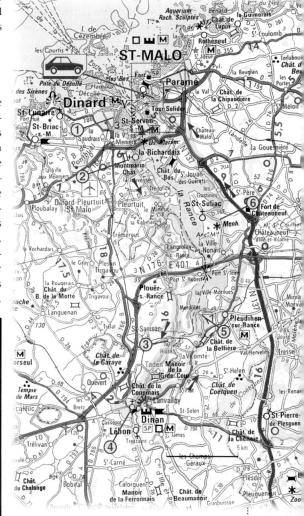

St Malo's cathedral is decorated with beautiful stained glass

ℒE MONT-ST-MICHEL

*L*e Mont-St-Michel is without doubt one of the most spectacular sights in Europe – a circular, rocky, island fortress rising dramatically out of a vast, sandy bay, crowned by a magnificent Romanesque and Gothic fairy-tale abbey.

The ramparts at Avranches offer an excellent view of le Mont-St-Michel across the mudflats

The abbey on le Mont-St-Michel was founded in 708 by St Aubert, Bishop of Avranches, following three visions from St Michael ordering him to construct an oratory on the rock. The third time, the impatient archangel poked his *doigt de feu* (fiery finger) in the bishop's skull, finally stirring him into action.

■ FAITH THAT MOVES MOUNTAINS ■

Over the centuries, Benedictine monks have transformed St Aubert's simple oratory into an imposing abbey, using granite rocks gathered from the Iles Chausey, 15km off the mainland near Granville. In an extraordinary act of faith, they carried each stone across dangerous quicksands to create one of Europe's most renowned pilgrimage sites, built from an extraordinary mixture of sacred architectural styles from the Middle Ages to the 16th cen-

The graceful arches in 13th-century cloister of Mont-St-Michel

Delicacies of the Baie

The sheep that graze on the scrubby pastures and wild samphire at the sea's edge around the Baie du Mont-St-Michel provide meat for the salt-meadow lamb renowned throughout France. This delicacy, known as *mouton pré-salé* (pre-salted lamb), is best grilled without further seasoning. At low tide, between here and Genêts, look out for *la peche a pied* – a 13th-century method of fishing, done on foot using huge wooden V-shaped fish traps. The main catch is *chevrettes* (grey shrimps), mullet and 'Genêts cockles'. Oysters and mussels thrive here too, gathered from the mud at low tide, and served fresh in many of Mont-St-Michel's restaurants.

tury. A gleaming gold statue of St Michael the Archangel surveys le Mont from its eyrie at the top of the abbey's spire, almost

80m above sea level; St Aubert's holed skull is on view in the church.

Its superb setting and splendid architecture has made le Mont-St-Michel into one of France's most popular attractions. The steep, cobbled climb up the Grande Rue to the abbey is lined with half-timbered houses, tempting the crowds with cafés, expensive restaurants, mediocre museums and endless souvenir shops. The ramparts offer a less crowded route as well as stunning sea views.

■ AT THE MERCY OF THE SEA ■

Le Mont-St-Michel is situated in a massive bay that has the highest tides in Europe. According to local legend – and such folklore is rife here – the water rises

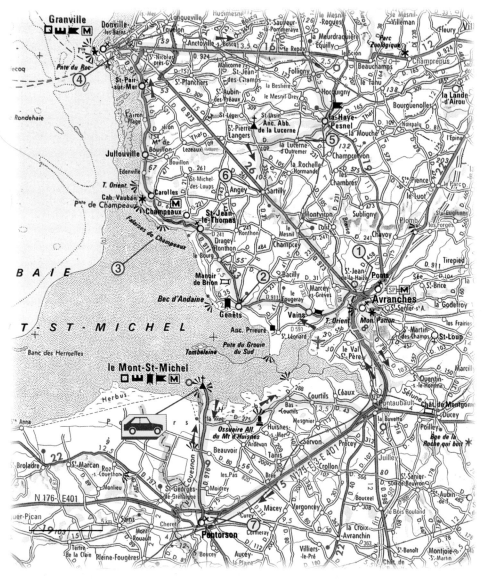

length of tour: 137km
time: 1 day
IGN Top 25: sheet 102

This tour offers several opportunities to view le Mont-St-Michel from a distance, across the sands. It takes in a museum of medieval manuscripts and a chance to wander on the tidal flats – but take a guide!

❶ Set off from **le Mont-St-Michel** along its ancient causeway, then turn left on the D 275 signed Avranches and *La Route de la Baie* (the Bay Route), across pancakc flat marshland and through a gaggle of seaside villages and farming communities. After Les Forges, join the N 175 to **Avranches**, the nearest main town to Mont-St-Michel, high above the bay on a rocky outcrop offering excellent views to le Mont-St-Michel from the Jardins des Plantes and the ruined castle. The town museum contains a fine collection of medieval illuminated manuscripts, mostly from le Mont-St-Michel.

❷ Leave Avranches on the D 973 signposted to Granville and Cherbourg. Cross a small bridge then turn immediately left onto the D 911 through rich, pastoral scenery to **Genêts**. This pleasant seaside resort was once a bustling port and salt works. Its tiny medieval church was the final stop on the pilgrim route to le Mont-St-Michel. From here pilgrims would cross, barefoot, the sand dunes and salt marshes of the broad bay, to the abbey. The walk can still be done today, starting from the broad sandy beach at Bec d'Andaine just north of the village, but the journey must not be attempted without a guide, as quicksand and rapid tides are a hazard.

❸ Continue northwards on the D 911. After St-Jean-le-Thomas, the road winds steeply over the clifftops of Les Falaises de Champeaux, carpeted with gorse and wild cherry in springtime, and affording memorable views across the vast bay with le Mont-St-Michel standing proud in its midst. The road passes through several small seaside towns before reaching Granville – the 'Monaco of the north' – a lively seaside resort jutting out to sea on a rocky promontory. It is also a busy port, with a vivid history of seafaring and piracy.

❹ Leave Granville on the D 924 and turn right onto the D 35 to **La Haye Pesnel**. From here follow signs to **La Lucerne d'Outremer** and l'Abbaye de la Lucerne, through narrow lanes and hamlets.

❺ This isolated abbey, tucked into the Thar valley on the D 105, was founded in 1143 by two monks with a donation by the great nephew of William the Conqueror. Its mass of ancient buildings includes a fine abbey church and cloisters, a chapter house, refectory, abbot's lodge and massive dovecote.

❻ Return along the D105 for 1.25km. Cross the D 109 towards La Rochelle-Normande then join the D 335 to **Sartilly**. Turn right at the T-junction onto the D 35 into Sartilly, left onto the main D 973 back to Avranches.

❼ Take the N 175 to **Pontorson**. From here, the D 976 leads back to le Mont-St-Michel alongside the River Couesnon, which defines the Normandy-Brittany border.

---

into the bay at the speed of a galloping horse. The extreme tides, with variations of up to 15m, are reputedly due to Gargantua. Passing through the region centuries ago, he felt an irresistible urge to relieve himself – after the excessive quantities of cider he had drunk earlier – just as he was about to stride across the gap between Carolles and Cancale!

During the Middle Ages, when it was separate from the mainland by a long causeway, the island was known as 'Mont-St-Michel at the mercy of the Sea'. Even today the car park is sometimes submerged. When the tides are at their highest, you can watch the meadows flood, the mudflats turn to sea and the waves pound against the abbey ramparts – an awesome and unforgettable spectacle as the water advances at an incredible metre per second over 16km.

RIGHT: the narrow streets bustle with life during the daylight hours

LEFT: the abbey on Mont-St-Michel was founded in 708 by St Aubert, Bishop of Avranches

BAYEUX

*H*istory – ancient and modern – surrounds Bayeux, an atmospheric old town just 10km from the coast, famous worldwide for the magnificent Bayeux Tapestry and as the first French town liberated by Allied forces the day after the D-Day landings in 1944.

The memory of the Normandy Landings in June 1944 is still powerful in Bayeux, with more British flags on show here than you are likely to find in London.

The old town, with its ancient stone and timber-framed houses, narrow streets, arched bridges, watermills and fishmarket, which miraculously survived the 1944 campaign, has recently been restored.

The American military cemetery at St Laurent, just above Omaha Beach

■ MOVING MEMORIALS ■

The display of guns and tanks parked on the lawn outside makes the Museum of the Battle of Normandy, on Bayeux's ring road, difficult to miss. The events, courage and sacrifice that brought Allied victory against Nazism – as well as the devastation wrought on Normandy's towns – are grimly recorded through photographs and newsreel footage, uniforms, guns and rifles, tanks, machine guns and newspaper clippings. Displays of kit, memorabilia and personal possessions are powerfully emotive.

Even more moving is the war cemetery opposite the museum – row upon row of well-tended graves and neat headstones, where 4,648 soldiers, mostly British, are buried. One of several in the region, the cemetery is dominated by a memorial arch bearing in Latin the words 'We, whose land William conquered, came to liberate William's land'. It is this earlier invasion – the Norman Conquest in 1066 – for which Bayeux is most famous.

■ ANCIENT TREASURES ■

Bayeux's greatest treasure, housed in the William the Conqueror Centre, is the Bayeux Tapestry – a remarkable, 70m embroidered scroll depicting the epic story of William of Normandy's conquest of England. The tour includes a slide display with detailed explanations of each of the tapestry's 58 scenes, while upstairs a cinema shows films about its history. Yet nothing quite prepares the

visitor for the sheer length of the tapestry itself, floodlit behind glass in a long, darkened room, nor for the extraordinary intricacy of the needlework, the brilliance of its colours and the dramatic, violent story it tells, enlivened throughout with scenes of medieval life and mythical beasts.

The fine detail includes a miniature Mont-St-Michel, Halley's

Elegant Bayeux cathedral still has its orginal towers and crypt

comet, the English, distinguished by their moustaches and long hair (including Harold with an arrow through his eye), clergy with shaved heads, and ladies (of which there are only three) with veiled heads and flowing robes. The tapestry – the most accurate and informative medieval document in existence – provides a unique and fascinating record of clothes, weapons, ships and lifestyles from the Middle Ages.

The origins of the tapestry are unknown, although it is believed to have been commissioned from Saxon embroiderers by Odo of Conteville, Count of Kent and Bishop of Bayeux, to grace his glorious new Cathédrale de Notre-Dame – a harmonious blend of Norman Romanesque and Gothic styles, with soaring spires and a magnificent, domed, lantern tower.

The famous Bayeux Tapestry illustrates the Norman Conquest

A model on display in the Musée des Ballons in the Château de Balleroy

TOUR

length of tour: 129km
time: 1 day
IGN Top 250: sheet 102

This tour is dedicated to Operation Overlord and the D-Day Landings. It includes a number of the important landing beaches and some museums specialising in various aspects of the operation. On a lighter note, it also includes a centre for pottery and a balloon museum.

❶ Leave **Bayeux** on the D 572 towards St Lô, passing through Noron-la-Poterie, a well-known centre for its salt-glaze ware. This dark brown pottery, made from local red clay sprayed with fine salt during baking to produce a bluish lustre, is used to make such traditional vessels as *bonbonnes* (large cider jugs) and *cruchons* (small calvados flasks). Continue on the D 572, turning right at a major roundabout onto the D 13 to the noble and spacious village of **Balleroy**, known for its stately château – the first masterpiece of Louis XIII's celebrated architect Farnçois Mansart – and its eccentric

Musée des Ballons, which outlines the history of France's great *montgolfière* (hot-air balloon) invention.

❷ Continue on the D 13 to **Tilly-sur-Seulles**. Cross the D 6 and turn left by the church, onto the D 82.

❸ Carry on past quaint villages and huge expanses of open farmland to **Creully**, a peaceful village which welcomed many wartime dignitaries, including Winston Churchill and King George VI when they were entertained by Field-Marshal Montgomery, in a straw-camouflaged caravan parked in the grounds of the château in 1944. That same year, a makeshift BBC studio was set up in the town hall here, to broadcast news updates of the Battle of Normandy.

❹ Leave Creully on the D 22. Turn right onto the D 12, following signs to **Courseulles-sur-Mer**, the first French port to be liberated on 6 June 1944. Leave Courseulles on the D 514, past the Juno Beach war memorial, through Ver-sur-Mer with its extensive views of Gold Beach, and on to **Arromanches-les-Bains**.

❺ At this small seaside town, synonymous with D-Day, remains of Port Winston, the giant Mulberry harbour that served the wartime landings, can still be seen. On the seafront, the remarkable D-Day operations are

vividly explained in the moving Musée du Débarquement.

❻ Further along the coast, on the D 514, lies **Port-en-Bessin-Huppain**, a small fishing port with an unusual museum of D-Day wrecks. Continue on towards Omaha Beach, the Americans' principal landing beach, which saw the most difficult and – in terms of human life – most costly of the D-Day assaults; the Military Cemetery at **Colleville-sur-Mer** has over 9,000 marble crosses.

❼ At St Laurent-sur-Mer, turn right down the D 517, past a prefabricated wartime building housing the Omaha Museum, then left along the waterfront to **Vierville-sur-Mer**, where the beaches and dunes are dotted with ruined bunkers, trenches and other sad remnants of war. Pass the seafront Normandy Landings Monument, then head uphill and left onto the D 514. Back in St Laurent, turn right on the D 517, left at the N 13 and back to Bayeux.

HONFLEUR

Honfleur, jewel of the Normandy coastline, is the France of all our fantasies – a picturesque port and seaside town with cobbled quays, narrow jetty houses and museums – once home to privateers and seafarers, today a town of fishermen, writers and artists.

Honfleur is centred around its Vieux Bassin (Old Harbour) lined with narrow, grey-slate, tall houses and plenty of outdoor cafés and restaurants. It is easy to while away the hours over a heaped bowl of *moules frites* (mussels and chips), watching the fishermen bringing in the day's catch, sold directly from their boats, or stands, along the pier.

■ ADVENTURERS AND EXPLORERS ■

It was from Honfleur that ships bound for the New World once set sail. In 1608 Samuel de Champlain sailed off in search of Quebec. In 1681 Cavelier de la Salle reached the mouth of the Mississippi from here, calling the area Louisiana in honour of King Louis XIV. These and other exploits are are vividly portrayed in the Naval Museum in the deconsecrated Eglise de St-Etienne on the harbour. The harbour bustles with yachts and pleasure craft, while the Avant Port (Outer Harbour) is home to Honfleur's fishing fleet, separated from the main harbour by the 16th-century Lieutenancy, the former residence of the town's royal governor and the only surviving part of the old town wall.

The heart of the old city, known as the Enclos because it was once enclosed by fortifications, lies to the east of the Vieux Bassin – a labyrinth of cobbled streets and alleyways, restaurants, shops and galleries which combine to create an atmosphere of traditional charm. The 17th-century *greniers à sel* (salt stores), built with stone from the old ramparts, once housed the salt used by the fishing fleet to cure its catch. It now hosts concerts and exhibitions. Another place to see is l'Eglise de Ste-Catherine – an unusual wooden church, built by shipwrights as a 'temporary measure' after the Hundred Years War. It has a vaulted roof, like the upturned hulls of two boats, and a separate belfry.

Half-timbered houses in Beuvron-en-Auge, one of the pretty villages on the Route du Cidre

■ ARTISTIC LINKS ■

The composer Erik Satie (famous for his Gymnopédies) was born in Honfleur, as was the artist Eugène Boudin, one of the first French artists to paint in the open air; he is still admired for his beach scenes featuring parasols and billowing dresses, dramatic skyscapes and his ability to 'paint the wind'. It was Boudin who persuaded Claude Monet, the young cartoonist from le Havre, to work outdoors and study the way in which changing light affects the subject. In 1864 Monet joined Boudin in Honfleur, mixing with such artists as Corot, Renoir, Sisley, Pissarro and Cézanne. Together they formed the Société Anonyme des Artistes-Peintres, whose works were to become the basis for the Musée Eugène Boudin. Honfleur's great art museum.

The old harbour in Honfleur is much loved by artists and photographers, and is home to a varied fleet of boats

La Suisse Normande

For a true taste of *la vie Normande* head inland to the Calvados *département*. This area captures the true character and charm of old Normandy, with its brown and white bespectacled cows grazing in lush meadows against a backdrop of gently undulating hills, half-timbered manor houses hidden amidst clouds of apple blossom, and high hedgerows dividing the countryside like lead in stained glass.

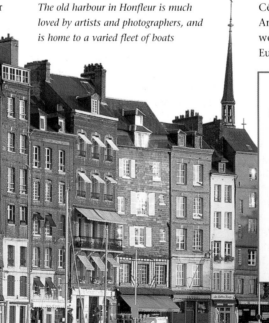

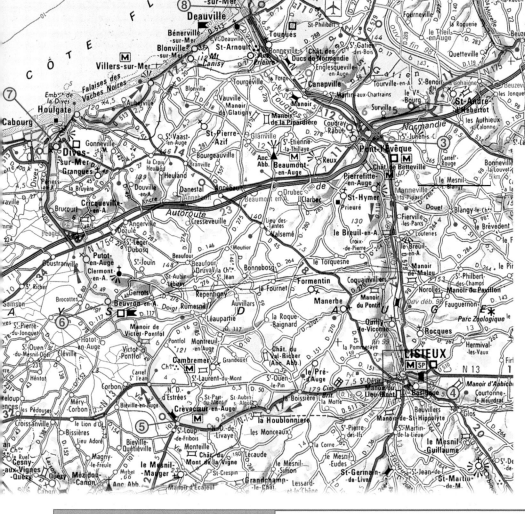

The magnificent Pont de Normandie at night

T O U R

length of tour: 150km
time: 1 day
IGN Top 250: sheet 102

Cheese and cider form a major part of this tour, which takes in several smart seaside resorts on a route which is easy going, but can be hilly in places.

❶ Leave **Honfleur** on the D 580, following signs to the A13 autoroute and **Pont de Normandie**, the beautiful, cable-stayed bridge, opened in 1995, crossing the Seine estuary between Honfleur and le Havre. Spanning 856m, it makes a spectacular sight when illuminated at night. Continue past the bridge, turning left on to the D 312 along the scenic Seine estuary and through the village of **Berville-sur-Mer**.

❷ At the junction with the N178 turn right, still on the D 312, then left in Toutainville on to the N 175 to **Pont-Audemer**, a pleasant old port on the River Risle, noted for its leather tanneries.

❸ Return to Toutainville on the D 175 and continue on through bustling Beuzeville to **Pont-l'Évêque**, which gives its name to one of Normandy's most famous cheeses. Another fine local product is Calvados, with many cellars open for tastings; just look for the signs.

❹ Turn left out of Pont-l'Évêque (opposite the police station) towards Lisieux. Follow a delightful country lane along the course of the River Touque to Lisieux, through the lush countryside, dotted with châteaux, a lake and pretty half-timbered cottages. This is the heart of the Pays d'Auge, a region boasting some of Normandy's most picturesque scenery. Its capital, **Lisieux**, is a provincial market town and important pilgrimage centre, with the relics of France's second patron saint, St Theresa, contained in its oversized basilica.

❺ Head west from Lisieux on the N 13, past the 11th- to 16th-century **Château de Crèvecoeur-en-Auge** – a magnificent, moated cluster of half-timbered, ochre-coloured buildings, including a chapel, dovecote and gatehouse – and continue as far as Carrefour St-Jean.

❻ Turn right here on to the D 16, then left on to the D 49 to **Beuvron-en-Auge**. This follows part of the *Route du Cidre* through typical Pays d'Auge countryside of high hedgerows, apple orchards and immaculate white fences, enclosing some of France's most prestigious stud farms. Beuvron is without doubt one of the prettiest villages in the Pays d'Auge – a delightful, almost entirely half-timbered tourist trap which thrives on its sales of farmhouse cider, Calvados and cheeses.

❼ Head north from here on the D 49. Turn left at the N 175 then immediately right on to the D 400 to **Dives-sur-Mer**.

❽ From here follow the D 513 east through Houlgate, Deauville and **Trouville**, smart resorts on the Côte Fleurie (Floral Coast). Ever since sea-bathing became fashionable nearly two centuries ago, these towns have drawn visitors to their grand *belle-époque* hotels, sandy beaches patterned with colourful parasols, elegant promenades, glitzy casinos and racecourses, and extensive leisure facilities. From Trouville, it is a short drive back to Honfleur.

ÉTRETAT

*F*rance's most famous stretch of coastline is undoubtedly the breathtaking chalk cliffs of the Côte d'Albâtre at Étretat, best summed up by 19th-century author, Alphonse Karr, who wrote, 'If I had to show a friend the sea for the first time, I would do so at Étretat.'

The Côte d'Albâtre (Alabaster Coast) stretches 100km from Dieppe to Étretat and beyond – a formation of imposing, white cliffs that seem to mirror the white cliffs at Dover just across the English Channel. At Étretat the seascape is at its most spectacular, with sheer cliffs pierced by massive arches and a solitary needle rock soaring to 70m a little way offshore. Whatever the season, the grandeur of these cliff formations and the crashing of waves on the pebble beach are unforgettable.

Ageless charm

For centuries the cliffs have drawn people to Etretat. The Romans built a road here from Lillebonne; Marie-Antoinette had her own private oyster bed here; and in the 19th century the humble fishing port was transformed into a highly fashionable seaside resort, attracting wealthy Parisians to its theatre, casino and fine bathing facilities. On the outskirts of town, the Château des Aigues was considered one of the most desirable coastal addresses for European aristocracy spending 'the season' at Étretat. However it was artists Corot, Boudin, Delacroix, Monet and Manet, composer Offenbach, and writers Dumas, Gide, Hugo, Karr and Maupassant who really put Étretat on the map. Today it is one of the most visited places in France.

Tucked neatly between the cliffs in a fold of verdant hills, the town has remained surprisingly unspoiled by the constant flood of tourists, with a proliferation of fine fish restaurants, an attractive, wooden-covered market *halle* (with gift shops), and a charming medieval church. A promenade fringes the curved shingle beach, rather spoiled by cheap cafés and *pommes frites* stands, but retaining some of its earlier charm at the far end, with its *caloges* (thatched cottages) and gaily painted, traditional fishing craft.

Porte d'Aval and Porte d'Amont

The town is tucked neatly between two main cliffs: Porte (or Falaise) d'Aval to the west and Porte (or Falaise) d'Amont to the east, both with imposing arches carved by wind and waves over the years. Guy de Maupassant compared the Porte d'Amont to 'an elephant dipping its trunk into the sea'. On top of the

Fishing boats moored neatly beside the promenade in the unspoiled resort of Etretat

Coastal impressions
At the turn of the century, the dazzling coastline of Normandy became the cradle of Impressionism, attracting Boudin, Monet, Sisley, Renoir and numerous other great artists to the open-air *ateliers* of Etretat, Honfleur, Dieppe, Deauville, Trouville and le Havre. It was Monet's masterwork *Impression, Sunrise*, painted at le Havre in 1874, that gave the movement its name. These stylish seaside resorts also gave inspiration to many famous writers such as Maupassant and Flaubert, and attracted many others to the area, including Hugo, Proust (left) and Sartre. Indeed, Normandy has inspired more great literature than any other region of France.

ABOVE: *the covered market at Etretat, and detail from the town's Musé Nungesser et Coli, right*

cliff sits a small, granite seafarer's chapel, Notre-Dame-de-la-Garde, a 1950 replacement for the original, destroyed in World War II, with charming seal gargoyles. Near by, a Concorde-like memorial stands as a tribute to aviators Nungesser and Coli, whose aircraft *Oiseau Blanc* was last seen over Étretat before disappearing during the first attempt to fly the Atlantic in 1927. There is also a small museum dedicated to them, and a life-size aeroplane set in concrete relief alongside the monument. The view from here across the sheltered bay to the windswept Porte d'Aval, with its dramatic arches and l'Aiguille (the Needle), is particularly unforgettable.

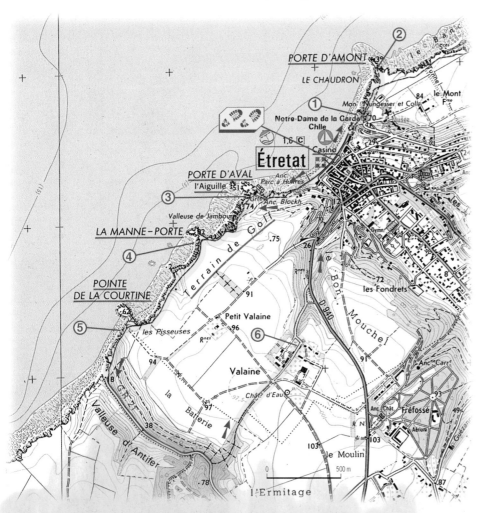

length of walk: 6.5km
time: 2½ hours
IGN Top 25: sheet 1710E

This scenic coastal walk offers glorious views from windswept clifftops. The going can be rough in places, but the breathtaking panoramas make it all worthwhile. Wear sturdy, non-slip shoes.

❶ Start on the promenade. Walk to the eastern end, then turn right, up a flight of 83 brick steps which then opens out onto a grassy clifftop pathway, past a children's theme park, and up to the top of the Porte d'Amont and the **Chapelle Notre-Dame-de-la-Garde**. Inland from the sailors' chapel is the memorial to the two aviators, Nungesser and Coli (see above).

❷ Continue along the cliff edge, past the chapel and go down some steps leading to the **arch of Amont**. A steep, slippery and narrow pathway, cut into the chalky stack, offers wonderful views of the alabaster cliffs to the east. A wooden handrail and a ladder assist in the final descent to a small beach.

❸ Retrace your steps, past the chapel and back down the brick steps. Proceed along the promenade, an unbroken curve of café-lined concrete above the steep shingle beach. At the far end, another flight of steps, followed by a steep, well-trodden, flint-filled path, leads up beside a scenic golf course to **Porte d'Aval**. Bear right along the cliff edge, crossing a narrow bridge, past an old pillbox and onto the top of the cliff arch — not for those with a fear of heights! — for spectacular views over the grey, slate roofs of Etretat and Porte d'Amont beyond. Legend has it that many centuries ago three beautiful sisters were imprisoned in a cave at the foot of these cliffs by an evil lord. Even today, fishermen sometimes hear their plaintive cries from inside the rock.

❹ Continue along the windswept cliff-edge, flecked with wild flowers, yellow gorse and purple sea cabbage, and on to a second arch, **La Manne-Porte**, with breathtaking views stretching as far as the port of Le Havre-Antifer.

❺ Just beyond the next headland, **Pointe de la Courtine**, follow a track inland (the GR 21, marked with a red-and-white stripe), branching left where two paths meet, to Valaine.

❻ At the next junction, depart from the GR 21 and head straight on down a narrow country lane, through the attractive brick and stone farm buildings of **Ferme le Valaine**. On the left, the lovely old farmhouse sells delicious home-produced cider, calvados and goats' milk cheese. Follow the road as it winds gently downhill, past grazing goats, until you reach the D 940. Turn left back into the centre of Étretat and left again back to the seafront.

Abbaye de Notre-Dame de Jumièges

The tiny village of Jumièges, surrounded by meadows and orchards in a sweeping loop of the River Seine, boasts one of the most impressive ruins in all France, the historic Abbaye de Notre-Dame de Jumièges, once the most powerful abbey in Normandy.

With the spread of Christianity in northern France, Normandy rapidly became one of the most important centres of learning in the Christian world from the 6th century onwards, when a string of monasteries developed as major centres of religious and intellectual life along the River Seine.

The *Route Historique des Abbayes* (Historic Abbey Route) follows the broad river valley between Rouen and le Havre, which provides a spectacular backdrop for many abbeys, including the most important, the 7th-century Benedictine Abbaye de Notre-Dame at Jumièges.

ABOVE: *the elegant façade of Musée Victor Hugo*
RIGHT: *the ruined 11th-century Benedictine abbey is one of Normandy's most striking sites*

A tragic tale

The beautiful village of Villequier on the edge of the Seine is associated with Victor Hugo, France's greatest 19th-century poet. In *A Villequier* he mourns the death of his daughter, Léopoldine, and her husband, Charles Vacquerie, who drowned here in 1843 in the Seine's then notorious tidal bore. Their riverside house today contains the Musée Victor Hugo. At the eastern edge of the village is a statue of Hugo bearing two poignant lines from his poem:
Il faut que l'herbe pousse et que les enfants meurent;
Je le sais, ô mon Dieu!
(Grass must grow, and children must die; I realise that, O Lord!)

■ FROM SPLENDOUR TO RUINS ■

The abbey was founded in 654 by St Philibert, and destroyed two centuries later during the Norman invasions. It was rebuilt in about 942 during the reign of William Long Sword, Duke of Normandy, and consecrated in 1067 in the presence of William the Conqueror on his triumphant return from England. The new abbey soon became known for its charity as the Jumièges Almshouse, and as a great centre of scholarship. The monks were, however, dispersed again during the French Revolution and in 1793 the abbey was sold at public auction for use as a stone quarry.

Now it is nothing more than a haunting ruin, with the nave open to the sky and the huge, ivory towers rising up above

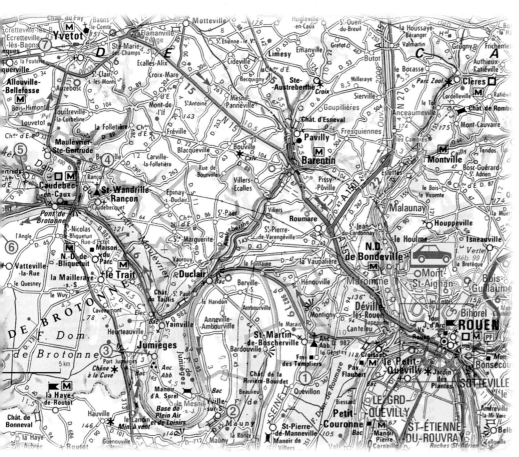

Wisteria smothers a half-timbered dwelling in picturesque Jumièges

the treeline. It is easy to imagine its former glory as you walk round the ruins, tracing out the vast dimensions of the original buildings which once represented one of France's most important and influential monastic institutions.

▪ TREASURES OF JUMIÈGES ▪

The actual village of Jumièges – a cluster of half-timbered houses and ancient cottages – sits snugly round the walls of the abbey and the triangular main square. Charles VII, Joan of Arc's king, often stayed at the abbey together with his favourite mistress, Agnes Sorel, who died here in 1450. A small museum in the former abbot's lodge contains the black marble slab that covered her heart, along with tombs, gargoyles, statues and other fragments all salvaged from the original abbey.

Hidden down by the river, the Auberge du Bac offers refreshments on the banks of the Seine. From here you can cross the river on a small *bac* (car ferry) to explore the Forêt de Brotonne.

The Seine Valley

The River Seine rises in Burgundy, flows through Champagne, then the Île-de-France and finally follows a snake-like course, looping through the picturesque countryside of Normandy, as if reluctant to reach the sea 770km later at le Havre. Its name is said to derive from the Celtic word *squan* (curve or bend). The Normandy stretch of the river is perhaps the most romantic and rural, so near to Paris yet so distant from Parisian chic. Napoleon once described it as a great highway linking the capital with the sea, declaring, 'Le Havre, Rouen and Paris are but a single town of which the Seine is the main street'.

TOUR

length of tour: 120km
time: 1 day
IGN Top 250: sheet 102

Taking in two of France's most beautiful and historic villages – Jumièges itself and Villequier – this tour starts and ends in Rouen, the historic capital of Upper Normandy. The city is well worth exploring in its own right for its wealth of interesting sights, including the 12th-century Cathédrale Notre-Dame, the medieval old town and the Musée de Beaux Arts.

❶ Head westwards out of **Rouen**, following signs to Dieppe, le Havre, then the D 982 to Canteleu, which eventually leads under the main road and out of the city. Go through Canteleu and continue on the same road to **St-Martin-de-Boscherville**, entering the Parc Naturel Régional de Brotonne, a region embracing the forest of Brotonne, the Seine valley, the chalky plateau of the Pays de Caux, the Vernier Marsh and the lower valley of the Risle. Turn left in St-Martin to visit the 11th-century church of St George. Formerly part of an important Benedictine Abbey here, it became St Martin's parish church at the time of the French Revolution, thereby saving it from destruction.

❷ Return to the D 982 and continue on along the banks of the Seine to Duclair. On leaving the town, turn left onto the D 65 to **le Mesnil-sous-Jumièges** on a delightful road, *La Route des Fruits*, which follows a gracious curve of the river past pretty, half-timbered cottages hidden among orchards of apples, cherries and plums.

❸ Continue on to **Jumièges**. Pass through the main square and continue up the hill, past the 12th- to 16th- century church of St Valentin, and on through Yainville until you reach a T-junction with the D 982.

❹ Turn left through Le Trait, then turn right just before the massive Pont de Brotonne toll bridge, on the D 22 to **St-Wandrille-Rançon**. For centuries the abbey was plagued by theft, fire and pillage, after Wandrille deserted his bride on their wedding night to devote himself to the service of God in 648. It has nevertheless survived as an active Benedictine monastery and you can still hear the monks sing the Gregorian chants at morning mass.

❺ Return to the main road and proceed to **Caudebec-en-Caux**, known for its Musée de la Marine de Seine and its flamboyant Gothic church, described by Henri IV in the 16th century as 'the most beautiful chapel in the kingdom'. Turn left in the town onto the D 81, which hugs the river bank all the way to **Villequier**.

❻ Head back to the centre of Caudebec, then turn left onto the D 131 following signs to **Yvetot**(❼), a large market town on the Caux Plateau. From here, the N 15 returns to Rouen.

$\mathcal{G}$IVERNY

*T*his delightful riverside village, spread across a hillside near Vernon, is the most visited site in Normandy. Crowds of art- and garden-lovers flock to see the home of Claude Monet and the world's most famous lily pond, immortalised in some of its best-known paintings.

*I*n 1883 Monet moved to a pastel-pink house with grass-green shutters in Giverny, near Argenteuil, the Paris suburb where he had worked with Renoir, Sisley and Manet for a number of years. Monet had spotted the village of Giverny out of the window of the train and immediately decided to move there.

■ MONET'S INSPIRATION ■

Monet designed the garden himself; it slopes down over nearly one hectare to the *chemin du Roy*, where a small, local railway connected to Vernon and Gasny. At the time, he had little money but was able to rent the house, thanks to the financial aid of a dealer-friend, Durand-Ruel. As he became more widely known and his canvases began to sell well, Monet decided to buy the house – he paid 22,000 francs (about £2,200) – and proceeded to lay out his famous gardens, considered by many of his friends to be his greatest masterpiece.

He also purchased a further plot of land at the bottom of the main garden on the banks of the River Epte, where he created his famous water-garden with its lilies and Japanese bridge; he continued to paint this scene until his death in 1926, at the age of 86.

It is best to visit in May or June, when the rhododendrons and the wisteria on the bridge are in bloom. Despite the crowds, it is easy to imagine the great master at work on one of his huge canvases. He used to say, 'I am good for nothing except painting and gardening!'

BELOW: the real bridge across the lily pond and, left, Claude Monet's Waterlily Pond: Pink Harmony, *1900 (© ADAGP, Paris and DACS, London, 1999)*

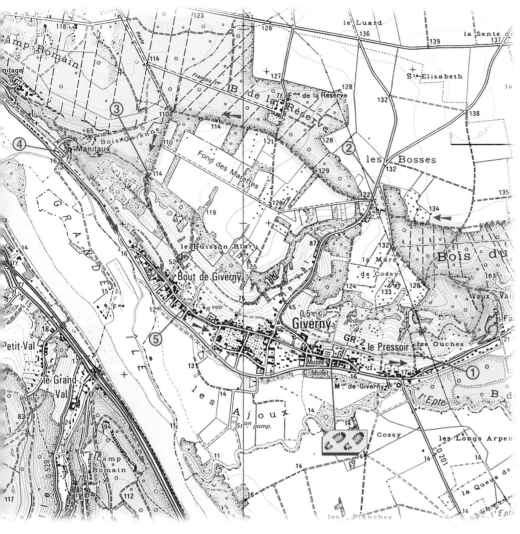

W A L K

length of walk: 9km
time: 2½ hours
IGN Top 25: sheet 21130

This walk is centred on the village where Claude Monet spent his time and where he attracted many friends and followers, both French and American. Sturdy, non-slip shoes or, ideally, walking boots should be worn for this excursion.

❶ Start outside the **Fondation Claude Monet** and head along rue Claude-Monet, heading towards the **Musée Américain**. Take the lane to the right, called Chemin Blanche-Hoschéde, then go right again almost immediately up the narrow rue Hélène-Pillon, which curves left before becoming a dirt track. Follow this path along the backs of houses, running parallel to rue Claude-Monet below, until you reach the end of the village. Turn left (signposted GR 2, and marked with red and white paint markers) up a steep path, then turn right at the first intersection, which snakes across open meadowland towards the woods, with sweeping views over the Epte valley below. At the next crossing of footpaths, go left and climb up through oak woods. At this point you leave the GR 2 and the path is now marked in yellow. At the next cross-roads, go right then at the edge of the woods, take the grassy path on the left, passing alongside pastureland then more woodland. As you reach the woods, turn right towards a small road.

❷ Turn left onto the road, which runs steeply downhill. After 50m bear right and right again along a track bordering the woods of La Réserve on the right and flanked by fields on the left. Continue straight on at a cross-roads level with a small yellow house on the left. Then branch left along the fringe of the Garenne woods.

❸ Turn to the right in the woods (once again following the red and white signs of GR 2). Soon afterwards, there is a promontory marked by a large cross, with a magnificent view of the Seine. Continue down a very steep, narrow path to the hamlet of **Manitaux**, which comes out on a small lane bordered by cottages.

❹ Turn left, following the course of a former railway track until you reach the edge of Giverny. Go along the grassy path behind the first houses in the village, until the path joins the Sente des Grosses Eaux and, soon afterwards, rue Claude-Monet.

❺ Back on the main street of the village, proceed past the church, where Monet lies buried, and **Hôtel Baudy**, the ancient boarding house and rendezvous of various painter friends of Monet – Rodin, Sisley, Renoire, Cézanne, Pissarro – and the majority of visiting American artists. It was also the venue of the first studio and the first art exhibitions in the village. Continue past the Museum of American Art and the galleries of various artists before returning to Claude Monet's great house and garden at the far end of the village.

▪ A COLOURFUL PALETTE ▪

The main garden – the Clos Normand –with its 12 resident gardeners, still follows Monet's design and is a dazzling palette of changing colours from spring to autumn. Each month has its own dominant colour, as does each room in Monet's immaculately restored house, from the colourful yellow dining room to the cool, blue kitchen, decorated with his collection of Japanese prints. Just a stone's throw from the house, his huge atelier has been restored and filled with huge copies of his finest works. It was built in 1916 so that the elderly Monet, despite failing eyesight, could paint the famous water lily series *Décoration des Nymphéas* at ease and in good light. Today much of

the series hangs in the Musée National de l'Orangerie in Paris, where the gigantic paintings are arranged according to the artist's precise instructions to run round the walls of two oval rooms.

Monet acquired this house in Giverny in 1883 and lived here till he died; today visitors can still see his furniture and personal mementoes

BAIE DE LA SOMME

A magical expanse of sand, sea and sky, the Baie de la Somme, home to several hundred species of bird, was classified a natural reserve in 1994. Its history is linked to invasions and conquests – it was from here that William of Normandy set forth to England in 1066.

With its muted colours and ever-changing landscapes, the Baie de la Somme invites investigation. Not surprisingly, nature-loving artists and writers such as Degas, Victor Hugo and Colette found inspiration in the bay's flat, humid expanses of land, where the receding sea leaves an irregular network of canals to mirror the luminous grey-blue skies. Watch just one sunset from the terrace of St-Valéry-sur-Somme, with its panoramic view over the bay, and you will see why this area is called the Côte d'Opale.

A DELICATE ECOSYSTEM

The slow-moving Somme – the longest river in Northern France (192km) – forms an estuary in the bay, stretching from the fishing port of le Hourdel to St-Quentin-en-Tourmont as it feeds into the English Channel. As the sea has receded over the centuries, silt-laden pastures have been created, which have doubled since the end of the 19th century, to provide fine grazing land for sheep (lamb bearing the Estran label is a local speciality) and the sandy-coloured Hensen horses. In the summer, these meadows are blanketed in sea fennel and other plants suited to the aquatic environment.

BIRD OF PARADISE

Come to the bay equipped with a pair of binoculars: the whole area is a privileged migration crossroads and nesting area for hundreds of species of bird, including greylag geese, pintails, oystercatchers and redshanks. If you're lucky you'll be able to spot seals basking in the sun on a sand bank at low tide, or out at sea. At low tide, fishermen venture out into the bay to collect clams, cockles and other shellfish.

Empty sand dunes lead north from the Baie de la Somme; INSET: the canal at St-Valéry-sur-Somme

■ ST-VALÉRY-SUR-SOMME ■

With its ramparts, medieval architecture and narrow, cobbled lanes lined with brick and stone cottages with lace curtains and flower boxes, St-Valéry-sur-Somme is the bay's most picturesque town, and also a good base for exploring. It was named after St Valéry, who brought Christianity to the local county in the 7th century. From here, William of Normandy set out to conquer England in 1066. Its strategic position has made for a turbulent history – the town underwent more than 20 sieges in four centuries. In 1475 Louis XI even ordered it to be burned rather than given up to the English.

Parc Ornithologique du Marquenterre

Set amid marshes, pine forests, sand dunes and moors in the northern part of the Baie de la Somme, the Marquenterre Bird Park offers bird lovers the chance to observe up to 320 species at different times during the year, including oystercatchers (below), white storks and spoonbills, of which there are only 15 couples in France. If you don't own a pair of binoculars, they can be hired at the park entrance.

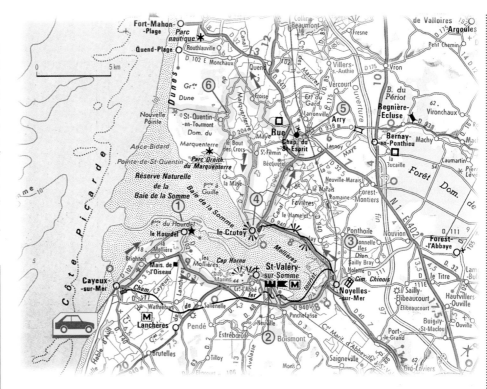

The small port of le Crotoy nestles on the north bank of the River Somme

T O U R

length of tour: 75km
time: 1 day, including visits
IGN Top 250: sheet 101

The wide, open feel of this estuary is combined with the charm of small fishing ports, the poignancy of a cemetery for those who perished thousands of miles from their homes and a chance to get close to nature and see rare birds at close quarters. This tour around the Baie de la Somme gives plenty of opportunity for walking as well as driving, and starts at Cayeux-sur-Mer.

❶ From the south of the bay at **Cayeux-sur-Mer** follow the D 102 to the harbour at le Hourdel. Here you can admire the spectacular landscape and watch the fishermen unloading their catch. Walk along the beach to admire the vast expanse of sea and land, with le Crotoy outlined at the other end of the bay.

❷ Continue along the D 102, past Cap Hornu, which offers another superb panorama over the bay, and take the D 3 to **St-Valéry-sur-Somme**. This town is best explored from the fishermen's quarter in the *ville-basse* to the quai Jeanne-d'Arc, a pedestrian promenade shaded by lime trees. The Musée Picarvie exhibits local crafts and trades. Enter the *ville-haute* through the imposing, twin-towered Porte St-Guillaume. A plaque commemorates Joan of Arc's journey here in 1430. Typical of the region is the church of St Martin, made of flint and stone in a distinctive chessboard pattern.

❸ From St-Valéry-sur-Somme follow the D 940 which crosses the Canal de la Somme, built between 1803 and 1827. A short detour along the D 111 takes you to **Nolette** (just after Noyelles-sur-Mer), where a Chinese cemetery is the last resting place of 870 Chinese workers recruited during World War I to maintain roads leading to the front. Many died in a flu epidemic.

❹ Return to the panoramic D 940 as it cuts between marshes and cultivated land. **Le Crotoy**, 'the only beach of the north facing southwards', is a small fishing port with claims on some illustrious names: from 1865 to 1871, Jules Verne wrote *Twenty Thousand Leagues under the Sea* while he was living here.

❺ Continue along the D 940 to **Rue**, a seaport disputed by the French and British throughout the Middle Ages. Here the Chapelle du St-Esprit, once a stopping point on the pilgrimage route to Saint Jacques-de-Compostella, is a jewel of flamboyant, 15th-century Gothic architecture.

❻ From here, continue to **St-Quentin-en-Tourmont**, at the heart of the Marquenterre, with its salt meadows, marshland, immense, sandy beaches and the largest group of sand dunes in northern France. At St-Quentin, look out for the *chemin d'accès à la mer*, an hour-long walk to the sea along a sand trail lined by pine trees. Towards the sea the landscape gradually changes until you reach a line of sand dunes covered by high grass, overlooking the vast beach of Fort-Mahon, great for sand-yachting. From St-Quentin go on to the Parque Ornithologique du Marquenterre, then rejoin the D 204 and D 4 back to le Crotoy.

CATHÉDRALE DE NOTRE-DAME, AMIENS

*A*miens – the capital of Picardy – is home to the largest cathedral in France, yet never seems far from the countryside, with its floating gardens, pleasant parks and meandering canals lined with cottages, bookshops and antiques dealers.

Described as the 'parthenon of Gothic' by the English author and art critic John Ruskin (1819–1900), Notre-Dame d'Amiens is the largest cathedral in France and one of the most accomplished examples of Gothic architecture. To appreciate its full magnificence, view it first from Parc St-Pierre, from where the 13th-century stone and glass architecture gives an impression of elegance, grace and ethereal light.

The cathedral probably owes its existence to wode, a plant cultivated in the region from which the famous colour *bleu d'Amiens*, was obtained.

■ THROUGH THE AGES ■

Amiens became a site of pilgrimage in the 11th century after Walton de Sarton, a local canon, returned from the 4th crusade with what he claimed was the skull of St John the Baptist. After the city's Romanesque church was destroyed by lightning, the clergy, textile merchants, noble families and King Louis VIII himself donated funds for the construction of a new cathedral on the same site. Designed by Robert de Luzarches and built in record time (about 50 years), Notre-Dame d'Amiens is renowned for its homogeneous style.

■ A BIBLE OF STONE ■

Start with the western façade, Ruskin's 'veritable bible of stone', with 3,000 carved figures. On the central portal, the impassive figure of the *Beau Dieu* (Beautiful God) is one of the cathedral's most striking sculptures. According to legend, Christ's face appeared to the sculptor in a dream. The right portal, dedicated to the Virgin Mary, has been restored, uncovering the warm, yellow tones of 12th-century local limestone. The noble expressions of these restored statues each displays a slightly different attitude.

■ A VERTIGINOUS NAVE ■

With its grand arcades, soaring 12m bay windows and high, ribbed vaults, eyes are naturally drawn upwards. The cathedral's three-tier elevation is breathtaking: the nave stretches 133.5m and rises to 42.5m, France's second highest after Beauvais. A 234m black-and-white maze (along which

ABOVE: the extraordinary display of sculpture on the cathedral's west front whets the appetite for the intricate carvings inside, left and right

worshippers once advanced on their knees) features at its centre the names of the cathedral's builders.

Behind the majestic, 18th-century, wrought-iron grille of the choir are 110 sculpted stalls of the canons, unique in France. The 4,000 figures, carved in oak by local craftsmen in the early 16th century, relate episodes from both Testaments. On the arm rests are lively, humorous carvings of local trades and traditions. Postcards of the little angel grieving on the tomb of the canon Guilain Lucas – sent home by Allied soldiers – made it a symbol of the liberation of Amiens in 1918.

Miraculously spared during the two world wars, Notre-Dame d'Amiens remained standing in the midst of a city which was mostly devastated by bombing.

LEFT: the massive but dignified Memorial to the Missing at Thiepval

Battle of the Somme

In 1916, one of the fiercest battles of World War I raged in the Somme. Aimed at breaking through German defences, the offensive began on 1 July 1916, preceded by a week of intensive shelling. Despite their superiority in numbers, British and French troops ran into unexpected resistance: in a few hours, 57,500 infantrymen were killed, incurring the heaviest loss of life on a single day during the war. Over the next five months, Allied forces advanced at a snail's pace, in a bitter battle of trench warfare. A grim total of 1,331,000 soldiers perished in the four-month Battle of the Somme.

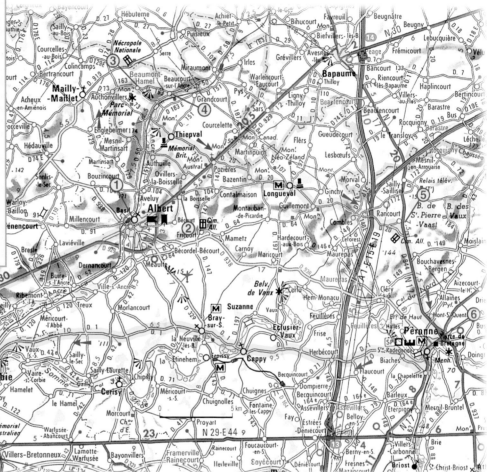

TOUR

length of tour: 80km
time: half a day
IGN Top 250: sheet 101

Starting from Amiens, this poignant World War I Circuit of Remembrance includes several battlefield memorials and related museums.

❶ From Amiens follow the D 929 to **Albert**, a town captured by the Germans in March 1918 and liberated by the British army the following August. Almost entirely destroyed, the town has been largely reconstructed, including the neo-Byzantine Notre-Dame de Brebières basilica. The golden Virgin surmounting the dome is a replica of the famous 'Leaning Virgin'. After being hit by a German mortar shell in January 1915, the statue stood tilting in the void until April 1918. The Musée des Abris retells the ordeal of trench warfare.

❷ Continue along the D 929 to **La Boisselle**. The 30m Lochnager Crater, the largest on the western front, is the only mine crater that remains accessible. In July 1916, several blasts, aimed at splitting the German front line, carved craters like this.

❸ Just outside La Boisselle, turn left onto the D 174 to Auchonvillers and then right onto the D 163 to the Newfoundland camp in **Beaumont-Hamel**. The statue of a caribou, the symbol of Newfoundland, recalls the tragedy of the regiment that was decimated on 1 July 1916, within hours of the start of fighting. With its trenches, barbed wire and graves, the park is a powerful reminder of the past. A statue in Beaumont honours Scottish soldiers from the Highlanders' 51st Division.

❹ Continue to **Beaucourt-sur-l'Ancre**, then follow the D 50 for 2.5km before turning onto the D 20 to Thiepval, where you will find the largest British memorial in the region. From 1 July to 20 September 1916, British forces fought to take back this hill and village, a pillar of German defence protected at its base by swamps of the Ancre River and a network of tunnels. A huge brick archway lists the names of 73,367 soldiers killed in the battle, whose bodies were never identified.

❺ Continue along the D 20 to **Longueval**, in the heart of the Delville forest – Devil's Wood in Marshal Haig's terms – where 90,000 soldiers fell. Memorials have been erected to South African and New Zealand forces. Further along is **Rancourt**, strategically located on the road between Bapaume and Péronne, an important communication link for German troops. The only site honouring French soldiers stands here.

❻ From Rancourt follow the N 14 south to the Historical de la Grande Guerre in **Péronne**, a museum inaugurated in 1992. This trilingual museum (French, English and German) studies Europe's cultural history from the pre-war to the post-war period, covering the complex causes of the war, the mobilisation of the population, the many military and technological developments, day-to-day survival on the front and civilian life. The museum also holds a collection of 50 etchings by the German artist Otto Dix denouncing the horror of war. From here return to Amiens west along the D 1.

FORÊT DE ST-GOBAIN

Majestic and luminous, the Forêt de St-Gobain is an oasis of tranquillity and a prized hunting ground which harbours vestiges of prosperous abbeys from the Middle Ages.

The vast 6,000ha Forêt de St-Gobain covered an even greater area when Gobban, an Irish monk, arrived in 647 AD to evangelise the region. The legend says that he made his base in the town that now bears his name after a water source sprang up where he planted his pilgrim's stick. After 20 years of evangelising, Gobban was decapitated by barbarian hordes and his body was buried in the church he had erected, making it a site of pilgrimage. The present church, built in the 13th and 14th centuries, probably stands on the site of the one that Gobban founded.

Four car tours, marked out by numbers and the silhouettes of animals, pass through this forest of oaks, beech and ash trees, with its deer and the vestiges of once influential abbeys. From St-Gobain, three walks, varying in length from 1½ to 4½ hours, are marked by coloured arrows.

■ THE LORDS OF COUCY ■

From the 10th to the 14th centuries, the forest belonged to the lords of Coucy, powerful feudal barons who fought in all the battles and crusades of their day. The most famous of them all was Enguerrand III, also known as 'The Builder'. He affirmed his independence from the royal crown, saying 'I am not king, nor prince, nor duke, nor count, I am the lord of Coucy.' His castle at Coucy is an ultimate expression of pride and ambition.

■ MIRROR, MIRROR ON THE WALL ■

St-Gobain is inextricably linked with the history of French glass manufacture. In 1692 the Manufacture Royale des Glaces (Royal

The magnificent choir of Cathédrale de Notre-Dame in Laon

There are some breathtaking routes through the Forêt de St-Gobain

Chemin des Dames

Once used by *les dames* (daughters) of Louis XV to visit their former governess, this stretch of land is now more closely associated with World War I, as German forces turned its underground rock quarries into a fortress. The French army's first unsuccessful attempt to recapture the area in April 1917 incurred heavy losses, and a second offensive in October 1917 forced the Germans northwards. After four years, the area had been devastated. The Chemin des Dames today runs along the D13 south of St-Gobain, lined with memorials such as the Caverne du Dragon, rock quarries carved with graffiti and sculptures which stand as poignant testimonies to a generation of young soldiers.

TOUR

length of tour: 60km
time: half a day
IGN Top 250: sheet 101

In St-Gobain, a monumental, wrought-iron gate marks the entrance to what was once the Manufacture des Glaces, which produced mirrors on a semi-industrial scale. Starting from this important pre-industrial site, this tour offers rocks to climb, quiet forest walks, pleasant picnic places and romantic ruined abbeys and castles.

1 From St-Gobain, take the D 554 towards the **Roches de l'Hermitage** site. A beautiful, leisurely hour-long walk is marked with arrows along a cleared path through the forest and around a quiet lake. Children will enjoy climbing the rocks, while picnic tables make this a good spot to stop off and take a break in the midst of the forest's majestic beauty.

2 Continue along the D 554 and turn right onto the D 55, then left onto the D 556 to **Le Tortoir**, a former 14th-century priory and chapel surrounded by ponds and meadows. Near by, in **St-Nicolas-aux-Bois**, are the ruins of an abbey, largely destroyed during the French Revolution. In around 1080 a few hermits made a clearing here to build a chapel. Fifty years later the site had blossomed into an influential congregation of Benedictine monks. Although it cannot be visited, the abbey, a retreat buried away in the heart of the forest, evokes an age when faith drove men to retire from the world (the word monk comes from the Greek *monos* – alone) and follow a vocation of prayer, meditation and manual labour.

3 A different type of abbey is found in **Prémontré**, reached via the D 55 to Suzy then the D 552. Founded in 1120 by St Norbert, the order observed a strict set of rules inspired by the Cistercian model and owned over 100 abbeys throughout Europe in the Middle Ages. Apart from the ruins of a church, little is left of the orig-inal abbey, which was reconstructed in the 18th century. It forms a very harmonious ensemble, only partially opened to the public and now housing a hospital.

4 Follow the D 14 then the D 5 to **Coucy-le-Château-Auffrique**. Built in record time (between 1225 and 1230) by Enguerrand III, Coucy-le-Château is a spectacular example of medieval defensive architecture. It was destroyed in 1917 by German forces, but the castle's keep was the largest specimen of its kind in the 13th century, standing 54m high with a 100m circumference. Inside the castle, a 58m ceremonial room was one of the largest in the Middle Ages. Follow the walk through the imposing gateways (flanked by massive towers) and around the ramparts – the path is marked – to take in the strategic grandness of this site, perched 70m above the Ailette and Oise valleys.

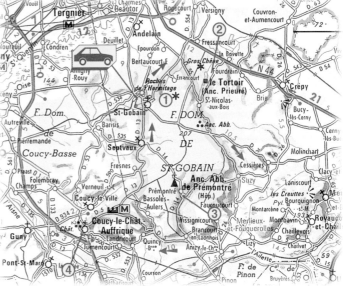

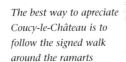

The best way to apreciate Coucy-le-Château is to follow the signed walk around the ramarts

Company of Mirrors), founded in 1665, was transferred to St-Gobain, due in part to the area's natural resources (sand and water) and in part to its proximity to the River Oise, a good route to Paris. Here, in the huge, underground galleries of a 13th-century fortress built by the lords of Coucy, the glass-casting technique, invented by a glassmaker from Orléans, was developed on a quasi-industrial scale. As a result, the Manufacture Royale broke a monopoly held by Venetian glassblowers and spurred development in the region. It eventually became the Compagnie de St-Gobain, now one of France's leading industrial groups.

The Manufacture Royale des Glaces, the glass factory, is an important part of St-Gobain

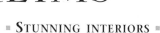

CATHÉDRALE DE NOTRE-DAME, REIMS

In the heart of champagne country, la Cathédrale de Notre-Dame in Reims stands as the most enduring and eloquent symbol of the French monarchy. Nearly all the kings of France were crowned under its nave, from Louis VIII in 1223 to Charles X in 1825.

Long before the cathedral's first stone was laid on 6 May 1211 by Archbishop Aubry de Humbert, Reims' destiny was linked with the monarchy's. The crypt and the baptistry, excavated after World War I, reveal the early cathedral where Frankish King Clovis was baptised on Christmas Day in 498, sealing the union between the Franks and Christianity.

The Cathédral de Notre-Dame at Reims is as awe-inspiring inside as out

■ CATHEDRAL OF ANGELS ■

Built to symbolise the strength of the monarchy of divine right, Notre-Dame rivals other splendid Gothic edifices, and despite its succession of architects, some continuity was preserved. Its Gothic façade, one of the most delicate and harmonious in France, was once decorated with 2,300 sculptures, many of which have been replaced by copies over the years. On the buttresses, angels with open wings mount a celestial guard of honour. The whole structure, with its perfect proportions and open work, gives a sense of astonishing brightness and refinement.

■ WHICH STATUE? ■

The statues adorning the three portals belong to different schools of sculpture, spanning between them 500 years. On the right, the Old Testament prophets, no longer standing squarely on two feet, their drapery infused with movement, exhibit a style influenced by classical Antiquity. In contrast are those devoted to the Virgin Mary on the central portal. On the left portal, the Angel of the Smile, dedicated to local saints, belongs to an ancient style characterised by elegant draping

and delicate features. The tympana are replaced by rose windows, accentuating the sense of lightness.

■ STUNNING INTERIORS ■

The slender, 138m nave, illuminated by the rose windows of the façade, gives an impression of depth and harmony, with its vaults soaring effortlessly to 38m. The Great Rose Window, a 13th-century masterpiece, is dedicated to the Virgin Mary – at sunset, its twelve petals send shafts of pastel light streaming down the nave. Contemporary stained glass harmonises with the cathedral's medieval masterpieces, such as the Champagne

Chalk, monks and champagne

The chalky rock on which Reims stands is riddled with miles of caves that provide ideal conditions for the production and storage of champagne, the region's most celebrated export. Although known as a wine since Roman times, it took a 17th-century Benedictine monk, Dom Perignon of Hautvillers (right), to invent the process that gives champagne its unique sparkle. Cellars in Reims rank among the most impressive of the champagne producers, and visitors can visit caves of such famous names as Veuve-Cliquot, Pommeroy and Moët et Chandon for tastings.

windows (1954, south transept) which tell the story of the making of this wine in medieval style. The figures in the windows of the axial chapel, drawn by Marc Chagall, dance in a luminous blue light.

■ WAR AND RECONCILIATION ■

Ironically, the cathedral that symbolised the monarchy was barely touched during the Revolution, but suffered extensive damage during World War I. Shells and subsequent fires destroyed the wood scaffolding of the north tower, mutilated a large number of its statues and blackened the stone. Reconstruction and excavations were led by the architect Henri Deneux, who replaced the wooden framework with a concrete structure – it was reopened on 18 October 1937. Reflecting its lasting symbolic significance, the cathedral provided the setting for the Franco-German reconciliation mass on 18 July 1962, attended by Charles de Gaulle and Chancellor Adenauer.

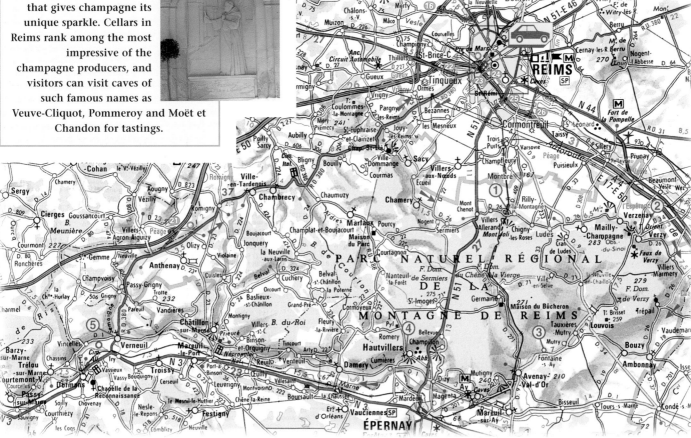

TOUR

length of tour: 90km
time: half a day
IGN Top 250: sheet 103

This tour, following the Champagne Route through the Montagne de Reims, offers the chance to stop in pretty villages and learn about the art of champagne-making from local growers and merchants. It takes in a fantastic beach forest and includes a visit to the capital of champagne.

❶ From Reims, follow the RD 380, turn left onto the D 26 at Jouy-lès-Reims towards Chamery, a *premier cru* vineyard dominated by its 12th-century church. This type of scenery is typical of the Montagne de Reims region, a plateau of forests and tidy vineyards planted with Chardonnay, Pinot Noir and Meunier grapes. The tender, chalky soil acts as a natural regulator, providing the vines with the required amount of humidity and warmth. Continue to **Rilly-la-Montagne**, an attractive town on the edge of the forest. Its church has beautiful,

16th-century choir stalls carved with vine motifs. For a panoramic view over Reims and the surrounding countryside of vines, hamlets and Romanesque churches, climb to the top of Mont Joli (274m).

❷ The D 26 then winds along to **Mailly-Champagne**, where in 1931, 23 vine growers formed a co-operative to counteract the monopoly and power of wine merchants. **Verzenay**, further on, boasts over 500ha of *premier cru* Pinot Noir grapes. Near by, **Mont Sinaï**, the highest point of the Montagne de Reims (288m), offers another magnificent panorama over the vineyards of Champagne. Further along, the outskirts of Verzy are noted for a forest of strangely-knotted beech trees (known as *faux de Verzy*), some of which are over 500 years old. Their contortions, once believed to stem from a divine curse, are now attributed to a genetic mutation.

❸ The route continues through the picturesque village of Ambonnay. Take the D 19 to Bouzy, which produces a light red wine, then the D 34 to Louvois, where Louis XIV's minister had a castle built for himself by Mansart, with gardens by Le Notre. From here, the D 9 leads to Avenay. Go right on the D 201 to **Fontaine-sur-Ay**, one

of the most charming villages in the region. Further along is Ay, a town once surrounded by ramparts where Henry IV, who fancied being addressed as the *Sire d'Ay*, owned land.

❹ Follow the road to Cumières, then turn right onto the RD386 toward **Hautvillers**, the cradle of Champagne, overlooking the Marne River. After walking up the steep, narrow streets of this picture-postcard village, with its wrought-iron signs illustrated with champagne motifs, you can make a pilgrimage to the former Benedictine abbey where Dom Pérignon conducted his experiments with double fermentation and wine-blending to obtain sparkling champagne. The property now belongs to a champagne house, which has reconstructed the cellar master's workshop.

❺ Return to the D 1, which runs along the Marne River to Damery and **Châtillon-sur-Marne**, dominated by a colossal statue of Urban II, the 11th-century pope from Champagne who launched the First Crusade. The Marne also evokes the celebrated episode from 1914 when 4,000 troops were driven up to the front in 600 Paris taxicabs to stop the German advance. From Verneuil, follow the RD 380 back to Reims.

CATHÉDRALE DE NOTRE-DAME DE STRASBOURG

*A*t the centre of an island embraced by the Ill river, Strasbourg's pink, sandstone cathedral soars gloriously skyward, a resplendent symbol of a city that has never lost its ancient tradition as a prosperous cross-roads of Europe.

*G*enerations of skilled craftsmen transformed this island city into a giant building site for three centuries, but few saw the fruits of their labours. Unlike most cathedrals, which were ostentatious proof of a wealthy Church, this fragile cathedral, built from the surrounding Vosges mountains, was financed by the bourgeoisie. The Oeuvre Notre-Dame, a civil institution founded in 1205, is still responsible for the cathedral's upkeep.

The Gothic façade of the cathedral never fails to amaze

■ A SUCCESSION OF STYLES ■

As a result of the immense time span involved – from when building began in 1190 to the completion of the spectacular single spire in 1439 – the cathedral encompasses a succession of architectural styles. The south side is Romanesque, while the grandiose west façade has intricate lacework and breathtaking grace, featuring a sculpted rose window, gables, pinnacles, stone needles and detailed ornamentation, including storks (symbols of spring and prosperity), lions (symbolising the tribes of Israel), angels, musicians and figures on horseback.

Indeed, the cast of characters sculpted on the three doors of this pure, Gothic façade seem about to speak. On the right portal, the Wise and Foolish Virgins are tempted by a seducer; on the left, the svelte figures of Virtues strike down Vices and in the centre, in stunning realism, is the Passion of Christ, framed by highly evocative scenes from the Old and New Testaments.

The south entrance is decorated with a remarkable couple, carved in classical style, representing the Church holding a cross and chalice on one side and the blindfolded Synagogue dropping the tablets of law on the other.

RIGHT: this superb aerial view of Strasbourg shows the cathedral dominating the skyline

---

The Astronomical Clock

Next to the graceful Pillar of Angels (*c*1230) depicting the Last Judgement, stands the Astronomical Clock, an 18m-tall engineering marvel designed by Conrad Dasypodius. Started in 1574, it worked until 1789, and was repaired by a local clockmaker in 1838. The march of time and the movement of planets can be read on the various dials. Each day a different deity appears in a chariot, and the 'ages of mankind' pass before the figure of Death. At 12.30pm, the 12 apostles file before Christ as the rooster crows three times and flaps its wings, recalling the denial by St Peter. Below, Death strikes the hour as an angel turns over a sand-timer.

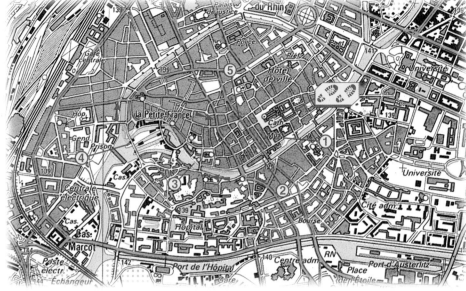

◾ LUTHERIAN REVOLT ◾

Inside, the darkness of the semi-circular Romanesque apse (painted in Byzantine style in the 19th century) contrasts with the harmonious proportions and elegant simplicity of the nave. The stained-glass windows – some of which were taken apart and hidden in salt mines during the Allied bombing in 1944 – are from the 12th to 14th centuries. Alsace is renowned for its organs, and the one in Notre-Dame is majestic, with florid, gilded carvings, painted wood, and figures of angels, merchants and Samson with his lion. Another fine piece is the chiselled octagonal pulpit

from 1485 depicting the Passion of Christ. When the clergy wanted to prevent a zealous reformer preaching from the Bible in this pulpit, they locked it with a key. Local woodworkers who had rallied to the cause struck back by carving a portable wooden pulpit.

The Ponts-Couverts add to the charm of Strasbourg

The city was profoundly influenced by humanism and the Reformation, and here the Lutheran doctrine won over. Mass, lavish ceremonies and other rituals were abolished for almost a century. When the city was added to France in 1681, Louis XIV promptly ordered a return to Catholicism and duly travelled with all pomp to the cathedral to kiss the holy crucifix.

WALK

length of walk: 5km
time: half a day
IGN Top 25: sheet 38160

Walk through the medieval heart of Strasbourg, with its wealth of architectural interest, including the Cathédrale de Notre-Dame de Strasbourg. On the cathedral square itself, note the 15th-century Pharmacie du Cerf at No. 10 (possibly the oldest in the country) and the 16th-century Kammerzell House (No. 16), with its abundance of sculptures and sparkling window panes. Boat trips, departing from the Embarcadère du Palais Rohan, also offer a leisurely 1½ hour tour.

❶ Pass in front of the post office to place du Chateau. To the right is the Musée de L'Oeuvre Notre-Dame, consisting of two houses from different periods, with a beautiful medieval garden. Next door, the 18th-century **Château des Rohan**, now housing several museums, is a model of classical elegance. From here, walk along rue des Rohan and rue des Cordiers to place du Marché-aux-Cochons-de-Lait. No. 1 is a rare example of a half-timbered building with outside balconies.

❷ Cross place de la Grande Boucherie onto rue du Vieux Marché-aux-Poissons. On rue de la Douane is the 14th-century Customs House, and alongside it is the **Pont du Corbeau** (Raven Bridge), where criminals were once locked in cages and drowned in the river.

❸ Continue along Quai St-Thomas to the Protestant **église St-Thomas**, in which can be found the handsome tomb of the Maréchal de Saxe by the sculptor Jean-Baptiste Pigalle. Follow rue de la Monnaie and rue des Dentelles, to the heart of 'La Petite France'. This picturesque neighbourhood of half-timbered houses, alleys and canal locks is named after a 16th-century

hospital that once stood here, where men afflicted with venereal diseases, referred to as *le mal français* (the French disease), were isolated. Rue du Bain-aux-Plantes includes splendid half-timbered and corbelled houses with sculpted orioles. Some of the best examples are at Nos. 40 and 42. Note the broad sloping roofs where tanners could lay their hides out to dry.

❹ Three **Ponts-Couverts** (covered bridges) are linked by square towers (prisons until 1823) that formed part of the city's defence system. Down-river is the Vauban lock. From the terrace, take in the striking view over the romantic Petite France quarter.

❺ Walk along Quai Turkheim and turn right on Grand' Rue, lined with houses dating from the 16th to the 18th centuries, following it straight to rue Gutenberg and **place Gutenberg**, dominated by the statue (left) of the inventor of the printing press, who developed his revolutionary discovery in Strasbourg. He is holding a scroll inscribed with the words 'And there was light'. Cross rue du Vieux Marché asux Poissons onto rue Mercière, which leads you back to the cathedral.

Route des Vins d'Alsace

Seemingly untainted by the upheavals of time, the Route des Vins is one of the most scenic journeys into the heart of Alsace, a region that – despite its turbulent history – preserves its heritage with discreet pride. Colourful, charming villages invite visitors to discover the fragrant wines that have been produced there for centuries.

The wines of Alsace have their own gods, traditions and heritage that unfold gradually during a leisurely drive along the Route des Vins, a 170km stretch from Marlenheim in the north to Thann in the south.

The Route des Vins is best explored in two to three days, but if you only have one, choose a few towns and soak up the atmosphere. The picturesque courtyards of medieval houses are museums in themselves, with vintners' tools adorning the walls, as well as ancient presses, carved barrels and wells with fancy, wrought-iron designs – and frequently a wine-tasting counter.

■ A PICTURE-PERFECT HERITAGE ■

The heart of Alsace is encapsulated along this route, where ruined fortifications lie deep in forests overlooking neat vineyards. Equally enchanting are the church bell-towers and half-timbered, ochre and pastel houses with flower-decked windows. Some of the oldest houses in Alsace trace their wine-making activities – a family tradition – back to the 12th century, when Alsatian wines were already being enjoyed across Europe.

Wine-making claims a rich variety of symbols, closely tied to the fertility cycle and the life of Christ. Crucifixes stand at the feet of vineyards, while pruning knives, sun rays and the coopers' emblem (a square-headed hammer and a barrel) are carved on house façades. The Wine Museum in Kientzheim records the art and history of wine-making.

The ritual of hearty foods and fruity wines can be savoured in the cosy atmosphere of a *winstub* – the convivial equivalent to a good English country pubs.

■ THE CLUB OF SEVEN ■

This is the only region in France which has maintained the tradition of naming wines by the type of grape used rather than geographical location. This 'Club of Seven', all presented in flute-shaped bottles are the delicate Riesling, the aromatic Gewürztraminer, the light Sylvaner, the refreshing Pinot Blanc, the fragrant Tokay Pinot Gris, the fruity Muscat d'Alsace and the Pinot Noir, the only Alsatian red or rosé. Alsaces *grands crus* come from 50 strictly defined pockets of land, and are exceptional wines made only during years with plenty of sun and little rain. Try the *Vendanges tardives*, made with over-ripe grape. These elite vintages are best savoured alone or with some *foie gras*, a Strasbourg speciality.

The beautiful setting of Little Venice in Colmar

The Unterlinden Museum

The capital of the Route des Vins, Colmar is a thriving city with a rich artistic heritage. The prestigious Unterlinden Museum, located in a former Dominican convent, houses treasures dating from the Middle Ages to the present. Particularly impressive is the 16th-century Issenheim altarpiece by Matthias Grünewald, a pessimistic polyptich before which the sick once prayed for miracles. The stark agony of Christ on the Cross, and St Anthony besieged by a tribe of mythical beasts contrast with the graceful representations of the Annunciation, the Nativity and the Resurrection. This masterpiece alone makes the trip to Colmar a must.

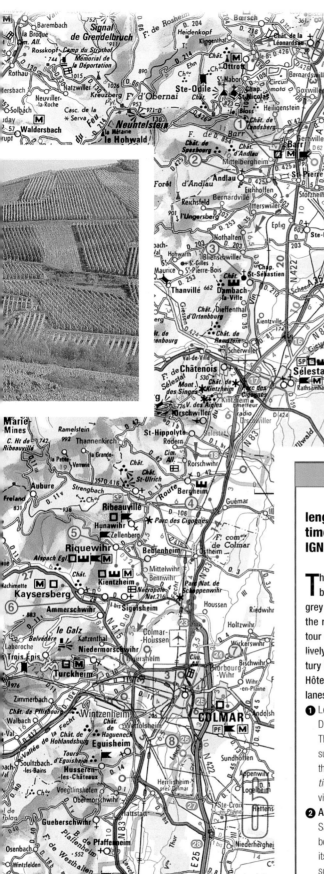

Sheltered by the Vosges are the vine-covered slopes of Alsace

The charming town of Riquewihr nestles among the grapevines

T O U R

length of tour: 120km
time: at least 1 day
IGN Top 250: sheet 104

The Route des Vins has its own logo featuring a bunch of grapes and a glass of wine against a grey background. There are some 100 towns along the route, each with its own special features. This tour covers an impressive selection and starts from lively, imposing Obernai. Its market square, 16th-century Halle aux Blés, the handsome, neo-Renaissance Hôtel du Ville (town hall) and surrounding maze of lanes still reflect a thriving trading centre.

❶ Leave Obernai on the D 426 and turn left onto the D 35, along the Route des Vins to **Mittelbergheim**. This proud place, with a 16th-century Hôtel du Ville surrounded by lovely Renaissance houses, is among the 100 most beautiful villages in France. It has a *sentier viticole* (a path cutting straight through the vineyards), which offers a perfect post-lunch stroll.

❷ **Andlau**, on the site of a 9th-century abbey founded by Sainte Richarde (wife of emperor Charles le Gros), boasts three *grands crus*. The abbey church still has its remarkable Romanesque tympanum. The market square has elegant 16th-century buildings and a Renaissance fountain. Andlau's Riesling is one of the region's finest.

❸ **Dambach-la-Ville**, one of the largest vineyards in Alsace, has survived the ages unspoilt. Dambach's Frankstein Grand Cru produces characterful Rieslings and Gewürztraminers.

❹ **Ribeauvillé**, dominated by vestiges of several castles, also produces Carola sparkling water. Here you can admire the architecture on the Grand' Rue, in particu-

lar the handsome Maison des Ménétriers with its decorated oriole. Louis XIV tasted the town's wines during a stop here in 1673.

❺ **Riquewihr**, the pearl of this route, is a pedestrianised town with no fewer than five museums, all located in magnificent old houses. Along rue du Général-de-Gaulle and adjacent lanes, the handsome townhouses, decorated with vaulted gables and orioles, evoke a prosperity that has survived the centuries.

❻ Fortified in the 13th century by Emperor Fredrick II, **Kayersberg**, just off the route, is another prosperous town; the parish church houses one of the rarest carved wooden altarpieces in Alsace. The fortified bridge spanning the Weiss gives a wonderful view over the town. Kayersberg is the birthplace of Dr Albert Schweitzer: an adjacent cultural centre features this Nobel Peace Prize laureate.

❼ The pedestrianised historic centre of **Colmar** offers an enchanting stroll past medieval, Gothic and richly ornamented Renaissance buildings. The tourist office provides an itinerary taking in the city's landmark houses, the tanners' quarter, the romantic quai de la Poissonnerie and 'Little Venice', formerly inhabited by boatmen and fishermen.

❽ Dominated by the ruins of three castles, exquisite **Eguisheim**, birthplace of Pope Leon IX in 1002, has wonderful half-timbered houses, Renaissance stairways, stone archways and sculpted lintels, flower-decked courtyards and uneven lanes. Several inns have rooms overlooking the vineyards, which are among the largest in Alsace. There is a vintners' festival in August.

❾ Continue to Gueberschwihr, Soultzmatt and Thann, the southern end of the Route des Vins.

Forêt de Gérardmer

*G*érardmer, the pearl of the Vosges, has long attracted visitors to the shores of its magnificent lakes – Lac de Longemer, Lac de Retournemer and Lac de Blanchemer – framed by gently domed summits and pine forests crossed by numerous walking paths.

Enjoying the spectacular scenery around Gérardmer, with Mount Hohneck rising in the distance

According to legend, Gérardmer's flair for tourism dates back to when Emperor Charlemagne came to hunt in the thick forests of the nearby valley. As he paused to contemplate the landscape, his horse impatiently kicked at the rock on which it was standing, leaving a hoof-mark which is engraved on it to this day.

Legend aside, this resourceful lakeside town, standing at an altitude of 660m, is an ideal base for discovering the Vosges, a gently landscaped mountain ridge with rounded summits known as *ballons*. Despite its past, when silver, copper and other minerals once brought prosperity, the area is very sparsely populated, with a surprisingly low population of just 9,000 across the entire region.

■ HAVEN FOR TOURISTS ■

Ever since the first French tourist office opened here in 1885, Gérardmer has been a popular destination. In 1928, it even made an unsuccessful bid to stage the Olympic Games! Despite being almost entirely destroyed by bombing in 1944, Gérardmer managed to recover its past reputation, and

in addition to being a tourist centre, it is still renowned for the quality of its household linen, an industry that employs a sizeable part of the population. From swimming, sailing, windsurfing and boat tours to bike riding, tennis and well-marked walking paths, there's always something to do, and if that's not enough, there's a casino overlooking the lake, as in most fashionable resorts that flourished during the *belle époque*.

Lac de Retournemer in the Vallée des Lacs is a peaceful spot

Les Fermes-Auberges

In summer, *marcaires* (local farmers) traditionally migrated with their cows to shingle-roofed, stone farms in the upland pastures of the Vosges, where they produced butter and cheese, notably the traditional, strongly flavoured *Munster*. Still made with local cows' milk (10l for 1kg of cheese), seasoned with caraway or aniseed, these cheeses are eaten fresh, sometimes with a dash of Kirsch. To boost incomes and maintain traditional methods, some dairy farmers have opened their farms to hikers – *les fermes-auberges* – serving rustic fare such as hearty soups, potato pies and home-made cheese. Some also provide no-frills accommodation. You can get a list from local tourist offices.

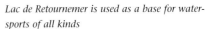

Lac de Retournemer is used as a base for water-sports of all kinds

occupation of Alsace, this forest is one of the best mapped in France, with 16,000km of marked footpaths, rest areas, information panels and chalets. In Gérardmer *Instants Nature* and *Montagne Evasion* organise trips to discover the fauna, flora and traditions of the Vosges. Nor do you have to be a seasoned mountaineer to reach the peaks – the gentle slopes provide a leisurely climb, with superb views over lakes, forests and valleys .

Joan of Arc defiant at the Ballon d'Alsace

■ A PROTECTED AREA ■

Gérardmer is in the heart of the massive Parc Régional des Ballons des Vosges, where the balance is between economic development and environmental protection. Above 1,000m, densely packed beech, spruce, fir and pine trees form a hypnotic bluish halo that gives the Vosges their distinct identity. Ancient glaciation has sculpted beautiful lakes, of which Gérardmer is just one example. Peat bogs and meadows harbour rare Alpine plants, while pastures on the bare, wind-swept summits provide grazing land for cattle in the summer. Thanks to the *Club Vosgien*, founded in 1872 during the German

TOUR

length of tour: 100km
time: 1 day
IGN Top 250: sheet 104

From Charlemagne's stone to an alpine garden, all can be seen on this tour, La Route des Crêtes, which includes waterfalls, forests and a spectacular view of the highest mountain in the Vosges.

❶ From **Gérardmer** follow the D 417 towards Colmar. Park next to the Hotel du Saut-des-Cuves and take the path towards the Saut-des-Cuves (marked with a green rectangle), an enchanting spot set among cascades and spruce trees, near the Pierre Charlemagne. Continue on foot along the GR 533 to the Pont des Fées, an 18th-century bridge spanning the Vologne. At the crossroads just before reaching the Saut-des-Cuves, take the D 67a towards **Xonrupt-Longemer** and continue to Longemer.

❷ **Lac de Longemer** and **Lac de Retournemer** (further along the D 67) are two magically serene spots, relics from the Ice Age, surrounded by meadows and forests of firs and spruce trees, and dominated by the Schlucht and Hohneck. A short but steep climb from a path near the Retournemer tunnel, the Roche du Diable offers an unrivalled view over the Valley of the Vologne

❸ Return to the D 417, heading towards Col de la Schlucht, a passageway linking the Vosges to neighbouring Alsace. Turn right off the D 417 along the D 430 towards the high-altitude **Jardin d'Altitude du Haut-Chitelet** which houses over 2,500 plant species from mountain areas around the world. Follow the Route des Crêtes (D 430), a strategic pathway built during World War I to join le Hohneck and le Grand Ballon, built during World War I. One of the spectacular sites of this mountain ridge is **le Hohneck** (1,362m). After the 1870 invasion of Alsace by Germany, this ridge marked the border between France and Germany.

❹ Continue along the D 430 past the lovely Lac de Blanchemer, Lac de Lauch and le Markstein, a winter sports resort, to le **Grand Ballon**. The view over lakes nestling in valleys, across to the Jura and the Alps is spectacular on a clear day. Slightly below the summit, the *Diables Bleus* (Blue Devils) monument witnesses that this area saw fierce fighting during World War I.

❺ Further along, **le Vieil Armand** was another major battle front, where fighting cost 30,000 lives.

❻ Follow the N 66 along the Thur Valley to **Bussang**, one of the highest villages in the Vosges and famed for the Théâtre du Peuple (The People's Theatre), an experiment started in 1895 by Maurice Pottecher. His descendants have upheld the tradition, drawing crowds every summer to the wooden theatre surrounded by forest.

❼ At **le Thillot**, a former mining centre, take the D 486 to return to Gérardmer.

CHÂTEAU DE VAUX-LE-VICOMTE

A masterpiece of 17th-century architecture, the magnificent château of Vaux-le-Vicomte is a perfect example of Louis XIV style. Lavishly decorated, it outshone all other châteaux at the time – a fact regarded with horror by Louis himself, the Sun King.

The stark interior of the 16th-century church at Champeaux

Vaux-le-Vicomte was built not by a king, but by Nicolas Fouquet, Louis XIV's finance minister and one of the most powerful – and corrupt – men under his rule. Vaux-le-Vicomte, in all its glorious splendour, owes its good looks to the fact that Fouquet spent outrageously, employing 18,000 people to construct his dream home, although the money was embezzled from the government.

■ EXPOSED! ■

Fouquet's downfall came suddenly. On 17 August 1661, he invited the king, along with 6,000 other guests, to a celebration so extrav-

agant that the jealous Louis XIV immediately questioned the source of all this splendour. Within a month Fouquet was in prison, where he languished for some 15 years until he died. The king wasted no time requisitioning the furniture, the artwork – and even the workers – for his ongoing project at Versailles.

■ THE CHÂTEAU ■

Vaux-le-Vicomte was conceived by the greatest artisans of the time, including the architect Louis Le Vau, the painter Charles Le Brun and the landscape designer André Le Nôtre. Many of the ideas used at Vaux-le-Vicomte were incorporated (with further embellishments!) at Versailles. Le Nôtre laid out the long vistas and the formal French garden in which light and water interplay so dramatically; for example, the château is surrounded by – and reflected in – a purely decorative moat.

INSET: the elegant library is one of the splendid rooms in Vaux-Le-Vicomte

The imposing château stands on a terrace amid landscaped gardens by Le Nôtre

Provins

This medieval town of Provins, east of St-Loup-de-Naud, was an important economic centre in the Middle Ages, Provins hosted two annual fairs, where traders brought spices and silks from the east, and woollen goods. In spring and summer, the town reverts to its historic past, and hundreds of actors dressed as beggars, knights, serfs, ladies and even lepers line the streets. There are jousting tournaments with knights on charging steeds, spectacular demonstrations of falconry and medieval weaponry, with catapults re-enacting an assault on the ramparts. A two-hour walking tour explores the town's ancient walls, and a multitude of events are scheduled throughout the summer. The main sights include the 12th-century Cesar Tower, a vaulted cellar with 10km of underground passages and mysterious inscriptions on the walls (the galleries were once used by the Freemasons) and the Maison Romane, a medieval museum.

Lavish as it is, the château is constructed on a more human scale that any of the royal châteaux. Fouquet's private apartments are on the upper floor, with the reception rooms below. The Grand Salon remained unfinished as his arrest was so sudden, and the proposed painted decoration by Le Brun progressed only as far as a set of studies (now on display).

Sixteen caryatids supporting the central dome represent the twelve months and the four seasons. The kitchens and wine cellar have been restored, and provide an idea of how servants catered to the needs of the more aristocratic residents.

The Saturday night candlelight tour in summer is a wonderfully atmospheric way of appreciating the château, which is also the venue for occasional concerts.

Flower-filled stone troughs add a splash of colour to the narrow streets of Blandy

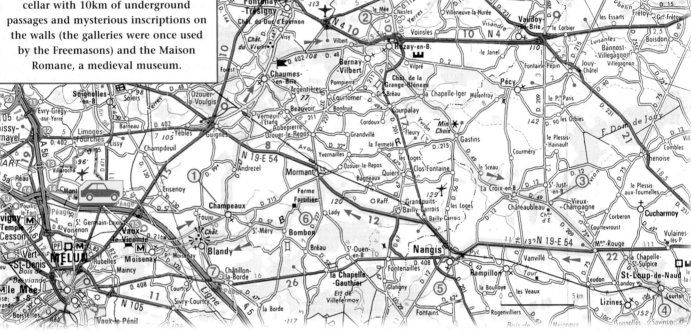

T O U R

length of tour: 100km
approximate time: 1 day
IGN Top 250: sheet 103

The medieval world is to the fore in this tour, which takes in a town once famous for its sacred music, calls in at an ancient and unique fortified farm and finishes with a relic of the Hundred Years War.

❶ From Vaux-le-Vicomte, follow the D 215 to **Champeaux**, a renowned centre for musical training in the Middle Ages. The annual Festival of Sacred Music brings to life this centuries-old tradition. The beautiful Gothic church has a fortified tower and lovely 16th-century stained-glass windows (if the church is closed, enquire at the town hall on the Place du Marché).

❷ From Champeaux, go north on the D 47. Cross the N 19 and continue to Verneuil. Follow signs to Chaumes-en-Brie. Leaving this town, turn right onto the D 48 to reach **Rozay-en-Brie**, where a few remains of the old fortified walls are still visible, along with the 12th-century church. Leave Rozay on the D 201, then turn left onto the D 49 towards Gastin.

❸ Follow the D 49 through **Châteaubleau** (from here the road becomes the D 209) leading to the N 19.

❹ Turn left and after about 2km turn right on to the D 49 leading to **St-Loup-de-Naud**. The little-known church is a jewel of Romanesque art, with 12th-century statuary on the portal rivalling that of Chartres. It was begun as a Benedictine chapel in the 10th century and completed in the late 12th: the apse, transept and first two bays of the nave are Romanesque, while the remaining architecture is early Gothic in style. A festival of classical music takes place in the church in September.

❺ Return to the N 19 and head west to **Nangis**. This town hosted a major fair in the Middle Ages. A few traces of its medieval past remain in the 13th-century church and the Château de la Motte-Nangis.

❻ Continue on to Mormant, and take the D 227 south, then turn right (signposted) to the **Fief des Epoisses**, a unique example of a 12th-century fortified farm (transformed in the 16th century), with turrets, high walls and a moat. The rooms inside contain an outstanding collection of furniture and art (closed Tuesdays).

❼ Continue south to Bombon and take the D 57 to **Blandy-les-Tours**. Recently renovated, the structure was fortified in the 14th century, during the Hundred Years War and is the sole remaining medieval fortress in the region. The round turrets, crypt and tall keep make this a fascinating example of medieval military architecture. Return to Vaux-le-Vicomte.

FORÊT DE FONTAINEBLEAU

The largest forest in the region, Fontainebleau is rich in natural wonders, including some 6,000 species of insects and 200 varieties of birds. Its confines shelter historic villages and beautiful landscapes, while its château is a historical and cultural landmark.

Every weekend, hikers, cyclists and rock-climbers swarm towards the Fontainebleau forest. However, with 300km of marked paths and 1,500km of forest lanes, there is plenty of room for everyone. Although the altitude never exceeds 147m, the terrain can be steep in places; indeed, the rocks at Fontainebleau are a well known training ground for serious climbers.

The kings of France had hundreds of lanes cleared for carriage rides through their domain and, in keeping with its past as a favourite royal hunting ground, horse-riding has remained a popular activity in the forest. The Fontainebleau tourist office can provide the necessary information for every type of excursion and activity.

Called the 'château of the centuries' by Napoleon, whose favourite residence it was, Fontainebleau contains eight centuries of French history within its walls. Like Versailles, this is an immense château, and far too big to take in on one visit. Several tours are on offer: the State Apartments, the Napoleon I Museum or the Chinese Museum. For an additional fee, the private apartments of the emperor and empress can also be seen. A scale model of the whole estate in the entrance to the château gives an idea of its exceptional size and the diversity of its gardens. Regional tourist information is also available in the main entrance hall.

The Fountain Courtyard and Carp Pond of the beautiful château

■ A ROYAL FAVOURITE ■

Some 30 sovereigns have taken up residence at Fontainebleau, beginning with Louis VII in 1137 and continuing up to the fall of the Second Empire in 1870, yet most of the construction and renovation was undertaken by just a handful of rulers. King François I was the first to take a serious interest in the palace, preferring it to all his other royal residences. He pulled down all the medieval buildings and rebuilt the château, employing Italian architects and decorators. The frescoes and stucco decoration from this period are still intact. François I was so enthusiastic about the Italian Renaissance style that he imported both art and artists to his palaces. Long before it reached the Louvre, the *Mona Lisa* hung on the walls at Fontainebleau.

■ NAPOLEON'S PREFERENCE ■

Henri II continued the work begun by his father, leaving as his greatest legacy the exquisite ballroom. King Henri IV enlarged the château considerably and redesigned the gardens completely, and Napoleon I often stayed at Fontainebleau, preferring it to

TOUR

length of tour: 100km
approximate time: 1 day
IGN Top 250: sheet 103

Impressionism and modern art are the main items of interest on this tour, with visits to two villages that have welcomed a host of famous artists. For variety, there is a beautiful château and a wood-framed market building dating from the 15th century.

❶ From Fontainebleau take the D 210 towards **Vulaines-sur-Seine**, where the Stéphane Mallarmé Museum is situated in the artist's former home (closed Mondays).

❷ Follow the D 138 to the intersection called the Croix de Toulouse, then turn left; take the first right onto Route de la Butte, which crosses the N 6 and winds around Mount Chavet. Cross the N 7 and continue on the road that leads through the Gorges de l'Apremont, leading to **Barbizon**. This picturesque little village played an important role in the development of modern art. It attracted landscape painters such as Corot and Millet, who contributed to the fame of the School of Barbizon. Galleries, antiques dealers and restaurants line the long main street, along with a museum in the former studio of painter Theodore Rousseau. Barbizon is also the starting point for a number of paths through the forest.

❸ Leave Barbizon on the N 37; at the first main intersection follow signs to **Courances**, which has a magnificent 17th-century château. Even more spectacular, however, are the gardens, originally designed by Le Nôtre and painstakingly restored by its present owners.

❹ Continue on the D 372 to **Milly-la-Forêt**, which is known for its 15th-century wood-framed market place.

❺ From Milly take the D 16 to **Larchant**. This old fortified town is dominated by the 59m ruined tower of the Church of St-Martin (late 12th century). The scene of the Last Judgement on the main portal was strongly influenced by the door of the Cathédrale de Notre-Dame in Paris.

❻ Leave Larchant on the D 16 and turn left towards Villiers-sur-Grez. Follow signs to **Grez-sur-Loing**. There is a superb view of the ruins of the Tour Ganne from the old bridge. From here, continue on to the D 40; turn left towards la Genevraye.

❼ Take the D 104 to **Moret-sur-Loing**, a charming old fortified town with an impressive *son et lumière* show on Saturday nights during summer. Impressionist painters came here to paint the 12th-century keep and the old stone houses lining the Loing. The artist Alfred Sisley moved to Moret in 1880, where he worked during the final years of his life. Return to Fontainebleau on the N 6.

The Gorges d'Apremont in Fontainebleu forest is known for its many unusual rock formations

Versailles, where he always felt overshadowed by the glory of his illustrious predecessor, the Sun King. It was at Fontainebleau that he abdicated in favour of his son, the Aiglon, on 20 April 1814. On being sent into exile, he stood on the Horseshoe Staircase and addressed his entourage: 'Soldiers of my old guard, I bid you farewell.' Don't miss the extravagant throne room, where gold bees (the emperor's emblem) are emblazoned over red velvet drapes.

▪ A FEEL FOR THE PAST ▪

The site is full of treasures, but one of the more curious aspects of Fontainebleau is the Chinese Museum, a rich collection formed by Empress Eugenie and housed in her private

Fontainebleau forest, once a royal hunting ground, is today popular with walkers, cyclists and climbers

apartments. For a flavour of the grandiose life at court, soak up the ambience of the Grand Apartments; in contrast, the private apartments reveal the more intimate aspects of château life.

The magnificent gardens alone, leading off in all directions from the château, are worth the trip to Fontainebleau. Visitors can stroll in the English garden, admire the immense pond, inspect the formal parterre and linger in the romantic Diana gardens.

During the summer there are carriage rides through the gardens; alternatively, a small train carries visitors on a guided tour of the town and the gardens.

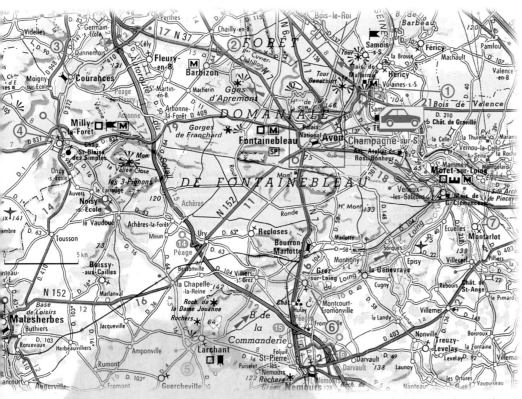

CATHÉDRALE DE NOTRE-DAME

For over 800 years, visitors and pilgrims have flocked to the magnificent Gothic cathedral of Notre-Dame, standing proudly on the Ile de la Cité, the historic and geographic centre of Paris.

The Cathédrale de Notre-Dame was not the first church to be built on the Ile de la Cité. During the Roman occupation of *Lutetia* – the early name for Paris – a temple dedicated to Jupiter stood on the tip of the island. Work on the majestic Gothic cathedral started in 1163, when Bishop Sully decided to replace two existing smaller churches dedicated to St Étienne and Notre-Dame with an edifice worthy of the capital of France. All that survived from the earlier structure was a portal, which is now part of the western façade (the St Anne portal).

It took nearly 100 years – and at least five different architects – to complete the present masterpiece. The initial structure had small windows and no flying buttresses, but in the 1220–30s the windows were enlarged to let more light into the building, and the famous buttresses (which also serve as drainpipes) were added.

On a fine, clear day, there can be few sights as memorable and as imposing as the cathedral of Notre-Dame, reflected in the Seine

■ CASUALTY OF THE REVOLUTION ■

The French Revolution took a heavy toll on Notre-Dame: the bells were melted down, the statues defaced and the cathedral became a 'Temple of Reason', and later a storehouse. Indeed, for Napoleon's coronation in 1804, the cathedral was so dilapidated that tapestries had to be hung inside to conceal the crumbling walls. After the publication of Victor Hugo's book *Notre-Dame de Paris* in 1831, a movement began to save the neglected monument, and Viollet-le-Duc was given the responsibility of returning the cathedral to its former glory.

The Gallery of Kings

In 1977, construction workers on a building site in the 9th arrondissement of Paris made an astonishing discovery: they unearthed 21 of the 28 stone heads from the Gallery of Kings along the front of Notre-Dame. The heads were pulled off in October of 1793, during the French Revolution, as it was thought that they represented the kings of France. They lay piled high in front of the church until 1796, when they were sold at public auction and acquired by a royalist who had them buried in the courtyard of the mansion he was building, where they stayed for 170 years. In the meantime, Viollet-le-Duc replaced them with heads of his own design. The originals are now displayed at the Cluny Museum.

The scale, detail and sheer beauty of the cathedral's rose windows are simply breathtaking

▪ SUPERB STAINED GLASS ▪

Notre-Dame is a masterpiece of Gothic architecture, a luminous temple of stone with shafts of light filtering through the glorious stained-glass rose windows. With the development of the ogival (intersecting ribbed vault), the weight of the building was taken by the pillars instead of the walls. As a result of this architectural innovation, windows of unprecedented size, almost from floor to ceiling, let in more light than ever before.

The north rose window, almost 13m in diameter, is a glorious testimony to the genius of Gothic architecture. The almost-intact, 13th-century rose window is devoted to the Virgin Mary, who sits surrounded by 80 figures representing prophets, judges and kings from the Old Testament.

▪ EXTERIOR MAJESTY ▪

Outside, the central portal of Notre-Dame portrays the Last Judgement; on either side are portals representing the Virgin Mary and St Anne. The statues on this portal are the cathedral's oldest, carved in about 1170.

Before the mid-19th century, the *parvis* (square) in front of the cathedral was much narrower than it is at present: a mere 18m separated the cathedral's façade from the houses before it. As part of his major urban renewal project to clean up what was still a medieval city, Baron Haussmann razed almost all the houses on the Ile de la Cité to create the square. The paving stones on the ground indicate the location of former streets, and a metal disc in front of the cathedral marks 'Point Zero', the place from where all roads leading to Paris are measured.

Roads leading out of Paris radiate from Point Zero

Before leaving the square, visit the archaeological crypt to admire the Gallo-Roman fortifications, bathed in an unearthly, bluish-green light, and get a feel for how the Romans lived here. To the left are ruins of Gallo-Roman rooms heated by hypocaust, a system used for bathing and heating private homes. Walk round the back of the cathedral for a view of the flying buttresses: they are most impressive at night, when they rise from the ground like stone lace.

▪ NOT TO BE MISSED... ▪

The Ile de la Cité has two other spectacular monuments: the St-Chapelle and the Conciergerie, both situated at the Palais de Justice complex. King Louis IX, known as 'St Louis', constructed the ethereal St-Chapelle as a giant reliquary to house the Crown of Thorns, which he purchased from the Emperor of Constantinople in the early 13th century (the crown, supposedly worn by Christ during his trial and crucifixion, cost three times what it took to build the St-Chapelle). The upper chapel is breathtakingly beautiful; the walls seem to dissolve together, in deep blue, red and green light from the magnificent stained-glass windows.

The Conciergerie was a citadel as early as the Gallo-Roman era, then became the seat of the first Merovingian kings (CAD 500–751) and a massive fortress under the Capetians (987–1328). It served as the royal palace from the 10th century to 1378, when it became the centre of the Parisian judicial system. Along the Seine is the oldest of the towers, the crenellated Tour Bonbec (meaning 'chatter', a grim reminder that this was once a torture chamber). During the French Revolution, the powerful Revolutionary Tribunal held court here, sentencing 2,700 people to die under the guillotine. Although law courts still occupy the upper floors, a museum on the ground floor now traces this period of French history, with reconstructed prison cells, including the cell in which Marie-Antoinette spent her last days.

The massive Salle des Gens d'Armes, one of the largest and most impressive examples of medieval secular architecture, was used as a refectory for the palace staff.

WALK

length of walk: 4km
time: 2–4 hours

The relatively compact area along the Seine and on the islands of the city offers stately historic buildings, breathtaking views, provincial charm and the liveliness of a great city.

❶ Start on the Right Bank at **place du Châtelet**, site of the monumental fountain commissioned by Napoleon on his return from Egypt.

❷ Walk along the quai de Gesvres, then across pont Notre-Dame to reach the refreshing sight of **Marché aux Fleurs** on place Louis Lépine. On Sunday, the market's flowers are replaced by birds.

❸ Now walk east along the embankment, turn right into rue des Ursins, then left and left again. The narrow streets of the medieval cathedral precinct have retained a few old houses. At the tip of the island is the underground **Mémorial de la Déportation**.

❹ Cross over to the Île St-Louis and turn left, following quai de Bourbon. Enjoy the peaceful atmosphere of this popular residential area.

❺ Turn right into rue des Deux Ponts and cross over to the Left Bank. Walk to square **René Viviani** to admire the fantastic views, then cross rue St-Jacques into rue St-Séverin in one of the oldest parts of the Quartier Latin. The gothic church of **St-Séverin** has a magnificent interior.

❻ From place St-Michel, cross back on to the Ile de la Cité. **Ste-Chapelle** is close by, and **place Dauphine** at the western end of the island is another peaceful spot. On offer here is a great view of **pont Neuf**, Paris's oldest bridge. Cross over to the Right Bank to finish at pont Neuf métro station.

Cimetière du Père-Lachaise

The Père-Lachaise cemetery may seem an unlikely tourist attraction, yet the greenery, history, celebrities and the 19th-century charm of the largest cemetery in Paris make it one of the most popular outings for tourists and locals alike.

The Père-Lachaise cemetery is the most prestigious and most frequented cemetery in Paris. Nearly one million people are buried there and more than two million visitors come every year. In 1626 the site was purchased by the Jesuits and was named Mont-Louis, in honour of St-Louis. The cemetery is named after the Jesuit priest de La Chaize, Louis XIV's confessor, who lived here between 1665 and 1709.

■ A NEW CEMETERY FOR PARIS ■

In 1803, Frochot, the prefect of Paris, purchased the property with the intention of creating a new cemetery for Paris. Although it now covers 44ha, the initial cemetery covered only 17ha. Asked to design the cemetery, the architect Alexandre Brongniart came up with a new concept which combined gardens and tombs of highly diverse styles. However, when it was first opened on 21 May 1804, the Parisians did not want anything to do with it, as they considered it too remote (at least until 1860, when the expanding capital once again outgrew its boundaries).

By 1815, Père-Lachaise contained fewer than 2,000 tombs, so the city officials came up with a brilliant publicity scheme: inter a few famous people and Parisians would soon want to follow. In 1817, the remains of lovers Heloïse and Abelard, along with those of Molière and La Fontaine (although their

> **Ashes to ashes**
> The large structure in the middle of Division 87 of the cemetery is the *columbarium*, which contains the ashes of those who were cremated, including those of Maria Callas, Isadora Duncan and Max Ernst.

authenticity is still questioned) were brought to the cemetery. By 1828, there were more than 33,000 tombs and the cemetery had to be expanded. Several parcels of land were purchased, creating the present 44ha cemetery.

■ AN OPEN-AIR MUSEUM ■

Père-Lachaise is roughly divided into two sections: the lower section is a romantic forest of tombs and vaults – some well tended, others seemingly abandoned – laid out along winding dirt paths and cobbled streets. A gentle

BELOW: the lifelike tomb of Victor Noir
RIGHT: peaceful walks through the cemetery increase its appeal

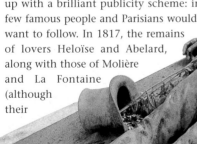

hill leads to the upper section, which has a more sober, grid-like layout.

The cemetery is a remarkable open-air museum of 19th-century funerary art. Every possible style is represented: flamboyant neo-Gothic, pompous Haussmannian, delicate wrought iron, rare marble and some surprising statuary. Keep your eyes open as you stroll around; the most interesting tombs do not necessarily belong to the most famous people.

Ask the guard at the entrance for the map giving the location of most of the tombs of the famous. You may need to wander off the paths to find the tomb you are looking for, as the map only gives a general indication of position. Start at the main entrance, on boulevard de Ménilmontant, where a long avenue leads to the impressive Monument to the Dead, sculpted in 1895 by Albert Bartholomé. Then follow your preferences: music fans head straight for the graffiti-covered tomb of Jim Morrison, who died in Paris in 1971 in mysterious circumstances. Classical music buffs flock to Frédéric Chopin's tomb; near by is the intriguing tombstone of Asturias, the Guatemalan winner of the Nobel prize for literature, whose tomb resembles a Mayan sculpture. Other famous writers buried here include Honoré de Balzac, Marcel Proust and Guillaume Apollinaire. Division 24 is home to a cluster of famous 19th-century painters, including Camille Corot, Charles-François Daubigny and Honoré Daumier.

The upper section is where celebrities such as Yves Montand and Simone Signoret, Sarah Bernhardt and Edith Piaf are buried. Oscar Wilde died in exile in Paris in 1900 and is commemorated by a striking winged sphinx. Initially the male figure was anatomically correct in every detail, but an anonymous visitor knocked off the offending parts.

▪ WAR MEMORIALS ▪

A series of monuments near the Mur des Fédérés(see box) forms a moving homage to the French who died in Nazi concentration camps. The inscriptions tell the grim story: of the 12,500 people deported to Mauthausen, 10,000 were exterminated; only 600 of the 13,500 sent to Neuengamme survived. The stark, bronze monument representing three skeletal men is a particularly emotional tribute to the dead of Buchenwald-Dora.

▪ HELOÏSE AND ABELARAD ▪

A Gothic canopy shelters the remains of this almost mythical pair of medieval lovers. The young Heloïse was staying with her uncle Fulbert who, some time around 1118, also offered his hospitality to the famous scholar Pierre Abelard, asking him to take charge of her education. She was only 17, he was 39, but they fell in love. Heloïse became pregnant and they married in secret. But the outraged Fulbert trapped Abelard and had him castrated. She entered a convent, and he retreated to a monastery. When Abelard died, Heloïse recovered his body and arranged for

WALK

length of walk: 4km
time: 2 hours

To round off a trip to the cemetery of Père-Lachaise, stroll through old villages in a little-visited part of the city to the peaceful setting of the Parc des Buttes-Chaumont.

❶ Leave the cemetery at place Gambetta and turn left into the avenue of the same name, then right into **rue de la Bidassoa**. This narrow street passes a couple of old but now much-changed roads (rue **Villiers de l'Isle-Adam** and **rue d'Annam**).

❷ Continue downhill past a small garden into rue Sorbier to reach **place de Ménilmontant**. This area was a hamlet in the Middle Ages, surrounded by woods and vineyards, and with a 17th-century château. Jean-Jacques Rousseau would gather plants for his collection up on the hill.

❸ Near by, on rue de la Mare, is the large 19th-century **église Notre-Dame-de-la-Croix**. The street dates from the 17th century and got its name from a pond close by. Continue along rue de la Mare in the heart of **Belleville**, once one of Paris's most charming villages, but blighted in the 1970s.

❹ Cross rue des Couronnes, take the steps along passage Plantin then turn left into rue du Transvaal to reach **Villa Castel** and a reminder of how the village once looked.

❺ Continue along rue de Transvaal to rue Piat and **Parc de Belleville**, one of the highest points of the city, offering views of many of the major sights.

❻ At the bottom of rue Piat, turn right along rue de Belleville, the main street of the old village. Cross the road and turn left into avenue Simon-Bolivar to reach the fine **Parc des Buttes-Chaumont**. Created in 1863–5 on the orders of Napoleon III, the park's lakes, grottoes, bridges and cafes provided a welcome retreat for local workers in this part of town formerly devoid of green spaces.

them both to be buried in the same coffin after her own death. But her plans were thwarted by a nun who placed them in separate coffins. Finally, in 1817 they were reunited when Alexandre Lenoir moved their remains to Pére-Lachaise.

INSET: the surprisingly modest Gassion-Piaf family tomb includes the remains of Edith Piaf.
BELOW: Oscar Wilde's monumental sphinx was sculpted by the British artist Jacob Epstein

TOUR EIFFEL

Built for the 1889 Universal Exhibition, the Eiffel Tower was intended to dazzle the world with the technological superiority of French engineering. For 40 years, this marvel of cast iron remained the tallest structure in the world, and it is still the universally recognised symbol of France.

The construction of the Eiffel Tower coincided with the centenary of the French Revolution. French engineer, Gustave Eiffel had already made his name with the railway bridges he had built throughout Europe, and he drew on this experience to construct the tower. The statistics alone reflect his technological expertise: 15,000 metal parts were prefabricated and numbered for assembly, while most of the 2½ million rivets were already in place before the structure went up.

The project proceeded almost without a hitch; although 132 construction workers laboured seven days a week for 26 uninterrupted months, there was not a single fatal accident, and the tower was complete (with the exception of the lifts) just seven days before the opening of the Universal Exhibition in May of 1889.

■ FACTS AND FIGURES ■

The tower was meant to stand for only 20 years, a fact that consoled its many detractors, who called it a 'hollow candlestick', a 'monstrous creation' and a 'bald umbrella'. The invention of wireless broadcasting was its saviour: in 1898 a radio link was established between the top of the tower and the Panthéon. It was the best radio mast the city could hope for and plans for demolishing it were shelved.

More than two million people flocked to the tower during its first year, overwhelmed by the delicate structure of metal and bolts. Today it is estimated that five million visitors come to see this most Parisian of monuments every year.

The four pillars of the tower are laid out along the points of the geographical compass. Three platforms are accessible to visitors, who can either climb the steps or take the lifts to the first floor (57m), site of the superb Jules Verne restaurant, and an incomparable view. There is an observation platform on the second floor (115m), located where the four giant legs converge. Finally, the third platform, at 276m, offers the best panorama in Paris. On a clear day the view extends for 72km.

The innovative tower created by Dijon-born Gustave Eiffel (1832–1923) was the world's tallest building until 1930

▪ NIGHT-TIME DELIGHT ▪

A spectacular sight at the best of times, the Eiffel Tower's full splendour really shines at night. It is a dazzling vision when illuminated, and an evening stroll is the best time to view this superb monument in all its finery.

▪ PALAIS DE CHAILLOT ▪

Although the Eiffel Tower is the most spectacular, there are many other worthwhile monuments in the area. Across the river rises the monumental Palais de Chaillot, built for a World Fair in 1937. Skateboarders from all over Paris converge on the vast plaza outside.

The building itself houses several museums, including the remarkable Musée de Monuments Français, which contains casts

and reproductions of monumental sculpture and architecture in France; the Musée de l'Homme, an ethnological and anthropological museum with exhibitions such as Six Billion People (about worldwide population growth) and The Mists of Time in the prehistory gallery, a chronological display that

traces mankind's evolution throughout the world from prehistory to the present; and the Musée de la Marine, a little-known treasure house containing scale models of warships dating from the 17th century to the present, including the famous tall sailing ships.

▪ HÔTEL DES INVALIDES ▪

Just west of the Eifel Tower, distinguished by its gleaming gilded dome, is the Hôtel des Invalides. Although most people associate it with Napoleon, the Invalides was actually constructed by Louis XIV in 1670 as a hospice for penniless veterans, the first of its kind in Europe. Visitors come to pay homage to Napoleon, whose remains were returned from Sainte Helena and placed here in 1840. His ashes lie within six coffins – one inside another – made of iron, mahogany, lead (two), ebony and oak respectively, placed

The superb gilded dome of the Hôtel des Invalides

within a massive red porphyry sarcophagus in a specially designed circular crypt.

▪ MUSÉE RODIN ▪

For a total change of ambience, walk a few steps to the nearby Rodin Museum, located in the Hôtel Biron on rue Varenne. The rose-filled gardens are studded with the artist's most famous sculptures, including *The Kiss* and *The Burghers of Calais*, *The Thinker* and *The Gates of Hell*, while the house, once used as a studio by Auguste Rodin (1840–1917), now exhibits his work, as well as treasures from his personal collection. Don't miss the room devoted to the intimate sculptures by Camille Claudel, Rodin's student and lover.

BELOW: Rodin's famous work Le Penseur

Daredevils

The Eiffel Tower has attracted its share of daredevils. In 1911, Mr Reichelt, a tailor, sewed himself a winged costume with which he intended to fly from the top of the Tower; instead of landing gracefully on the Champ-de-Mars below, he plummeted straight to his death. In 1923, Monsieur Labric rode his bicycle down the staircase from the first platform, and in 1948 Bouglione (of the famous Bouglione circus family) tried to get his elephant to climb up! In 1964, two mountain climbers scaled the west pillar to the top, and in 1987, two mountain bikers pedalled up to the second platform.

WALK

length of walk: 3km
approximate time: 1 hour (excluding visits)

This is a pleasant stroll from the Eiffel Tower to the Rodin Museum. Allow yourself plenty of time for climbing the tower and visiting the museum.

❶ The vast open space stretching from the Tour Eiffel to the École Militaire was originally designed as a parade-ground for the nearby military academy. Later it was used for major public festivals and World Exhibitions; almost half a million people gathered here in 1989 to celebrate the centary of the tower.

❷ Walk across the fountain-strewn formal gardens of the **Champ du Mars** and turn right into avenue de la Motte Piquet to the **École Militaire** (closed to the public). Designed by Louis XV's architect Jacques-Ange Gabriel, this magnificent neoclassical building was financed by a special tax on playing cards. Its

most famous cadet was Napoleon Bonaparte, who passed out with the comment "Will go far, given favourable circumstances'.

❸ As you walk round the building, you might enjoy a short detour to the antiques shops of the Village Suisse across avenue de Suffren.

❹ Continue along avenue de Lowendal and turn right on avenue de Tourville to reach place Vauban. Straight ahead is the fascinating **Hôtel des Invalides**.

❺ After your visit, emerge from the Invalides at place des Invalides. Turn right and right again into boulevard des Invalides. Now turn left into rue de Varenne to round off the walk with a visit to the often forgotten but superb **Musée Rodin**, set in beautiful private gardens.

LE LOUVRE

The glass-walled pyramid by Pei, a new Egyptian department, and a giant underground shopping centre have given the Louvre a much-needed facelift, bringing light and space into one of the world's greatest museums.

The foundations of the Louvre were laid in 1190, when King Philippe Auguste constructed a massive, stone keep on the western edge of Paris to protect the city from invasion by the English. Over the centuries, subsequent sovereigns have expanded, renovated, demolished and remodelled the Louvre, transforming it from a fortress to a lavish royal residence and finally to the present magnificent museum.

The Louvre houses some of the world's best collections of art, sculpture and antiques

shopping centre, with food court, auditorium, exhibition spaces, record stores and high fashion. One section was designed specially as a venue for twice-yearly fashion shows.

There are seven main departments, with works of art exhibited in one of the three main wings. These are called Sully (the Cour Carrée), Richelieu (running parallel to the rue de Rivoli) and Denon (stretching alongside the Seine). The Louvre is enormous, and certainly much too large to be appreciated in a single visit. The best strategy is to choose a few specific topics. There are guided tours (available in English) devoted to different themes: choose either a general tour or thematic itineraries, then pick up one of the excellent maps from the information desk to plot your route.

PAINTINGS GALORE

The collection of paintings is divided into works from France (with most on the upper floor of the Sully and Richelieu wings) and Europe. Every period of French art, from the 14th century to the mid-19th century, is well represented in the Louvre. Two of the more interesting rooms, situated alongside the

Once a royal palace, the Louvre is today one of the largest museums in the world

THAT PYRAMID

During its construction, many people were shocked by I M Pei's towering glass pyramid, an early part of the Louvre's modernisation scheme. Most now agree, however, that the pyramid, inaugurated in 1989, provides not only a spectacular entrance and improved illumination but also, with the cool spray of the surrounding fountains, a moment's respite for weary tourists.

REORGANISATION

The Louvre has been thoroughly reorganised; most departments have been rearranged and the brand-new Egyptian section, with nearly 55,000 exhibits, is one of the best such departments in the world. Indeed an entire town, the Carrousel du Louvre, now stretches beneath the museum, and includes a vast

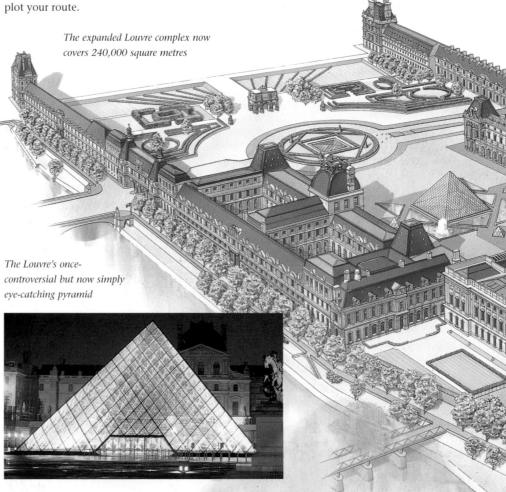

The expanded Louvre complex now covers 240,000 square metres

The Louvre's once-controversial but now simply eye-catching pyramid

Italian paintings, in the Denon gallery, are devoted to the Romantics – represented by Gericault and Delacroix – and the Neo-Classical painters, spearheaded by David and Ingres. Note especially Gericault's *Raft of the Medusa*, a work based on real maritime tragedy of his time. When it was first exhibited, the painting caused an outcry: not only was it not a classical subject, but it actually depicted a current event. After the ship capsized and the captain and crew had escaped with the lifeboats, those still stranded were forced into cannibalism.

The museum's impressive collection of Flemish paintings includes two rare masterpieces by Vermeer – *The Lacemaker* and *The Astronomer* – along with a number of works by Rembrandt van Rijn.

Of course, most visitors troop straight to the 16th- to 17th-century Italian paintings to see Leonardo da Vinci's *Mona Lisa*, but the vast Salle des Etats also contains an enticing number of other masterpieces, including several Titians, a Caravaggio and the recently restored *Marriage Feast at Cana* by Veronese, which stretches along the entire back wall.

The curved glass roof makes the most of the natural light in the Louvre

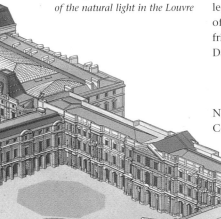

One of the many magnificent sculptures in the restored Cour Marly

---

St Germain l'Auxerrois

Just opposite the eastern end of the Louvre was this royal parish church for the Valois kings while they resided in the palace across the street. Most of the original decoration has disappeared, except for the superbly flamboyant Gothic porch (1435), the only such original left in Paris. The church has associations with a number of artists, and many of the architects, sculptors, painters and engravers who lived and worked in the Louvre are buried here.

▪ EGYPTIAN TREASURES ▪

The Egyptian section in the Sully wing is an ideal place to start. To reach it, walk through the medieval section of the original building, uncovered during the renovation work. A walkway leads around the foundations of the 12th-century Philippe-Auguste keep and sections of the old city wall.

Using its vast collection of pieces, the curators of the Egyptian department, have created a two-part exhibition: the ground floor is arranged thematically with exhibits devoted to every aspect of ancient Egyptian life, from writing to games, jewellery, farming and burial customs (with the *Crypt of Osiris*). The upper floor is arranged chronologically and includes such famous works as *The Seated Scribe* and a *Head of Akhenaten*.

▪ ORIENTAL ANTIQUITIES ▪

This section is devoted to the region stretching from north Africa to the borders of India. Two of the most spectacular pieces in this collection are the winged bulls from the palaces of King Sargon of Assyria (720 BC) and the frieze of the winged archers from the palace of Darius (late 6th century BC).

▪ SCULPTURE ▪

Not far from the Oriental antiquities section is Cour Marly, which includes Guillaume Coustouís sculptures of the marble horses that originally stood in the gardens of the Château de Marly, Louis XIV's country residence, then were moved to Place de la Concorde. Light streams in from the overhead skylight, creating a luminous effect even on a gloomy winter's day.

▪ GREEK, ROMAN AND ETRUSCAN ANTIQUITIES ▪

This section of the Denon gallery forms a museum in itself. The world-famous *Venus de Milo* epitomises the Classical period of Greek art, but for sheer energy, nothing matches the *Winged Victory of Samothrace*, which stands, wings outspread, at the top of the monumental staircase. This work (dated 190 BC) is by an unknown sculptor from Rhodes and is the finest known example of Hellenistic art.

The prestigious Opéra House and the elegant Palais-Royal epitomise the grandeur of this walk, which passes just outside the Louvre.

❶ Starting from place de l'Opéra, cross boulevard des Capucines then turn right, along **rue de la Paix**. Formerly rue Napoléon, the street has become a symbol of luxury and is lined with expensive jewellers, including Cartier. This leads to place Vendôme, with Napoleon atop the column.

❷ Cross the square, walk along rue de Castiglione and turn left into rue St-Honoré. The church of **St-Roch** halfway down the street once stood on a hillock know as the Butte St-Roch; it was levelled for the building of avenue de l'Opéra. Further along, on the right, rue des Pyramides leads to the square of the same name, where a 19th-century gilded statue of Joan of Arc stands on the very spot where she ws wounded trying to deliver Paris from the English.

❸ Follow rue St-Honoré, which leads to the grand **Palais-Royal**. This magnificent 17th-century palace, formerly home to Cardinal Richelieu, is now the Council of State office and not open to the public. Across the square is the **Théâtre-Français**, home of the famous Comédie-Française. Near by is place Colette, entrance to the Palais-Royal gardens.

❹ Walk through the **Jardin du Palais-Royal** and turn right into rue des Petits-Champs. You'll come to the charming covered arcades of Galerie Colbert and Galerie Vivienne and, near by, 17th-century **Notre-Dame-des-Victoires**, famed for its paintings by Van Loo, its monument to the composer Lully and its beautiful organ.

❺ Continue along rue Notre-Dames-des-Victoires, turn left past the Palais de la Bourse (Stock Exchange), then left again into rue de Richelieu. You will see a 19th-century fountain, dedicated to Molière, not far from the house where he died.

❻ Turn right into rue Thérèse, then follow rue Ste-Anne back to rue des Petits-Champs; on the corner stands Lully's house, adorned with musical motives. Walk back along avenue de l'Opéra.

CHANTILLY

***C**hantilly is one of the prettiest châteaux in Île-de-France, standing in isolated splendour surrounded by a moat and in the midst of lush forest. Chantilly is a world in itself, with parks and gardens, grand works of art and a wealth of history.*

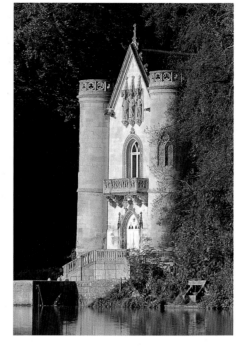

The Château de la Reine Blanche, a hunting lodge in the forest of Chantilly

ABOVE: *dressage demonstrations take place in the stable buildings of the Château de Chantilly*

Visiting le Château de Chantilly is like stepping straight into the world of the 18th-century aristocracy. The perfectly restored rooms are still furnished, books line the library from floor to ceiling, and the private apartments look as though its occupants have just stepped out.

▪ LE CHÂTEAU ▪

The château has two parts – le Petit and le Grand. The Grand Château, although Renaissance in style, is an entire reproduction. The original château, which once belonged to the Prince de Condé (who was fortunate enough to escape during the French Revolution), was transformed into a prison and ultimately dismantled, its furniture dispersed. The château as it stands today is the work of one man, le duc d'Aumale. After he inherited it – along with a colossal fortune – from his godfather, he devoted his energies to restoring the property, whilst amassing one of the richest art collections in France. On his death, he bequeathed both the château and the collection to the Institut de France.

The duc d'Aumale's spectacular art collection stemmed from his passion for rare books. His representatives scoured Europe for treasures to grace his personal museum, which eventually grew to include almost a thousand works from the Italian, Flemish, French, German, Dutch and English schools, dating from the 15th to the 19th centuries, as well as almost 2,000 drawings.

The Condé Museum includes paintings by Filippino Lippi, Raphaël, Poussin, van Dyck and Watteau. Perhaps the most interesting pieces are the magnificent, medieval,

The Château de Chantilly is surrounded by beautiful gardens and a lake

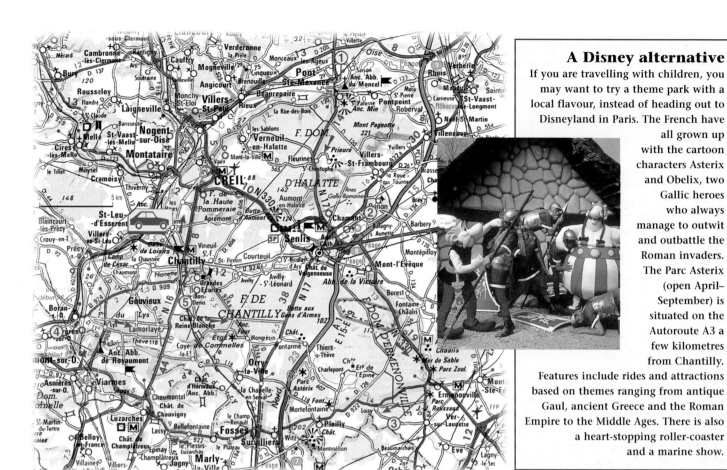

illuminated manuscripts, many of which come from Books of Hours, or Psalters, and from great literary texts. The most famous are the illustrations from the *Très Riches Heures de duc de Berry*, from the early 15th century.

▪ FOUNTAINS AND HORSES ▪

The gardens reflect the original formal design created by André Le Nôtre, who altered the course of the nearby stream, the Nonette, to form the Grand Canal, and laid a complex system of pipes and valves to create ephemeral displays of fountains and waterways.

Although famed for the splendid châteaux and grounds, Chantilly is also a favourite place for horse-lovers from all over the world who come for the races and to visit the Musée Vivant du Cheval et du Pony (Horse and Pony Museum), housed in what is probably the most beautiful stable block in the world, and featuring lavish stalls.

Chantilly is distinguished from other châteaux by these stable buildings. Henri-Louis de Bourbon, who owned the château in the early 18th century, commissioned the architect, Jean Aubert to design a grandiose structure to house his 240 horses, a pack of

over 300 hounds, all the carriages, a manège for the training school and accommodation for 100 stable boys, coachmen and grooms. The main building alone is 186m long. Visitors can view the popular dressage demonstrations or watch the thoroughbred horses train on the racetrack.

Chantilly is also the site for two of the most prestigious horse-racing events in the social season: the Prix du Jockey Club-Lancia and the Prix de Diane-Hermès, both held in June, and which, reminiscent of Royal Ascot, attract the cream of Paris society, behatted and bejewelled in their designer best.

TOUR

length of tour: 100km
time: 1 day
IGN Top 250: sheet 103

Starting with a ship-shaped abbey and a bishop's palace turned technology museum, the tour progresses to a romantic ruin with Giotto paintings. From the last home of Rousseau, see how a silent order of monks dealt with the necessities of life. Finally, after pausing at a white queen's castle, see how the monks of another abbey met their desire for fresh fish.

① Leave **Chantilly** and head the north on the N 16 towards Creil. Follow the D 120 from Creil to Verneuil-en-Halatte. Continue on the D 120 past Pont-Ste-Maxence, and follow signs to **l'Abbaye Royale de Moncel**, a remarkable 14th-century wooden-framed structure shaped like the hull of a ship.

② Take the N 17 south to Senlis, a charming town with narrow streets and a 12th- to 13th-century

cathedral. The former Bishop's Palace now houses an art and archaeology museum. Leave Senlis, following signs to Meaux, along the N 330. At the edge of the Forêt Ermenonville is **l'Abbaye de Chaalis**, where the romantic 13th-century ruins of the former Cistercian monastery have been partially restored. The museum houses two painted panels by Giotto.

③ Continue to **Ermenonville**, where the philosopher Jean-Jacques Rousseau lived in the château and spent his last days. He was buried here in 1778, but in 1794 his remains were transferred to the Panthéon in Paris.

④ From Senlis turn onto the D 922 and continue past Luzarches toward Viarmes. Turn right at the intersection with the D 909 and follow signs to **l'Abbaye Royaumont**. This abbey, founded in 1228 by Saint Louis, became vastly wealthy through royal patronage. Although the church was destroyed, the foundations are still visible and the abbey palace and cloisters are in remarkably good condition. The former refectory (where 60 monks once used to eat in total silence) is now used for music concerts. Visit the kitchens and the latrines,

where the monks devised a system of running water through the building.

⑤ Continue north on the D 909, then turn right onto the D 118 to **Lamorlaye**. Turn right onto the N 16 and go on for about 1km; turn left again onto the D 118 towards Coye la Forêt. Follow le Route des Etangs, which leads to the **Château de la Reine Blanche** (Castle of the White Queen), a former mill that was transformed into a hunting lodge in 1825. Take the road towards the *étangs* (ponds), created by the monks of the Chaalis abbey (there are two roads, one running along the north edge, the other to the south; they meet at the far eastern edge). Several footpaths lead around the ponds. Continue on to the Carrefour de la Table de Mongresin. Turn left on to the D 924a back towards Chantilly, to appreciate the impressive view of the château.

VERSAILLES

*V*ersailles is not the oldest, nor the largest, nor the most perfectly designed château, but for the millions of visitors who converge here every year, it epitomises the essence of what a royal palace should be, the reflection of the radiant glory of Louis XIV, the Sun King.

The sumptuous l'Opera at Versailles was built by Ange-Jacques Gabriel in 1768

Although Louis XIV was responsible for the grandiose château and grounds that extend over 800ha in the town of Versailles, it was his father, Louis XIII, an avid hunter, who in 1623 built the original modest lodge in the heart of the forest. Later, he asked Philibert Le Roy to build a more spacious manor, which was completed in 1634.

Louis XIV was only five years old when his father died in 1643. He inherited the small

ABOVE: *the Apollo Basin and, below, the Galerie des Glaces, dazzling at every turn from its 17 mirrors*

château and slowly initiated a rebuilding and renovation project that would last throughout his entire 72-year reign. He spent lavishly, giving him the name Le Roi Soleil (Sun King), and used the talents of the best artisans: the architect Louis Le Vau (succeeded after his death by Jules Hardouin-Mansart), the painter Le Brun, and the landscape designer Le Nôtre. In 1611, Le Vau constructed the Orangerie; by 1668 the king decided to expand the château toward the gardens; and in 1678, Hardouin-Mansart eliminated the terrace overlooking

---

History in the making

Versailles is more than a historical monument and popular tourist destination; it has also been the site of numerous historical events:

- The declaration ending the American Revolution was signed here by British and US representatives on 20 January 1783 (the definitive peace treaty was signed that same year in Paris).
- Headquarters of the German armies laying siege to Paris during the Franco-Prussian War of 1870–71.
- Seat of the Allied War Council during World War I.
- The Treaty of Versailles was signed in the Hall of Mirrors on 28 June 1919.

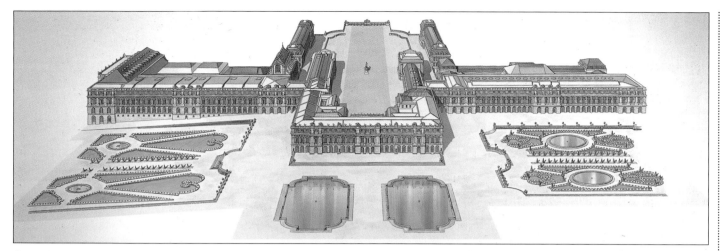

the gardens to create the splendid Galerie des Glaces (Hall of Mirrors).

An inveterate builder, when Versailles became the seat of government in 1682, Louis XIV expanded the construction projects to accommodate the entire court as well as government administrators and all the servants involved in running the palace. He continued to increase his domain, adding the north wing, the Grand Trianon and the chapel (completed in 1710, five years before his death). Louis XV continued the extravagant projects, adding the Hercules Room, the magnificent Opera and the Petit Trianon.

■ THE CHÂTEAU ■

Versailles, like the Louvre, is far too extensive to explore in a single day. Visitors have a number of options. Guided tours of various sections – helpful but not obligatory – are available during the day. The main sections of the château – the King's Apartments, the Queen's Apartments and the Hall of Mirrors – can be visited without a guide. Headsets can be rented for these areas.

The tour of the royal apartments starts in the upper vestibule of the chapel. The King's Apartments consist of a series of seven rooms designed by Le Brun. From 1684 onwards they were used for royal audiences and official functions, as Louis XIV actually resided in the rooms facing the inner Marble Court. The King's Bedchamber, a lavish celebration in crimson and gold, has been restored to look just as it did when Louis XIV died here on 1 September 1715.

The spectacular Queen's Room is just as gilded and splendid as the King's Room

The Queen's Room rivals that of the king for gilded splendour. A succession of three queens and two dauphines (wife of the current dauphin – the reigning king's eldest son) lived here from 1672 to 1789. No fewer than nineteen children were born – in public – in this room.

Louis XIV set out to make his palace the most glorious in Europe, and part of its fame is due to the 73m-long Hall of Mirrors, where 17 large mirrors run the length of the hall, reflecting the light from the 17 windows overlooking the formal gardens.

■ THE GARDENS ■

Everything about Versailles was intended to reflect the magnificence of the Sun King, and the gardens are no exception. Le Nôtre created possibly the most perfect example of a formal French garden, integrating long, straight avenues with enclosed groves and fountains, adorned with bronze, marble and gilded statues. He undertook immense earth-moving and drainage work to create a series of linked terraces, and created the Apollo Basin, just below the windows of the Hall of Mirrors, to reflect the façade of the palace, the water and the sky, much like the Hall of Mirrors reflects the chandeliers and windows.

Take time to explore the small groves and labyrinthine paths; many were created as part of the grand festivities organised periodically under Louis XIV to accompany complex displays of waterworks. The most extraordinary was the fête in 1664, a week-long celebration including tournaments, ballets, fireworks and several new plays by Molière, written specially for the event. The 32 pools and fountains are switched on as part of the 'Grand Eaux' musical display every Sunday from early May to early October.

■ LE GRAND ET PETIT TRIANON ■

After Louis XIV moved his court to Versailles, the palace was overrun with people – nearly 10,000 were housed in the château and its grounds. To escape the constant crush of people in the palace, Louis XIV commissioned Jules Hardouin-Mansart to build the Grand

The impressive symmetry of the royal palace of Versailles is the epitome of grandeur

Trianon, a small, pink-marble palace. It took less than a year to build and was completed in 1688. The king used to bring his family here during the summer for short breaks from palace life. Louis XV later constructed the Petit Trianon in 1768 for his mistress, Madame de Pompadour, as a private meeting place. When Louis XVI became king, Marie-Antoinette took over the Petit Trianon and created the Hameau, a miniature farm around a small pond. For those who do not like to walk, a small train runs between the palace and the Trianon.

T O U R

length of tour: 95km
time: 1 day

Starting from Porte de St-Cloud, this picturesque drive takes you through the wooded Vallée de Chevreuse to Rambouillet, with its castle and park.

❶ From Porte de St-Cloud follow signs for Chartres/Orléans. After 17km leave for Saclay and take the N 306 towards **Chevreuse**. This little town is dominated by the ruins of its medieval château, which houses the Maison du Parc Naturel Régional de la Haute Vallée de Chevreuse.

❷ From Chevreuse take the D 906 southwest to **Rambouillet**. The 14th-century fortress is now an official residence of the the Rupublic. In the park, criss-crossed by canals, look for the Laterie de la Reine (Marie-Antoinette's dairy).

❸ Drive back on the D 906 for 10km and turn left on the D 91 towards **Dampierre**, with its 16th-century stone and brick château.

❹ Continue on the D 91 across the River Yvette, negotiating the '17 bends' to the ruined former Cistercian **Abbaye de Port-Royal-des-Champs**.

❺ Continue along the D 91 to Versailles, and return to Port de St-Cloud along the Route de Paris (D 10).

CHARTRES

*E*ight hundred years after Chartres Cathedral was built, the sight of the church soaring over the surrounding plains is still awe-inspiring from a distance, as well as breathtakingly beautiful from within, illuminated by its boldly coloured stained glass.

In the Middle Ages, holy relics were the single most important possession of any church, and in its treasury, Chartres has one of the most highly prized: the Sancta Camisia, the garment supposedly worn by Mary when she gave birth to Christ. Charlemagne's grandson gave this relic to the cathedral in 876, and since then pilgrims have flocked here from all over Europe.

The north window in the cathedral depicts scenes from the Old Testament

■ RESURRECTED FROM ASHES ■

Chartres was also among the most prestigious centres of learning, attracting scholars from all over Europe. References to a church on this site date from 743, and a series of fires destroyed several earlier cathedrals. The worst disaster was in 1194, when a great fire burned down both the cathedral and the entire town. Three days after the fire, while the ruins were still smoking, the cardinal appeared in front of the cathedral, holding the holy relic. The people were convinced that this miraculous

Magnificent Chartres Cathedral, a medieval master-piece that took only 31 years to build

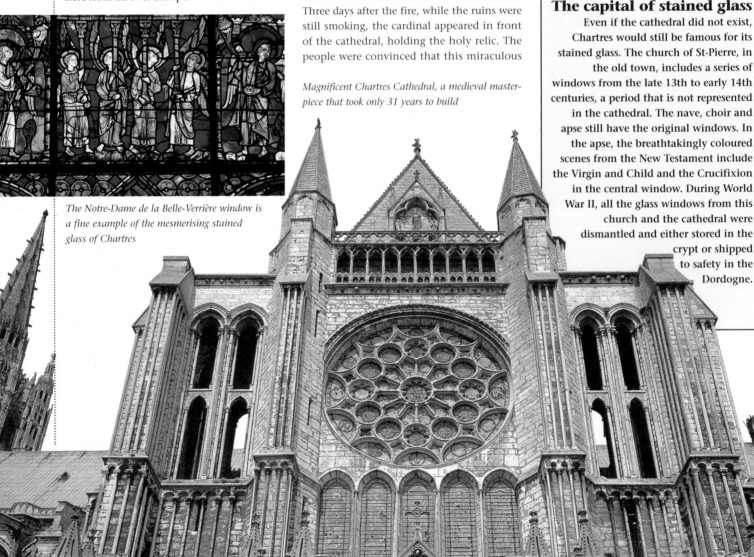

The Notre-Dame de la Belle-Verrière window is a fine example of the mesmerising stained glass of Chartres

The capital of stained glass

Even if the cathedral did not exist, Chartres would still be famous for its stained glass. The church of St-Pierre, in the old town, includes a series of windows from the late 13th to early 14th centuries, a period that is not represented in the cathedral. The nave, choir and apse still have the original windows. In the apse, the breathtakingly coloured scenes from the New Testament include the Virgin and Child and the Crucifixion in the central window. During World War II, all the glass windows from this church and the cathedral were dismantled and either stored in the crypt or shipped to safety in the Dordogne.

▪ SACRED STAINED GLASS ▪

The cathedral is justifiably world famous for its stained glass, but it is the harmony of the architecture, sculpture and glass that gives such an overwhelming impression of ethereal stone and dazzling jewels. Apart from the 12th-century Royal Portal, which alone survived the great fire, the cathedral was completely rebuilt in just 31 years (1194–1225), and is one of the earliest fully Gothic churches.

At 16m, the nave of the cathedral is the widest in France, and has on its floor the only surviving stone labyrinth. In the past, pilgrims made their way through the 290m maze on their knees.

Chartres' collection of medieval, stained-glass windows is the most complete of any cathedral. Along with the sculptures outside, they were created to provide religious education to a largely illiterate population. Many of the scenes portray Old and New Testament figures; others depict images of princes and court figures and even representations of daily

The cathedral can be seen from all over Chartres

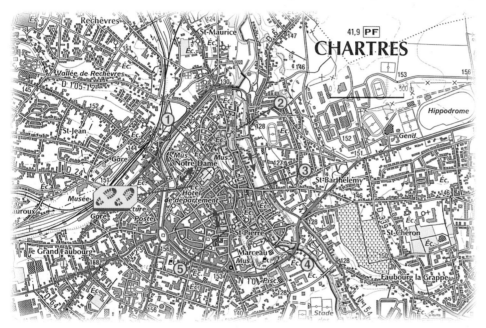

event was a sign from the Virgin Mary that a new church should be built. Again, funds poured in from royal sources, resulting in the present cathedral, which dates from the 12th to 13th centuries.

Tranquil backwaters of the River Eure just add to the town's charm

life, including industrious butchers, shoemakers and weavers. A number of the windows were financed by the guilds, and these scenes signify the benefactors. Some of the most famous include the Blue Virgin (c1150), the three rose windows, and the Tree of Jesse over the Royal Portal. The windows were meant to be 'read' like immense picture books, from bottom to top and left to right, and easily understood by everyone. The windows are arranged so that taken in order, the north wall shows scenes from the Old Testament and the south depicts the New Testament, culminating in the Resurrection; finally, the Last Judgement faces the setting sun to the west.

WALK

length of walk: 3km
time: half a day
IGN Top 25: sheet 21160

While in Chartres, visitorswill find a clearly marked tour of the old city, with plaques indicating '*circuit touristique*' placed strategically along the way. This walk gives you a flavour of the ancient city. Visit a stained-glass centre, cross the river over fascinating bridges, indulge an interest in archaeology and finish with fresh salmon in a charming restaurant.

❶ Leave the cathedral and turn left, taking rue du Cheval Blanc along the northern side, to the **Centre International du Vitrail**, an exhibition and research centre, inaugurated in 1980, for old and new stained glass. Return to the cathedral through the arched passageway (rue St-Yves) and turn left.

❷ Just behind the cathedral, housed in the former Bishop's Palace, is the **Musée des Beaux-Arts** (closed Tuesday). The museum houses 12 remarkable enamels of apostles by Léonard Limousin, commissioned by King François I in 1545. Continue through the gardens, which offer a splendid view over the old town below. Go down the steps and out through a small doorway on the left – but before leaving the gardens, turn and look at the choir of the church above. Steps lead down to the Romanesque **église St-André**.

❸ Cross the river by the stone and iron bridge and turn right along rue du Massacre. Recross the river by the iron bridge, where a small stone building protects **la Fontaine de St-André** – once the main water supply for the city, and used again in 1944 after the city was bombed. Turn left and cross the river once again over the le Pont des Minimes.

❹ Follow the river to the next stone bridge, called the Bouju Bridge. Cross the bridge and continue along rue du Bourg to the corner of rue des Ecuyers. Look out for the 16th-century sculpted wooden staircase of the **Reine Blanche** (White Queen). Turn left and follow the cobblestone street past the timber-framed house on the left. Immediately after this house turn left into Tertre du Pied Plat, which leads to rue aux Juifs. Follow this road to the 12th- to 13th-century **église de St-Pierre**, with magnificent 13th- to 14th-century stained-glass windows representing figures from the Old Testament.

❺ Follow rue St-Pierre in front of the church and up the hill to the **Maison de l'Archéologie**. After visiting the museum retrace a few steps and turn right just past the timber-framed house into the small passageway, which leads up to the église St-Aignan. Continue up rue des Grenets, which leads to the marketplace. Just past here is **rue de la Poissonnière** to the right, with a splendid 16th-century half-timbered house, le Maison du Saumon (Salmon House), now a restaurant. Stop for refreshments before returning to the cathedral.

VALLÉE DU LOIR

The small Loir River meanders through some of the most picturesque scenery in the Loire region – past charming villages, châteaux and gently rolling countryside quilted by orchards, prestigious vineyards and fields of bright yellow mustard, sunflowers and golden wheat – earning the valley the apt sobriquet 'Gentle France'.

The tranquil, little-known river called Le Loir – not to be confused with its bolder neighbour, La Loire – meanders through the *douceur de vivre* of rural France, with its 'scenes of vineyard, orchard, meadow-ground and tilth, calm waters, gleams of sun and breathless trees ...' (William Wordsworth).

GENTLE FRANCE

From its source in Île-de-France, the Loir travels 350km to meet with the Sarthe near Angers; it passes through an unhurried, unchanging landscape bordered by gentle hills, verdant forests and rich farmlands, with châteaux and country manors at every bend. Originally the river was navigable up to Château-du-Loir but now the only boats, tied up to the silvery willows at the water's edge, belong to fishermen. On its banks grow the grapes used to produce the Côteaux du Loir – some of the region's finest wines.

■ AN INSPIRATIONAL LANDSCAPE ■

The Vallé du Loir's deserted country roads, lined with slender poplars reflected in the slow, lazy river, follow the Loir's course across

LEFT: the 14th-century St George's Gate guards the way into Vendôme from the river
BELOW: the lush Loir valley at Lavardin, site of a massive ruined castle, inset

some of the richest, most fertile countryside of France. Over the centuries the white tufa towns, the soft green landscapes, the blues of

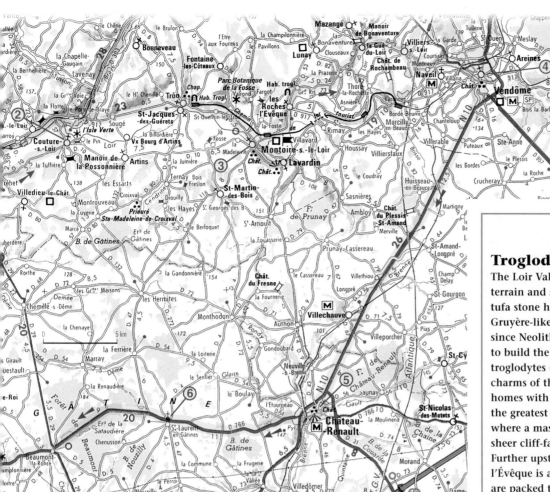

Troglodytes

The Loir Valley is renowned for its chalky terrain and steep, riverside bluffs, where white tufa stone has been hollowed out leaving Gruyère-like holes in the cliffs, used as shelter since Neolithic times. Later, the stone was used to build the region's châteaux. Today, these troglodytes (cave-dwellings) are one of the great charms of the valley, and many are permanent homes with all modern conveniences. One of the greatest troglodyte settlements is at Trôo, where a mass of narrow, rocky passages along a sheer cliff-face link these extraordinary homes. Further upstream, tiny flower-filled Les Roches-l'Évêque is also famed for its troglodytes, which are packed tightly into its wooded cliffs.

the river, the silvery sands and the creamy-grey stone of the fairy-tale châteaux have provided a rich source of inspiration for writers, artists and poets.

The Manoir de la Possonière, a beautiful Renaissance manor house richly decorated with carved details and set amongst fields and woodland south of the Loir in Couture, was birthplace and home to the 16th-century poet, Pierre de Ronsard. Here he wrote sonnets and odes, unappreciated during his lifetime but now greatly admired for their outstanding lyricism. The ancient village church contains the Ronsard family effigies.

Just north of Le Gué-du-Loir, The Manoir de Bonaventure belonged in the 16th century to Henri VI's father Antoine de Bourbon-Vendôme, who entertained his friends here, including some of the poets of the Pléiade. Later, in the 19th century, it belonged to poet Alfred de Musset.

◾ HIDDEN TREASURES ◾

Other gems in the valley include Vendôme, a picturesque medieval town, spanning several branches of the Loir and famed for its beautiful old buildings, riverside walks, ruined castle

and exceptional regional cuisine. There is also Montoire, with its huge main square and bandstand, castle ruins, and priory, attractively set on the river, and the neighbouring flower-bedecked village of Lavardin with its spectacular ruined fortress, which resisted attacks by two English kings in the 12th century. In the Middle Ages, pilgrims on the road to Santiago de Compostella followed the upper reaches of the river before heading south to Tours, their religious fervour leaving its mark in the valley's many churches and chapels, notably those at Montoire and Lavardin, with their ornate frescoes.

T O U R

length of tour: 190km
time: 1 day
IGN Top 250: sheet 106

This tour gives you a more unusual idea of the Loir, as it visits a motor racing bar, and inhabited cave dwellings, taking in water mills and a leather museum as well as ruined castles and pretty châteaux.

❶ Start in Château-du-Loir, named after its ruined fortress. Head south on the N 138 to Coëmont, then left along the D 64, following the northern bank of the Loir to Vouvray-sur-Loir, a tiny village, known for its wine cellars, housed in caves dug out of the cliffs. Continue on the D 64 then take the D 61, following signs to Marçon. Turn right at Le Port Gautier, crossing the river past the Lac des Varennes, a large lake popular for fishing, sailing and swimming. The sleepy village of

Marçon has a small square, lined with lime trees and framed by quaint cream stone houses, a church and small shops selling wine and other local produce.

❷ Turn left through lush, open countryside to la Chartre-sur-le-Loir, a small town, known for its Jasnières wine-caves and the ivy-clad Hôtel de France, which attracts motor-racing teams from the Le Mans 24-hour race and their fans, who come to see the signed photographs in the bar. Leave la Chartre on the D 154, closely following the course of the Loir through Tréhet and onto the D 10 to Couture-sur-Loir, birthplace and home of 16th-century poet Pierre de Ronsard.

❸ Head towards Poncé on the D 57. Cross the river, then turn immediately right onto the D 305 to Pont de Braye. At the end of the village, fork right across the River Braye and continue through the great troglodyte village of Trôo and on to the bustling provincial town of Montoire-sur-le-Loir on the D 917. From the main square, head towards the ruined castle, over the bridge and first left onto the V 3, a narrow country lane beside

the river, through woodland to the showcase village of Lavardin, its mighty ruined château dominating the skyline. Cross the small stone bridge and circle back to Montoire on the D 108. In the main square, turn immediately right, leaving town towards Vendôme.

❹ Pass through Les Roches-l'Évêque, a beautiful village famed for its troglodyte houses, and on to Le Gué-du-Loir and Villiers-sur-Loir, on the D 24 then the D 5, until you reach the lively market town of Vendôme.

❺ Head south from Vendôme on the N 10 to old-fashioned Château-Renault, with its ruined medieval castle, ancient riverside mills and leather museum.

❻ Back on the N 10, turn right at the first roundabout onto the D 766, through St-Laurent-en-Gâtines, notable for its remarkable church – a converted 15th-century red-brick manor, with an added stone apse.

❼ Continue across sparsely populated farmland, through Beaumont-la-Ronce, with its attractive turreted château and on to Neuillé-Pont Pierre, where a right turn on to the N 138 heads back to Château-du-Loir.

CHÂTEAU ET JARDINS DE VILLANDRY

Gardeners will delight in Villandry, one of the last great Renaissance châteaux to be built in the Loire, where the magnificent, ornamental gardens – among the finest and most fascinating in Europe – are even more famous than the splendid castle itself.

Villandry enjoys worldwide fame for its gardens, with over 250,000 flower and vegetable plants laid out with mathematical precision and framed by hundreds of vine trellises, shaded bowers and alleyways, over a thousand lime tree, and 52km of box hedgerow. The gardens were restored to their original state by Joachim de Carvallo, founder of 'La Demeure Historique' (French Historic Houses Association), who acquired the château in 1906. They represent the most complete example of formal Renaissance style in France today.

The guided tour of the château explains the significance of the formal gardens

■ CHANGING HANDS ■

The château itself was once an early medieval fortress, rebuilt in the early 16th century in the Italian Renaissance style by Jean Le Breton, Secretary of State to François I. Little remains of the early structure, except the keep – a robust tower harmoniously integrated into the Renaissance architecture – which offers a spectacular panorama of the rivers Cher and Loire and a bird's-eye view of the gardens. The castle was saved from deterioration by Spanish conservationist Dr Carvallo at the same time as the gardens; his influence is reflected in the furnishings of the splendid state rooms with their fine 18th-century Spanish furniture, a family collection of 16th- to 18th-century paintings, including works by Goya, Velázquez and Murillo, and a beautiful Moorish mosque ceiling, purchased by Carvallo in 3,000 pieces and painstakingly reconstructed inside the château.

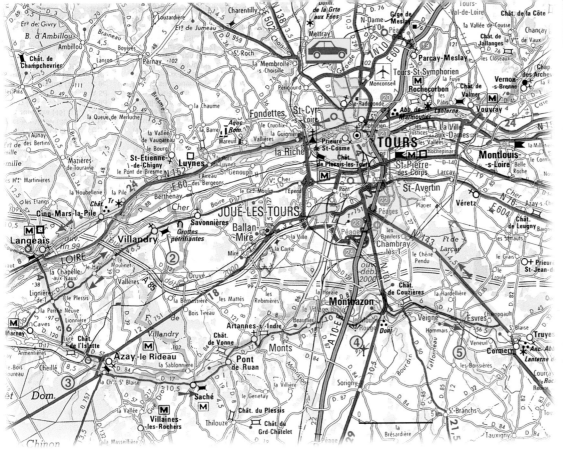

The ornamental gardens are the main attraction at Villandry

The splendid kitchen-garden lies between the château and the village church. The vegetable garden was created in the Middle Ages, when monks took great pleasure in growing their vegetables in geometrical patterns. The many crosses in this kitchen garden are a reminder of these monastic origins.

In the 16th century the vegetables grown here were prized as much for their ornamental value as for their flavour. Pink-hearted cabbages, today so popular in garden centres around the world, were cultivated here. There is also a small, medieval-style herb garden dedicated to aromatic plants and herbs used in cooking and as medicines.

■ MUSIC, LOVE AND CABBAGES ■

The divided gardens are best viewed from the top of the keep or from the terraces behind the château. The upper terrace features a peaceful water garden designed around a large lake in the shape of a Louis XV mirror, and shrouded by greenery. The lake feeds the fountains, cascades and canals of the lower levels, which include the superb ornamental gardens, with geometric designs based on the Maltese, Languedoc and Basque crosses and outlined in manicured box hedge.

Four neatly laid-out squares represent an allegory of the 'Gardens of Love': 'Tender Love', symbolised by hearts, flames of love, and domino masks traditionally worn at balls; 'Passionate Love' with the same hearts broken by passion, represented by intricately crossing hedges forming a swirling maze; 'Fickle Love', portrayed by love letters, the horns of the jilted lover, and four fans to symbolise the volatile nature of emotions, with yellow as the dominant colour, the colour of untrue love; and 'Tragic Love', with the blades of daggers and swords used during duels provoked by lovers' rivalry, and red flowers to symbolise the blood spilt during these fights.

On the other side of a narrow canal, a second box garden symbolises music with lyres and harps.

The Garden of France

The Loire valley is the birthplace of French gardening, with many fine château gardens, including those at Villandry, Chenonceau and Angers as well as the gardens of Chameroles and Ussé, designed by the great André Le Nôtre, creator of the royal gardens at Versailles. The Loire also claims some of the richest, most fertile countryside in France; it is particularly famous for fruit, flowers, vegetables and its world-renowned wines, earning it 16th-century writer Rabelais' well-chosen title, the 'Garden of France'.

T O U R

length of tour: 88km
approximate time: 1 day (including visits)
IGN Top 250: sheet 106

This tour, starting appropriately from Tours, can easily be extended to take in three more of the Loire's celebrated châteaux, by incorporating the tour on pages 74–5. In this case allow two days. The time includes about 1½ hours for the walk in Villandry.

① Leave Tours on the N 152 west past Luynes with its early medieval fortress, to **Langeais**, a characterful town nestling beneath Louis XI's 15th-century fortress-castle.

② Head south on the D 57 across the Loire to Lignieres-de-Tours and turn left along the D 7 to **Villandry** on the right. At the far end of the village, turn left into rue du Commerce and double-back into the village. After a couple of minutes the road opens out into a small square, shaded by lime trees, with a small memorial dedicated to those who died in World War I. At the end of the square, take the right-hand fork in the road, signed to Druye, up rue Emile Peltier. Turn left at the end and circle Villandry's beautiful Romanesque church, with its austere 11th- to 12th-century interior and simple stained glass. The path beside the church affords spectactular glimpses of the château and gar-dens through a grand gateway. Continue downhill, over a small crossroads and back to the main road. Go straight across the D 7, down an avenue of chestnut trees, which arch over the road like a cathedral nave. Halfway along tho lano, turn lcft, following signs to Les Petites Rivières, Promenade à Cheval riding stables, through rich pasture land which soon gives way to paddocks. A right fork at the riding stables leads you through a clutter of farm buildings and up onto a raised path alongside the river Cher, offers impressive views across fields to Villandry. Turn right and continue along the riverbank path, past an old stone cross where the river broadens, until you reach the main D 7 road once more and continue back to Lignieres.

③ From Lignieres follow the D 57 towards **Azay-le-Rideau**, whose castle competes with Chenonceau for the title of 'most beautiful château on water'. Leave Azay-le-Rideau on the D 757, following signs to Chinon.

④ Turn left onto the D 17 at la Chapelle St-Blaise, past Saché, a charming medieval village where Honoré de Balzac wrote many of his novels while resident in the 16th-century château, then on to **Montbazon**.

⑤ Join the N 10 to Tours momentarily, cross the Indre and turn immediately right onto the D 17 again, which follows the course of the river through Veigné and **Esvres**. Briefly follow signs to Cormery, then turn left onto the N 143, with the Forêt de Larçay on the right. Join the A 10 back to Tours.

LOIRE

CHÂTEAUX DE LA LOIRE

***T**o visit the Châteaux of the Loire is to take a step back in time to past centuries of French aristocratic life. No other stretch of river can boast so many royal residences, with over 120 fairytale castles and mansions lining the river.*

The Loire – the longest river in France – flows lazily for 1,020km from its source in the Massif Central to the Atlantic at St Nazaire. The Loire valley has the finest concentration of Renaissance châteaux and medieval citadels in Europe, built by a succession of French kings. Indeed, it has been a valley of kings since the days of the powerful Plantagenets – Henry II, Eleanor of Aquitaine and Richard the Lionheart – who controlled most of France.

The Royal Bedroom, inset, in Château de Chambord, which was built on a daunting scale

■ A MASTERPIECE AT EVERY TURN ■

The main period of building began in the 1500s, when architects blended late Gothic with new Italian Renaissance influences, rivalling each other to create the most lavish and magnificent châteaux. These include such masterpieces as legendary Chambord, former hunting lodge of Francois I in the heart of forestland, with over 350 chimneys; Catherine de Medici's Chenonceau, one of France's top attractions, with the inscription

'S'il vient à point, me souviendra' ('When it's finished, they'll remember me') over the entrance; and the enchanting castle at Ussé, whose fairytale towers and turrets were the model for Charles Perrault's tale of *The Sleeping Beauty*.

On the banks of the Loire are some of the most grandiose mansions, palaces and fortresses of the region, including Blois, Amboise and Chaumont, each with its own unique legends and features; other equally impressive châteaux line its graceful tributaries, including Azay-le-Rideau on the Indre, Chinon on the Vienne, Villandry on the Cher and Angers on the Sarthe. Most stage spellbinding *son-et-lumière* spectacles on summer evenings, bringing the battlements to life by recounting the history of the castle and town with a cast of hundreds, often including horses, boats and fireworks.

■ LADIES OF THE LOIRE ■

Not only kings, but also countless ladies of the Loire Châteaux – whether peasant, mistress, seductress or queen – have left an indelible mark on the history of France. Without Eleanor of Aquitaine, the Hundred Years' War between England and France would never have taken place: married first to King Louis VII of France, she later married Henry II of England, making her queen for the second time. Joan of Arc rode into Chinon to rouse Dauphin Charles VII into regaining his throne in 1429. Agnès Sorel became Charles VII's favourite mistress at Loches. She died carrying a child in 1450, allegedly poisoned. Henri II's mistress, Diane de

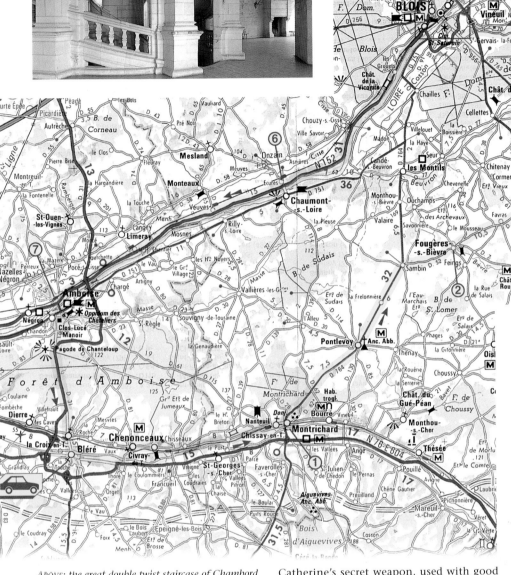

Fine wines

Mention the Loire and such names as Sancerre, Vouvray, Pouilly-Fumé and Anjou spring to mind. The region boasts a seemingly endless choice of excellent wines – red, white and rosé, dry, medium and sweet, still and sparkling. The valley is perhaps most famous for its light, fruity white and rosé wines and its dessert wines. Among the best reds are the robust Bourgueil, Chinon with its violet bouquet, and the lighter Saumur-Champigny. Saumur is home to an important sparkling wine industry, ranking second only to Champagne, and the Savennières dry whites, from the area just west of Angers or Jasnières in the little-known Loir valley, are exceptional.

Poitiers, was given Chaumont on his death, while his Queen, Catherine de Medici, took over power and control of Chenonceau.

Catherine's secret weapon, used with good effect to further her ambitions, was a group of beautiful women, called the *Escadron Volant* (Flying Squad), who enlivened festivities at the château by seducing her male opponents.

T O U R

length of tour: 140km
time: 1day
IGN Top 250: sheet 106

This tour, taking in three of the Loire's most celebrated châteaux, can easily be extended to two days by incorporating the tour of Villandry and Azay-le-Rideau on pages 72–3. In this case Chenonceaux and Cheverny are both ideal for overnight stops, with accommodation to suit all tastes and pockets.

❶ Starting from Bleré, just over 20km east of Tours, follow signs to Chenonceaux, crossing the Cher, and turning right in Civray de Touraine on the D 40 to the **Château de Chenonceau**, undoubtedly the Loire's most photographed castle, so aptly described by

Flaubert – it 'floats on air and water' – with its magnificent gallery spanning the river. Continue on the D 40 along the Cher valley, passing **Chissay**, with its late Renaissance château, and the crumbling medieval keep at **Montrichard**.

❷ From here, take the D 764 as far as Sambin, then fork right onto the D 52 past the **Château de Fougères-sur-Bièvre** – a marvellous example of medieval architecture softened by a Renaissance gallery, housing a living museum of traditional building techniques and crafts.

❸ Continue on through vineyards following signs to Cheverny, one of the Loire's finest château, set in magnificent grounds, scene of a prestigious summer garden festival.

❹ From here follow signs to Chambord. Cross the D 765, joining the D 102 to Bracieux. Turn left on to the D 120/D 112 through the dense **Forêt de Boulogne**

straight to **Chambord**, largest of all the châteaux, its pinnacles, spires, domes and chimneys piercing the skyline.

❺ Now head to **Blois** on the D 33 and D 956. Blois's palace is famous for its unusual architecture and its tales of love and intrigue.

❻ From Blois the N 152 on the north bank of the Loire leads to Amboise, past turreted **Chaumont** on the south bank, where Catherine de Medici lived briefly after the death of Henri II, and where the stables have porcelain troughs.

❼ At Amboise cross the river to the old town and château, one of the most visited in the Loire, and former seat of the Kings of France. Take the D31 through the Forêt d'Amboise and then back to Bleré. To form the longer tour, continue west along the N152 to Tours to join up with the route for Villandry and Azay-le-Rideau (see pages 72–3).

St-Benoît-sur-Loire

*T*he superb abbey church of St-Benoît-sur-Loire (St-Benedict-on-the-Loire) – the final resting place of St Benedict, regarded as the father of western monasticism – is one of the most famous Romanesque buildings in France.

The massive basilica, which dominates the village of St-Benoît-sur-Loire and the surrounding countryside, is all that remains of the Benedictine abbey of Fleury, founded in 651. The abbey acquired renown when the relics of St Benedict (480–547) were brought here from Monte Cassino in Italy in 672 and from then on Fleury became known by its present name.

The abbey of Fleury, built on an ancient site of Druid worship

■ LOSS AND RECOVERY ■

In ancient times, Fleury was reputed to be frequented by the Druid priests of ancient Gaul. In medieval times, it became famous as a great centre of learning and manuscripts, but was repeatedly pillaged by the Normans, the English, and finally the Huguenots in 1562, during the Wars of Religion. They sold its magnificent library of precious manuscripts and

ABOVE RIGHT: the house where poet Max Jacob lived in St-Benoît

EN CETTE MAISON DE 1939 A 1944
VÉCUT LE POÈTE
MAX JACOB
NÉ A QUIMPER LE 12 JUILLET 1876
MORT AU CAMP DE DRANCY
LE 5 MARS 1944
A.M.J.

Famous names

Over the centuries the abbey has been associated with dignitaries, royalty and heroes. The recumbent statue of King Philippe I of France (1060–1108) lies near the main altar. His remains are buried beneath the choir. Joan of Arc was received here in 1429, together with the young Dauphin, Charles VII, on the way to his coronation in Reims. More recently, poet and surrealist artist Max Jacob (1876–1944) a Jewish convert to Catholicism, retired to the abbey in 1936. He was, however, arrested by the Gestapo and deported to a concentration camp where he died in 1944. His remains are buried in the abbey cemetery, according to his wishes, and a permanent exhibition in the tourist office portrays his life and works.

melted down its treasures – the gold casket containing the relics of St Benedict alone weighed 17.5kg.

Spiritual and intellectual life was restored by Cardinal Richelieu during the 17th century, only to be destroyed during the French Revolution. Thankfully, however, the abbey church was spared and a lengthy restoration project (1836–1923) returned it to its former glory. Benedictine monks finally returned in 1944, at the end of World War II, to rebuild the abbey buildings, and they continue to follow their monastic life according to the Rule of Saint Benedict.

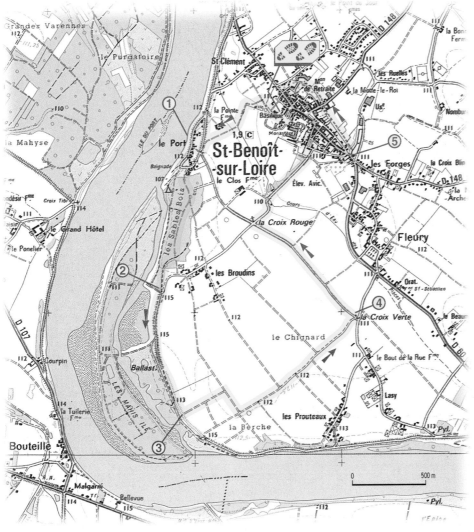

length of walk: 9km
time: 3 hours
IGN Top 25: 23200

Starting from the Benedictine abbey of St-Benoît, this walk takes you to a 19th-century river port, passing through flat, riverside farmland with raised, 15th-century flood protection banks. Don't miss the moated village, where gossip was actively encouraged!

❶ From the abbey take the chemin du Port past Hôtel du Labrador, and follow a small sign marking out a cycle path to Sully. Cross a tiny bridge onto a gravel path and turn left, then walk across open meadowland until you reach a cluster of buildings called the Hameau du Port. This attractive hamlet, marking the **Port of St-Benoît**, was an ancient landing place for river boatmen who lived in these small, white-washed cottages, mostly dating from the mid-19th century. Turn right, then first left along the water-front, passing several flat-bottomed, barge-style fishing boats tied up on the narrow strip of beach.

❷ Turn left just before the entrance to a campsite, up a path through woodland beside a wooden hut. After a few minutes, the trees clear at a crossing in the path above a farm. Turn right along a raised path, following the curve of the river to your right, with flat farmland to your left. Such raised banks (*levées*) are common along the Loire. This one was built during the 15th century to prevent flooding.

❸ After about 2km you reach several buildings on the left-hand side. Turn left, past some farm buildings, onto the **chemin de la Levée**. Turn right at the T-junction, past a jumble of lovely old stone buildings, and left at the next junction back towards the abbey – its vast silhouette stands proud above the village. Turn left again following the cycle-path signed Châteauneuf, across more farmland until the next cross-roads. Turn right and return to St-Benoît.

❹ Cross a small bridge and turn first left into tree-shaded **place du Grand Arcis** and the village school. Cut diagonally across the small square. **Rue Jean de Fleury** leads to the main square with its *caquetoir* (from *caqueter*, to gossip) or covered porch at the corner, so-called because parishioners used to gather here to exchange their news.

❺ Turn right here, past sleepy, sun-baked streets of cream-stone cottages, and over another small bridge. Turn immediately left down a path alongside a small *fossé* (ditch) – brilliantly coloured with bright green weed – which encircles the village. You will pass neat vegetable allotments and rows of unkempt private gardens, each accessed by tiny wrought-iron bridges. Cross **rue Max Jacob** and continue along the *fossé* past a large retirement home on the right. The path swings round to the left and returns to the main road. Turn left towards the village centre, then second right down the tree-lined **avenue de l'Abbaye** back to the basilica.

■ PROUD MONKS ■

Village life revolves around the abbey church, its services, work and religious celebrations. Six times a day the basilica comes to life as it is filled with the sound of Gregorian chant and prayers dedicated to St Benedict. Between services, the monks offer guided tours of their magnificent church – an impressive edifice of simple, solid design, built between 1004 and 1218. Entrance is through the oldest part of the church, a two-storey belfry porch in golden stone, surmounted by a square bell tower. The Romanesque pillars are crowned by intricately carved capitals portraying scenes from the Book of Revelations, the last book of the Bible, and events from the life of Christ and the Virgin Mary.

Once inside, the soaring nave, with its white stonework and high vaulting creates a feeling of space and light. Under the dome in the transept, the choir stalls date from the early 15th century: the carved choir screen was presented to the abbey in 1635 by Richelieu, when he was Commendatory Abbot here. The floor is paved with an ancient Roman mosaic transported from Italy in 1531. The lintel of the carved northern portal shows the transfer of St Benedict's relics to Fleury. Below the choir, the dimly lit crypt consists of a series of tiny chapels radiating from a large, central pillar which houses the modern shrine of St Benedict, whose relics have been venerated here since the 7th century.

A Romanesque capital in St-Benoît's church

Cardinal Richelieu presented a carved choir screen to the abbey in 1635

VÉZELAY

Known since medieval times as the Eternal Hill, Vézelay is a town to be discovered slowly, for it has a spirituality and inner peace that have attracted pilgrims, writers and visitors for centuries.

From almost any vantage point in this town, the eye is drawn to the façade of the basilica, dominating rows of vineyards that slope down the valley of the River Cure. Along rue St-Etienne and rue St-Pierre, the town's two main streets, there are art galleries, tea-rooms, crafts shops and regional speciality stores. These have taken over the ground floors of medieval dwellings, built in the region's pale white limestone that catches the light in a singularly gentle fashion.

▪ PRECIOUS RELICS ▪

Although the population of the modern town is only 300, in medieval times it reached 10,000, not including the many worshippers who flocked to Vézelay in the 12th century. The town was a gathering point on the pilgrimage route to Santiago de Compostella; it was also believed to hold the relics of Saint Mary Magdalene, the repented sinner and first witness to the Resurrection of Christ.

BELOW: The town of Vézelay is a charming medieval cluster, with the basilica of Saint Madeleine its most prominent feature

> ### A bible of stone
> The capitals of the pillars bear a blend of mythical, fantastic and religious images, depicting episodes from the Old and New Testaments of the Bible, as well as scenes from daily life. They offer a rare insight into the psychology and theology of the medieval period. One of the most well known of the capitals (in the south aisle) depicts the 'Mystical Mill'. A man can be seen pouring grain into a mill while another gathers the flour. The first, dressed in the slave's short tunic, is Moses, representing the Ancient Law. The second man, barefoot and dressed in the long toga worn by a free man, represents Saint Paul, while the mill, with its four-spoked wheel, symbolises Christ. Mingling art and philosophy, this scene depicts the basic message of the Christian Gospel – the transformation of grain into the new bread, or new life.

While the abbey's origins date back to the 9th century, its present layout, composed of a beautiful nave, a vast narthex (an ante-chamber at the entrance) and a graceful Gothic chancel, dates from 1140–90.

After the 13th century, the abbey fell into decline: Saint Mary Magdalene's relics were claimed to have been discovered elsewhere,

ABOVE LEFT: The faultlessly beautiful interior of the Basilique Ste-Madeleine

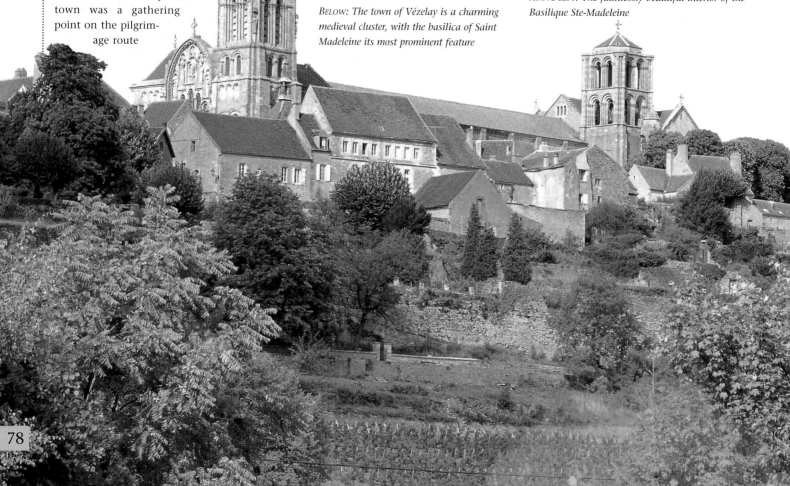

narthex is dominated by the fluid figure of the Resurrected Christ. Rays radiate from his outstretched hands as he entrusts the Apostles with their evangelical mission while in the pleats of his robe can be seen spirals of air, palm leaves and aquatic motifs representing the Creation. One of the finest examples of Romanesque art, this sculpture emits tremendous energy. The alternating light and dark stone of the nave's arches and columns give a comforting sense of peace and harmony. The play of stone and light makes full use of the changing seasons.

On the summer solstice (21 June, the feast of Saint John the Baptist), the midday sun shines through the basilica's south windows, falling upon the ground in pools of light along the centre of the nave. At noon on the winter solstice (21 December), the light shining through the same windows strikes the very top of the west-facing pillars. The three-level chancel, a representation of heaven, is one of the earliest examples of Gothic architecture. Built entirely of white stone, its great arcades, tall windows and slender colonettes allow the light to flood in, especially at sunrise, when the basilica is seen at its most beautiful.

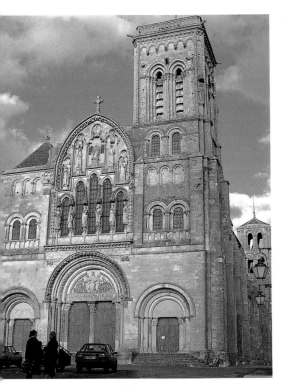

The magnificent Basilique Ste-Madeleine, at the top of a single street, is visited by hordes of tourists every year

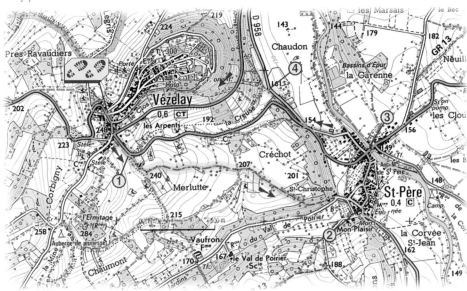

then the Reformation, followed by the French Revolution, left the building nearly derelict. When Prosper Mérimée, the first inspector of Historic Monuments, visited it in 1840, he immediately dispatched the young Viollet-le-Duc to begin restoration work that ended up lasting 20 years.

▪ FROM DARKNESS TO LIGHT ▪

In medieval times, pilgrims compared a visit to the basilica to an inner journey from sin and darkness towards truth and light, mirroring the life of Mary Magdalene. Even in its present state, it is easy to see why. Beyond the main façade, the visitor enters the dim interior of the narthex, an area of purification, before moving on to the nave, a path of light. The tympanum above the portico of the

The wines of Vézelay

The shaded terrace garden behind the basilica offers a panoramic view over the surrounding vineyards and the hills of the Morvan. A stay in Vézelay would not be complete without tasting the local wines. In the 13th century a Franciscan friar wrote about their 'delicious bouquet' that produced a 'sense of tranquillity and well-being'. The town's vineyards, mainly planted with Melon, Chardonnay and Pinot Noir vines, remain modest in size after a phylloxera epidemic. They were granted the official 'Burgundy' appellation in 1988 and are slowly regaining their reputation for excellence.

WALK

length of walk: 4km
time: 1½ hours
IGN Top 25: sheet 27220

Leave your car at the bottom of the hill, at place du Champ-de-Foire, and become a pilgrim as you pass between the columns of the Porte du Barle into this village, widely known as the Eternal Hill. The going is easy, but the terrain is hilly in places.

❶ From **place du Champ-de-Foire** follow the road towards Avallon, going straight over the first two crossroads. At the next bend, fork off on the dirt path to the right (a wooden sign marked with a red and white symbol marks the way). Walk past an abandoned wooden barn and keep on the left-hand side of the path as it starts descending towards **St-Père-sous-Vézelay**. Along the way, there is a wonderful view of Vézelay on the hilltop, protected by ramparts, its basilica looking massive and unshakeable.

❷ Upon entering St-Père, follow the Cure River. At the first crossroads, turn left then right (the path is marked by a yellow symbol). The story of Vézelay actually started in St-Père: the knight Girart de Roussillon founded a Benedictine monastery in this area in the 9th century, but Norman invasions forced its community to seek refuge on the hill.

❸ At the end of the street turn left, passing in front of the Gothic **Église de Notre-Dame**, built in the 12th and 14th centuries. Near by are the **Fontaines Salées**. In the 2nd century BC, a sanctuary was built around these salt-water springs. Recognising their therapeutic virtues, the Romans constructed a spa complex on the site, but this was largely destroyed during the Germanic invasions of the 3rd and 4th centuries. Vestiges of the site were excavated in 1934. The regional archaeological museum, next to the church in the former presbytery, houses several interesting ceramic and bronze artefacts from the Fontaines Salées, as well as an Etruscan statuette (700 BC) and a head of Venus, in white marble (1st century BC).

❹ Continue for about 400m and cross the D 957 to the road opposite. Follow it until it crosses the road to **Asquins**. Continue in this direction. After about 300m there is a marked path forking off on the left, leading to the **Fontaine Sainte-Madeleine**, once the closest water source to Vézelay. Follow the path on the left, which climbs through the vines towards the southern ramparts. At the top, either turn right and follow the road around the ramparts (allow about 45 minutes), or turn left and return to the entrance of the town.

BOURGOGNE
Canal de Bourgogne

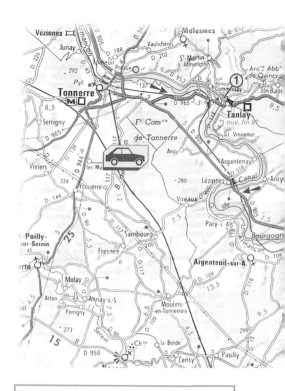

To the modern traveller, this ancient watery highway seems at first unimpressive and quaint and there is scant water traffic for much of the year. This, and the fishermen casting for carp, give the feeling that the canal has been abandoned. There is little to show that this thread of water links the Mediterranean to the Atlantic Ocean.

Although the Romans were the first to think of linking their sea with the ocean by means of a canal, it was not until 1606 that the Canal de Briare was dug, between the Saône and the Seine. This was soon followed by the Canal du Midi linking the Mediterranean to the Gironde basin near Bordeaux. Plans for the Canal de Bourgogne (Burgundy Canal) were made in 1727, but work did not begin until 1774. Despite an enthusiastic start, it was not completed until 1843, hampered by the French Revolution, a lack of interest during the Napoleonic era, and a lack of funds. The canal was finally

Technical information

In all, the canal has 189 cut stone locks, each 5m wide and 38.5m long, scattered over its entirely stone-lined length of 242km. The official water depth is 1.8m, with a clearance under bridges of 2.2m. There are six enormous water reservoirs holding a combined capacity of 29 million cubic metres of water.

LEFT: the crypt at Flavigny's abbey

BELOW: Tanlay's château has a superb courtyard as well as bell-shaped domes and swans in the moat

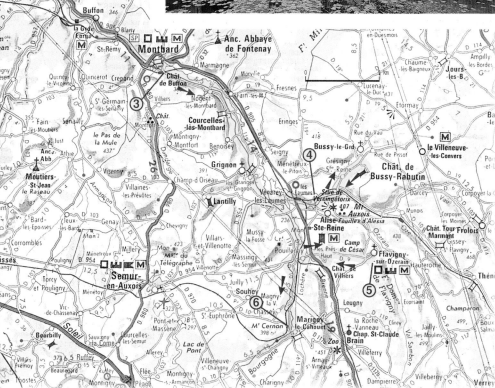

TOUR

length of tour: 100km
time: varies according to stage
IGN Top 250: sheet 108

Boats can be hired in several places along the canal – Tonnerre and other bases on the Yonne River at the northern end, Marigny le Cahouët and Montbard near the middle, and St Jean de Losne, Pont d'Ouche and Pouilly en Auxois at the southern end. Locks close for lunch every day, all day Wednesday between Dijon and Tonnerre, and all French holidays. Hours also vary according to season, so check before setting out. This only includes a section of the canal from Tonnerre to Marigny, but there are plenty more interesting towns and villages to visit if you have time to explore the full length of the canal.

❶ From the former Gallo-Roman settlement of **Tonnerre**, first stop is the village of **Tanlay**, unassuming, but graced by a beautiful French Renaissance château. Built in 1550 for François de Coligny, the château is surrounded by a moat and splendid gardens.

❷ The **Château d'Ancy-le-Franc** is considered to be one of the finest examples of Renaissance architecture to be found anywhere in Burgundy. The interiors are especially interesting, having been restored in the 19th century and sumptuously redecorated. Built between 1546 and 1622 by Antoine de Clermont Tonnerre, the château hosted Henry IV, Louis XIII and Louis XIV.

❸ Next stop is **l' Abbaye de Fontenay** at Montbard, without doubt one of the most beautiful in France. Set in a cool wooded valley, and largely undamaged, it is a perfect example of a Cistercian abbey. The abbey church, with its earthen floor, is often used as the setting for classical concerts in the summer months and the sculpted cloister is one of the best preserved in France. The gardens are a joy, with their fountain and fish pond. The abbey was once owned by the Montgolfière family, pioneers of hot-air ballooning. The abbey is now a UNESCO world heritage site.

❹ The important historical site of **Alise Ste Reine** is also an interesting stop. Here Gallic warriors led by Vercingetorix retreated after their failed attack on Caesar. Caesar's legions dug double trenches and fortified earthworks around the Gallic camp to prevent the Gauls from escaping and to defend themselves from relief troops coming to save their besieged allies. After six weeks of trying to break through these barriers, Vercingetorix was forced to surrender and was subsequently paraded through the streets of Rome, imprisoned for six years and finally strangled. An imposing statue of Vercingetorix now dominates the place.

❺ **Flavigny**, a tiny, fortified hilltop village, was once the religious centre of the Auxois region. There are remains of an important abbey, with a Carolingian crypt. The ancient fortress gates are still standing, as are houses dating from the 13th century. It is here that Anis de Flavigny, the aniseed sweets produced since the 9th century, are made.

❻ Final stop on this section is **Marigny**, where you can visit the Maison des Lacs museum.

A tranquil section of the canal at Châteauneuf

completed on private funds but by then it was undermined by the Paris–Lyon railway.

▪ THE CANAL TODAY ▪

The Burgundy Canal is practically obsolete as a transport route: barges use only its farthest sections. But this solemnly majestic waterway has instead become one of the most popular waterways in France for boating. In summer all manner of craft jostle for position in the

queues to get through the succession of locks that takes them past sleepy villages and up and down the rolling terrain, dotted with grazing cows and sheep. The traffic-free towpaths offer peaceful avenues for reflection and discovery. Boating requires a pretty open schedule, as a good day's navigation may sometimes take you only a few kilometres. Exploring nearby towns and villages will further slow your progress, so the key is to relax and enjoy some of the historical places along the way. You could spend days just floating, so choose your itinerary in advance to get the best out of the canal's diverse route.

PARC RÉGIONAL DU MORVAN

*I*n sharp contrast to the wealth of the neighbouring wine country, the character of this mountainous region, a granite massif in the heart of Burgundy, has been shaped by its inaccessibility, its rugged climate and the relatively poor land.

Early in the morning, a blanket of mist often floats above the steep valleys and gentle hills of the Morvan, revealing only the dark outline of pine trees. This air of mystery suits the Parc Régional du Morvan, which was created in 1970. With altitudes of 350–900m, the countryside can change rapidly. Thick, coniferous forests alternate with soft-rolling farmland criss-crossed by hedges and trees. There are tumbling streams teeming with trout, broom-covered moors and nestling hamlets of stone homes with slate roofs.

■ CELTIC ORIGINS ■

The first mention of the Morvan dates back to the 5th century, when a priest from Autun wrote about a retreat in the *deserta morvinni* (deserts of the Morvan), although human presence in the region has been traced back to the Neolithic era. Around 100 BC, the Eduens, a Celtic tribe, colonised the area and established their capital at Bibracte on the summit of Mont Beuvray.

The site was abandoned around 85 BC for Augustodunum (Autun), where a Roman theatre (once the largest in Gaul), a temple and gateways witness a thriving past. In this region, marked by pagan rites, the transition to Christianity was slow. At first, the Church staunchly condemned all pagan practices. Eventually, though, it adopted a more conciliatory approach, accepting pagan sanctuaries and transforming them into chapels. The Morvan was divided into rival political entities and was ravaged several times by local conflicts, as well as the Hundred Years War and the Wars of Religion. It was also repeatedly impoverished by harsh winters and several recorded famines.

BELOW: Bridges span the River Cure at Pierre-Perthius
INSET: tracks through the forest in Morvan

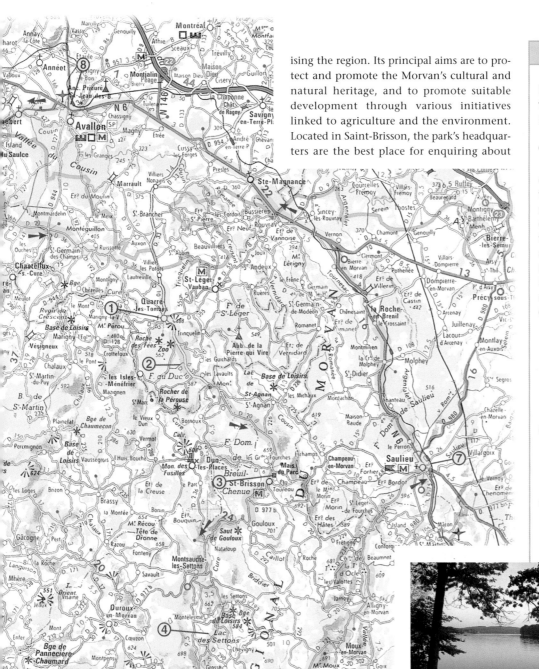

ising the region. Its principal aims are to protect and promote the Morvan's cultural and natural heritage, and to promote suitable development through various initiatives linked to agriculture and the environment. Located in Saint-Brisson, the park's headquarters are the best place for enquiring about

accommodation and excursions, whether on foot (the park has over 1,200km of walking trails), horseback or bicycle.

■ CULTURAL DISTINCTION ■

Ancient dialects, legends and songs have been proudly preserved in this region where hardship and isolation have bred a distinctive culture. As one old saying goes: 'It's an ill wind and an ill folk that come from the Morvan...' One man who has helped bring the region into a more favourable light is François Mitterrand. Twice president, he was mayor of Château-Chinon for over 22 years. The town's Musée de Septennat, housed in an 18th-century convent, displays 750 gifts received by the president.

■ A LAND FOR NATURE LOVERS ■

The whole region is sparsely populated and is permeated with a tranquil, almost mystical quality which comes from nature's dominant – though domesticated – influence. Apart from tourism, two main sources of income for the region are the raising of the robust Charolais cows and the cultivation of coniferous trees for the Christmas season. The regional park has played a key role in revital-

length of tour: 137km
time: 1 day
IGN Top 250: sheet 108

The winding roads of the Morvan make driving quite tiring. But to really appreciate the region's natural beauty, choose one or two destinations along the way and explore some of the region on foot. The Maison du Parc in Saint-Brisson publishes cards with maps detailing excursions of various lengths and difficulty.

❶ Starting from Vézelay, stop off briefly at St-Père-sur-Vézelay and follow the D 958 to Pierre-Perthuis, a village nested around the ruins of a 12th-century castle above the tumultuous waters of the Cure River. Take the D 353, then turn on to the D 36 to **Quarré-les-Tombes**, with its granite church surrounded by 112 empty tombs, believed to date from the end of the 7th century.

❷ Continue on the D 20, a road that dives into the heart of the hills and forests of the Morvan, offering superb views. Stop, for instance, at the Roche des Fées (D 128) or the Rocher de la Pérouse, off the D 10 in the **Forêt au Duc**.

❸ Follow the D 20 to the Maison du Parc in **Saint-Brisson**, with deer and donkeys and a nature trail around the Etang du Taureau. It also has exhibitions, displays of local crafts and a museum showing the decisive role played by Resistance fighers in occupied Morvan in 1942–4.

❹ Now follow the D 236 to **Montsauche-les-Settons**, then the D 193 to **Lac des Settons**, an artificial lake formed by a dam built to facilitate the floating of logs along the River Cure and to regularise the flow of the Yonne. With elegant villas and hotels, today, it is a popular site for watersports.

❺ Follow the D 37 south to medieval **Château-Chinon**, with its bright fountain by Niki de Saint Phalle in front of the *mairie*, the Musée du Septennat and the Musée du Costume. For a view over the town and hills of the surrounding region, follow rue St-Christophe and rue du Square to the top of the Butte du Calvaire, once the site of an *oppidum* and later a medieval castle.

❻ Retrace your route back to **Lorient** (just before Frétoy) and turn right on to the D 294 and then the D 121 northeast across the national park, through Alligny-en-Morvan.

❼ Take the D 26 to **Saulieu** (a place of pilgrimage for gourmets with its excellent three-star restaurant).

❽ From here follow the N 6 up to **Avallon**, overlooking the Vallée du Cousin, then take the D 957 back to Vézelay.

The tranquil waters of Lac des Settons

BOURGOGNE
HÔTEL-DIEU DE BEAUNE

*F*rom flamboyant coloured roofs hidden behind high façades to vaulted cellars lined with some of the world's most precious wines, the capital of Burgundy coquettishly unfolds its treasures of art, history and gastronomy.

The early city of Beaune sprung up around the sacred source of the Aigue River, dedicated to Belenos, the god of spring waters. At the crossroads of Celtic trading routes, the city built its wealth on cloth, iron and wine. It was fortified in the 12th century and the Dukes of Burgundy established their palace and parliament here. In the 15th century, under Philippe-le-Bon, Burgundy was one of

The striking tiling and façade of the Hôtel-Dieu

the most powerful kingdoms in Europe, with territories stretching over most of present-day Belgium and Holland.

◾ A HOSPITAL FOR THE POOR ◾

But not even this region was spared by the Hundred Years War, and Beaune's most exceptional building is not a palace or an abbey church, but the Hôtel-Dieu, a charity hospital founded in 1443 by one of the most influen-

tial and astute figures in Burgundy, Nicolas Rolin, chancellor of Philippe-le-Bon, and his wife, Guigone de Salins. At the time, Rolin was 67 years old, he had built up an immense fortune and was undoubtedly concerned about his eternal salvation. In the institution's founding act, he evokes a 'fortunate transaction' by which the temporal goods he had received through divine bounty would be exchanged for heavenly, eternal ones.

◾ A PRESTIGE OPERATION ◾

Self-interest notwithstanding, this was a prestigious operation and nothing was too beautiful for the poor. Remarkably preserved, the Hôtel-Dieu is a jewel of medieval architecture, inspired by hospitals that Rolin had seen in Flanders. In the impoverished environment of the age, it was best not to flaunt wealth, so the façade is rather austere, with its immense slate roof punctuated by dormers and surmounted by Gothic pinnacles. But upon crossing into the court of honour, the visitor is greeted by a feast of colour: the roof's design of glazed tiles lined by lead lacework combines with timber and Burgundian stone to form an exceptionally harmonious ensemble.

Inside, the Great Hall of the Poor exudes the same sense of perfection and humanity. Above the entrance is a profoundly expressive Christ, carved from a single block of oak. From their beds framed by red curtains, the sick could follow mass in the chapel that was once decorated with the polyptych of the Last Judgement (see box).

■ ARCHITECTURAL RICHES ■

The hospital aside, Beaune harbours a rich architectural heritage, notably the Collégiale Notre-Dame with its collection of tapestries on *The Life of the Virgin*, a striking ensemble of Renaissance façades along rue de Lorraine and the Town Hall, installed in a former convent of the Ursuline nuns. One of the most pleasant and relaxing strolls is a tour of Beaune's ramparts. Some of the bastions have been turned into cellars, while the 15th-century castle along the route offers another radiant example of the glazed tile roofs, believed to have originated in Central Europe.

■ FROM WATER TO WINE ■

Beaune sits upon some of the world's most prestigious wine cellars, so a visit must include a *descente de cave*. In underground vaults you can savour some of Burgundy's best wines while learning how to describe their colour or decipher a wine label. The former residence of the dukes of Burgundy is now a viticulture museum and includes a rare collection of wine presses.

The Hospices de Beaune labels deserve special attention since the hospital owns some of the most prestigious vineyards in France. Every year, on the third Sunday in November, its wines are auctioned, with proceeds going to the hospital and other charities. The event attracts buyers from all over the world. A candle is ceremoniously lit when the first offer is made, followed by a second one when the bidding ebbs. In 1997, casks fetched up to 400,000 francs.

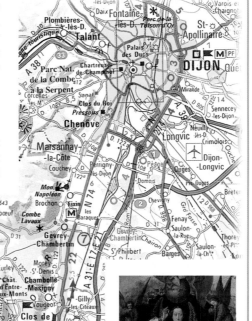

The Last Judgement
This polyptich (above) by the Flemish artist Rogier van der Weyden, commissioned by Chancellor Rolin, is an artistic treasure now exhibited in its own room, where a magnifying glass allows visitors to inspect the richness of its details. The outer panels reveal the central figure of Christ shrouded in red against a gold heaven, the impassive expression of the Archangel Michael weighing souls, the ardour of the apostles and saints, the resurrection of bodies and images of hell and paradise.

T O U R

length of tour: 75km
time: 1 day
IGN Top 250: sheet 108

The Route of Great Wines is a must in Burgundy. The beauty and tranquillity of the landscape is breathtaking. The wine region is a narrow stretch of land made up of a mosaic of small properties, and vineyards only a few kilometres apart produce wines of different character. Take time to visit the cellars of local growers, who are more than willing to share their knowledge.

❶ Leaving **Beaune**, follow the D 973 to **Pommard** on the Côte de Beaune, a region that produces some of the best *premier cru* reds. The 19th-century Château de Pommard is surrounded by a vineyard. Further along is the picturesque village of **Volnay**, known for the finesse of its reds.

❷ Continue along the D 973 through Auxey-Duresses, where 9th-century monks from Cîteaux planted vines. Further along, **la Rochepot** is dominated by a striking medieval castle with a roof of multi-coloured glazed tiles. Follow the D 33 through St-Aubin until reaching the D 113A and D 113B.

❸ **Puligny-Montrachet**, along with neigbouring **Chassagne-Montrachet**, is home to arguably the greatest dry white wines in France. Alexandre Dumas claimed this *grand cru* had to be savoured 'kneeling down and with the hat off'.

❹ Continue back towards Beaune along the D 113B to **Meursault**, where the annual *paulée*, a dinner celebrating the end of the harvest, is held in the 15th-century château.

❺ Return to the D 973 and cross to the north side of Beaune, following the D 2 to **Savigny-les-Beaune**, where vines have been cultivated since the 9th century. Pernand-Vergelesses and Aloxe-Corton mark the northern limit of the Côte de Beaune. Charlemagne reputedly owned vines here while Corton's reds have been cherished by figures such as Voltaire and John F Kennedy.

❻ Follow the N 74 north to Nuits-St-Georges and the 'Champs-Elysées of Burgundy'. This kingdom of the Pinot Noir grape, a stretch known as the Côtes de Nuits, boasts nearly all of Burgundy's red *grands crus*. Nuits-St-Georges earned lasting fame after king Louis XIV was ordered by his doctor to have a daily dose of 'vin de Nuits'. The route continues through **Vosne-Romanée**, home of Romanée-Conti, one of the world's most expensive wines. Along the road is **Clos de Vougeot**, founded by the monks of Cîteaux in the 12th century. The estate stages the Chevaliers du Tastevin ceremony, when wine worshippers are knighted, swearing 'to serve the great wines of France, and especially of Burgundy'.

❼ **Gevrey-Chambertin** nestles around a 15th/16th-century castle. Chambertin was the favourite wine of Napoleon and Alexandre Dumas.

❽ From here, you can continue to Dijon or return to Beaune through the vineyards of the Haute Côtes de Nuits, following the D 31 to Semezanges and along the D 35 to Ternant. Then take the D 104 and the D 2 via Bouilland back to Beaune.

FRANCHE-COMTÉ

ARC-ET-SENANS

The director's house at Saline Royale is an imposing classical-style building

Situated close to the River Loue, Arc-et-Senans is the home of the Saline Royale, one of the most interesting industrial architectural structures of the 18th century. It is a memorial to the salt extraction industry, which has all but disappeared.

Traditionally, salt has held an important role in the economy for centuries as a vital commodity both for the preservation of food and as a constituent part in various remedies. It has also been used in many industrial processes, including tanning of hides, dying of cloth and soap-making.

Grottes d'Osselle

These caves, in the cliffs overlooking the River Doubs, are just 30km from Arc-et-Senans. Discovered in the 13th century, the caves have interested visitors since the 16th century. The long, dry galleries served as a hiding place and a chapel during the French Revolution. Remains from this time are still visible. Numerous galleries exist in these cliffs. In the earliest of these, which still contain fresh water, the walls and ceilings have been blackened by the smoke of generations of torches. Other caves boast stalagmites ranging in colour from purest white from the lime in the rock to other hues caused by salts of iron, copper and magnesium.

▪ WORTH ITS SALT ▪

In the 16th century salt was heavily taxed by the French monarchy. Not surprisingly, this was highly unpopular with the common people, and an active black market in salt developed. The state, which was running its own monopoly, took ruthless action against the tax evaders, since the trade in salt was of prime importance to the monarchy and virtually a symbol of its power. As a result, the various *salines royales* (royal salt works) were effectively fortresses, operating behind high walls. Every effort was made to protect the process and avoid fraud and smuggling.

▪ UNITING THE COMMUNITY ▪

Until the middle of the 18th century, salt was produced at Salins, but with the depletion of natural resources – wood for the furnaces and salt itself – a new site was needed. In 1773 a decision was taken to build a new centre to extract salt from waters with lower salt content. The site for the new salt works, between Arc and Senans along the banks of the River Loue, was chosen because it provided ample

The buildings of the 18th-century Saline Royal were arranged in a semicircle; today the complex is a modern conference centre

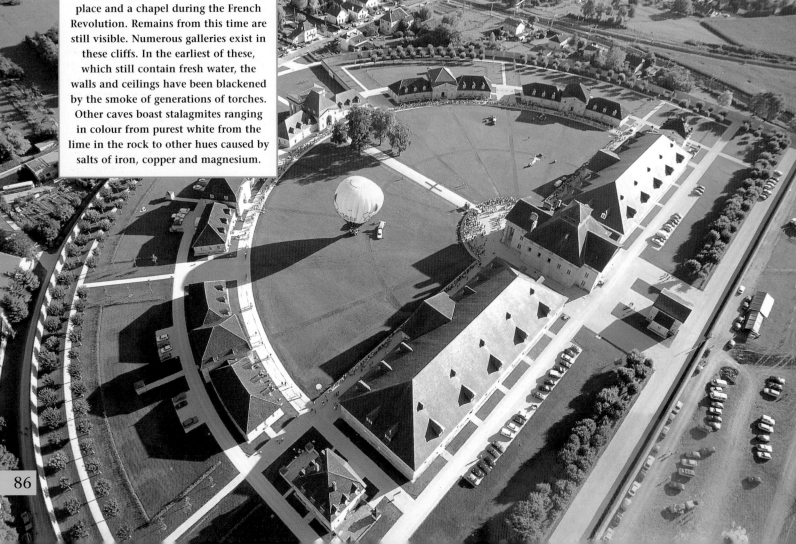

space and was close to the vast royal forest of Chaux. This new salt works, built by Ledoux under the orders of Louis XV, would be both a factory and an integrated community. The bringing together of living quarters and factory into one site was a great innovation in industrial architecture for the 18th century.

One of the important aspects of this great project was the departure from the usual square layout centred around a vast courtyard, and the introduction of the semicircular format. The focal point in this design was the director's house, around which all activities, both industrial and domestic, took place.

The choice of this layout satisfied several criteria, as the various buildings were placed according to their functional relationships. It is comparable to an ideal urban layout and represents the most advanced ideas on town planning of that time. The design was thought to encourage the free circulation of air which, given the nature of the factory, was of prime importance. The separation of activities into different buildings or areas also greatly reduced the risk of fire. A less obvious benefit of the aesthetic design of the compound was that everything could be easily overseen from the centre – the director's house. This same principle would later be applied to prison architecture.

■ MODERN TIMES ■

The making of salt at that time was a long, arduous process. Salt water was boiled and evaporated, using large wood-burning furnaces. The salty residue was collected and sold, either in granular form or shaped into loaves, similar in appearance to bread.

With the emergence of new techniques, the Saline Royale soon became obsolete and was closed in 1895. In 1927 it was purchased by the state and progressively restored. The restoration of the gardens was completed in 1996 and constituted the third phase of restoration.

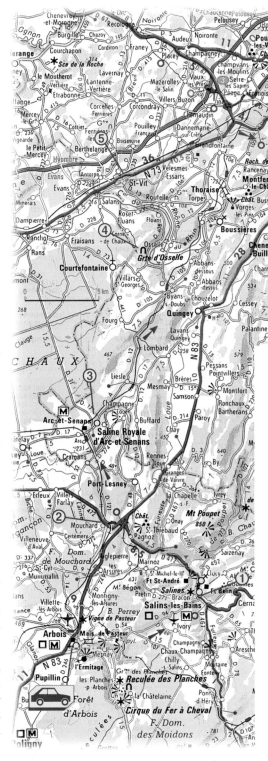

ABOVE: the old salt works at Saline-les-Bains and, right, the underground salt-water duct

The Saline Royale is now a modern conference centre with full facilities, and complete information is available which explains the history and the use of the various buildings. The entrance is by the former guard buildings, directly opposite the director's house.

TOUR

length of tour: 80km
time: half to 1 day
IGN Top 250: sheet 109

Starting from the historic town of Arbois, this short but picturesque drive takes in Salins-les-Bains, the Saline Royale and the Grottes d'Osselle, the striking approach to which is not to be missed.

❶ From **Arbois**, follow the D 107 then the D 94 east to **Salins-les-Bains**, a charming village in the narrow valley of Furieuse. Very long and narrow, Salins still has many remains of its old ramparts and towers. Stop to visit the church of St-Anatoile, one of the best examples of 13th-century Burgundian gothic architecture in the region.

❷ Now take the D 472 through Panoz to join the D 121 at Mouchard.

❸ From Mouchard turn right on to the D 274 to reach the **Saline Royale** and **Arc-et-Senans**, which opens all year round and offers guided tours.

❹ After leaving Arc-et-Senans, follow the D 12 north to Byans-sur-Doubs and then turn left to the **Grottes d'Osselle**.

❺ From here follow the D 408 round to St-Vit and turn right on to the N 73 towards Besançon, via the city's historic Citadelle and Porte Noire.

❻ From here it's just a short journey to finish in **Besançon**, capital of Franche-Comté.

FRANCHE-COMTÉ

SAUT DU DOUBS

The Doubs, one of the main rivers of the Jura region, is known for its ever-changing and dramatic landscapes. The river rises in a cavern at the foot of the Noirmont Forest, at an altitude of 937m, and winds through the Jura for 430km.

Take to the river on one of the many different types of watercraft which can be hired at Villers-le-Lac

Visiting this region is like embarking on a journey into the past. This spectacular area has been important to mankind since the Stone Age. Cro-Magnon Man lived here, and there are traces of villages and encampments dating back to 7000–5000 BC. Archeologists are still hoping to find evidence of a population living here between 6000 and 3500 BC.

HARNESSING NATURE

Until the end of the 19th century, the water was used for industrial purposes. The energy of the waterfall was harnessed, to be used by wood and iron mills. The introduction of electricity, at the beginning of the 20th century, enabled industry to move to places that were more accessible, thus making these mills obsolete; only a few remains are still visible.

The Saut du Doubs, now a nature reserve, nestles along the French–Swiss border. Its lake, Chaillexon (called Brenet by the Swiss), is 3.5km long, yet is never wider than 250m. The river snakes between towering rock cliffs 200m high, stretching up into the sky. As this narrow gorge opens up dramatically, the river loses its limpid appearance and forms a series of powerful rapids which end in a spectacular waterfall 27m high. The water crashes thunderously in a breathtaking burst of white mist and spray that is hard to equal.

HIGH DIVING AND WILDLIFE

It is in this setting that athletes have fought to establish records in high diving. In 1936, the world record was established by Girard, from a platform 40m high. In 1987, Olivier Favre established yet another world record by diving from a height of 54m, entering the water at an incredible speed of 117kph.

Another attraction of the Saut du Doubs is its abundant wildlife. The lake has more than 30 different types of fish, including pike, trout and perch, and is a birdwatcher's heaven. Among the more noteworthy species are swans, crested grebes, mallards and herons.

The Saut du Doubs plunging into Lac de Chaillexon

scenes as the Gorges du Doubs, taking in some of nature's most colourful and amazing vistas. This region is frequently called 'The Land of Blue and Green'. As the name implies, there are shades and contrasts of blue and green scarcely to be seen elsewhere and of which Monet could only have dreamt.

LEFT: a leisurely cruise down the Doubs is an ideal way to enjoy the scenery

BELOW: the tranquil waters of the River Doubs at the Swiss border

▪ THE DOUBS IN WINTER ▪

The River Doubs freezes every winter, transforming the Chaillexon Lake into one of the largest skating rinks in Europe. The temperature frequently sinks as low as –30°C and, as a result, the ice is exceptionally thick (more than 60cm). This extraordinary thickness turns the lake into an adventure playground; on some days, thousands of people can be seen walking and skating. There are even refreshment stands and vendors selling roasted chestnuts. Lumberjacks take advantage of the ice to use tractors to haul wood from places that are inaccessible at other times of the year.

Between Easter and the end of October the ideal way to explore the area and the waterfall is by boat, following the loops and meanderings of the Doubs, passing such spectacular

TOUR

length of tour: 14km
time: half a day
IGN Top 250: sheet 109

This scenic tour includes a boat ride and some walking to get the most out of the waterfalls. The Saut du Doubs is accessible only by water. Boat tours start from Villers-le-Lac and offer a superb view of this natural wonder. Lunch or dinner cruises are available and, although the boats can accommodate wheelchairs, they are not equipped with ramps. Allow about 2 hours for the boat trip. The departure point for the boat tour is on the right-hand side of the road at the entrance to Villers-le-Lac, just before place Clipillard. The boats stop over at Saut du Doubs and

give ample opportunity for travellers to see the 27m drop of the Doubs to Lac de Chaillexon. This unique waterfall is best seen from one of the two viewpoints with their unequalled positions. On the return to the boat, keep to the left to find another spectacular viewpoint, offering one of the best glimpses of the falls.

❶ After returning to **Villers-le-Lac**, take the road to le Pissoux. At the entrance to this village, turn right on to a road which ends at a viewpoint overlooking the **barrage** (dam) **du Chatelot**.

❷ Return to le Pissoux and continue straight to Barboux. Then turn right on to the D 211. After Blancheroche, turn right on to the D 464 and head towards **les Echelles de la Mort**. At the Swiss border, indicate to the customs officials that you do not intend to cross into Switzerland. Turn left on to the access road to the hydro-electric plant and follow this to the gorge.

❸ Leave your car to the left of the fence and follow the

footpath, which is clearly marked, to **Belvédère des Echelles de la Mort**. You must climb three sturdy iron ladders to reach the 100m viewpoint for a sensational view of the **Gorges du Doubs**.

❹ Return to the D 464 and follow it towards Charquemont, then take the D 10 to the car park 'de la Cendrée'. After 200m there are two paths leading to the **Belvédère de la Cendrée**, from which there is an excellent view of both the Gorges du Doubs and Switzerland.

❺ From Charquemont take the D 414 to le Russey, then the D 437 south to Morteau. From there the D 461 takes you back to Villers-le-Lac.

CASCADES DU HÉRISSON

Situated in the heart of the Jura mountains, the Vallée du Hérisson is known for its romantic setting, primeval forests and abundant wildlife. The Cascades du Hérrison generated a good deal of the industry in the area, as well as offering spectacular scenery.

The name of Hérisson was given to the river by a 19th-century cartographer. But this is a phonetic interpretation and has little to do with the original name.

When first mentioned in 1388, it was spelt Yrison; over the centuries it became Uraisson, Uresson, Hurisson, Huresson and even Hurrisson. More serious studies tell us that Yrisson had in fact a double meaning: 'water' and 'sacred'. Hence it means 'sacred water' and has nothing at all in common with the hedgehog, which is the present day translation of Hérisson.

The importance of the Vallée du Hérisson dates back to the Middle Ages, when three different monastic orders fought for control of the river and the right to build various kinds of mills and forges. The area still relies heavily upon its abundant natural resources to maintain its way of life.

■ DEVELOPMENT OF INDUSTRY ■

The first mill in the area was recorded in 1329. A village grew up around it in around 1471. However, this way of life was interrupted and this and other mills were destroyed in about 1637, during the French conquest of the Franche-Comté. It was not until 1674 that some mills were rebuilt. These included a hemp mill, a saw mill and a forge with its water-powered bellows and hammers. This industrial development, although providing well for the people who exploited the land, did much to deplete its natural resources. It was not until the 19th century that painters, poets and novelists discovered this area and worked towards restoring its natural beauty.

The Jura is now one of the most wooded parts of France, with forests covering over 45 per cent of the land. The town and local government own approximately 45 per cent of the wooded areas, the state owns 10 per cent; the rest is privately owned and managed. An important source of income, the forest is now scrupulously managed along strict guidelines that have long-term growth and development in mind. If the past was a time of destroying the forest and pillaging the land for profit, the present is one of preservation and conservation. Today's Jura breeds and houses a great variety of wildlife, much of which, although flourishing here, is in fact endangered in the world as a whole.

■ ROMANTIC HÉRRISON ■

Xavier de Montepin made the area the heart of the Comtoise Resistance to the King of France. There is now a cave which bears the name of one of his characters, Captain Lacuzon. It was in 1820 that the writer Charles Nodier brought this region into vogue with other writers of the Romantic period. He described the area as 'A little Scotland'.

The Vallée du Hérisson, however, has a rich oral tradition of stories and legends which go back much further than the 19th century.

BELOW: the heavily wooded limestone cliffs of the Vallée du Hérisson

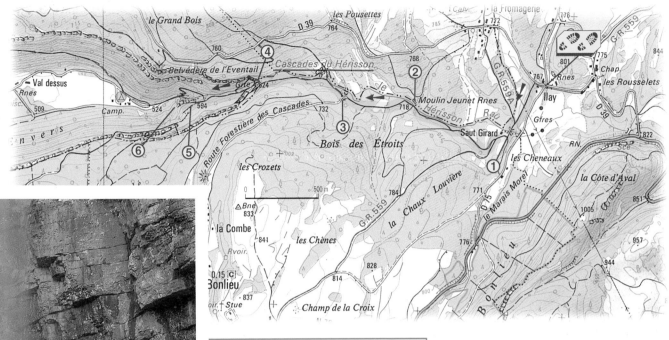

Myths and legends

One story from the region tells of a mythical monster which haunts the ruins of the Château de l'Aigle. It appears each time the Franche-Comté is threatened, pointing its sword in the direction of the enemy. Another story tells of the Chevalier de Bon-Lieu who was killed by a pack of black cats. He will forever haunt the banks of the lakes, covered in blood, lamenting his fate.

LEFT AND ABOVE LEFT: a spectacular translucent curtain of water, the Cascades de Hérisson are among the finest in the region

RIGHT: the attractive medieval town of Lods on the banks of the River Loue

Unsurprisingly, these are most frequently connected to water, springs and forest. The landscape here has long inspired the creation of all sorts of characters, legends, tales and myths which frequently have much to reveal about the customs and traditions of bygone times.

W A L K

length of walk: 4km
time: 3 hours
IGN Top 25: sheet 33270

The Jura makes for superb touring, and the area around the Cascades du Hérisson is an ideal spot to explore the landscape on foot. Wear sturdy footwear and, although easy, this walk from Ilay is hilly in places.

❶ At **Ilay**, park at the auberge du Hérisson and follow the signs to **Saut Girard** about 500m to the south, through tree-covered pathways and fields. The site formerly produced iron, and in 1811, 65 tonnes were produced in this factory workers' village. Half a century later Saut Girard was a marble works. During the Middle Ages, and up to 1714, a bridge over Saut Girard joined Lons-le-Saunier with Saint Laurent en Grandvaux and Geneva and was used to transport salt, wine and other products.

❷ Next, walk on to **Saut du Moulin** beside the ruins of Le Moulin Jeunet which can be seen 20m below the path. In 1434, it was known as the Moulin de Frasnois.

In the 17th century it fell into ruin after a war which devastated the lake region and was rebuilt by Frasnois villagers in 1663. At the end of the 19th century, Seraphin-Francois Jeunet became the proprietor and he kept it up until the beginning of the 20th century.

❸ **Le Saut de la Forge**, another former ironworks, is the next site on the walk. Proceed on to the **Gour bleu**, a romantic spot which is reached via a tree-covered path. The transparent blue waters are so clear that you can see right through to the gleaming river bed. Relax and enjoy the soothing, soft sound of the waterfalls.

❹ Cross the Hérisson River by the footbridge and climb the steep path to reach **la Grotte Lacuzon** at the foot of the waterfalls of **le Grand Saut**, which are best seen from below the towering 60m drop.

❺ From here, after a 400m hike, you find yourself at the foot of **Cascade de l'Eventail**, another spectacular waterfall. The water flows down for 65m over a succession of zigzag steps known as 'the Great Organ'.

❻ You can climb to the summit of l'Evantail, taking the Sarrazine footbridge which takes you to the **Tuffs belvédère**, offering a wonderful view of the Hérisson valley and the Cascades du Hérisson.

*L*ES RECULÉES

***T**aking their form from their environment, the villages of les Reculées blend into the surrounding stone cliffs, the lush greeenery and cascading rivers. The location is truly picturesque. The sheer grey cliffs are stark, but their tops are alive with greenery.*

RIGHT: white rivers tumble over lush green cliffs in les Reculées

This area takes its name from le Reculé, which burrows 900m into the cliffside. In the dry weather, fantastically shaped rock formations and features can be seen. After rain, the river tumbles down through pools, in its frenzied journey.

▪ BAUME-LES-MESSIEURS ▪

It was the Benedictines who founded Baume-les-Messieurs. According to tradition, at the end of the 6th century the Irish monk, Saint Colomba, established a community at the foot of these cliffs, much as he did at Luxeuil. In 910 some of the monks left Baume to help found the famous Abbaye de Cluny. The 12th and 13th centuries saw the peak of their influence. Over time, monastic life became less ardous, less strict: candidates were accepted only if they were from the nobility. Some of the monks even went so far as to forsake religious clothing, dressing instead as members of the gentry. It is at this time that Baume-les-Moines became Baume-les-Messieurs.

During the French Revolution the abbey was disbanded and its belongings were sold. It was not until the 19th century that Prosper Mérimée, Inspector General of National Monuments, had the abbey classified. Then began a restoration programme that lasted for a whole century.

The abbey resembles Baume-les-Dames and Château-Chalon. Of particular note are the bell-tower, the 16th-century Flemish reredos (given to the Abbot Guillame de Poupet by the city of Ghent), the museum and the tombstones, as well as other examples of religious architecture ranging from Jurassian Roman to Gothic.

The *grottes* (caves) of Baume-les-Messieurs are also well worth a visit, with their vaulted ceilings 30–80m high. During the summer concerts are given in these caves 120m underground! The caves are open from the end of March to the end of September, and the guided tour lasts about 40 minutes.

LEFT: the village of Baume-les-Messieurs, along with its ancient abbey, below, nestles in the 'V' where three valleys meet

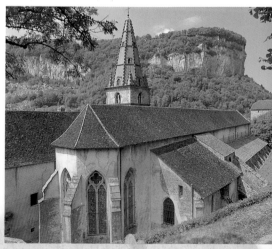

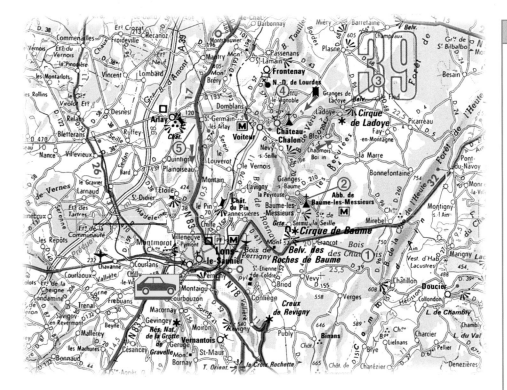

T O U R

length of tour: 60km
time: half a day
IGN Top 250: sheet 109

Taking in a few of the villages and sights of les Reculées, this drive is easy going but hilly in places. It starts some 12km south of Arlay in Lons-le-Saunier, birthplace of Rouget de Lisle, composer of La Marseillaise.

❶ From Lons-le-Saunier follow the D 471, making sure to stop at the viewpoint at **des Roches de Baume**, shortly before Crançot.

❷ At Crançot, turn left on to the D 4 and head for the **Abbaye de Baume-les-Messieurs**. After visiting the abbey, continue down to **Baume-les-Messieurs** itself. At the bottom of the hill, turn left on to the D 70 which will take you to the **Grottes de Baume-les-Messieurs**. These caves were formed by the Dard River which, after heavy rainfall, overflows and runs through them. Particularly notable are the accoustics in the *salle de fête*.

❸ Rejoin the D 70, which becomes the D 204, and head towards Granges-de-Ladoye, stopping at the belvédère du **Cirque de Ladoye** on the way.

❹ At Granges-de-Ladoye turn left on to the D 5 to **Château-Chalon**. The 12th-century church of St-Pierre is an attraction of this village, the reputation of which would otherwise rest solely upon the merit of its wine.

❺ From Château-Chalon, follow the D 120 through Voiteur to reach the N 83, then drive south to return to Lons-le-Saunier.

Ruined Charlemagne tower, covered in greenery, is in the clifftop village of Château-Chalon overlooking the valley of the Seille

▪ CHÂTEAU-CHALON ▪

Perched as it is on its rocky spur, the site of this village is as unique as the wine produced here. A lonely sentinel along the cliffs, for centuries it has guarded the entrance to Baume-les-Messieurs and les Reculées. The Charlemagne tower, ruins of a keep, is testimony to the dukes of Burgundy and their influence. The tower of the 12th-century church of Saint Pierre offers a view of the entire valley of the Seille.

▪ WINES OF THE JURA ▪

Most parts of France have their own speciality wines, and this region is no exception. The surrounding mountains have effectively isolated the entire Jura region, and this has given rise to some of the country's most individual wines. In this remote corner of eastern France on the borders of Switzerland, grape varieties are grown with flavours that are not to be matched anywhere else. The grapes are used to produce not only reds, but also whites and rosés, both still and sparkling.

The overall appellation here is the Côtes du Jura, which covers all the vineyards not included in the other small appellations of Château-Chalon, L'Etoile and Arbois. In addition to the local grape varieties, white Savagnin and red Trousseau and Poulsard, the historical links with Burgundy are maintained with Pinot Noir and Chardonnay. White wines may be pure Chardonnay or Savagnin or a blend of both, or even include some Poulsard; likewise reds and pinks may come from a single variety or a blend of two or three varieties.

Château-Chalon is the appellation of Vin Jaune, an unusual white wine, made solely from Savagnin grapes, that is left to mature for six years in small barrels, without any topping up, thereby upsetting the accepted rules of wine-making. Jean Macle is the best producer of Château-Chalon, while Christian Bourdy makes a stylish Vin Jaune. L'Etoile is a white appellation, at its best in the hands of Jean Gros at Domaine de Montbourgeau.

Arbois is better known for its red wines, and is also home of the Jura's largest producer, Henri Maire, who – more than anyone – has put the Jura on the wine map of France. Other good Arbois producers include Rolet Frères and Lucien Aviet, while names to look out for in the Côtes du Jura include Château d'Arlay, Luc Boilley, Château de Bréa and Jacques Richard.

Fêtes and festivals

The villages of les Reculées have a highly developed sense of community. This is particularly clear in the various festivals, such as the fête of Saint Vernier in Château-Chalon on the last weekend of July, when artists, musicians and actors flood the streets. And in Arbois and other villages, the Sait-Just is also celebrated.

At Christmas, *fayes* (torches of lime wood) are lit and hung from the highest points of the village, in memory of a time when the various cliff-top communities used this method to signal to each other.

LAC D'ANNECY

F*ed by several small springs and surrounded by breathtaking mountains, from early spring until the autumn colours arrive, you can stroll by the lakeside, walk in the mountains, go biking or horse riding and also swim or sail in Europe's cleanest lake.*

In prehistoric times, the lake was divided into two sections by a bar between Duingt Point and the Roc de Chere. Now the north Grand lac and the south Petit lac are joined by the Duingt Strait to form one lake. The main streams feeding the lake are Eau Mort and an abundant spring called the Boubioz. Thanks to waste-water purifying stations around the lake, Lac d'Annecy has been restored to its natural state. This operation is considered to be the pilot project for similar lakes all over the world. Fishing conditions are perfect, with species such as trout and perch living in the water. Boat trips offer relaxing and interesting tours of the lake, and several boat companies leave from Quai Napoleon III behind l'Hôtel de Ville (Town Hall).

The colourful old quarter of Annecy at the head of the lake is a delightful place for a stroll, but perhaps the the best way to enjoy the lake itself is from a boat, above

■ ROMAN REMAINS ■

The discovery of the remains of lake villages on the margins of Lac d'Annecy has proved that Annecy dates back to the neolithic period (4000 BC). The Gallo-Roman civilisation left its mark by founding the Roman city of Boutae, on the Fins plain, in 50 BC. Then during the Middle Ages the banks of the River Thiau were chosen as the site for a small burg which quickly became the regional capital because of its economic importance. The construction of a fortified castle followed. In the 16th and 17th centuries, *Annessi* was regarded as the Rome of the Savoie, because of its religious and intellectual character. Today Annecy, although a little less significant, remains the capital of the Haute Savoie.

▪ MOVING BACK IN TIME ▪

Visiting the old parts of Annecy is like taking a journey back in time. The imposing outline of its castle, with the mountains as its backdrop, dominates the old town. It was originally a stronghold, the oldest portion being the Tour de la Reine (the Queen's Tower) dating back to the 13th century. In 1394 the castle became the official residence of the Counts of Geneva, and remained so for generations. In 1514, the Duke of Savoy assigned the castle to Philippe, his brother, who was given the dukedom of Nemours 14 years later by Francois I of France. The astonishingly elegant Nemours Logis dates back to this period. Abandoned in the 18th century, the castle was turned into barracks in 1742, and so it remained until 1947. After World War II, the castle was used by the homeless until it was auctioned off. After a fire in the castle in 1952, the city of Annecy bought it in 1953 and began its restoration as a museum. It houses collections belonging to the city, with emphasis on regional and local work.

LEFT: stained-glass in Église St-Maurice in Annecy
BELOW: set above the east shore of Lac d'Annecy, silhouetted against snow-capped mountain peaks, is the imposing Château de Menthon

Château de Menthon

Well worth a visit, this château still belongs to the 22nd generation of the Menthon squires, who have owned the castle for over 1,000 years. The building has 105 rooms, 166 doors and 272 windows. It was built between the 13th and 15th centuries and was the birthplace of Saint Bernard de Menthon. The furniture is extraordinary and there is also a very rich library.

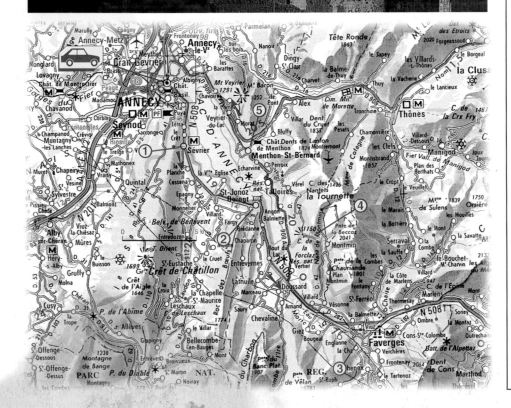

TOUR

length of tour: 90km
approximate time: 1 day
IGN Top 250: sheet 112

Starting from Annecy, this scenic tour includes a walk around the old city and optional boat trip, and a visit to Menthon-St-Bernard and its château.

❶ In Annecy, follow signs to '*centre ville*' to avenue du Rhône. Cross avenue de Chambery and continue to avenue du Cret du Maure. Turn left and carry on to place du Paradis and turn left again, keeping to the left. You will come to chemin du Tour which will take you to the château's car park. You can leave your car here while you visit the château and the old part of town, and take a boat tour of the lake. About 100m further along, the Palais de l'Isle (an old prison) sits on an islet. This 12th-century home houses exhibitions on the history of Annecy and the Savoy. Continuing, you will come to the quai Eust Chappuis. Cross this and walk to your left to the entrance of l'Hôtel de Ville. Go through the building to enter the park. To your right is quai Napoléon III, where there are several boats that tour Lac d'Annecy. While you are waiting to board a boat, pass the time by taking a stroll through Jardin de l'Europe, from where there are fine views of Annecy. After the boat tour, go back through l'Hôtel de Ville and cross the street again, this time carrying straight on, to the left of l'église St-Maurice, into rue Grenette. Take the first left and go straight ahead, back up rampe du Château.

❷ Back at place du Paradis, go straight on to boulevard de la Corniche. Take the first left on to avenue de Tresum, drive down the hill and then turn right on to rue des Marauisats (N 508) to reach **Sevrier**. Its church is situated on a hill overlooking the banks of Lac d'Annecy. Driving on, you come to **St-Jorioz Duingt**, where an 11th-century castle dominates the lake.

❸ Go on, passing through Bout-du-Lac, to reach **Faverges**, known for woodworking and manufacturing machines, household appliances, as well as lighters and pens. From here you can see another 13th-century castle. You might want to stop at the archeological museum in nearby **Viuz**, with its collection of regional Gallo-Roman artefacts.

❹ Drive along the D 42 as far as le Villard, then turn left and go to the **Col de la Forclaz**. Park your car and take the path on your right which climbs for about 100m. Turn left to reach the viewpoint (1,157m), with splendid views.

❺ Now carry on to l'Ermitage de Saint Germain and take the D 42 north to **Menthon-St-Bernard** to visit the château. Finally, head back to Annecy along the D 909 via **Veyrier-du-Lac**, where you can see interesting examples of French agriculture.

CHAMONIX-MONT-BLANC

Chamonix-Mont-Blanc, with its spectacular setting in the French Alps, is the country's capital for mountain climbing, with many viewpoints and over 300km of paths for skiing and hiking. But possibly the most impressive viewpoint is the Aiguille du Midi.

Founded in 1821, Chamonix has long been a favourite spot for mountain lovers and over the years has become a magnet for climbers. The large number of very impressive viewpoints has contributed to the popularity of this amazing region. The first Winter Olympics were held here in 1924. An obvious choice for a ski vacation, it is also a spectacular environment in which to spend a summer holiday. In addition to endless footpaths, the area offers many opportunities for other sports including swimming, tennis and golf.

■ SCALING THE HEIGHTS ■

Although modern history in this area begins in the 19th century, the site and its inhabitants go much further back. From the 1st century BC to the 4th century AD, the area was under Roman control. In 1609 Louis XIV conquered the area; in the mid-1700s a few tourists began visiting, attracted by the fresh air and natural beauty. In 1741, the Englishmen Whindham and Pococke went as far as the Mer de Glace. Some 20 years later, a prize was offered to the first person to scale

Mont Blanc, but it was another 26 years before this was accomplished (8 August, 1786 by Dr Paccard and Jacques Balmat). The first woman to conquer Mont Blanc was Marie Paradis, a waitress, who scaled its heights in 1808. The invention of the first skis in 1893, which coincided with the building of the first ice rink in this area, led to Chamonix becoming a tourist centre.

■ AIGUILLE DU MIDI ■

Another site worthy of attention is the Aiguille du Midi. Of all the viewpoints in the area, this is by far the most impressive and is reachable either by cable car or a mountain train. From the main terrace of the northern point, at an altitude of 3,842m, there is a view of the valley of Chamonix from a height of 2,800m above it. The series of four terraces provides a full 360 degree panorama.

RIGHT: from the viewing point at the Aiguille du Midi, there are impressive views of the busy alpine town of Chamonix-Mont-Blanc nestling in its valley, below

▪ MUSÉE ALPIN ▪

Opened in 1969, the Musée Alpin at la Résidence, avenue Michel Croz, was the work of Cusin Berlincourt and houses an interesting collection on the history of this area. This museum was installed in the 1840s hotel, formerly the Chamonix-Palace, and looks out over the first mountain refuge called the Temple de la nature, which was restored in 1974. Run by the Association des Amis du Vieux Chamonix, the museum's collection provides much information about day-to-day life in this area, during the 19th century. It includes furniture, tools, post cards, writings and clothing.

The vast majority of the collection is related to the conquest of the local mountains: the mountain gear is of particular interest. There is also a collection of older artefacts, engravings and crystals. The final room houses around 30 paintings of the area by the artist Gabriel Loppe (1825–1913).

The snaking Mer de Glace, right, is best appreciated from the lower slopes of the mountain or from a cable car

Mer de Glace
One of the major attractions of this site has always been the Mer de Glace, a glacier some 7km long, 1,200m wide and 200m thick. The glacier, which takes its name from its appearance of frozen waves, moves at a speed of 8mm per hour, or 70m per year.

W A L K

length of walk: 5km
approximate time: half a day
IGN Top 250: sheet 112

At Chamonix, follow the signs to the Téléphérique de l'Aiguille du Midi (cable car). There is a large car park beside the cable car take-off platform (which is only 5 minutes from the city centre). It is a good idea to book tickets roughly 10 days in advance.

The trip up to the top is in two stages, each taking roughly 10 minutes. The first takes you from 1,030m to 2,317m over the forest. On the right there is a view of the Massif and the Mont Blanc summit, below is the Bossons glacier and on the left a view of the Aiguille Verte, the Drus and the Aiguille de Chamonix. The second stage takes you up to an altitude of 3,842m and the north side of the Aiguille de Midi.

❶ The visit includes four sites. The first, **Piton Nord**, is where the visit begins and ends. It has restaurants, snackbars, gift shops and toilets. The **Piton Central**, which is reached via a footbridge, has a lift to the terrace at the summit (the price of the lift-ride is not included in the cost of the round trip ticket). The Mont Blanc terrace has the best view of Mont Blanc. From here follow the path to the end with its vantage point of the Vallee Blanche, (departure point of the Helbronner cable car), be careful because the ground is slippery. The visit takes approximately 2 hours.

❷ Next, visit the **Musée Alpin** which is a short 5-minute walk away. From the entrance to the cable car, follow rue du Lyret past the casino to avenue Michel Croz. From the car park of the Aiguille du Midi, the route Blanche will take you directly to the Mer de Glace departure point. From here you can take a cable car to the chill galleries (caves) carved into the glaciers (these galleries are recarved every year as the glacier moves). Alternatively, there is a footpath to the right of the cable car station.

PARC DE LA VANOISE

*T*he first national park created in France, the Vanoise occupies approximately one-third of the Savoie region, between the Italian park Gran Paradiso to the east, and the valleys of Isère to the north and Arc to the south.

Created in 1963, the Parc National de la Vanoise, together with its Italian neighbour the Gran Paradiso, form the largest single protected area in Europe (1,250sq km). The two parks have been twinned since 1972. The park's central area contains over 500km

The high mountain region of the Parc de la Vanoise is dotted with traditional old villages of squat buildings roofed with rough stone tiles

of footpaths and 35 shelters with a total of 1,000 bunks. In the high mountains, many of them over 3,000m, are several glaciers and innumerable valleys and gorges. The mountains protect the area from rain-bearing winds from the ocean, resulting in a sunny and very dry climate.

The wide variety of rock types, the complex geological structure and the unusual climatic conditions all contribute to the remarkable diversity of flora and fauna. The many types of rock to be found here include limestone, quartz, gypsum, sandstone, schist and gneiss.

Four distinct types of vegetation exist in the park, each controlled in part by the altitude. At its lowest level, up to 800m, the oak is representative and dominant. The second level, which are the foothills at 800–1,500m, is typified by the Sylvester pine. The third level, at 1,500–2,000m, is the sub-alpine level, with shrubs and bushes such as rhododendrons and blueberries. The final level, located above the tree line, is the alpine level. The central part of the park is made up primarily of the sub-alpine and alpine levels.

Although the ibex is disappearing throughout the world, it has found a refuge within the Vanoise National Park, along with a great many other animals. As well as the largest French population of ibex in the Alps, other mammals flourishing here include hares, hedgehogs, foxes and stoats. There are also more than 125 species of birds, the most impressive being the golden eagle, the rock partridge, the grand duke owl and the tridactyl woodpecker (which lives only in the Savoie and the Haute-Savoie regions).

▪ EXPLORE AT YOUR LEISURE ▪

The national park offers many opportunities for exploration on foot. In addition to its several hundred kilometres of well-marked footpaths, there are a few circuits which allow a complete tour of the area. For the most part, the paths are accessible from early June to the end of October but there is always a risk of

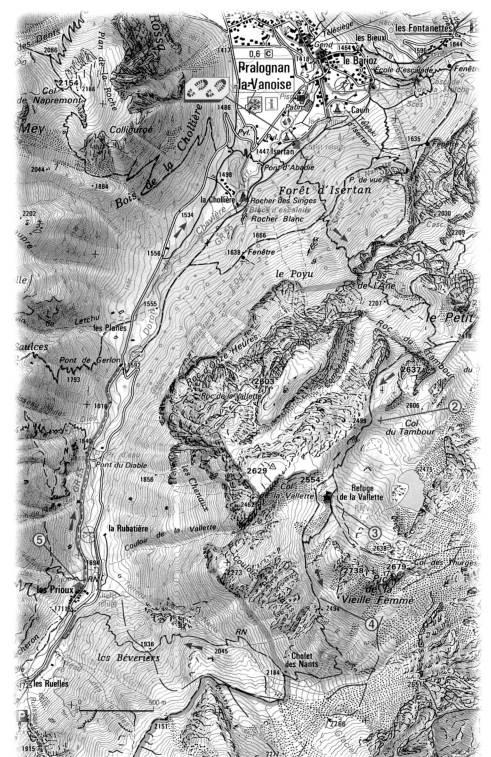

Pastel coloured houses line the banks of the River Isère in Moûtiers

snow at the beginning and end of the season. Before setting out into the mountains, it is vital to be well prepared, and to check the weather forecast.

The park also offers several paths designed for newcomers to the outdoors. These are to be found at Orgere (Villarodin-Bourget), at Mont Bochor (Pralognan-la-Vanoise), at Fornet (Val d'Isère), and at Bois (Champagny-le-Haut); the last one being designed for visitors in wheelchairs.

W A L K

length of walk: 26km
time: 6½ hours
IGN Top 25: sheet 35340T

Although some roads pass through the Parc de la Vanoise, cars are banned from its heart. This stimulating walk, which includes a total change in altitude of 1,200m, is of average difficulty but becomes slightly dangerous in wet weather. Start from the campsite ground (camping de l'Isertan), just south of Pralognan-la-Vanoise.

❶ Enter the **Forêt d'Isertan** by a path that soon joins a woodland road. Follow this to the right for approximately 250m. The path then leaves the road and veers to the left. As you climb, leave to the right the path marked 'rocher blanc' and then the one to the left marked 'nanette'. (Both paths merit a separate visit to explore the forest.) The path follows the edge of the forest. Higher up you'll see the upper part of the nanette path but do not follow it. Instead keep climbing. Cross the rocky edge of the '**pas de l'Âne**'.

❷ To reach the Col du Tambour, ignore the first two paths to your left and keep climbing. A little higher the path veers to the right and crosses under the Roc du Tambour. You then reach the **Col du Tambour** by crossing a small valley with unusual vegetation.

❸ The final part of the climb is the 30-minute hike to the **Refuge de la Vallette**, which is clearly visible from the col and offers an exceptional panoramic view.

❹ Go behind the refuge and cross under **le Pic de la Vieille Femme** to take a small path to the **Couloirs des Nants**.

❺ The path then descends on the left side, past Chalet des Nantes, to the hamlet of **les Prioux**. Continue by following the left bank of the Doron de Chaviere, to Pralognan-la-Vanoise and some well-earned refreshment.

*M*ASSIF DU VERCORS

*T*he forests and plateaux of the Vercors have sheltered mankind since prehistoric times, when the Celts built the first villages in these highlands. And more recently, the region has provided refuge for the French Resistance movement during World War II.

*O*riginally inhabited by the Voconces, a Celto-Ligure tribe, during the 6th century BC, the Roman writer Pliny the Younger explains the origin of 'Vercors': in the upper valleys of the Voconces, there was a township called Vertacomacores, which over time was shortened to Vercors. Others have suggested that it was based on Celtic words: *vers* signifies 'big' or 'elevated' and *cor* meaning 'hills'.

Little is known about the Vercors during the Middle Ages, but a couple of centuries later, the Marquis de Sassenage and the Bishop of Die often fought over ownership of the plateau. By 1698, the population of Villard-de-Lans was already 1,160 and prior to the French Revolution the area was ruled by Sassenage. In 1770 Lans became the county town, but was replaced by Villard-de-Lans in 1796. The last major reorganisation was in 1857, when Correncon was separated from Villard-de-Lans, to become a town in its own right. Between 1940 and 1944, the remoteness of Vercors made it a refuge for members of the French Resistance Movement.

■ MOUNTAINS AND PLATEAUX ■

The Dauphine, a mountainous region of the Vercors, is a limestone plateau surrounded by thick forests. The spectacular roads were con-

A series of hairpin bends and a tunnel take motorists through the magnificent mountain scenery beneath the Col de Rousset

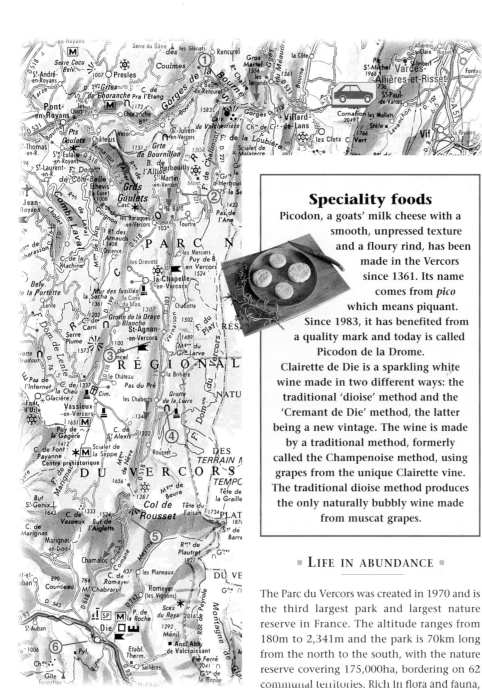

length of tour: 80km
time: 1 day
IGN Top 250: sheet 112

This scenic tour, through the the steep, winding and rugged roads of the Vercors, starts in the popular winter tourist resort of Villard-de-Lans, about 30 minutes' drive from Grenoble.

1 From Villard take the D 531 west, passing les Jarrands; after 7km turn left, just before reaching la Balme de Rencurel. The road ascends through rough and rugged scenery, with imposing rock cliffs on the left and an impressive drop on the right. Travelling south, the landscape opens out as you approach St-Julien-en-Vercors.

2 The next town, **St-Martin-en-Vercors**, is interesting for its traces of ancient footpaths. The Ancolie café, beside the church, has a 400-year-old lime tree and is a good place to stop for refreshments.

3 Upon leaving the town, turn left at the next junction and head into the Vernaison valley, in the direction of the Col de Rousset. This road winds through meadows and past the Hauts Plateaux falls. It passes by typical farms of the region, giving a good idea of local agriculture. Stop at **St-Agnan-en-Vercors** to look at its imposing village church.

4 A little further on, visit the **Grotte de la Luire**. It opens on to a vast chamber which was the site of a tragedy in World War II: it was used as a hospital for members of the *maquis* until July 1944, when it was discovered by the Germans, who killed both the wounded and orderlies.

5 Next, head towards the village of Rousset along the D 103. From here, the road climbs continuously up to 1,300m, where you find the Col ski slopes. At the **Col de Rousset**, you can climb up to the crests on foot. In July and August it is also possible to take a chair-lift, which gives the most spectacular view of the region. From Col de Rousset, a tunnel goes through the crest of the mountain and opens up onto a wonderful panoramic view of the Vercors' scenic splendour: the Diois ridges and the Alpes-de-Provence. The climate here seems to change completely. In summer, thyme and lavender perfume the air. Stop on the left, just after the tunnel, to take in the view.

6 After enjoying the view head off in the direction of Die. From Die, go southeast on the D 93 (then the D 993) for 60km until you reach Aspres-sur-Buëch. Head north in the direction of Grenoble on the N 75. From Die, it's about 2 hours back to Grenoble north along the N 75.

Speciality foods

Picodon, a goats' milk cheese with a smooth, unpressed texture and a floury rind, has been made in the Vercors since 1361. Its name comes from *pico* which means piquant. Since 1983, it has benefited from a quality mark and today is called Picodon de la Drome.
Clairette de Die is a sparkling white wine made in two different ways: the traditional 'dioise' method and the 'Cremant de Die' method, the latter being a new vintage. The wine is made by a traditional method, formerly called the Champenoise method, using grapes from the unique Clairette vine. The traditional dioise method produces the only naturally bubbly wine made from muscat grapes.

▪ LIFE IN ABUNDANCE ▪

The Parc du Vercors was created in 1970 and is the third largest park and largest nature reserve in France. The altitude ranges from 180m to 2,341m and the park is 70km long from the north to the south, with the nature reserve covering 175,000ha, bordering on 62 communal territories. Rich in flora and fauna, it boasts 1,800 plant varieties, the most precious of which are the lady's slipper orchid, the Martagon lily and the Sylvestre tulip. Forty species of mammal have been recorded in this principally mountainous region. And today the Vercors protects rare animals such as wild antelopes, wild sheep, boar and even ibex since their return in 1989. There are also over 100 bird species, including the majestic golden eagle, the peregrine falcon and the grand duke owl.

structed in the last century, taking several years to complete. Arriving on the plateau, you are immediately impressed by the green valleys and forests and the crisp fresh air. The plateau, at an average altitude of 1,000m, has its own micro-climate, a subtle blend of Alpine and Mediterranean influences.

Villard-de-Lans in the valley, below and above left, is an ideal base for exploring the area

PÉROUGES

A picturesque, medieval, walled stone village near Lyon, Pérouges remains much as it was in the 19th century and has found new life, thanks to some enterprising preservationists, and tourists.

Medieval Pérouges is ideally suited for relaxing al fresco surrounded by elegant stone buildings

Ironically, the economic decline of the ancient village of Pérouges at the beginning of the 20th century preserved a little piece of the past for posterity.

Perched on a knoll 35km north-east of Lyon, the village was once home to prosperous weavers, wine-growers and farmers. Its houses are built of local tufa, the limestone rock formed from the bed of the sea that covered the area in prehistoric times. The holes that riddle the stones were created by mussels and vegetation that lived in them aeons ago.

The town's ancient links with Italy are strong. Pérouges was founded by a group of Gauls returning from Perugia (*Pérouse* in French) in Italy – hence, the name of the village and the coat of arms that is identical to that of Perugia. The local patois also owed something to these Italian connections: local members of Napoleon's armies were amazed to discover that the Milanese understood their dialect when they arrived there in 1796. The principal occupation of Pérouges, the weaving of hemp, is also widely practised in Perugia.

▪ SAVED BY A FEW BRICKS ▪

In 1468 the ingenuity of the residents saved Pérouges from destruction during a siege. When the attackers forced their way through the lower gate, they found that the townspeople had hastily constructed a brick wall to block their way. The frustrated enemy ripped the doors off their hinges and retreated with them. The town was thus 'saved by a few bricks'. Prosperity followed, aided by the Duc de Savoie's decision to reward the Pérougians for their bravery by exempting them for 20 years from tolls, salt taxes and other levies.

From its peak of 1,500 inhabitants in the 16th century, the town's population declined to only 500 in 1900. New roads and railways had bypassed the town, taking commerce elsewhere, and its wooden marketplace burned down in 1839, never to be rebuilt. The weaving profession died out. Residents left for greener pastures, and neglected houses began to crumble. In 1909, the mayor ordered many home-owners to repair or demolish their houses in the interests of public safety. Ten

Not a museum

An effort has been made to ensure that Pérouges does not become a museum. The 100 or so people who live there are committed to restoring (not rebuilding) their properties, and some have taken up such traditional activities as weaving, pottery and bookbinding . Archaeologists and film-makers who use it as a set have also taken an interest in Pérouges, not to mention the tourists who provide the revenue that keeps the town alive. The most famous recent visitor was US President Bill Clinton, who visited the town during the G7 summit meeting in Lyon in 1996, focusing the attention of the international press on this unique remnant of the past.

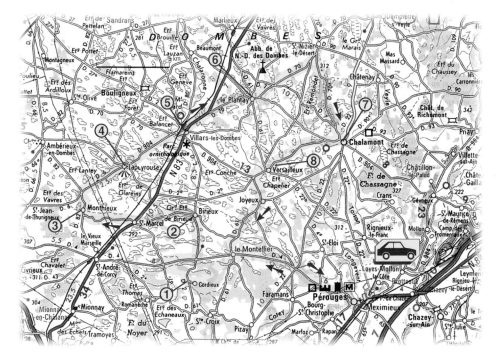

1,000 artificial *étangs* (ponds) that have been created over a period of eight centuries. They are used for fish-farming, mostly of carp; the other main activity is growing cereals. The area's ponds, forests and meadows attract hundreds of species of birds, making the area a birdwatcher's paradise.

The wetlands are populated by woodcocks, snipe, nightingales, hoopoe, shrikes, grebes, pochards and other ducks, coots, herons, egrets, and so on. In the forests are a variety of woodpeckers, tits, owls, cuckoos, hawks and nuthatches, to name just a few.

were destroyed within two months, and more were condemned to the same fate. This inspired a native son, Anthelme Thibaut, to sound an alarm in the press, attracting archaeologists, photographers and the curious to the village. Thanks to his efforts, a committee was formed to preserve and restore Pérouges, and the town was eventually declared an historic monument and protected from further destruction. The still-active committee has even seen to it that all electrical wires are underground and out of sight.

▪ VISITING PÉROUGES ▪

This tiny walled village can be visited on foot (no cars are allowed) in an hour or two, but it is well worth stopping in the fine restaurant of the Ostellerie du Vieux-Pérouges for a meal. This is where the local delicacy, the Galette Pérougienne, was reinvented from a local recipe by Madame Anthelme Thibaut, wife of the saviour of the town, in 1912. Shaped like a pizza, its delicate brioche pastry base is topped with caramelised butter and sugar. It can also be purchased by the slice at stands in the streets. Don't leave without trying it.

The ornothological park, which attracts many migratory species, is open all year to visitors

Flat-soled shoes are recommended for the visit as the uneven cobblestones make walking difficult. Park alongside the church or on rue les Terreaux and enter through the fortified Upper Gate (Porte d'en Haut), with the adjoining 16th-century church on the left. Rue des Rondes circles the town, but don't miss the side streets leading to the place de la Halle, where the Ostellerie and museum (with a fine view from its tower, and a collection of local artefacts, including old looms, porcelain, furnishings and documents), a sundial, and the 'tree of liberty' (a lime tree planted during the French Revolution) are located.

Around the corner, on rue du Prince, is the 15th-century Maison du Prince, with its round watchtower, charming walled gardens and arcaded courtyard. To visit the interior, with its Gothic furnishings and Aubusson and Flemish tapestries, enquire at the Ostellerie. Wander the streets and enjoy the quaint half-timbered houses with brick- and stone-studded, vine-covered façades. A 15th-century wine press can be seen on rue des Contreforts and an ancient well in place des Puits.

▪ DIVERSE HABITATS ▪

Just north of Pérouges, the peaceful landscape of the Dombes plateau is dotted with about

T O U R

length of tour: 65km
time: half a day
IGN Top 250: sheet 109

The Route des Étangs de la Doubs is particularly beautiful in the early evening, when the colours of the sunset are reflected in the water of the ponds. Springtime, when the birds are nesting and the wildflowers are blooming, is the best time to visit.

❶ From Pérouges, take the D 4, passing la Glaye, to le Montellier. From here, follow signs to Route des Étangs de la Dombes, passing Étang Romagne, to **Cordieux**, which still has vestiges of its ancient tower and ramparts and is home to Notre-Dame des Marais, a classified historical monument.

❷ Continue on to the Étang du Cazard, where the road takes a sharp right turn and, shortly after, a left turn on to the D 2, heading toward **Birieux**, where Étang du Grand Birieux is the largest in the Dombes.

❸ Drive on to St-Marcel-en-Dombes, with the area's oldest pond, Étang Conches, dating from the 11th century. At **Monthieux**, take a look at the 12th-century Romanesque church built of pink brick.

❹ The next town on the route is **Lapeyrouse**, site of the 14th- to 15th-century Château de Glareins.

❺ The **Parc Ornithologique**, located in **Villars-les-Dombes**, is a refuge for some 2,000 birds of 400 species and is open all year.

❻ The next town, **le Plantay**, has a 12th-century Romanesque church and a red-brick castle tower standing next to the remains of a feudal château.

❼ From here continue along the D 70 to St-Nizier-le-Desert, where the road turns south towards **Chalamont**, the highest point in the Dombes, which has restored its old quarter, notably a 15th-century house on rue de l'Hôpital.

❽ The next stop is **Versailleux**, home to a 19th-century brick château, a Romanesque church and a 15th-century chapel. Turn south on the D 61, past Étang Chapelier before reaching Joyeux, followed by Étang Neyrieux, Étang Le Fay and the Château de Montellier, a lovely sight with horses grazing on its lawn. At le Montellier turn left to take the D 4 back to Pérouges.

CRÊT DE L'ŒILLON, PARC DE PILAT

***T**he Crêt de l'Œillon, one of the highest peaks in the Parc Naturel Régional du Pilat, offers dramatic panoramic views over the peaceful Rhône Valley and the snow-capped Alps. The park has a variety of natural and artificial environments, each with its own distinct characteristics.*

The 70,000ha Parc du Pilat, located between the city of St-Étienne and the River Rhône, is a small world unto itself, encompassing mountain peaks, bucolic meadows, vast forests, rivers, lakes, châteaux and charming villages. Nature seems to have made peace with mankind here, and mankind is now trying to undo some of the damage caused by previous generations.

At some 1,430m, Crêt de la Perdrix is the highest peak in the park. However, it is Crêt de l'Œillon (1,370m) that offers the unsurpassed views. The cross that once marked the site has been replaced by a transmitter and its red-tipped tower. As you walk around the fenced-in white building, you will have a splendid 360° view of the surrounding area, including the Rhône Valley (to the east), the Jura, Mont Ventoux and the snow-capped Alps (to the southeast), Mts Lyonnais, the Chaîne des Puys, Mt Mézenec and Mt Gerbier de Jonc (from the northwest to the south).

The landscape on the slopes consists of moors, pine forest and expanses of granite *chirats* (boulders) that appear to be the result of a rock slide but were actually formed by aeons of freezing and thawing that cracked the solid granite.

■ WINES AND WOODPECKERS ■

On the eastern side, the park takes on a peaceful Mediterranean aspect, with vineyards and fruit trees surveyed by the eagle owl. Some of the finest wines of the Côtes du Rhône are produced here, including the excellent white wine of Condrieu, made exclusively of Viognier grapes, the legendary white wines of

Woolly ecologists

The park authorities are making efforts to preserve the open spaces of the area. In 1997, they sent a shepherd (a rustic sight with his long, white beard and walking stick) and his flock of 600 sheep to camp on a hillside, hoping that as the sheep graze on the woody vegetation, they will help to stop the encroachment of the forest. They will come back every year between June and September.

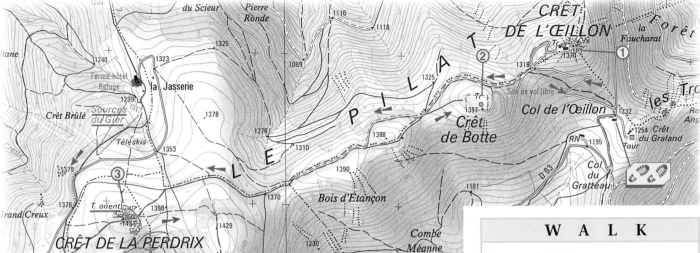

Château Grillet and Saint-Joseph (both red and white). The exceptional Côte-Rotie, produced on a tiny area of sunny slopes in Ampuis and Tupin-et-Semons, is becoming increasingly scarce since its popularisation by US wine critics.

In the highlands, the wilder landscape consists of impressive fir forests – with a sprinkling of beech trees – that are inhabited by roe deer. Cool, sunny glades harbour tall ferns, pink evening primroses and giant-leafed adenostyles. The forest is filled with the song of crested tits, coal tits and wrens, and the tapping of the black woodpecker.

▪ PEACEFUL COHABITATION ▪

Pilat's *crêts* (peaks) have an interesting ecological history. Made of granite, they rose during the Tertiary period, and the *chirats* (boulders) that cover the hillsides like streams of rock flowing between the fir trees were formed by alternating periods of freezing and thawing over the ages, that cracked the once-solid rock. When humans arrived, they changed the landscape to suit their needs, enriching the soil, creating pastures and planting forests. Now that grazing has declined, the forests are advancing up the hillsides, threatening the area's natural ecology, with its plant and animal species that thrive in open spaces, as well as the stunning views from the peaks.

Pastures with grazing goats, moors and forests alternate on the dry, rocky slopes of the southern flank of the peaks. Five pairs of short-toed eagles soar over this area hunting the small reptiles that inhabit it.

To the southwest, dairy cows graze on the plateaux and valleys where the meadows blossom in a riot of colour in the early summer, when blue bachelors' buttons, orchids, larkspur and other wild flowers make their appearance. Rock sparrows, whinchats and wheatears are some of the birds that populate the area, and the insect-eating sundew plant can be found in the occasional peat bogs.

Along the waterways, the old mills and *passementerie* (fancy trim for textiles) workshops that were once the main economic activity of the area can still be seen, and the locals continue to produce honey, cheeses made from goats' and cows' milk, *charcuterie* and fruits (especially apples).

Numerous leisure activities are available to visitors to the Parc du Pilat, including hiking, mountain biking, rock climbing, canoeing and kayaking, para-gliding and hang-gliding, horse riding, cross-country skiing, snow shoeing, donkey and carriage rides and go-karting.

▪ STE-CROIX-EN-JAREZ ▪

The 60 residents of this tiny, peaceful village in the Parc du Pilat have the unusual privilege of living in a former Carthusian monastery, said to have been founded after Béatrix de la Tour, wife of Guillaume de Roussillon, devastated by her husband's death during the final Crusade, followed a vision of a cross of stars to the site. She built a chapel in 1280, and it was soon surrounded by the constructions of the

LEFT and RIGHT: *Ste-Croix-en-Jarez, a former monastery, was founded by Béatrix de la Tour, who lived there until her death in 1307*

W A L K

length of walk: 7km
time: half a day
IGN Top 25: sheet 2933E

For this walk you need stout shoes and a good level of fitness, as there is climbing involved and the rough paths can be steep and rocky. Viewpoint indicators explaining what you are seeing from the peaks are located at Crêt de l'Œillon and Crêt de Perdrix. Leave your car in the car park at Col de l'Œillon.

❶ From the car park walk up the rocky path to **Crêt de l'Œillon** to sample the spectacular views.

❷ When you've had your fill, return to the car park and take a look at the signboard that describes the area and has a map of the path. Follow the arrows on the wooden signposts, which indicate the route and show exactly where you are and at what altitude. Each crossroads is clearly signposted. If you take the northern path, you'll pass **Crêt de Botte** and **Crêt du Rachat** and arrive at **Crêt de la Perdrix**, the highest peak at 1431m.

❸ From here the trail turns back to the south and passes Crêt de la Chèvre, Crêt de l'Arnica and Crêt de l'Étançon before returning to the car park.

---

monks. Béatrix lived there until her death in 1307, and she still rests under the alter of the Gothic church, which boasts 15th-century frescoes and a painting by Andrea Mantegna of Saint Sebastian. The monks were evicted after the French Revolution, and the building was sold in parcels to local residents.

Nothing much has changed since then. Beyond the imposing fortified façade with its arched portal and two round towers is a large courtyard and a passageway leading to another courtyard surrounded by ancient residences. Here the entire school population of a few children plays under the watchful eyes of two teachers seated on folding chairs. Another arched passageway leads to a stream lined with gardens. The monastery, whose kitchen and bakery have been restored, houses a modest hotel/restaurant, Le Prieuré.

VALLÉE DU RHÔNE

GORGES DE L'ARDÈCHE

For more than 100 million years, the emerald waters of the Ardèche River have been carving a deep, twisting canyon into a limestone plateau, creating the Gorges de l'Ardèche, a spectacular natural site covered with scrubby vegetation, riddled with caves and adorned with strange rock formations.

The Gorges de l'Ardèche is a protected natural preserve, where the cliffs provide housing for the rare Bonelli's eagle (above right) and chattering colonies of swifts. During the day, lizards sun themselves on the rocks and, at night, beavers build their homes in partly submerged caves along the river. Boars roam the forests, and wild goats clamber along steep, rocky slopes.

In the past, the caves carved out of the same cliffs by underground rivers provided shelter for another species: mankind. Over a period of some 350,000 years, prehistoric mankind left behind such traces as sepulchres, engravings, paintings, dolmens and other remnants of ritual life.

■ LIFE UNDERGROUND ■

Some caves, such as the Grotte de la Madeleine, Aven Marzal and the Grotte de Saint Marcel d'Ardèche, with their dramatic stalactites and stalagmites, are open to the public (except in winter). More adventurous visitors can go cave hunting on their own in such places as the Goule de Foussouble. More than 2,000 caves have been discovered to date, including the Grotte Chauvet Pont-d'Arc, the oldest known painted cave in the world, which was recently discovered by amateur speleologists. The plant life found along the gorge includes spruce, chestnut and beech trees; Douglas firs, sessile oaks, holm oaks, poplars, willows, alders, thyme, wild asparagus, boxwood, arbutus, honeysuckle and broom.

■ RIDING THE RAPIDS ■

One of the best ways to enjoy the Gorges de l'Ardèche is by canoe or kayak. However, in the peak summer months (July and August),

The Ardèche River snakes below steep cliffs, right, and the natural archway of Pont d'Arc, above, as it slices its way through the mountains

106

traffic on the river can reach phenomenal proportions, with around 10,000 people on the water every day. But at least it's not the motorway at rush hour: canoes are quiet and don't emit exhaust fumes. Boats can be rented for short treks or by the day at numerous, well-signposted spots along the river.

Hardy visitors might want to park the car at the lower end of the gorge, at St-Martin-d'Ardèche, for example, take two days to hike to the other end, then rent a boat at Pont d'Arc and take another two days to float tranquilly back down the river – that is, until they hit the rapids in 25 places.

Alternatively, you can rent a canoe or kayak at Pont d'Arc and the *concessionaire* will drive your car to the other end, where it will await your arrival. Camping along the river is allowed at Gaud and Gournier, as sudden flooding can occur elsewhere. Both campsites are equipped with toilets and drinking water. In all, more than 40 commercial campsites are accessible from the road. Other activities available in the warm months (everything closes in winter) include swimming, fishing (a licence is required), horse riding, biking, hiking and rock climbing.

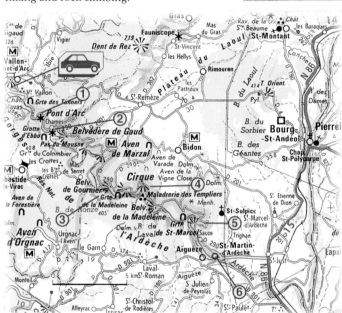

Canoeists can meet the odd challenge along the river near Vallon Pont-d'Arc

Grotte Chauvet Pont-d'Arc

This is a true treasure among the many caves in the Gorges de l'Ardèche. Discovered only in 1994 by three amateur speleologists, the Grotte Chauvet Pont-d'Arc is one of the world's finest – and oldest – known Palaeolithic sites. More than 30,000 years old, the cave proves that Cro-Magnon Man's artistic abilities were even more advanced than other cave paintings, such as those at Lascaux, had shown. Here we find rare images of lions, woolly rhinoceroses and aurochs (extinct wild oxen), as well as horses and bison, beautifully drawn and engraved with great sophistication. Over 300 animals of 13 species are represented. The fragility of the paintings means that the cave will never be opened to the public, but it is worth visiting the exhibition in Vallon Pont-d'Arc for a film presentation, or the new museum, built for the year 2000.

T O U R

length of tour: 35km
time: half a day
IGN Top 250: sheet 115

There is only one road that runs along the Gorges de l'Ardèche, on the northern side. It is a dramatic, twisting drive that offers spectacular views and numerous opportunities to stop at viewpoints or for hiking, canoeing, swimming and other activities.

❶ Start at the town of **Vallon-Pont-d'Arc** and follow the signs for the Route Touristique des Gorges de l'Ardèche. The road cuts through rock wall as you drive alongside the swift-running river. The rock face is riddled with holes and caves, and there are vineyards and olive groves tucked into the land between the curves of

the road and the meanders of the river. Be sure to stop at **Pont d'Arc** to see the famous 66m natural stone arch that has been carved out by the river. A short walk takes you to the river bank for a closer look.

❷ Further on, the nearby hamlet of **Chames** has the ruins of a 14th-century chapel and a charmingly simple little church built in the 18th century.

❸ At **la Serre de Tour** there is a spectacular open view of the river and the valley. Here the river's meandering forms an almost perfect circle around a small peak. A short detour at **Autridge** takes you to a lookout point that makes a good picnic spot. At **Gournier**, hikers might want to walk down the little road (no cars allowed), through the forest to the river, where there is a bivouac for campers. It's a steep walk back up to the main road, however.

❹ **Cirque de la Madeleine** offers a naturist beach, plage

des Templiers, as well as the 2-million-year-old Grotte de la Madeleine.

❺ Not far down the road is another cave open to the public, **Grotte de Saint Marcel**. Near the entrance, a 2.3km nature walk with signs describing the plant life passes by an ancient menhir. There is a boat-launching site at Sauze and a riverside park with picnic tables.

❻ The gorge comes to an end at the town of **St-Martin-d'Ardèche**.

From here you can retrace your steps and see the views from the opposite direction, or continue your travels in the valley.

ℒE PUY-EN-VELAY

***T**he first impression of le Puy-en-Velay is of a lively, bustling city, its boulevards busy with traffic, but, once away from the main streets, you find the charming old quarter, steeped in history.*

Three diverse and unmistakable monuments dominate the skyline of le Puy, capital of the Haute-Loire *département*: a chapel, improbably built on the summit of an extinct volcano, the cathedral's tower, and a huge pink statue of Notre-Dame. No trip to this fine, town would be complete without a visit to all three, and walking is the best way to enjoy the sights on offer.

The town's history is inextricably linked with the Christian faith. Following an appearance by the Virgin Mary and the subsequent healing properties attributed to a slab of volcanic stone, a first church was constructed in AD 430 on a pagan site; the first pilgrimages date from this time. Le Puy is, with Chartres, one of the oldest holy towns dedicated to the worship of the Virgin.

■ A POINT OF DEPARTURE ■

In AD 950 Gothescalk, the bishop of le Puy-en-Velay, set a trend which has lasted centuries by leading the first French pilgrimage to Santiago de Compostella (St Jacques de Compostelle) in Spain. On the bishop's return, a chapel dedicated to St Michel was built on the rock, inappropriately known as the Dyke d'Aiguilhe, reached by 268 steps. Among the treasures found in 1955 during the restoration of the altar was a magnificent 10th-century reliquary of Spanish origin.

The town's fame grew throughout the Middle Ages as a point of departure for pilgrimages along one of the four main routes to Santiago de Compostella, as well as to St Gilles du Gard in Haute Provence. Modern-day pilgrims are still made welcome.

The Dyke d'Aiguilhe, with the chapel of St-Michel perched on top

▪ A FAMOUS VICTORY ▪

The French victory at Sebastopol in 1855 during the Crimean War motivated the bishop of le Puy, Monseigneur de Morlhon – with the permission of the emperor Napoleon III – to commission a cast-iron statue dedicated to Notre-Dame de France, made of 213 melted-down cannon from the battlefield, in celebration and gratitude. The 16m-tall statue (22.7m including the pedestal), by Jean-Marie Bonnassieux, was unveiled on 12 July 1860 in front of 120,000 pilgrims. Remarkably, it is hollow, and you can enter through a doorway in the base and climb a narrow spiral staircase to neck level for a vertiginous view over the town through small peep-holes.

With its colourful, sensitively restored houses, le Puy is lively all year round: its Italian-style carnival in March or the Fêtes du Roi de l'Oiseau in September recall splendours of Renaissance times.

Lace, lentils and liqueurs

Le Puy-en-Velay is famous for its lace which, according to legend, was invented by a young embroidress here in 1407. You can learn more about this meticulous craft by visiting the Lace Museum and teaching centre in rue Raphael, with its fascinating exhibition of both old and creative con-temporary lace designs. Another symbol of the city is the green lentil, which grows particularly well in the micro-climate of the Velay plateaux. Considered a delicacy because of the fineness of its skin, it is the base of many local dishes. Finally, to help digest your meal, sample le Puy's renowned green Verveine liqueur from the impressive Pages boutique in rue du Faubourg St Jean.

The Moorish cathedral contains some superb frescoes

WALK

length of walk: 5km
time: half a day
IGN Top 25: sheet 2735E

This town walk takes in all the major landmarks. You can complete your visit with a walk in Jardin Henri Vinay, behind the Préfecture, where le Musée Crozatier displays paintings, sculptures, crafts, machines, furniture and lace. Wear sturdy shoes as many streets are steep and/or cobbled.

❶ Start from the tourist office in place de Breuil. Cross the boulevard and take rue Porte-Aiguière to reach place du Martouret and the Hôtel de Ville. Continue through place du Clauzel, where a bric-à-brac market is held every Saturday morning.

❷ Turn left along rue Courrerie to place du Plot, the former departure point for pilgrimages, and still the beginning of a torch-lit procession every 14 August. Take rue Chenebouterie, where General Fayolle of World War I fame was born in no. 9 (the house dates from 1592). On rue Raphael, don't miss the Lace Museum at no. 38.

❸ The steep, cobbled streets, leading to the cathedral, particularly rue des Tables, are a delightful sight. But before entering the cathedral, take a detour to the Rocher d'Aiguilhe: turn left along rue Becdelièvre or rue de la Visitation and follow rue Gouteyron through the gate for a splendid view of the rock.

❹ Returning to the cathedral, visit the maze of the Cité Episcopal to see the statue of the Black Virgin, the Fever Stone (believed to cure those who lie on it), the frescoes and cloisters, the Penitents' Chapel and the baptistry. Climb rue du Cloître and the steps which lead up to the statue of Notre-Dame de France, and the staircase inside it.

❺ Descend rue St-Georges and rue de la Manecanterie, making a mini detour to place du For to admire another view of the town. Walk down rue Cardinal de Polignac and rue Rochetailla de (which means 'carved out of rock'). Turn left along rue de Bouillon, cross place de la Platrière. Go along rue Jules Valles and turn right down rue Ste-Marie, leading to rue Ste-Claire and its monastery to visit the chapel. The narrow streets of this quarter are among the oldest in the town.

❻ Now head towards rue Saint-François Regis, rue du Bessat and rue Crozatier and return to the tourist office in place du Breuil at the start of the walk.

$\mathcal{V}$IADUC DE GARABIT

$\mathcal{T}$he hand of Gustave Eiffel, one of the best-known names in France, can clearly be seen in the viaduct at Garabit, which predated his famous tower in Paris. Spanning the Gorges de la Truyère near St-Flour, in the département of Cantal, the viaduct is easily accessible from the A 75 motorway.

The Viaduc de Garabit was not originally Eiffel's idea. That honour belongs to Léon Boyer, although without the support of Eiffel's superior experience and reputation the project might never have seen the light of day. The problem facing the engineers of the Paris–Béziers railway line in the 1870s was how to cross the Gorges de la Truyère in the Massif Central, which was hindering its completion. The improbable solution dreamed up by the 29-year-old Boyer was this spider's web of meccano, 125m high and 565m long. The scale of the project was made clear to the French people of the time by a drawing which showed the cathedral of Notre-Dame (70m high), with the column of the Bastille (47m) superimposed upon it, underneath the arch of the viaduct.

PRECISION ENGINEERING

Work began in the spring of 1880, and the last piece completing the arch was slotted into place on a sunny afternoon in April 1884; even the expansion of the metal in the heat of the day was included in the engineering cal-

Ecomusée le Domaine de Longevialle

A visit to this fascinating museum helps to fully appreciate the impressive viaduct at Garabit, its history and the various stories associated with it. Created in the 18th-century château known as le Domaine de Longevialle, just off the N 9 south of the viaduct, this lively museum, particularly appreciated by children, forms one section of a four-part Ecomusée. Another section is the completely unmodernised Ferme de Pierre Allègre at Loubaresse.

At Longevialle you can visit a reconstruction of the bistro where the workmen drank, marvel at original photographs of the viaduct's construction and learn about the films that have been shot around this magnificent site, including some of its less happy moments (such as stunts that went wrong and suicides).

▪ IN AND AROUND ST-FLOUR ▪

The medieval market town of St-Flour has two advantages: it occupies a magnificent viewpoint in the heart of the empty and unspoilt Cantal, and is easily accessible from the A 75, built to link Paris and Barcelona.

At first sight its 15th-century cathedral, built from the region's black volcanic stone, appears bleak and unwelcoming, but inside its stained-glass windows and frescoes create a much more joyous atmosphere. The town has two museums: the Musée de la Haute-Auvergne in the former Bishop's Palace houses an archaeological collection, furniture and religious art; the Maison Consulaire in St-Flour's oldest house is an architectural delight. It is from here that the best view over the surrounding countryside can be enjoyed.

Apart from the viaduct, one of the most spectacular sites in the region is the Château d'Alleuze. From 1383 onwards it was the haunt of a bandit chief, Bernard de Garlan whose brigands, terrorised the local countryside. When they finally disappeared in 1394 St-Flour celebrated with three days of wine and cakes distributed by the municipality.

St-Flour, built on a steep bluff, is a picturesque old mountain town; at Loubaresse you can see how country folk lived in the écomusée, left

culations. During this time, a whole village sprang up to house the workmen in what had previously been a virtually uninhabited valley. The total cost of the construction was 3.383 million francs, against an estimate of 3.2 million francs. The precision of the estimate has to be admired! The price of its construction today would be multiplied by approximately 1,500.

Since the construction of the Barrage de Grandval hydroelectric dam, the viaduct dominates an artificial lake 122m below, in the former gorge, but it is no less impressive for that. It now stands out against the surrounding valley, with its coat of red anti-rust paint, a change from its original grey; it is painted approximately every 20 years. In 1992 another 'viaduc de Garabit' was built, this time in concrete, to carry the A 75 motorway.

ABOVE RIGHT: a trail of simple crosses along the steep slopes leading to the Château d'Alleuze
LEFT: the viaduct resplendent in its anti-rust paint

T O U R

length of tour: 80km
time: half to 1 day
IGN Top 250: sheet 111

Starting from St-Flour, note that this tour is not recommended in winter: there is often snow in the region and the narrow, winding roads can be icy and treacherous at this time of year.

❶ After exploring **St-Flour**, leave the lower town on the N 9, signposted Garabit, avoiding the A 75 motorway. Travel down into the spectacular **Gorges de la Truyère**: the view of the viaduct is impressive. If you are not visiting the écomusée, cross the viaduc de Garabit

and take the D 13 direct to Faverolles. If you are visiting the museum at **le Domaine de Longevialle** turn left after crossing the bridge, pass under the viaduct and continue on the N 9 until you turn left to le Domaine on the D 48. Follow this winding road for 6km passing through Claviers d'Outre. Also worth seeing is la ferme de Pierre Allègre at Loubaresse, which is part of the same écomusée. The buildings and interiors of this farm, which was never modernised, faithfully depict the life of country people in the last century.

❷ Backtrack to the original route and take the D 48 under the motorway, signposted Faverolles, passing through Bournoncles. At **Faverolles** is the Château du Chassan, with its elegantly furnished rooms. Also here is a crafts centre, le Bouffadou, where local artists exhibit their work during the summer.

❸ Continue along the D 13 (signposted Chaudes Aigues), taking in the view of the Gorges de la Truyère at Auriac, and continue to Fridefont, where you turn right on to the D 40. Follow this road, signposted Alleuze, to the **Barrage de Grandval**, which forms an artificial lake in the former gorge, was built to generate hydroelectricity.

❹ Visit the spectacular Château d'Alleuze, once occupied by bandits, which is accessible by a steep footpath.

❺ Return to St-Flour along the D 116 and D 10, pausing at **Villedieu** to visit its listed red-stone church with an 11th-century tower.

PUY DE DÔME

A chain of extinct volcanoes dominates this part of the Auvergne and the Puy de Dôme, the highest of these peaks, gives its name to the **département** in which it is found. A climb to the top is rewarded with superb views of the surrounding wild landscape.

The 1,464m summit of le Puy de Dôme offers a view of ten *départements*, and an occasional glimpse of Mont Blanc. Not surprisingly, this symbol of the eponymous *département* has been venerated by the locals since time immemorial. In the first century AD the Romans built a temple to the god Mercury, the ruins of which are still visible.

The history of le Puy de Dôme, however, predates the Roman temple by some 25 million years, to the time when the volcanic activity in the region began. The emergence of the 40km Chaîne des Puys, the range of 100 or so volcanoes which include le Puy de Dôme, is relatively recent in geological terms, dating back a mere 7,500–15,000 years.

■ WONDERFUL WATER ■

A fortuitous by-product of this volcanic activity was the emergence of springs with health-giving properties that were recognised in ancient times. Today, the waters are bottled and consumed in large quantities, under such famous names as Volvic (the town of that name lies just north of le Puy). The water often comes to the surface at temperatures exceeding 35°C, giving rise to the fashionable spa towns in the area. The *département* of Puy de Dôme alone has six such *stations thermales*, where the springs are said to cure everything from arthritis and allergies to respiratory, kidney and gynaecological problems.

■ GETTING TO THE TOP ■

Le Puy de Dôme has been the site of some memorable events. In the 17th century, Blaise Pascal conducted his experiments on air pressure here, and in 1872 a meteorological observatory was constructed. By the end of the 19th century it had become so fashionable to visit the summit of le Puy that the possibilities of constructing a railway were studied; finally, between 1906 and 1922, a steam tramway was created, which enabled passengers to make the ascent from Clermont Ferrand (the nearby capital of the Auvergne). This was superseded by the present-day road, constructed in 1926. The Tour de France included the ascent to

An aerial view of the Puy de Dôme, one of the volcanoes in the Chaîne des Puys, below

Of volcanoes and men

La Chaîne des Puys is part of *le Parc des Volcans*, a natural regional park which seeks to protect but also to enhance appreciation of the area's natural assets and heritage. Unique to France, the PNR (*Parc Naturel Régional*) is created as a result of local initiative. It represents a living, rural system, usually in an area affected by rural decline.

Created in 1977, le Parc des Volcans is the biggest such park in France. It has eight *maisons* which house exhibitions on subjects as diverse as flora and fauna, water, cheese and peat bogs. Its headquarters at Montlosier, not far from le Puy de Dôme, has a fascinating exhibition on volcanoes, the park and the role of man in the landscape.

W A L K

length of walk: 7km
time: 3–4 hours
IGN Top 25: sheet 102

The climb to the top of le Puy de Dôme is extremely steep and should only be attempted by those who are reasonably fit. Sturdy non-slip shoes, preferably walking boots, are essential, and walkers should keep to the footpaths. The summit is often snow-covered in winter. A road spirals to the top of the peak, but this route is closed between 1 December and mid-March. When open, it may not be used by walkers or cyclists, and there is a toll for cars and motorbikes.

❶ Start from **le Col de Ceyssat** to the south of le Puy de Dôme, where there is parking. Take the GR 4-441 (red and white markings) which leads from the car park of l'Auberge des Grosmanaux and follows the former mule track – also used by the Romans – to the summit (allow 45 minutes for the climb). Spend time at the summit resting, admiring the view or picnicking. Unfortunately, there is no public access to the ruins of the Roman **temple of Mercury**.

❷ To begin the descent, continue along the GR 4-441, signposted Col de Goules. At first, this follows the tarmac road, then branches off right (red and white markings). There is a steep descent at first, levelling out through woods and then into the open where it crosses with another footpath marked in yellow.

❸ Turn left here and follow the yellow markings (still the GR 4-441). After 10 minutes turn left again at a fork in the pathway – the GR 4-441 continues straight on, but follow the yellow markings now: a yellow X indicates the wrong path. The walk is mostly level from now on, but the path is often quite narrow, through hazel woods and is much used. You should beware of mountain bikers!

❹ After another half-hour's walk, bear left where the path forks, again avoiding the route marked by a yellow X. Another 20 minutes brings you to a wooden footbridge, and shortly afterwards you arrive back at the

the summit in its itinerary for the first time in 1952. By the end of the 20th century, its slopes presented a challenge for *aficionados* of the VTT (*vélo tout terrain*, or mountain bike).

The Puy de Dôme is also a favourite rendezvous for aviators of all types: in 1911 Eugène Renaux won the Grand Prix Michelin by flying from Paris in 5 hours 10 minutes, and landing on its slopes. Today, it makes an impressive launching place for hang-gliders, microlights, parachutes and hot-air balloons.

Le Puy, above, is set in an old crater basin with giant volcanic outcrops rising up from the town's streets. It's a popular site with aviators of all sorts, below

ℱORÊT DE TRONÇAIS

Known as the finest oak forest in Europe, the Forêt de Tronçais is a different world, where every crossroads is named and every parcel of woodland numbered. Its little-known attractions include listed oak trees, lakes and ancient springs.

The Forêt de Tronçais near the heart of France is a *forêt dominiale*, which means that it is state-owned, and visitors are actively encouraged to roam its 11,000ha, which include numerous picnic areas, footpaths, cycle tracks and bridlepaths. With a map it is impossible to get lost, thanks to a system of 442 numbered plots of woodland and individually named crossroads (known as *ronds*).

Understandably, the floor of the Fôret de Tronçais is carpeted with acorns

■ A CULTIVATED CROP ■

Though at first glance the trees in the forest may all look alike, closer examination reveals that different parcels contain trees of different ages. It is, in fact, a very carefully managed and cultivated 'crop'; one of the few tasks still left to nature is the sowing of new trees: otherwise there is very little that is truly wild about it. Therein lies its interest, particularly since some of the oldest oak trees are about 350 years old, and were planted on the orders of Colbert, prime minister of Louis XIV, in the mid-17th century. At that time he wanted high-quality oak to build French ships; it is likely that oak from Tronçais was

also used in the construction of the Louvre. Some of the most remarkable of these giant trees, attaining heights of 30–40m, are listed and have been given names.

Until the mid-17th century, the forest belonged to the noble family of Bourbon, who used it mainly for hunting. The sport is still encouraged, as the only viable means of controlling what would otherwise be an excessive population of deer and wild boar.

■ FORGES AND FOUNTAINS ■

In the 18th century much more of the forest was cut. About two-thirds of its area was used to provide fuel for the forges which were installed by Nicolas Rambourg, in the village of Tronçais. It was at this time that four of its five lakes were created – that of St-Bonnet is natural – to provide water for the forges. The forges later became a wire factory which man-

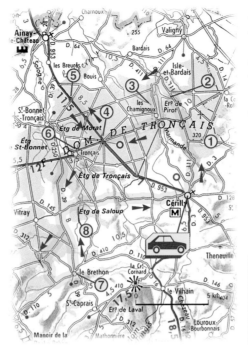

ufactured, among other things, the cables for the Eiffel Tower.

The very best oak is used for veneer, furniture and making the barrels in which the fine wines of Bordeaux and Burgundy – as well as Cognac – are aged; the remainder of the wood goes for carpentry and heating.

Several prehistoric sites have been found in the forest, dating from 15,000 to 8,500 BC. It is probable that one of the attractions of the area were the numerous springs of water, around which the earliest inhabitants would have settled. There are still around 40 of these springs, known as *fontaines*, some of which have legends attached to them.

Sacred springs

The *fountaines* of Tronçais were worshipped by the Celts, a cult which continued throughout the Middle Ages and until very recently was still alive. The springs were lovingly cared for and their water was sacred. Each has its legend: at la Fontaine de la Goutte d'Argent, a young man died of love for an enchanted princess; at la Fontaine de Viljot young girls would throw a pin into the water to see whether they would marry within the year.
The legend of Saint Mayeul concerns the Abbot of Cluny, who visited the monks at nearby Menesser in AD 994. When told that they lacked water, he struck the ground with his cross and a fountain gushed forth. It was subsequently visited by religious processions in years of drought; the last such occasion was in 1893.

The ideal place to enjoy walking, cycling and other outdoor pursuits, the Fôret de Tronçais is particularly peaceful at sunset

---

TOUR

length of tour: 70km
time: half to 1 day
IGN Top 250: sheet 111

Start from the town of Cérilly, but first obtain a map of the forest from the tourist office. All sights mentioned are clearly signposted.

❶ Take the road in front of the church (worth a visit) past the cemetery, and take the D 111, in the direction of Isle-et-Bardais. At le Rond de Brot turn right along one of the many forest roads to le Rond de Thiolais. Stop here if you wish to visit la Fontaine de la Goutte d'Argent. Return to le Rond de Brot and continue in the direction of Isle-et-Bardais.

❷ Continue past le Rond Bernard. Of note are the old primitive houses on the right. Just afterwards turn left towards le Rond des Pêcheurs, where you can stop for a swim g de Pirot.

❸ Return to the road and continue on to Isle-et-Bardais. Turn left and follow the road along the shore of the lake, passing through les Chamignoux village to the crossroads of the same name. Turn right on to the D 978. Just before le Rond de Viljot, stop to visit the fountain of the same name, the most famous of the springs in the forest. Continue on the D 978 and stop at le Rond de Viljot to visit a listed oak tree, the *Chêne Carré* (Square Oak), which is on your left. Two more trees on the right 1km further along the road are named *Charles Louis Philippe* and *Emile Guillaumin* after two local writers.

❹ At le Rond Gardien turn right, towards Ainay le Château. At le Rond Buffévent turn left and follow directions to visit the oaks called *Chêne Chevalier* (Cavalier Oak), *La Sentinelle* (the Sentry) and *Les Jumeaux* (the Twins), all magnificent specimens over 300 years old. Follow the one-way system of forest roads to regain le Rond Buffévent and return to le Rond Gardien. Turn right in the direction of Tronçais.

❺ Just after le Rond Desjobert take a sharp right turn (after a house on a bend) to take the forest road, turn-ing left after 50m to go to le Rond Neuf. Stop here to visit la Réserve de Colbert, a section of forest planted in the mid-1600s and, a little further on, *le Chêne Stebing*, named after a Scottish professor.

❻ Return to the D 978 and continue to the village of Tronçais, past the forges of Nicolas Rambourg. Continue to le Rond Raffignon, turn left on to the D 39, towards le Brethon, and continue past the Carrefour des Loges. After 5km turn right down a forest track marked la Bouteille to visit the charming little chapel of Saint-Mayeul and the two springs: le Fond du Tonneau and la Fontaine Saint-Mayeul.

❼ Continue to **le Brethon**, which has a Romanesque church. Return along the D 39, turning right at the Carrefour des Loges to visit **l'Ètang de Saloup** (D 145).

❽ Continue to le Rond du Chêne Aragon, pausing to visit le Font des Porchers, then turn right for la Clef des Fossés and le Rocher des Andars. Return to the D 145 back to Cerilly.

Suc-au-May

*I*n a region best known for its wooded hills and wide, open spaces, on a clear day the orientation table at the Suc-au-May viewpoint, situated at one of the highest points of the Corrèze, gives breathtaking views over seven départements.

Local markets are full of fresh produce, including this mouthwatering array of cheeses which offers something to suit every palate

The Corrèze is one of the lesser-known *départements* of France with possibly the lowest crime rate – with good reason, though, as it also has one of the lowest populations. The first thing that strikes you, when you look at the map of the region surrounding Suc-au-May, is the emptiness. Even in the peak summer months you are unlikely to find crowds. What you will find is utter peace and tranquillity, spectacular plunging, wooded hills and valleys, wild, open spaces, *étangs* (lakes) and solid granite and slate farmsteads.

Suc-au-May forms part of the Massif des Monédières, with its *puys* (peaks), *cols* (passes) and the Cirque de Freysselines (a horseshoe-shaped range). From the orientation table itself (inaugurated in 1935 and an IGN triangulation point) the neighbouring *départements* of Dordogne, Haute Vienne, Creuse, Puy de Dôme, Cantal and Lot can be surveyed. Most impressive and easily distinguished during the winter are the distant snow-capped peaks of the Plomb de Cantal and the Puy de Sancy.

The lush green landscape around Suc-au-May

Rural life

The bread oven in the hamlet of le Tourondel, with its turreted *manoir*, epitomises rural life here, and it is easy to imagine the simple implements on display still being used in the last 50 years. The region is also known for its accordionists, most notably Jean Ségurel, famous for his song *La Bruyère Correziene*.

Solid stone buildings in Freysselines are typical of this rural area

■ DÉPARTEMENT, RIVER, TOWN ■

Corrèze the town has its origins in the 9th century. It was known as one of the main stopping places for pilgrims on the route to Santiago de Compostella, as was Chaumeil, which is also visited on this circuit. The town belonged to the Vicomté de Ventadour and only became a free commune in the 15th century. Two of the town's gates are still visible today, as well as several of the fortified houses; it is said there were underground passages. The church has an impressive 18th-century baroque altarpiece carved in walnut, which can be illuminated by the visitor, at the touch of a button.

Religion played an important role in life in the region, as demonstrated by the innumerable crosses found at many of the road junctions. At Meyrignac-l'Église, near the *étang* of that name, to the north of Corrèze, a priest hid in a barn at the time of the French

Revolution and continued to celebrate clandestine masses. The same hamlet was the setting of a film *Le Moine et la Sorcière* (The Monk and the Witch) set 800 years ago. In the direction of Bar, to the southwest of Corrèze, is a shrine near the village of Lacour, Notre-Dame de Chastres, which hosts a fête on 8 September each year.

■ THE PILGRIM'S ROUTE ■

The Limousin region, which includes the Corrèze, has always been a land of journeys and people passing through: knights and warriors, merchants and craftspeople, monks, nuns and pilgrims. Famous for its saints, in the Middle Ages it developed as a place of pilgrimage, mostly as a result of the relics kept by the monks in their abbeys and priories. Walled towns often grew up around these imposing buildings.

This development was particularly noticeable during the 12th century, with the beginnings of pilgrimages to Santiago de Compostella in Spain (known as St Jacques de Compostelle in France). The Limousin lent its name to one of the four main routes that crossed France: the route Limousine, which crosses the *département* from Crozant in the north to Châlus in the south. Along the way a wealth of evidence of the route can be spotted in architectural details, the best known being the cockle shell.

■ A MARTYRED APOSTLE ■

Known in English as St James, St Jacques was one of the fishermen whom Jesus called to be his disciple. He was the first apostle to be martyred and, according to the apocryphal letter of Pope Leo in the 9th century, his body was laid in a boat and drifted to the Spanish port of Iria, where it was buried by his followers and a monument built. Here he gradually acquired legendary associations and his reputation spread as a slayer of the Moors, with his alleged appearance and promise of victory to the Christian king of Spain on the eve of his battle against the Emir of Cordoba. The saint is supposed to have led the army to victory the next day, astride a shining white steed.

Apart from his prowess in battle, St Jacques is known by the symbol of the cockle shell, and the pilgrims following his route traditionally carried a staff (*bourdon*) and pouch (*besace*) which they would ask a priest to bless before moving on. It is not unknown today to see pilgrims, sometimes with a cockle shell strapped to their rucksack; each evening they will look for a free place to sleep.

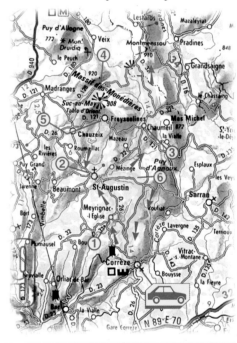

Jacques Chirac

One of the region's most celebrated sons is Jacques Chirac. Elected to the National Assembly to represent Corrèze in 1967, he proceeded to build a powerful base here, launching a career which would see him elected to the French presidency in 1995.

T O U R

length of tour: 60km
time: 3 hours
IGN Top 250: sheet 111

This car tour follows a 'figure of eight' from the square in Corrèze, the town straddling the river of the same name, where a market is held each Monday. The route is steep, and beware of icy roads and poor visibility in bad weather.

❶ From the square in front of the *mairie* (town hall) and the tourist office, take the D 26 towards St-Augustin. Turn left at l'étang de Meyrignac, where you can bathe and picnic in the summer, to visit **Meyrignac l'Église**.

❷ Rejoin the D 26 by the little white road and continue north to **St-Augustin**, where the *mairie* (open mornings) sells details of walks or mountain-bike tours.

❸ Turn right on to the D 32, to **Chaumeil**, capital of the Monédères, with its pretty pointed church spire against a backdrop of wooded hills, and listed porch. Note the public weighbridge with its little granite building beside the church, and houses decorated with cockle shells.

❹ Continue on the D 32, which starts to climb, following signs to Suc-au-May. Turn left at the Col des Géants crossroads on to the D 128. At the car park for **Suc-au-May** park and walk up the rocky track to the orientation table, with its spectacular view.

❺ Backtrack to the junction and turn left on to the D 128, towards Chauzeix, and continue to **Freysselines** on the D 121, passing the Cirque de Freysselines. At Freysselines take the first right, signposted Beyssac, to reach St-Augustin.

❻ Take the D 26 back towards Corrèze, but turn left after 1km on the D 142, following signs to the bread oven at **le Tourondel** and its thatched mini-museum. Continue on the D 142 for 1km, then take the first right and follow this minor road until it rejoins the D 26 just after l'étang de Meyrignac. Follow the D 26 back to Corrèze.

CHÂTEAU DE MEILLANT

***W**ith its flamboyant façade, rich history and verdant grounds, the Château de Meillant is packed with treasures collected over the centuries and stands close to one of the premier Cistercian abbeys in France.*

The Château de Meillant, with its impregnable medieval towers and extravagant Gothic façade, stands as a perfect example of how fortified castles abandoned their defensive role at the end of the Hundred Years War to evolve into graceful residences. Between 1430 and 1550, at least half the castles in the Berry region were reconstructed, ushering in a revolution in taste and style profoundly influenced by the Italian Renaissance.

■ AN IDYLLIC SETTING ■

Set in magnificent grounds, with a lake reflecting its lacy domes, towers and spires, the château seems to spring straight from a fairy tale. The story begins in the Celtic age, since Meillant stems from the Celtic word *Mediolanus* (meaning 'middle plain'). A sanctuary was founded near by. From an *oppidum*

The angular grace of Meillant's château

RIGHT: the ornate cloisters of l'Abbaye de Noirlac contrast with its simple exterior, below

(fortified camp) in Gallo-Roman times, Meillant evolved into a feudal fortress in the 11th century under the lords of Charenton, defended by ramparts, towers, moats and the surrounding marshes and thick forests. In 1453, the castle was acquired by Pierre d'Amboise, a councillor to King Charles VII. His grandson, Charles d'Amboise embellished it and, since he was a governor in Milan, called upon the talents of sculptors, painters and architects from across Italy. As one local saying goes: 'Milan made Meillant.'

■ A FLORID STYLE ■

The polygonal Tour du Lion, designed by Fra Jocondo, a collaborator of Michelangelo, stands as the most exuberant illustration of florid Gothic style, with its narrow spiralling columns, open-work balcony and profuse ornamentation of interlaced hearts, family ini-

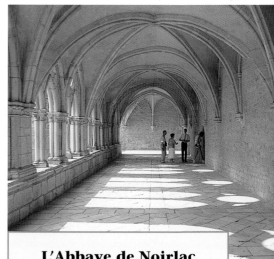

L'Abbaye de Noirlac

The strict geometry of l'Abbaye de Noirlac, built in pure white local stone without ornamentation, seems to invite order and purity. Founded in 1130 by Saint Bernard's cousin, Robert de Clairvaux, the abbey prospered in the 12th and 13th centuries as monks, after earlier privations and hunger, turned the surrounding forests into farmland. For Saint Bernard, the founder of the Cistercian order, the abbey was 'a prison with open doors'. Sold in the early 19th century, it was eventually returned to the state, and a vast restoration programme has transformed it into one of the best-preserved Cistercian complexes in France.

Detailed carving from the Château de Meillant

tials, emblems and sculpted figures. Inside, about 12 of its 75 rooms are open to the public, offering an overwhelming array of pieces collected over the centuries, from Chinese porcelains and ivories to 16th-century tapestries from Bruges depicting scenes from the Old Testament, Turkish carpets and a succession of portraits, some still unidentified.

Somehow, the styles fit together, although the eye has little time to rest: in the dining room, the walls are covered with embossed leather from Cordoba, the Renaissance coffered ceilings are painted in gold, blue and red, the windows decorated with floral designs and the table set with priceless Baccarat crystal.

In the vast Grand Salon, where feasts were held about 120 times a year, the sculpted chimney is surmounted by a musicians' gallery. For the rest, the guide will treat you to anecdotes, such as why people once slept sitting up and why bathing went out of style under Louis XIV.

In an adjacent building, children will revel in a series of miniature models that cleverly depict the changing lifestyles from medieval times to the 19th century, while in the park, a game invites them to discover some 20 different species of tree.

■ SURVIVING THE REVOLUTION ■

The Duc de Charost, owner of the château in the 18th century, could be described as a

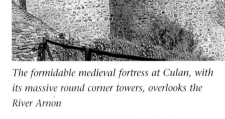

nobleman somewhat ahead of his time. He had abolished taxes on his estate; he took care of his retired employees and had set up a farming school on his grounds. However, he was arrested during the French Revolution and taken to the nearby prison of Saint Amand. But the good citizens of Meillant obtained his immediate release.

The Duke was then arrested and imprisoned a second time, but this time further from home. Despite this, once again the people of Berry petitioned the Convention, which decided to free the Duke and – what's more – enshrine him as a 'father of suffering humanity'. Buried in the chapel of Meillant, his epitaph reads: 'In all places, at all ages, he did nothing but good.' Unlike many around the country, Meillant's steadfast castle suffered no damage during the Revolution.

The formidable medieval fortress at Culan, with its massive round corner towers, overlooks the River Arnon

---

TOUR

length of tour: 90km
time: 1 day
IGN Top 250: sheet 108

Some time spent exploring the château at Meillant is the ideal preparation for this rewarding drive, taking in the history of the Cistercians.

❶ From Meillant, follow the D 92 west to **Bruère-Allichamps** where a Roman milestone was discovered at the N 144 and D 92; the spot now

symbolises the geographical centre of France. Turn left on to the N 144 to **l'Abbaye de Noirlac**. Note the simplicity of its 12th-century church with capitals and windows stripped of any decoration; the cloister with its lovely ribbed vaults; the 13th-century refectory, and the immaculate grounds. The abbey also houses a centre on illuminated manuscripts and organises exhibitions.

❷ At **St-Amand-Montrond**, continue on the N 144 to **Ainay-le-Vieil** on the D 1. Here an impressive octagonal fortress, protected by a moat of running waterr, encloses a gracious Renaissance dwelling and lovely gardens with 150 varieties dating back over 500 years.

❸ Continue along the D 1 (which becomes the D 62) to St-Christophe-le-Chaudry, then turn left on to the D 997 to **Culan** and another medieval fortress castle.

❹ Turn right along the D 65 to **l'Abbaye de Puyfferand** at le Châtelet. From here follow the D 3 until it meets the D 925. Turn right to St-Amand-Montrand, then take the D 10 back to Meillant.

CATHÉDRALE ST-ÉTIENNE

The powerful silhouette of Bourges' cathedral dominates the entire plain of the Berry region. Its towers, visible from afar, beckon visitors to climb the medieval streets of Bourges, which Julius Caesar described as 'one of the most beautiful cities in Gaul'.

Long before the present cathedral was built, religious buildings had succeeded one another on the same site for 1,000 years, since the foundation of a Christian community in this prosperous city. Bourges was once called *Avaricum*, from its proximity to water springs.

Printemps de Bourges

This musical extravanganza, established in April 1977, has become the city's major festival. Each April thousands of musicians and singers flock to Bourges for a celebration of all genres of music, from rock, folk and jazz to modern rap styles. The festival prides itself in popularising world music, attracting artists from all over the world and serves as a springboard for new French talent. Having grown enormously over the last 20 years, the festival takes place at several venues around the city, accommodating tens of thousands of performers and massive crowds.

13th-century Bourges Cathedral with a colourful floral display in the foreground

◾ THE CATHEDRAL ◾

The present cathedral was completed in the 13th century by an anonymous architect, commonly referred to as the Master of Bourges – his name has been forgotten over the years. At the time, the city was walled by ramparts, remnants of which may be seen along rue des Trois Maillets.

A Romanesque cathedral was built in the 11th century, a period when Bourges was at the head of a particularly vast diocese. Following a fire in 1193, Archbishop Henri de Sully decided to build a larger edifice. Work began in 1195 and continued throughout the 13th century, making St-Étienne the first Gothic religious building to rise up south of the Loire. The south tower, known as the

deaf tower because of the absence of bells, had to be consolidated with an enormous buttressing pillar shortly after its construction. The north tower collapsed in 1506 and was rebuilt with interesting Renaissance and Gothic decorative elements. Although threatened by destruction during the French Revolution, St-Étienne's Cathedral ended up housing a theatre where the cult of the Goddess of Reason was celebrated!

◾ UNIFIED SPACE ◾

Shaped like a basilica with chapels surrounding the nave, the cathedral gives an impression of majesty and strength, making a clear statement about the Church's power. One of its most remarkable characteristics is the floor plan comprising four side aisles instead of a transept, which differentiates Bourges from all other Gothic cathedrals. The purpose of the Master was to create a unified interior, unhampered by any partition.

The sense of unified space and light is accentuated by the absence of a tribune (bishop's throne), which left room for the large arcades to be higher, and allowed for the direct lighting of the intermediary nave. The five doors of the main porch are richly decorated, but the tympanum of the Last Judgement over the central door stands out as a masterpiece of 13th-century Gothic sculpture, representing the Resurrection of the Dead, the judgement by Saint Michael and the figure of Christ the Redeemer.

▪ PAGES OF LIGHT ▪

It is rare in any of the great Gothic cathedrals of France to be able to stand no more than a metre away from stained-glass windows and contemplate them, practically at eye level. It is also remarkable to stand in front of a story book of glass that has survived seven centuries. The figures are stylised and somewhat stiff, but they portray Bible stories such as the Good Samaritan, the Prodigal Son with a raw immediacy and sense of detail. Note, for instance, in the stained-glass window depicting the life of Saint Mary Magdalen, the fish on the table and the devoted expression of the saint as she anoints Christ's feet and dries them with her hair.

Finally, the astronomical clock is a magnificent piece, both for its mechanical precision and its decoration. The 12th-century crypt, lit by 12 stained-glass windows of the prophets, houses the recumbent white marble statue of Duke Jean de Berry, the only vestige of a large mausoleum executed by Jean de Cambrai. In the summer, an organ music festival is held in the cathedral.

Village rooftops

TOUR

length of tour: 120km
time: 1 day
IGN Top 250: sheet 102

This tour takes in some of the castles in the area. It also includes some of the local crafts, and some of the regions vineyards and wine-makers.

---

❶ From Bourges, follow the D 940 to **Menetou-Salon**, a village nestling among forests and vineyards. The grandiose castle, which was once part of Jacques Coeur's estate, was rebuilt completey in the 19th century. Now inhabited by the Prince d'Arenberg, it includes an impressive collection of vintage cars. It is also well worth visiting one of the town's cellars to taste Menetou-Salon's fine wines, made from Pinot Noir and Sauvignon grapes.

❷ Continue along the D 59 towards the **Château de Maupas**, owned and inhabited by the same family since the 17th century. It retains its original 13th-century towers and the remaining part dates from the 15th century. It houses a fine collection of faience plates, as well as beautiful Aubusson and Gobelain tapestries.

❸ At Morogues (D 59), turn left on to the D 46 to **la Borne**. Stoneware pottery was long one of the main resources in this region, a land rich in sandstone, and the craft has enjoyed a renewal. A local association of potters includes some 50 members of different nationalities. The chapel houses a pottery museum and showroom, with visits available on request. Another interesting museum is devoted to Vassil Ivanoff, a Bulgarian ceramicist who settled in la Borne in the late 1940s and spent the next 30 years perfecting his art.

❹ From la Borne, follow the D 22 east to **Sancerre**, a town perched above vineyards, overlooking the Loire and the hills of the Sancerrois, and justly reputed for its high-quality wines and goats' milk cheeses. The picturesque old town is dominated by the Tour des Fiefs, a 14th-century vestige of a Huguenot citadel. The view from Porte César stretches to the ridge of the Morvan.

❺ Leave Sancerre by the D 923 to Menetou-Râtel, then continue along the D 85 to **Boucard**, a medieval castle with corner turrets, a keep, drawbridge and moat. From here, the D 89 leads to the **Château de la Verrerie**, an elegant Renaissance residence built by Béraud Stuart of Scotland – worth the visit for its beautiful lakeside setting, its Renaissance frescoes and alabaster mourners that formed part of Jean de Berry's tomb.

❻ The D 39 leads north to **Blancafort**, its 15th-century red-brick castle set in a pleasant French garden. Nearby, the **Musée de la Sorcellerie** recalls the history of witchcraft in Berry, with exhibits illustrating the world of witches, fairies, dragons, elves and alchemists, with historical tales from early times to the Middle Ages.

❼ Follow the D 30 to picturesque **Aubigny-sur-Nère**, with its collection of half-timbered, 16th-century houses that belonged to the Stuarts, a link honoured every summer by the Franco-Scottish festival. From here, follow the D 940 back to Bourges.

ÎLE D'YEU

*S*haped like a narrow oyster and situated some 17km from the mainland, Île d'Yeu is one of the smallest, least populated and least visited of the string of islands stretching between Brittany and the estuary of the Gironde.

A hundred thousand years ago the island was connected to the mainland, a geological link preserved in a local legend about a magic bridge across the sea, said to survive intact to this day beneath the waves. The island's first inhabitants walked over from the mainland at low tide. They buried their chiefs on high places facing the westering sun. Only as recently as 5,000–6,000 years ago was Yeu cut off from the mainland.

Wandering monks came here in search of seclusion. One of them, St Martin de Vertou, is said to have clambered to the top of a pagan megalith and preached to the islanders, con-

verting many of them to Christianity. The stone is still there, a short distance from the Romanesque church of St-Sauveur, marked by three mysterious Celtic indentations and a Christian cross.

■ HISTORY'S INTRUSIONS ■

Thereafter the island's history was marked by long periods of neglect, during which the islanders went about their business – fishing, smuggling and raising sheep – without much contact with the mainland, interrupted occasionally by sudden incursions from across the sea. Île d'Yeu was raided by Saracens, ransacked by Normans and occupied by English troops during the Hundred Years War. In 1795, 6,000 royalist French and English soldiers landed on the island, in what was to be the first stage of an invasion of mainland France. A few weeks later the invasion was called off, the troops returned to England and Île d'Yeu was once again forgotten. In November 1945, Marshall Pétain, the World War I hero who headed the collaborationist Vichy government, was imprisoned in the grim 19th-century citadel of Port Joinville.

That says something about the way the mainland French have always looked on the island.

Shaped like a narrow oyster, Île d'Yeu is not quite 10km long between the foghorn at Pointe du Brut and the lighthouse at Pointe des Corbeaux. From Port Joinville, the island's commercial and administrative centre, an hour's leisurely walk brings you to the only other port, La Meule, nestling between the rocks of the southern coast.

■ BLACK SEAS AND HIBISCUS ■

Depending on the season and the weather, you may be reminded of the Cornish coast in southwest England, or the Greek Cyclades. Look eastwards from Pointe du Châtelet and

---

Le Vieux Château

Built on the jagged south coast, on the site of an earlier fortress, the stronghold known as le Vieux Château was erected in the 14th century for the island's châtelaine, Jeanne de Belleville. Described by the chronicler Froissart as 'The most beautiful woman of the realm', she was widowed at an early age and became a formidable warrior in her own right and, according to tradition, something of a pirate as well. Brooding over the waves, surrounded by the sea at high tide, the castle changed hands repeatedly during the Hundred Years War. The typically 16th-century star-shaped ravelin defending it is a later addition. It did not serve long: King Louis XVI had the fortifications destroyed to prevent them from falling into enemy hands and being used against vessels of the Royal French Navy. The castle has been partly restored. Standing on the watchpath, you get a spectacular view of Plage des Sabias across the bay and the open sea beyond the wild headland of Pointe du Châtelet.

Waves crash at the foot of the imposing 14th-century stronghold le Vieux Château

you will see black waves breaking on the rocks at the foot of the Vieux Château – reminiscent of Tintagel, in Cornwall. Yet only minutes away, on the other side of the island, you will stroll among hollyhocks and hibiscus, down the narrow white lanes of Port Joinville, where the shadows cast by the low, tiled roofs are the same blue as the painted windows and doors of the fishermen's cottages.

▪ ETERNAL OUTPOST ▪

Except for the presence of motorcars, satellite dishes, a small airfield and a high-speed ferry service to the mainland, with departures daily from Fromentine and, in summer, from St-Gilles-Croix-de-Vie, the island today is still the sleepy fishing community it has been for centuries. One out of ten of its 5,000 permanent residents makes a living from fishing, and many others have jobs connected with the fishing industry.

Tourism provides some seasonal work, but when the last of the summer visitors leave and the gales of the equinox sweep in, Île

ABOVE: the fishing village of Port Joinville is the main centre on the island and is also the starting point for a number of walks

BELOW: empty beaches are not difficult to find on this quiet island

d'Yeu withdraws into itself. The colourful shutters slam shut; the wind thrashes the holm oaks above Port Joinville; the only creatures about are migratory birds, resting here before departing for milder climes, far south across the dark Atlantic.

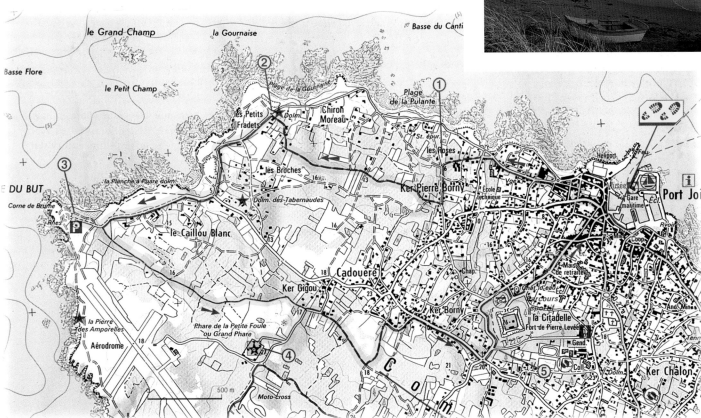

WALK

length of walk: 10km
time: half a day
IGN Top 25: sheet 1126OT

This walk is not suitable for wheelchairs or pushchairs. If you prefer cycling, bikes can be hired from several shops on the port. Free maps and instructions (in French) for cycling tours are available from the tourist office on place du Marché.

❶ From the tourist office, follow rue du Général de Gaulle to rue Ker Pierre Borny. Carry on west to rue des Moines. Turn right, and right again into rue Surcouf.

❷ At the end of rue Surcouf, turn on to a dirt track running west across a heath of furze, blackthorn and the occasional windswept pine. This takes you, in a little under 1km, to the asphalted road running along the island's northwest coast. As you reach the road, notice the dolmen about 50m to your right.

❸ Turn left on the road or, better still, cut across country between the road and the sea, skirting the inlet of **le Caillou Blanc** (an outcrop of dazzling white quartz

sloping down towards the dark grey rocks below) until you reach the car park at **Pointe du But**.

❹ After enjoying the view from the cape, turn inland on to the grassy track opposite the car park access, heading straight towards the lighthouse.

❺ Turn right at Ker Gidou and head back towards Port Joinville via Cadouere – or, if you don't mind stretching the walk by another kilometre, return by Ker Borny, straight southeast to **rue St-Amand** which leads, through a green wood past **la Citadelle** (worth a quick visit), down to the port and a restorative dish of *patagos*, a local dish of shellfish in cream.

*L*E MARAIS POITEVIN

*W*ith its labyrinth of waterways and canals choked with duckweed, the eastern portion of the low, slow, silent country between Niort and La Rochelle – once a pest-infested swamp – is known as la Venise Verte. *But you will see no grand* palazzi *here, only simple farmhouses sheltered by rows of poplars.*

The Marais Poitevin – much of it now protected in a regional park – is something of a paradox. One of western Europe's finest unspoiled habitats, where mankind and nature continue to live in harmony, it is a manufactured paradise – and a relatively recent one at that. In the early Middle Ages, much of its territory lay under water. At high tide the sea came almost as far east as Niort, as far north as Luçon and as far south as the village of Mauzé-sur-le-Mignon. Scattered here and there in this great gulf were small settlements built on islands, inhabited by fishermen, monks and farmers who made a living of sorts by drying salt from the sea.

Over the centuries the Golfe des Pictons, as it was called, filled with silt. A swampy, insalubrious country, it was forever being flooded. And so its inhabitants, foremost among them monks, began digging ditches to drain away the floodwaters. By the mid-16th century, it had evidently acquired its present-day character, for it was then that, travelling across it, Henry of Navarre, the future King Henry IV, is said to have likened the area to 'a great natural Venice' and to have appointed a Grand Master of Dykes and Canals with a brief to drain the marshes permanently.

◼ MARSHES WET AND DRY ◼

The elaborate network of dykes and – literally – thousands of kilometres of ditches and canals, built from the 17th to the 19th centuries, reclaimed almost 100,000ha of land and created two very different ecological zones. To the west, sheltered from tides by rows of dykes, the virtually treeless 'dry marshes' sustain an agriculture of wide-open spaces: extensive pastures, fields of rippling rye and wheat. To the east, roughly between Thairé-le-Fagnoux and Coulon, on either side of the meandering courses of the Sèvres Niortaise and the charmingly named rivers Mignon and Jeune Autize, the 'wet marshes' are wooded and often flooded.

The farmers of the wet *marais mouillés*, are called *Maraîchins* to distinguish them from the wealthier *Marouins* of the dry *marais desséchés*. Typically, each will own a cow or two, a narrow field of *mojettes* (white beans) on an embankment of rich silt dredged from a *conche* (ditch), a low, narrow, whitewashed farmhouse and a flat-bottomed boat tarred black.

LEFT: the Sèvres Niortaise River winds past lush meadow

RIGHT: the ruins of the Abbey of Maillezais

Colourful fishermen's cottages line the banks of the Sèvres Niortaise River and its tributaries

▪ L'ABBAYE DE MAILLEZAIS ▪

The ruined abbey of Maillezais stands on a rise above the River Jeune Autize, on the edge of the town of the same name, a little under 10km northwest of Damvix. Scattered over a broad, green meadow, dwarfed by vaulting

---

Local delicacies

The farmers of the *marais mouillés* supplement their meagre income by selling wood, hunting and fishing. If you stop in one of the villages of the Venise Verte – Maillé, Damvix, Arçais, and especially Coulon – you will have no trouble finding a restaurant serving the great *maraîchine* speciality: eels fricasséed with garlic and parsley, washed down with a tart white wine from Poitou.

Gothic cathedral arches, lie the remains of one of the richest abbeys in the Vendée and, judging from the stone carvings excavated on the site and preserved in the hostelry across from the gutted nave, a treasure trove of Romanesque and early Gothic art.

Built on a promontory overlooking the Golfe des Pictons, on the site of a stronghold belonging to the dukes of Aquitaine, the abbey owes its existence to a miraculous hunt, if we are to believe the Chronicle of the monk Peter, written in 1060. One day, while out hunting, the lord Guillaume Fier-à-Bras and his men pursued a boar so fierce and large that it could only have been the Devil himself. They succeeded in running the beast to ground beneath the altar of a deserted chapel deep in the forest, and killed it – whereupon the Duke vowed to establish an abbey. The story doesn't say whether this was in penance or thanksgiving.

Some two centuries later, Maillezais' prestige was such that Pope John XXII elevated its abbot, Geoffroy Pouvreau, to the rank of bishop. In the 16th century one of his successors, Monseigneur d'Estissac, a dedicated humanist, engaged Rabelais as his personal secretary. The author of *Gargantua* spent four years in the abbey, poring over the volumes in the bishop's library, before going to Rome to study medicine.

Maillezais' decline started shortly thereafter. In 1589 the abbey was captured by the Protestant commander (and great tragic poet) Agrippa d'Aubigné, who held it for 30 years. Much damaged during the Wars of Religion, it never regained its past glory. During the French Revolution it was auctioned off to an unscrupulous entrepreneur who dismantled it and sold its stones to local builders.

W A L K

length of walk: 5km/10km
time: 1¼ hours/3 hours
IGN Top 25: sheet 1428E

This takes place at the village of Damvix, on the left bank of the Sèvres Niortaise about 20km east of Marans. Park on place du Port. A map in front of the Salles des Fêtes shows two routes marked in yellow; one covers 5km and the other 10km. The terrain is easy, but unsuitable for wheelchairs or pushchairs. At Damvix and other villages of the Venise Verte you can rent a boat and glide along the *conches* under a tunnel of green leaves. Boats hold up to six people and can be rowed or poled. You can also hire a guide at an extra charge.

❶ Cross the pretty arched bridge to the opposite bank of the **Sèvres Niortaise River** and follow the yellow trail markers. This takes you along a *motte*, or embankment, parallel to a *conche* (narrow canal), the **Conche du Mauvais Bout**. Leaving the village, you soon enter a timeless green world. After 1km turn right then, after about 800m, turn left until you come to the banks of the River Mignon.

❷ Turn right and follow the River Mignon downstream to **Bazoin**.

❸ From Bazoin you can return to Damvix either by keeping to the left bank of the Sèvres Niortaise and walking along the D 104 or by crossing the bridge and turning right to the hamlet of **la Barbée** and back to Damvix via **les Loges** (adding an extra 1km to your walk).

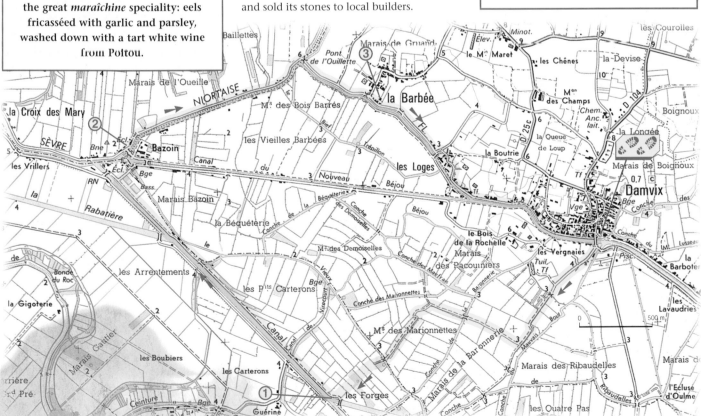

Île de Ré

Scoured by the wind and the sun, in places l'Île de Ré rests so low in the sea that it resembles a Pacific atoll. And with its fine sandy beaches, its tamarisks and flowers, and its gleaming white villages, it is as exotic a spot as anywhere north of the Pyrenees.

The 19th-century writer Eugène Fromentin described l'Île de Ré as shimmering like 'dreams of the Orient'. What saves the island from being a playground for holidaymakers is that many of its 11,000 year-round residents still make their living in much the same way as their forebears. Attracting crowds of cultivated sophisticates, the island can be seen as the antithesis of St-Tropez.

▪ A TRIPLE ISLAND ▪

The island, which is no longer as isolated as it was since the construction in 1988 of the graceful 3km bridge linking it to the mainland, is really a string of three separate islets connected by dykes. The largest and most densely populated islet is St-Martin-de-Ré, an agricultural an wine-making community.

▪ ST-MARTIN-DE-RÉ ▪

Though some of its buildings date back to the 15th century (among them the Renaissance arcades of the Hôtel de Clerjotte) – originally the mansion of the island's military governor, then a convent, later an arsenal, now a shipping museum – St-Martin-de-Ré's time came in the 17th century. Ransacked in 1627, when troops led by the Duke of Buckingham unsuccessfully laid siege to its fortress, the town and its port were fortified in the 1680s, on what was then a state-of-the-art plan designed by Louis XIV's military strategist and engineer extraordinaire, Marshal Vauban.

Vauban's defences include the town gates, the star-shaped fortifications above the grassy moat (used as grazing grounds for the island's last remaining donkeys), the port's tidal lock and breakwaters and the brooding citadel, which is the first sight greeting visitors from the mainland. Throughout the 19th and early 20th centuries the citadel's small harbour served as a departure point for ships carrying convicts to a brutish – and often short – life of hard labour in French Guiana.

Painterly views

The cure for any sombre thoughts the citadel may inspire is to follow the sea wall to the fishing port. Arriving there on a sunny day is like walking into one of Matisse's views of Mediterranean fishing ports: the flags of the yachts and trawlers, the grey-green shutters of the houses, the blue awnings of the shops, the pink hollyhocks and the terracotta roofs would melt the heart of the dourest gaoler.

For a panorama of the town climb the steps of the church's fortified bell-tower. Flags recalling the 17th-century battles between the French and the English hang in the nave below. The shadows of the past are never far from the festive colours of the present.

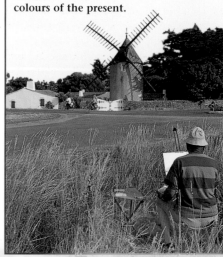

LEFT: walking along l'Île de Ré at low tide
ABOVE: the Moulin de Bellerre is popular with artists

■ A LAND OF SALT ■

To the east, connected to St-Martin by a narrow strip of land, lies Ars-en-Ré – and lies is the *mot juste*, for much of it consists of salt pans, all of them below sea-level. In its heyday in the 19th century, the island produced

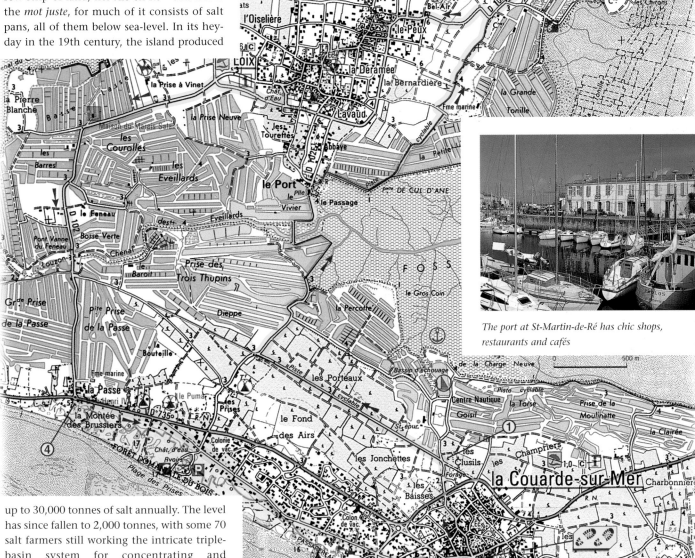

The port at St-Martin-de-Ré has chic shops, restaurants and cafés

up to 30,000 tonnes of salt annually. The level has since fallen to 2,000 tonnes, with some 70 salt farmers still working the intricate triple-basin system for concentrating and evaporating tidal waters and crystallising their precious saline cargo. Formerly the damp salt, dredged up by wooden scrapers on poles, was brought out of the marshes on donkeys wearing red-and-white striped leggings to protect them from the mosquitoes that made salt-gathering a distinctly less serene occupation than might be imagined.

An excellent way to visit the salt flats is to walk along the cycling track behind the restaurant at La Martray towards the church spire of Ars-en-Ré.

■ OYSTER FARMS ■

The third of l'Île de Ré's islets is little more than a large sandbank, reached by a road on a dyke between salt pans. Huge flocks of Brent geese winter in its western marshes. From Pointe du Groin to the east, you will glimpse St-Martin-de-Ré across the bay. At low tide you will see some of Ile de Ré's largest oyster banks. Oysters are now a mainstay of the island's economy, replacing the equally arduous but less profitable cultivation of salt. You will find a café, restaurant or oyster-producer almost anywhere on the island where, provided it's winter or early spring, you can feast on a dozen fresh-from-the-sea *fines de claire*.

TOUR

length of cycle tour/walk: 15km
time: 2½ hours
IGN Top 25: sheet 13290T

This is an easy, level cycling tour on well-marked, mostly paved tracks. On warm, summer days it is thronged by cyclists, some apparently bent on 'doing the loop' as fast as possible, so watch out for them.

Bicycles may be hired from the shop opposite the church in la Couarde-sur-Mer.

❶ From la Couarde, head north through the village until you reach the N 735. Cross over and take the road marked 'Centre Nautique'. After 250m turn left on to the *piste cyclable*. In 1.5km turn right across the salt flats towards Loix. Keep on until you reach the D 102.

❷ Follow the D 102 right, north as far as Fort du Grouin, a small 18th-century fort rebuilt in the 19th century. Climb to the top of the dyke behind the fort for a view of the oyster beds.

❸ Return on the D 102 towards Loix, then turn right on to the first road leading into the village. Cross the village and at the water tower turn left and rejoin the D 102 towards la Passe.

❹ At la Passe turn left on to the D 735, then, 500m further on, turn right on to Chemin de la Diligence. Keep straight ahead, skirting the woods on your right where Henry of Navarre is believed to have hunted before he became King Henry IV. At the roundabout at the entrance of la Couarde, turn right on to the street leading back into the village.

LA ROCHELLE

*O*riginally a Gallo-Roman fishing village built on an outcrop of limestone (whence its name, Rupella, *Little Rock*) in a marshy bay shielded from westerly gales by the Île de Ré, La Rochelle owes its pre-eminence to salt, Poitou wines – and a queen.

A dark trade

It was from la Rochelle that fleets sailed to the French possessions in Canada and Louisiana, and to here they returned, laden with sugar, tobacco and furs. The walk along the rampart between the Tour de la Chaine and the Tour de la Lanterne is paved with Canadian river stones used as ballast in returning vessels. Many of the 18th-century houses in the centre of town owe their refined elegance to the fortunes made from trade – including the slave trade – with the New World.

It was at Eleanor of Aquitaine's bidding that the old harbour was dug, and it was thanks to the tariff privileges she granted medieval Rochella that, for centuries, this was one of France's leading Atlantic ports.

■ A QUEENLY PORT ■

Modern La Rochelle's harbour is filled with yachts. Its fishing fleet may have shrunk to a fraction of its former size and its commercial harbour moved to La Pallice, about 5km to the west, but thanks to wise local management the town is poised for the 21st century, as prosperous, urbane and elegant as it was in its heyday in the 18th century. The old town has been beautifully restored, and several of its handsome arcaded streets are now closed to motor traffic. It is one of the few cities in the world that visitors can enjoy in the rain, even without an umbrella. The arcades originally sheltered street traders.

Before the advent of the car the city's paved streets were meant for pedestrian traffic – with the occasional pushcart, wheelbarrow or horse-drawn carriage. On bright days, visitors can while away the hours on the terrace of one of the old port's cafés, watching the endlessly absorbing spectacle of small craft chugging out through the channel between the towers guarding the harbour. Spellbound by this activity, it is very easy to forget that La Rochelle has not always been a peaceful and civilised haven.

The old port of La Rochelle, dominated by its massive towers, has plenty of stylish yachts and traditional fishing boats

The port is overlooked by smart cafés, while the streets are lined with Renaissance arcades

W A L K

length of walk: 4km
time: 1½ hours
IGN Top 25: sheet 1329ET

This walk is entirely on surfaced roads and is therefore suitable for wheelchairs and pushchairs. Start from the unfinished cathedral designed by Jacques V Gabriel (father of the architect of Paris's place de la Concorde), built on the site of the Protestant church destroyed in 1648.

❶ Follow the arcaded **rue Chaudrier** along the left side of the cathedral. The **Maison Henri II**, an elegant Renaissance house and now a local museum, is a short distance down the third street to the left (rue des Augustins). Return to rue des Chaudrier which becomes rue du Palais, flanked by some of the town's most handsome buildings, most particularly the **Hôtel de la Bourse** (built in 1764) and its neighbour, the **Palais de la Justice** (1783–89).

❷ At the 13th-century **Tour de la Grosse Horloge** (remodelled in the 18th century), turn right along rue Vieljeux, then left into rue Verdières, which leads down to the massive towers guarding the entrance of the old port. Take a stroll along the ramparts to the **Tour de la Lanterne**, before returning to the **Tour de la Chaine**.

❸ Follow the port's esplanade with its open-air cafés to the Quai Dupérré. Turn left into rue du Port, which leads to the **Hôtel de Ville**. Enter the flamboyant Gothic portal and you will find yourself in the paved courtyard of la Rochelle's finest Renaissance building.

❹ Leaving the Hôtel de Ville, turn right, and then left into **rue des Merciers**, one of the oldest streets in La Rochelle. Several of its houses date back to the 14th century. In the covered market at the end of the street, built in the 1830s, you will see plenty of fish and shellfish freshly caught from the sea. Return to the start of the walk at the cathedral by following rue Gargoulleau past the **Musée Bibliothèque**.

▪ A CHEQUERED HISTORY ▪

Heavily fortified since the Middle Ages, La Rochelle became a bastion of French Protestantism, thanks partly to its trading connections with northern Europe. In 1573 it successfully withstood its first Catholic siege, but 50 years later its citizens sided with the Duke of Buckingham's forces on the Île de Ré, and Louis XIII and his 'grey eminence' the Cardinal of Richelieu personally directed a second blockade of the port and the town.

Literally starved out, the Rochellois surrendered after 414 days. The toll was heavy. A quarter of the town's population perished during the siege and, with the exception of the three towers guarding the old port, its fortifications were razed. So were its Protestant churches. But the Rochellois are nothing if not resilient. Less than two decades after the great siege, the town was prospering again, and for the next 150 years it was one of France's busiest ports.

Take the time to soak up the local atmosphere at one of the many open-air cafés

▪ THE HARBOUR TOWERS ▪

All three towers at the gateway of the old port date from the 14th century. The oldest is the massive keep of the Tour St-Nicolas (reached by circling round the port and crossing the footbridge over the channel to the 19th-century dock). Visitors brave enough to climb the twisting stone stairs to the top of the tower are rewarded with a superb and incomparable view. The foundation of oak pilings on which the massive tower rests has slipped slightly to one side, giving the tower its characteristic lean.

Across the entrance to the port stands the Tour de la Chaine, so named because a smaller structure connected to it, but no longer existent, housed a capstan which served to stretch a chain anchored to the Tour St-Nicolas across the mouth of the port, barring it to unwanted visitors from the sea. The high, vaulted, eight-sided ground floor of the tower now houses a gift and bookshop.

The tallest and least military of the trio is the flamboyant Gothic Tour de La Lanterne set a short distance back from the port. Before the advent of electricity, a huge candle flicked at night in the glassed-in turret at the tip of its pyramidal flèche, to guide incoming vessels. Between the 17th and 19th centuries captive Spanish and English sailors languished within its walls. They left a huge collection of graffiti, some of them showing real artistry, many of them quite moving, like the simple words: 'Henry Tidcombe, 17, of the Royal William. Was cast on shore on Le Tranch'.

FORÊT DES LANDES

*I*magine a forest so vast that you could drive through it for hours without coming to its end. There are, of course, such places in Russia and Canada, but this is Gascony, the flat plain between the estuary of the Gironde and the foothills of the Pyrenees.

Historians tell us that 1,000 years ago France was covered with forests, and that the great task of the early Middle Ages was the clearing of fields needed to feed a population engaged in such energy-burning activities as building cathedrals. The forest of Landes reminds us of just how much the French countryside has changed since the days of Charlemagne.

■ FRANCE'S PREMIER PARK ■

The huge Parc Naturel Régional des Landes Gascogne was created in 1970 in an irregular quadrangle roughly 40km wide by 100km long. At the heart of the park are the valleys

The vast pine forest of the Landes, created in the 19th century, is now a regional park

of the Petit Leyre and the Grand Leyre rivers that flow together near Mousthey to form the River Eyre, which empties into the Bay of Arcachon. Canoes and kayaks can be rented at several locations. Perhaps the best way to get to know the forest is by gliding along its quiet rust-coloured waters, discovering the life in its depth, far from roads and towns.

■ A LAND OF PINE ■

The trees – mostly pines, which thrive in the sandy Gascon soil – dwarf the houses of those who live in their midst. They even tower over the church spires of the few isolated villages. This quality of a life lived among silent giants makes the Landes a place like no other.

Landes, however, means 'moor', and the fact is that large tracts of this seemingly time-less expanse of evergreens was, until not so long ago, virtually treeless. Poor drainage, acid soil and sand-laden Atlantic winds made this one of France's least prosperous provinces. The kind of farming it sustained – small rye fields and large sheep flocks – was much like that still encountered today on the arid plateaux des Causses.

Routes des Lacs

A pleasant detour from the forest car tour can be had from Mimizan, which lies on the Routes des Lacs, hugging the coast form Arcachon to Capbreton. Leaving the tour at Mimizan, some 50km south along the D 652 is the pretty Étang de Soustons. Fringed with roses and almost entirely surrounded by pine trees, this tranquil site is ideal for care-free walks unhindered by cars.

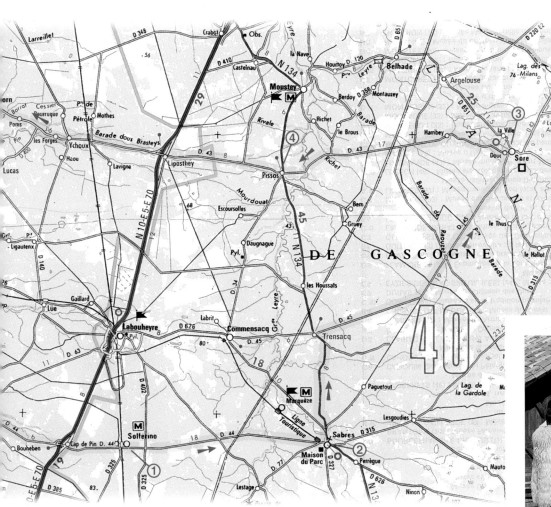

Trees in the forest are tapped for their resin

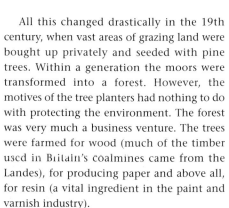

The Marquèze Ecomusée has traditional buildings in the local style

All this changed drastically in the 19th century, when vast areas of grazing land were bought up privately and seeded with pine trees. Within a generation the moors were transformed into a forest. However, the motives of the tree planters had nothing to do with protecting the environment. The forest was very much a business venture. The trees were farmed for wood (much of the timber used in Britain's coalmines came from the Landes), for producing paper and above all, for resin (a vital ingredient in the paint and varnish industry).

Since World War II these forest-related industries have languished, gradually being replaced by a more environmentally friendly economy based on tourism and leisure.

▪ A STEP BACK IN TIME ▪

On a bank of the River Escamat, just northwest of Sabres, the farming community of Marquèze was acquired by the Landes Regional Park in 1968. Its superbly restored early 19th-century buildings are fine examples of rural Gascon architecture before the seeding of the great pine forests. The three-sided roofs, timber frames, wattle-and-daub walls and tall porches are characteristic. So is the distribution of the owner's house, the tenant's farm and barns around an *airial*, the local equivalent of an English village green. It all looks idyllic: an oasis of the past nestling deep in the forest, it can be reached only on foot or by riding the little train from Sabres.

Community farming at Marquèze owes much to the past and is a tribute to old traditions in this age of chemicals and modified foods. The sheep are the old *landais* stock which have all but disappeared elsewhere, the apples and pears in the orchard belong to species unavailable since World War II, the field is planted with the rye and the small-kernel maize that were the local farmers' staple before the advent of chemical fertilisers and hybrid seeds.

TOUR

length of tour: 125km
time: one day
IGN Top 250: sheet 110

This loop takes you through the coastal forest down to the southernmost part of the regional park. The terrain is easy: the roads are straight, level and (once you leave the coast) traffic-free.

❶ Start at **Mimizan**, a pleasant resort town surrounded by forest, some 70km south of Arcachon. There's a good beach 5km west at **Mimizan-Plage**. Or you can explore the ruins of the 12th-century Benedictine abbey or those of the manor which the Duke of Westminster built in 1913 on the shores of the charming Étang d'Aureilhan. Drive east on the D 44 to **Solférino**, a model farming community built in the 1850s on land owned by Emperor Napoleon III. (See box for detour south along the Routes des Lacs.)

❷ Continue on the D 44 to **Sabres**, from where you can take a short train ride to the old farm at **Marquèze**.

❸ From Sabres head north on the N 134. At Trensacq, turn east onto the D 45 to **Sore**, a medieval town destroyed in the wars of religion (except for a portion of its Romanesque church and a fortified gate).

❹ Then drive west on the D 43 to **Pissos**, whose church, with its distinctive steeple, contains 14th-century frescoes. The village has a crafts shop displaying local wares, across the road from a glassblower, which is also open to the public.

❺ Continue on the D 43 to **Parentis-en-Born**, 'a village where life flows as smooth as honey', according to Antoine de Saint-Exupéry, the aviator and writer who took off on countless missions from the hydroplane base at Hourtiguets, across the Étang de Biscarosse.

❻ Follow the D 625 southwest towards Mimizan, skirting the southern shore of the lake. At the village of **Gastes** you get a good view of the lake and its oil rigs: France's largest oil field lies beneath these waters.

CÔTE ATLANTIQUE
DUNE DU PILAT

The sight is unexpected – as you leave the villas and gardens of Arcachon and approach the eerie vastness of the Landes pine forests, you suddenly encounter the awesome sight of Europe's largest sand dune towering high above the trees.

Pilat or Pyla – either spelling is correct – both come from the Gascon word for 'pile' and that is exactly what the dune is: a shifting heap of sand. Originally the name described a sandbank to the north of the present dune, which does not seem to have existed until the early 19th century. In 1855, when much of the land on which Arcachon stands was bought up by the developers who planned to turn it into a seaside resort, the dune was a mere 35m tall. Since then its height has more than trebled to some 115m. Added to this is a length of just over 2.5km and a width of 500m, creating a remarkable natural feature.

■ A TOWN ON THE MOVE ■

The neatly laid-out boroughs surrounding the Bay of Arcachon have an air of permanence that belies the physical reality of a coast that is constantly on the move – albeit not, geologically speaking, on the fast track. The bay itself is a recent development. Some time between the Bronze Age and the arrival of the Romans, it acquired its characteristic triangular shape. At first no more than a thin wedge in the coastline, the bay gradually widened as the tides and the River Eyre shifted its mud flats and sand banks.

It is only over the last 200 years that the long finger of Cap Ferret has begun to reach down towards the Arguin sandbanks, a few cable lengths off the Dune du Pilat. (The sandbanks are a bird sanctuary and can be visited by boat from Arcachon during July and August.) Unless the process is stopped artificially, eventually the tip of Cap Ferret will stand opposite the dune, across a narrow tidal channel. When that happens, and the sandbanks are covered with summer houses and

The dune is one of several, providing endless sandy beaches south of Arcachon

Climb the magnificent Dune du Pilat, especially recommended at sunset, and visit the Teich bird sanctuary at the mouth of the Eyre

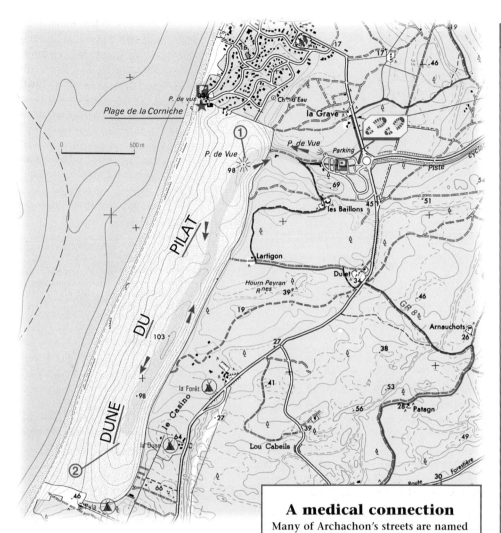

WALK

length of walk: up to 6km
time: 1½ hours
IGN Top 25: sheet 1337ET

It is a stiff but rewarding 15-minute climb up to the top of the dune, offering spectacular ocean and forest views. Naturally, the steep, shifting sand is not suitable for wheelchairs or pushchairs.

❶ Start from the northwest corner of the car park and follow the pedestrian road past a row of souvenir shops, to the viewpoint midway up the steep eastern bank of the dune. Visitors daunted by the 30° slope can stop for refreshments at the well-shaded café. If you're lucky, the steps that lead to the summit will have been dug out from the sand that is forever drifting over them. Otherwise, you'll discover why, in the movies, travellers who have lost their way in the desert always look so exhausted when they get to the top of the rise from which they hope to catch sight of the next oasis.

❷ Once at the top, there are three options: turn back, walk down to the beach on the dune's western side – and climb back later – or follow the ridge southwards as far as you like. There are no trails, no signposts, no benches, only sand sloping gently towards the sea on one side and very steeply towards the forest on the other. You cannot get lost but it is best not to get too close to the landward slope. When you have had your fill of sea, sun, sand and wind head back north to where the crowds are struggling up from the car park. Do not attempt to return by any other route. Negotiating the descent is not as difficult it looks.

---

pine groves, the ocean winds will cease heaping sand on Pilat and the dune will wear down until it sinks beneath the treetops.

▪ ARCACHON ▪

Arcachon's elegant 'winter town' was the brainwave of two 19th-century financiers, the brothers Emile and Isaac Pereire, who bought up 400ha of woodlot overlooking the seafront and then parcelled it out to the rich and the titled of the Second Napoleonic Empire. The Moorish-style casino that stood at its centre burned down in 1977, but the park surrounding it is still there to give the modern visitor the flavour of Arcachon in its heyday when, among other luminaries, the King of Spain came here to celebrate his engagement to Archduchess Maria Christina of Austria.

A stroll around the winding streets laid out by the architects Régnault and Alphand is an education in late 19th-century eclecticism, from Elizabethan Gothic to Wagnerian Baroque. The Villa Faust (allée Faust) recalls Gounaud's stay in Arcachon during the 1870s. A steel footbridge designed by Gustave Eiffel spans rue Pasteur.

▪ TEICH BIRD SANCTUARY ▪

A few kilometres east of Arcachon in the marshes at the mouth of the Eyre, the Parc Ornithologique du Teich covers over 100ha of

---

A medical connection

Many of Archachon's streets are named after great medical scientists, for the town was a leading health spa, its sea air considered salutory for lung ailments. The Anglican church and former Franco-British chemists (Villa Rochefoucaud) on place Fleming bear witness to what was once a sizeable English colony.

---

wetlands and is home to a large resident bird population. Also a favourite stopping-off site for migrants on their great annual voyage to and from Canada, Siberia and the sub-Arctic regions, as many as 260 different species are claimed to have been observed here.

A paradise for the birds that find plenty to eat in its swamps and shallow ponds (originally salt pans, then fish hatcheries) and a heaven for birdwatchers, the sanctuary is an enthralling place even for the average city-dweller who can't tell a teal from a tern. The visitor follows a path along a maze of tree-lined dykes leading from one unobtrusive observation post to another. Everything has been designed to allow visitors to approach the birds without disturbing them. Not only can you observe them at close quarters but you feel you are being privileged with a rare glimpse of a world where humans are passing intruders. Swans thrashing the surface of the water as they take off, storks clacking their bills, honking geese pursuing each other in

---

endless rituals of seduction and rejection – it is a clamorous world and yet a breathlessly still one too. The snowy egret poised on one leg, the cormorant standing on a rotting post with its wings outspread to dry are the idols of a cult of infinite patience.

Row upon row of yachts moored in the wide bay of the stylish resort of Arcachon

GROTTES DE LASCAUX

Prehistory helped establish the Dordogne, and nowhere more so than at Lascaux: probably the best-known and most-visited prehistoric site in France. The original caves are closed to preserve the paintings within, but visitors can inspect the replica, Lascaux II.

The story of the discovery in 1940 of Lascaux, with its multi-coloured paintings, is legendary: four young boys were looking for their dog, which had fallen down a hole, when they found they were in a cave full of coloured paintings. They rushed to tell their schoolteacher, who informed the prehistorian Abbé Breuil, who coined the phrase 'The Sistine Chapel of the Périgord'.

Animal paintings discovered at Lascaux, the area's most famous prehistoric site, have been faithfully recreated in the replica caves Lascaux II

■ PREHISTORY'S 'SISTINE CHAPEL' ■

The cave was opened to the public in 1948 but proved so popular that in 1963 it had to be closed for its own protection. Carbon dioxide from the breath of a million visitors – and moss and algae from the outside world – were starting to damage the irreplaceable paintings. It was decided to construct a replica of the original, and this was opened in 1983.

The original cave is made up of four chambers, and their paintings of horses, bison, reindeer, bears, aurochs (a type of extinct wild oxen) and woolly rhinoceros were perfectly preserved thanks to an impermeable roof and a fall of clay, which blocked the original entrance.

The Cult of the Bear

In 1954 numerous objects and bones were found at the prehistoric site of Le Regourdou, right in front of the home of Monsieur Roger Constant. The most important among them was the 70,000-year-old skeleton of a man, now displayed in the Périgord Museum in Périgueux, and named Regourdou Man after the site. Also found were bones of bears which, according to M Constant, were arranged in such a way as to provide evidence that the bears had been ritually buried, leading him to deduce that the bear had once been a sacred animal.

To reinforce his belief, he has created a small museum on the site and, more spectacularly, introduced live brown bears which he feeds in front of visitors. The bears are safely kept in large concrete enclosures and a notice outside warns of electric fences. Particularly revealing of M Constant's belief in bear worship is another panel which reads: 'You are in a solemn place. It belongs to the origins of man and the cult of the bear. Respect this sacred place.'

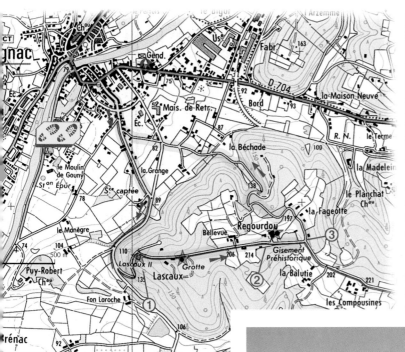

ABOVE: Le Thot visitor centre brings prehistory to life with displays and videos

BELOW: a jumble of old houses lines the banks of the River Vézère

W A L K

length of walk: 5km
time: 3 hours, including visits
IGN Top 25: sheet 20350

Lascaux is open every day during July and August, and every day except Monday during the rest of the year. Tickets for the caves are only available at Montignac, so remember to buy them underneath the arches of the tourist office (*syndicat d'initiative*). You can buy a single ticket for Lascaux only or a twin ticket for Lascaux and le Thot visitor centre. Tarmac roads make the terrain easy.

❶ Starting from the tourist office at **Montignac**, leave the town by taking either rue du Barry or rue Émile Lajunias; whichever you choose, you'll find yourself on the GR 461 footpath. Follow this to **Lascaux II** about 2km away.

❷ After you have visited the caves, take the small road signposted le Régourdou (still the GR 461), noting the original Lascaux (now closed) on the right as you ascend. Take time to visit the site of **le Régourdou** 1km away.

❸ After the visit continue along this road. Turning left at the T-junction, leaving the GR 461, take the winding road down through the woods keeping ahead until you rejoin the GR 461 and then follow signs back to Montignac.

■ THE MAKING OF LASCAUX II ■

The 'new' Lascaux is located some 200m from the original cave, and consists of a replica of two of the four galleries: the Bull's Hall, including the famous bull which has become the symbol for the department of the Dordogne, and the Axial Gallery, which between them contain the majority of the paintings at Lascaux.

Thanks to modern technology and rigid scientific discipline, the contours of the facsimile are accurate to within 5mm of the original. In order to accomplish this, the Institut Géographique National (IGN) carried out a photogrammetric survey of Lascaux in 1966, using three-dimensional scenes of the cave. This enabled a shell to be constructed in reinforced concrete, using shipbuilding techniques. The site is an open-cast quarry.

Once the cave walls had been reproduced, the painter Monique Peytral copied the cave paintings using not only detailed photographs but also the same methods and materials as the cave artists, for example paints made from natural pigments.

Any visit to Lascaux must start at the pretty town of Montignac, where tickets for the caves can be bought at the tourist office, situated in the 14th-century former Hospital of Saint-Jean l'Évangéliste.

■ MONTIGNAC ■

The town of Montignac itself warrants exploring, with its 18th-century stone bridge straddling the Vézère River, the restored tower of the château and the half-timbered houses

dating back to the 13th century, many in rue de la Pègerie. It is also famous because of the local writer Eugene le Roy, who died here in 1907, and who captured the feel and detail of rural life in the last century in his novels. The most famous of them, *Jacquou le Croquant*, was made into a French television series. Inside the tourist office is a museum dedicated to the writer's life and works, and his statue is found in the shady Square Pautauberge.

■ LE THOT ■

Although Lascaux can easily be reached on foot from Montignac (2km), it is worth making a car trip, either before or after your walk, to the 'Espace Cro-Magnon' known as Le Thot, a visitor centre with background explanations about Lascaux and its prehistory. The museum includes a fascinating video about the construction of Lascaux II, while in the park there are animated examples of species of animals found in cave paintings. Attractions even include a moving mammoth and a woolly rhinoceros to amuse the children and help bring the prehistory alive!

Just opposite the turning to Le Thot on the D 706 is the 16th-century Château de Losse on the banks of the Vézère River. This Renaissance castle includes sumptuously furnished rooms with 16th- and 17th-century cupboards, coffers and tapestries, as well as a garden and terrace overlooking the Vézère.

In a picturesque setting on the banks of the Vézère, the Château de Losse dates from the 16th century

SARLAT-LA-CANÉDA

*T*he best time to visit Sarlat is probably out of season, as its popularity means that it gets very crowded during the peak tourist times – understandably, given the charm of its ancient buildings and narrow streets. This walk includes a circuit in the wooded hills above the town to appreciate the beauty of its setting.

The cathedral of St-Sacerdos is one of the architectural treasures of Sarlat

Sarlat grew up around a Benedictine abbey founded in the 9th century, and its abbots were all-powerful until the 13th century when, because of political unrest, the abbey became a cathedral. After the ravages of the Hundred Years War the town had privileges awarded by the king to reward its loyalty, and entered a golden age of reconstruction, resulting in a pleasing architectural unity: most of the town houses were built by the prosperous bourgeoisie during 1450–1500 and are known as hôtels. Their steep-pitched roofs were designed to allow most of the enormous weight of the stone tiles (*lauzes*) to be supported on the thick walls.

A SLEEPING BEAUTY

After prospering throughout the 16th to 18th centuries, Sarlat fell into a period of dormancy as it was too far from the mainstream. This turned out to be a blessing in disguise, as it escaped modernisation in the 19th and 20th centuries. It was only when roads replaced rail and river transport, in the 1960–70s, that it awoke. Fortunately, its revival coincided with the passing of the loi Malraux in 1962, which decreed that financial aid should be given to the restoration of old towns; Sarlat was one to benefit.

Sarlat is especially colourful on market day

Part of the charm of exploring Sarlat is the pleasure of losing yourself in the old streets, all too easy with its abundance of winding streets and passages. Market days are Wednesdays and Saturdays and, in addition, there are no end of shops offering regional delicacies: preserved duck and goose, *foie gras*, sometimes garnished with truffles, and the wines from the Bergeracois, including Pecharmant and Monbazillac.

Étienne de La Boétie

The Maison de La Boétie (right) must be one of the most famous and most photographed buildings in Sarlat; it is hard to imagine it as newly built, as it was at the time when the most famous of Sarlat's sons, philosopher and poet Étienne de La Boétie, was born there in 1530. His father, Antoine, was a criminal lawyer, and Étienne himself became a brilliant attorney in the parliament at Bordeaux, as well as becoming famous for his writing from an early age. He was only 18 when he wrote an impassioned appeal for liberty, his *Discours sur la servitude volontaire ou Contr'un* (Against One), which later inspired Jean-Jacques Rousseau when he wrote his *Du contrat social* (Social Contract). La Boétie became lifelong friends with the writer Michel Montaigne, a friendship which has been immortalised in the latter's 'Essay on Friendship', in which Montaigne wrote: 'If I am urged to explain why I loved him, I feel I can only reply: because he was himself and I am myself...' His statue can be seen in place de la Grande Rigaudie.

RIGHT: the restored town with its honey-coloured buildings is popular with holiday-makers

WALK

length of walk: 5km
time: 3 hours
IGN Top 25: sheet 2036O

This walk takes in a town visit and a stroll outside the town. The latter includes an extremely steep climb at the beginning and the descent of a rough lane at the end. Other places of interest to visit include the Musée Automobile offering a collection of some 60 cars dating from as early as 1890; the Musée Aquarium, relating the history of the River Dordogne; and the Musée des Mirepoises, a Renaissance manor housing a collection of old armour, weapons and furniture. Start from place de la Grande Rigaudie, where you can park outside the town's former walls.

The town walk

❶ Enter the old town by rue Tourny and proceed to place du Peyrou. Note the **Maison de La Boétie**, one of the most spectacular early Renaissance houses in Sarlat, with its delicately carved mullion windows. Enter the **Cathédrale de St-Sacerdos**, leaving by the southern door and pass the remains of the old abbey cloisters. Continue with the Cour des Fountaines and the Cour des Chanoines. Pass through the archway to the right into the **Jardin des Enfeux**, where the tombstones and sarcophagi of the notables of 14th-to16th-century Sarlat can be found. Climb the steps leading to the 12th century Lanterne des Morts. Go through the little doorway in the wall and come out into rue Montaigne, opposite the birthplace of Sarlat historian Jean-Joseph Escande.

❷ Cross rue Montaigne and walk up rue Sylvain Cavaillez, continuing along rue d'Albusse. On your right up a little alley is the Hôtel de Génis. Go down rue d'Albusse and turn into rue du Présidial. The latter was the royal court of justice created by Henry II in 1552. Turn around and go down rue de Salamandre to come out in the town's main square, place de la Liberté, flanked by the Hôtel de Ville on its north side, and the old secularised **église Ste-Marie**, with its fine gargoyles. The church was sold and its chancel destroyed, leaving an open space where summer open-air theatre productions benefit from the magnificent setting. Behind the former church is **place du Marché aux Oies** (goose market), with its fine bronze statue of the geese which were once sold here. Take rue des Consuls, passing the 15th-century Hôtel Vassal on the corner, and further along on the left the 14th-century Hôtel Plamon and the Hôtel de Bétou. Enter the courtyard to see the magnificent wooden staircase. Immediately opposite is the Fontaine Ste-Marie.

❸ Emerge on to rue de la Republique (or Traverse) which cut the town in two in the 19th century; cross it and climb the steep rue des Armes. Coming out through the ramparts on to the main boulevard Eugène Le Roy, turn left and do down the second street on your right (rue de la Charité). Turn right along rue Jean-Jacques Rousseau, which leads to the former **Couvent Ste-Claire**. Turn left by this building, down rue de la Boétie, then right up rue Cordil and rue de Trois Conils.

❹ Leave the walled town by the high arched gateway next to the 15th-century **Tour du Bourreau** (Hangman's Tower), one of 18 towers which once guarded the town. Follow the Boulevard back to place de la Grande Rigaudie.

The country walk

❺ To do the walk in the hills, known as the **Route des Pechs** (*pech* means a 'high point' in Occitan, the former language of the south), take the lane alongside the Jardin Public du Plantier. This route is signed in blue. Pass the small car park on your left, and start to climb. As you pass the houses built by the modern Sarladais bourgeois, take some time to catch your breath and admire the views of the town below.

❻ Turn right at the junction at the top, and start down the gentle descent, following the road. Look out for the blue markings on posts, and turn right down a steep lane marked with a 'No through road' sign. This becomes a rough track which descends very steeply between ivy-covered walls. Note the *borie*, or dry-stone circular cabin, on the right. Turn right at the bottom, passing an old *lavoir* (public washing place) and follow the road to place Pasteur and so back to place de la Grande Rigaudie.

PÉRIGORD & QUERCY

ROCAMADOUR

Perched high on the rocky plateau known as the Causse du Quercy, the village of Rocamadour seems to defy gravity. The site of the oldest pilgrimage in France, it continues to astonish its numerous visitors with its breathtaking setting.

There is probably no more succinct description of Rocamadour's construction than in this local song:

> 'The houses on the stream
> The churches on the houses
> The rocks on the churches
> The castle on the rocks'

The builders in the Middle Ages made use of a natural phenomenon: a 140m-deep canyon of the River Alzou. According to legend, the origins of this rocky site stem from its inhabitant, the hermit Amadour, whose perfectly preserved body was discovered in the 12th century (hence the name, the *Roc Amadour*).

From that time on miracles began to occur, and crowds of up to 30,000 pilgrims would attend the site on certain holy days. Henry Plantagenet of England was among several kings to climb the famous 'great staircase' (the really devout did it on their knees) and pay homage to the miraculous virgin, or Black Madonna, a small statue carved in walnut and blackened from centuries of candle smoke; also to see the miraculous bell, which rings of its own accord to foretell miracles.

Stuck in the cliff face above the chapel door is a great iron sword, Durandal. According to legend the sword belonged to Roland, who planted it in the rock to prevent it falling into infidel hands.

Rated with Jerusalem, Rome and Compostella as among the four most important cities in the Middle Ages, Rocamadour's wealth and fame grew throughout the 12th, 13th and 14th centuries. With it came the need for defence, as it was threatened first by covetous neighbouring abbeys, then by plundering soldiers during the Hundred Years War. Despite the eight remaining gateways, ram-

Rocamadour, in a dramatic setting on a steep rock face, has attracted pilgrims for centuries
INSET: frescoes from a church in the village

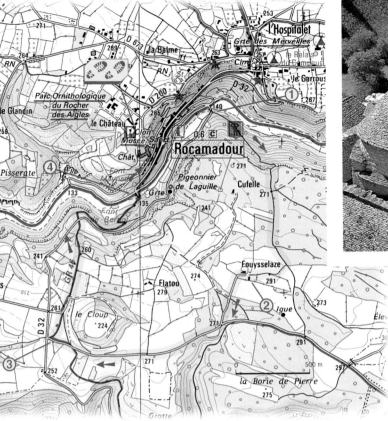

Singes (Monkey Forest), where a population of over 100 Barbary macaques live freely in a 10ha site, offering direct contact with visitors.

Still on the subject of wildlife, there is the Maison des Abeilles (House of the Bees) where up to half a million bees live. As well as a permanent exhibition on the life of the bee and all aspects of apiculture, there is a demonstration of bee handling. If this is not to your taste, the aquarium offers an exhibition of freshwater fish, with the *pièce de résistance* being Veronique, a 16kg carp.

Rocamadour, situated midway between the spectacular caves of Lacave to the west and Padirac to the east, also has its own prehistoric cave, the Grotte des Merveilles, with paintings dating from nearly 20,000 years ago.

ABOVE: the Cité Religieuse, with its shrines and chapels is reached by a steep flight of steps

RIGHT: the 14th-century château stands guard over the narrow streets of Rocamadour

parts and – its crowning glory – the château, the town was laid waste during the Wars of Religion and was only rebuilt in the 19th century when the bishop of Cahors revived the pilgrimage.

■ OTHER ATTRACTIONS ■

In case the tour of the town fails to catch your imagination, Rocamadour is surrounded by a number of other attractions, to suit all tastes and ages.

To help you see the beauty of Rocamadour

illuminated at night, there is 'le Petit Train' which offers a 30-minute evening tour (Easter–September). Or for an alternative *son et lumière*, La Féérie du Rail offers a miniature illuminated fairyland which took its inventor 15 years to create.

For those drawn towards wildlife, there is the Rocher des Aigles (Rock of Eagles) near the château, where a variety of species of birds of prey can be admired. An effort has been made to reconstruct their natural environment and their trainers will also make them perform spectacular dives. Not far away is the Fôret des

---

WALK

length of walks: 1km or 8km
time: 1½ hours or 3 hours
IGN Top 25: sheet 2136ET

Rocamadour can be approached on two levels, both with car parks: via the D 673 from the upper plateau on foot or by lifts, or from the Alzou valley, by foot or by a small train. Both approaches offer spectacular views. This tour starts from the top, and includes a walk in the town as well as a circular walk in the Alzou valley through the surrounding countryside. There are some steep ascents and descents.

The town walk

❶ From the car park near the château, visit the ramparts for an unforgettable panorama of the site and its rocky setting. Go down the steeply winding **Chemin de Croix**, with the Stations of the Cross at each turn of the pathway. Pas through a tunnel under the basilica to arrive in the **Cité Religieuse** which includes seven chapels.

Don't miss **Chapelle de Notre-Dame**, to the left of the basilica, site of the statue of the Black Madonna. Visit also the **Musée d'Art Sacré Francis Poulenc**, dedicated to the composer (1899–1963) who had a vision during a visit to the town in 1936 and subsequently composed *Litanies la Vièrge Noire de Rocamadour*. The museum contains an interesting collection of sacred art and artefacts.

Walk down the 223 steps of the **Grand Escalier** to visit the village at the lower level. Turn left along the main street to pass the *office de tourisme*, next to the Hôtel de Ville. Just before one of the old town gates, Porte Salmon, turn right down the lane and then descend one of the flights of steps; go towards the lower car park by the river.

The country walk

❷ This is marked with an image of a dragonfly (*libellule*) and is signposted to Fouysselaze at the start. Cross the **River Alzou** by the stone bridge, and take the lane on the left. After about 150m a little path on your right leads to the **fontaine de la Filiole**. Climb the hill amongst hazel and oak trees. Once on the plateau,

continue towards the farm of **Fouysselaze**, where the farmers make the delicious little goats' milk cheeses known as *cabécou*. Once past the farm, join the small tarmac road which joins another road after about 500m; keep straight on. In the wall on your right a sheep passage has been made.

❸ Skirt the large hollow on your right, known as le cloup de Magès; on the left is a dolmen, which is at least four or five thousand years old.

❹ Leave the road and take the GR 46 footpath, which descends to Rocamadour, crossing the D 32, and offers a magnificent view of the town. Cross the Alzou by the little bridge near the Moulin de Roquefraôche, enter the town by Porte Basse, then pass through Porte Hugon. If you can't face the Great Staircase again, take the lift and funicular railway through the rock back up to the plateau where the tour started.

GOUFFRE DE PADIRAC

*T*he Gouffre de Padirac is an extraordinary natural phenomenon even by the standards of other impressive geological features of France – a yawning chasm, hollowed out of the limestone mass of the Causse de Gramat by an underground river.

The Gouffre de Padirac was, understandably, a source of fear and superstition to local people right up until the 19th century, as its creation was said to be the work of the devil. How else can such a spectacular chasm be explained?

■ SATAN'S HANDIWORK ■

The legend has it that St Martin was returning from an unsuccessful expedition, looking for souls to save, when suddenly his mule stopped. Satan was blocking his path, with a sack full of souls on the way to hell. Satan proposed a bargain with the saint: he would give him the lost souls if St Martin would make his mule cross an obstacle created by Satan. The saint agreed, Satan stamped his foot and a great chasm opened in the ground. St Martin urged his mule to jump, which it did with such force that the imprint of its hooves can still be seen in the rock.

Despite this superstition, the Gouffre would certainly have served as a refuge for people living on the *causse* during times of war. Padirac was opened to tourists for the first time in 1898; at about the same time, the underground galleries were discovered by the speleologist Edouard Martel, who undertook several expeditions between 1889 and 1900. Since then, various expeditions have discovered 22km of underground passages. In 1947 it was proved, by colouring the water in Padirac's underground river, that it resurfaces 11km away at the Cirque de Montvalent, near the Dordogne River.

Prehistoric remains have been found not far away, including bones of mammoths, rhinoceroses, bison, bears and lions dating from between 150,000 and 200,000 years ago, as well as flint tools dating from between 30,000 and 50,000 years ago.

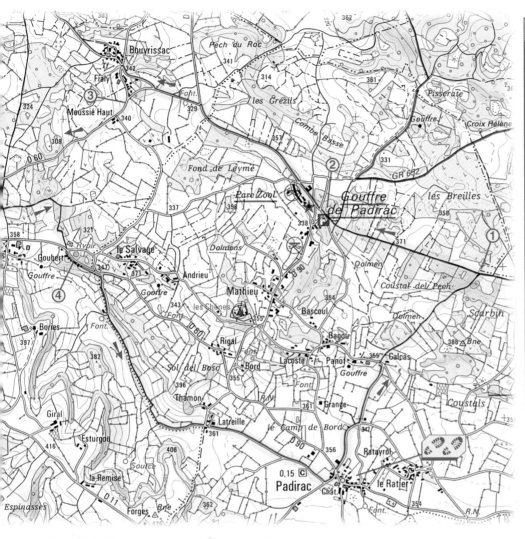

WALK

length of walk: 10.5km
time: 5 hours
IGN Top 25: sheet 2136ET

This walk starts from Padirac village then – to get a flavour of the *causse* and see some of its many dolmens and fountains – approaches the site of the Gouffre via tiny country lanes and hamlets. It also provides a pleasant contrast with the crowds of visitors to the town itself that you are likely to encounter in high season. The terrain is fairly easy, but it can be chilly, at 13°C, in the caves. The going may be very hot in midsummer.

1 Take the D 90 towards the Gouffre de Padirac and turn down the lane signposted to **Panot**, which is on your right before you leave the village. At the first crossroads turn left, at the next T-junction turn left and immediately right to follow a marked footpath to the Gouffre. You will pass a dolmen on your left.

2 After 500m turn left at the T-junction of paths and continue straight to the **Gouffre de Padirac**. The underground journey extends over 2km, 700m of which is by boat. Two lifts and several flights of stairs lead down into the chasm, which is approximately 100m in circumference and 75m deep. From the bottom the view upwards is impressive. The surrounding rocky walls are covered in stalactites and precariously-rooted vegetation.

It starts with the **Galerie de la Source** (300m long) at the far end of which is the landing stage. From here a flotilla of flat-bottomed boats carries visitors along the Rivière Plane, where the depth varies from 50cm to 4m. The height of the rocky roof above gradually increases to reach a maximum of 78m, the height of the impressive **Grande Pendeloque** (Great Pendant) stalactite, which nearly touches the water.

The visit continues through the **Pas du Crocodile**, a narrow passage linking the underground river with the next caves. Not to be missed are the **Grand Pillier** (Great Pillar), a stalagmite 40m high, the **Salle des Grands Gours**, which has a series of pools separated by *gours* (limestone dams), the **Lac Supérieur**, at a level 20m above that of the river, and the **Salle du Grand Dôme**, with its impressively high roof (91m) the most beautiful of all the Padirac caverns. Lifts take visitors back to the entrance, to save them climbing 455 steps. Visit the site and the Zoo de Tropicorama, if you wish. There are picnic facilities in the area between the Gouffre building and the entrance to the zoo.

3 After leaving the site, follow the D 90 in a north-westerly direction. Turn left by the impressive granite fountain of **Fialy**, with its three stone basins, following signposts to Miers. Keep left at the next fork, then turn left at the T-junction to join the D 60.

4 Follow this road for 1km, then turn left to follow the signed footpath which turns sharply left and then right. Pass the **ferme de Goubert**, and join the D 60 briefly, then follow the footpath to the right, passing another fountain (Goubert) on your right, and arriving back at Padirac village via Latreille.

The Causse de Gramat (main) is a suitably dramatic setting for the Gouffre de Padirac (inset)

The lift structure (left) descending down into the chasm seems to cling precariously to the cliff face

■ THE CAUSSES DE QUERCY ■

The Causse de Gramat is, strictly speaking, one of the four Causses de Quercy that make up the limestone plateau that stretches for approximately 100km, from the borders of the Dordogne and Correze in the north to the *département* of Tarn-et-Garonne in the south.

The *causse* has suffered from extreme rural depopulation, but even before this began in the 1850s, life must have been hard in this infertile stony region. Its limestone landscape has been shaped by the rain over the centuries into *pechs* (rocky outcrops), and *cloups* (hollows). The water, filtering slowly though the porous soil, has led to the formation of underground caves, caverns and rivers, often with spectacular stalactites and stalagmites, such as at Padirac. The water emerges again as springs. Pools to conserve the precious water are also a feature of the landscape.

It is a land where stone reigns supreme. As many as 750 dolmens are to be found on the *causse*, evidence of a high level of social organisation by early mankind. More recently, the building of dry stone walls and cabins shows that the art of building with natural stone is not lost, with even the roofs made of *lauzes* (stone tiles).

St-Cirq-Lapopie

*O*ne of the most spectacular beauty spots of the Lot valley, the little village of St-Cirq-Lapopie is perched on a cliff 100m above the river. The walk, from the neighbouring village of Bouziès, follows the old towpath along the river.

*W*hen the surrealist poet André Breton first saw the village of St-Cirq-Lapopie in the 1950s, he described it as 'an impossible rose in the night'. It was love at first sight and once he had settled in the old sailors' inn in Place du Carol, he declared that he wanted to live nowhere else. He was not the only one to succumb to the spell; many painters came to live and work in the village, among them the Post-Impressionist Henri Martin, and Pierre Daura, who carved the beams of his house in the Ruelle de la Fourdonne. Today the village is still full of craftspeople and artists in the summer months.

ABOVE: The medieval village of St-Cirq is crowned by its simple but elegant church

■ A TURBULENT HISTORY ■

In the Middle Ages, St-Cirq-Lapopie was the main town of one of the four viscountcies that made up the Quercy. It was divided among four feudal dynasties, the families of Lapopie, Gourdon, Cardaillac and Castelnau. The village was dominated by a fortress built on Lapopie rock, where its foundations are still visible; from here the view over the Lot valley is breathtaking. The fortress was regularly besieged through the centuries, by Richard the Lionheart in 1180, again by the English during the Hundred Years War, and by the Huguenots during the Wars of Religion. Its final demolition was ordered by the future Henri IV in 1580.

Below the fortress are the narrow twisting streets, with many of the houses dating back as far as the 13th century. The houses have steep tiled roofs and some have half-timbered

BELOW: St-Cirq-Lapopie clings to the the cliff above the River Lot

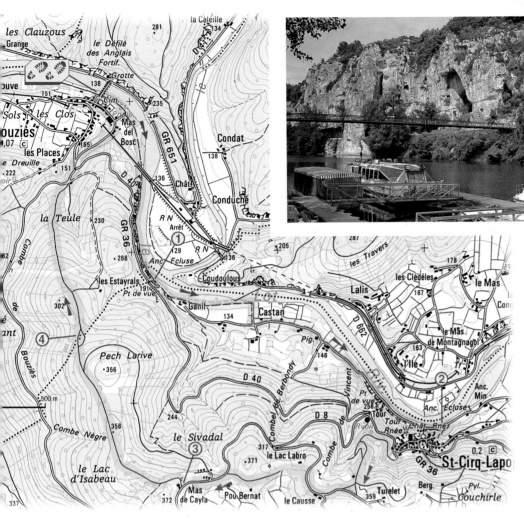

Boats trips from Bouziès are a popular and leisurely way of discovering the magnificent scenery of the Lot valley

Some of the old houses of St-Cirq have been restored by artists and craftspeople attracted to this beautiful village

fronts and mullion windows. Some houses are separated from the street by a narrow space called an *entremi*, which carried away rainwater as well as waste from sinks and latrines.

Beneath the cliffs of St-Cirq are watermills, weirs, harbours, locks and towpaths, recalling the days when river transport was the glory of the Lot valley.

▪ QUERCYRAIL ▪

An alternative way to see the beauty of the Lot valley, instead of driving, cycling or walking, is to let the train take the strain. At a stately 40kph the Quercyrail trains depart from either Cahors or Capdenac, at opposite ends of the Lot valley line and provide the means of enjoying views of spectacular cliffs, châteaux and the river valley not normally accessible from the road. Both trains pass near Saint-Cirq-Lapopie and Bouziès, with the option to get off and either walk along the towpath as described here, or take a boat trip to admire Saint-Cirq from the river.

The Cahors-Capdenac line was inaugurated on 14 July 1886, bringing civilisation to this very rural and inaccessible region. It presents some incredible feats of engineering: tunnels, viaducts and any number of level crossings. The line was important for carrying coal from Decazeville, but was finally closed to passengers in 1980 and to freight traffic in 1989. The Association Quercyrail was created in 1985 to rescue the line and its locomotives from dereliction and to preserve a part of the local heritage that would otherwise have disappeared, for the enjoyment of visitors to the region.

To commemorate the 'birth' of the line, the Association organises a special event each 14 July (Bastille Day) with the arrival of a steam train from Toulouse. Although it is not able to run steam trains on a regular basis, the 1950s diesel Micheline locomotives (named after their creator, the Michelin company) which ply the line will soon become antiques in their own right.

For information or reservations (which are essential) contact the Quercyrail office at Cahors station.

W A L K

length of walk: 10km
time: 3 hours
IGN Top 25: sheet 2138E

This walk starts at St-Cirq's neighbouring village of Bouziès. The route follows footpaths and minor roads, and some sections are steep. Bouziès is situated opposite the magnificent cliffs, known as the defilé des anglais, a sort of natural fortified château. Start from below the suspension bridge at Bouziès.

❶ From the bridge, follow the red and white markings of the GR 36 footpath which follows the River Lot. Pass underneath the railway bridge and follow the river towpath, which is hewn out of the rock face, and has bas-relief sculptures by the artist D Monnier.

❷ Go past the junction with the River Célé on the opposite bank, and the lock and keeper's cottage; still following the GR markings, turn sharp right and join a tarmac road. After 500m, notice an old *pigeonnier* (pigeon house) perched on a rocky outcrop. After passing the foot of the cliffs, climb the steep path on the right, which leads to **St-Cirq-Lapopie**.

❸ Take the time to climb the Lapopie rock, visit the church, the old houses and the crafts workshops in this lovely village. Finish the tour of the village by climbing one of the roads which joins the main road encircling the village (the D 8). Go into the main car park, opposite the post office, where another footpath is marked with orange signs. Follow this footpath as far as a chicken house on the left; 50m after this, follow a little lane on the right which leads to a road; turn right. Pass a turning on your left, then 200m further on, leave the road on a right-hand bend to follow the track on the left. It becomes a path bordered with boxwood hedges. Keep straight on until you join a road. Continue straight on to the **Mas de Cayla**; turn right.

❹ Follow this path through the woods for about 1km, keeping to the left each time it forks. Descend towards the valley and join a tarmac road. Continue straight on, descending and heading back towards the centre of Bouziès and the beginning of the walk.

CHÂTEAU DE BONAGUIL

The ruined 15th-century Château de Blanquefort is on the route of the drive

Standing on the borders of the départements of Lot, Lot-et-Garonne and Dordogne, this majestic fortress is one of the finest examples of late 15th-century military architecture. Capable of sheltering and sustaining a garrison of 100 men, it was never attacked and remained intact until the French Revolution.

If Bonaguil's setting, on a rocky promontory in the wooded hills of the Quercy, is impressive from a distance, it is no less so close-up; exploring the castle is a delight for those who love history and architecture, and especially for children.

■ AN IMPREGNABLE FORTRESS ■

The defences start with a massive outer wall, complete with an enormous bastion with its own garrison, powder store and armouries; inside this wall lies the second line of defence, consisting of five round towers. The biggest, la Grosse Tour, at 35m high, is one of the strongest round towers ever built in France. Inside again is the keep, overlooking everything and built in the shape of a ship's prow, to resist attack by cannonballs. A spiral staircase gives access to the top, from where the view from the battlements is almost vertiginous.

The castle was clearly designed to be self-sufficient, with a well sunk through the rock, bakeries, provisions stores, and covered tunnels which enabled troops to move about quickly. In addition, at a time when other castles – in the Loire, for example – were being built as symbols of leisure and wealth, Bonaguil's defences must have seemed something of an anachronism, despite the fact that they were designed to facilitate the use of newly invented firearms.

The creator of this masterpiece of defence belonged to one of the oldest families of Languedoc: the powerful and cruel baron, Bérenger de Roquefeuil, whose manner of ruling eventually incited rebellion. To crush the opposition, he strengthened the castle, which had existed since the 13th century, into an impregnable fortress, a transformation which began in 1480 and took nearly 40 years to complete. Perhaps not surprisingly, it was never besieged, and, despite being seen as a symbol of the old feudal system, was only partially destroyed during the French Revolution.

An excellent example of medieval architecture, the Château de Bonaguil was never besieged

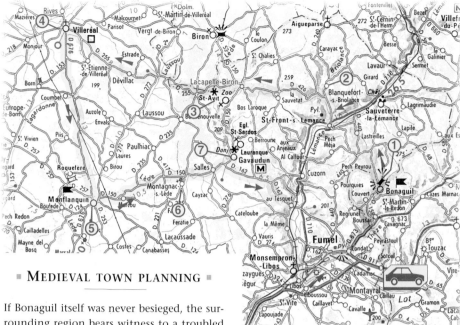

■ MEDIEVAL TOWN PLANNING ■

If Bonaguil itself was never besieged, the surrounding region bears witness to a troubled history, especially during the Hundred Years War and the Wars of Religion, by its remarkable number of châteaux and *bastides*, or new fortified towns, developed in the 13th and 14th centuries. One of the main founders of the *bastides* was Count Alphonse de Poitiers (1220–71), brother of St Louis, King Louis IX of France. He was responsible for founding Monflanquin and Villeréal, among others; other founders were the counts of Toulouse and English commanders, who founded Beaumont and Monpazier.

By the end of the 12th century a significant increase in the population had created a need for new towns, which were built in order to stabilise the population and stop the spread of the English. In contrast to the narrow, winding streets which grew up naturally in any small medieval town of this period, the streets in the *bastides* were laid out in the form of a grid.

The central square was surrounded by arcades, with the church, often fortified and representing a 'last refuge', in the corner of this square. From here the streets led straight to the town's gateways. Sometimes the towns had outer fortifications; otherwise they were surrounded by deep moats.

In addition, the creation of a *bastide* was marked by the passing of an official act, setting out clearly the rights and duties of the population. Although the *bastide* towns changed hands regularly during the conflicts between the French and the English, in times of peace they grew into prosperous commercial centres, as a result of having regularly organised fairs and markets

ABOVE: Villeréal's unusual two-storey market hall
BELOW: the streets of the exceptional bastide of Monflanquin are well worth exploring

length of tour: 75km
time: 1 day
IGN sheet: Top 250 sheet 102

Start from Fumel, where there are hotels and restaurants. The *gabares*, or river boats, which offer river trips to visitors from April to September, are a remnant of the time when the River Lot was an important means of transport.

❶ Take the D 911 to Condat and turn on to the D 673 to visit the **Château de Bonaguil**. There are restaurants in the village, as well as an auberge.

❷ After the visit, take the little road at the foot of the château, marked St Front and from here continue to **Blanquefort-sur-Briolance**, with its ruins of a 15th-century château and Romanesque churches. Backtrack 1km to take the turning right to **Lacapelle-Biron**, via la Sauvetat and St-Chaliès to see 12th-century Romanesque churches dominating tiny hamlets. Visit la fontaine du curé, the moulin de Courrance, the memorial to those deported to German prison camps during World War II.

❸ In the nearby village of **St-Avit** is the house of Bernard Palissy (16th-century potter and enamellist). The village hosts an international pottery fair on the second Sunday in August.

❹ Take the D 255 to **Villeréal**, one of the *bastide* towns. Look out for the unusual two-storey market hall and fortified church, once protected by a moat and drawbridge, as well as the half-timbered houses. Villeréal has a long tradition of being associated with horses. The Maison de la Campagne (place Jean-Moulin) has information on local wildlife, and at nearby Lac de Brayssou (5km to the north) visitors can watch migrating birds from an observatory.

❺ Take the D 676 south to **Monflanquin**, another remarkable *bastide*, constructed on a hill. Here the house of Alphonse de Poitiers, founder of the town in 1256, can be visited. Park near the church where there is an orientation table and a splendid view, as well as information about the town and a suggested tour. The market is held in the superb central Place des Arcades, where the Black Prince was said to have stayed during the Hundred Years War.

❻ Take the D 150 east in the direction of Montagnac-sur-Lède, turning left off this road after 6km to visit the 16th-century **Moulin du Cros**, where six generations of the same family of Caumières have ground corn and baked bread since 1833. Today, their descendants offer a guided visit as well as the opportunity to make and taste different breads (bread-making by reservation only).

❼ Continue along the D 150 for 5km, then turn left just after the village of Salles to visit **Gavaudun**, with its impressive six-storey tower built on a vertical cliff, accessible by a footpath. Return to Fumel either via **Monsempron-Libos**, a fortified village with magnificent 12th-century Romanesque church and priory, or direct by the D 162 and D 710.

CIRQUE DE GAVARNIE

*T*he Cirque de Gavarnie, a massive, natural amphitheatre of semicircular precipices in three towering limestone tiers, is a world apart: the numerous caves, ice-bridges, rivers of scree, glaciers and waterfalls all contribute to its magnificent splendour.

Gavarnie and Mont Perdu (3,353m) form the highest limestone massif in Europe, while the central rock rampart provides a strong climatic barrier. The French side, with its lush vegetation and many lakes and streams, is mild and damp with heavy rainfall (2,000mm per year). The Spanish side, with its arid canyons, is hotter and drier.

■ A TOWERING WALL OF ROCK ■

The cirques de Troumouse, Estaubé and Gavarnie stretch 20km from east to west, and all face north. The rocks, all now over 3km above sea level, were once part of the seabed, but millions of years ago they were folded by immense forces and raised to their present level. The landscape was later carved by rivers, glaciers and their meltwater.

Just 800m wide at its base, but 14km around its summit, the Cirque de Gavarnie rises 1,789m and is capped by several peaks over 3,000m. The waters of the Grande Cascade, originating in Spain, plunge 420m into the cirque, and freeze during winter.

■ A MEDIEVAL MOUNTAIN PASS ■

Despite having a reputation as an impassable barrier, the Pyrenees have always seen a certain two-way flow of travellers. The Port de Boucharo (2,270m), accessible by car, is the lowest pass in the central Pyrenees; over the ages it has been travelled by pilgrims, shepherds, soldiers, bandits, smugglers, deserters and refugees.

Gavarnie, at 1,350m the highest village in the Hautes-Pyrénées, was originally an insignificant hamlet inhabited by shepherds. During the Middle Ages, a Knight Hospitallers *commanderie* (local headquarters) protected the Boucharo Pass on the pilgrim route to Santiago de Compostella. Later transformed into a church, it houses an unusual 12th-century statue of the Virgin Mary holding a pilgrim's flask.

The Prade de Gavarnie, a natural meadow between the cirque and the village, is the traditional site of the agreement of the *lies et passeries*, Franco-Spanish treaties governing grazing rights. In place since the Middle Ages (1390), these treaties reduced the conflict which had previously endangered pilgrims and travellers.

■ FLORA AND FAUNA ■

The Jardin Botanique du Parc supports 400 native species of plant, including saxifrage,

---

Parc National des Pyrénées

Although confined to a narrow alpine strip, this park is over 100km long, stretching from the Hautes-Pyrénées to the Pyrenées-Atlantiques, with hundreds of lakes and mountain torrents. The central zone (all above 1,000m) is uninhabited, although used for grazing in summer; the peripheral zone is inhabited but protected.
The park's major role is the preservation of its indigenous species and its landscape, but it is also a centre for research and public information.
Access is free and unrestricted. Each of the six major valleys has a park 'house' visitor centre.

The Brèche de Roland

The Brèche de Roland (2,807m) is traditionally the spot where the tragic hero of the 10th-century French epic *Chanson de Roland* tried to smash his faithful sword, Durandal, so that it would not fall into the hands of the Saracens who had attacked Charlemagne's rearguard as they were crossing the Pyrenees back into France. The unyielding warrior, close to death but victorious even in defeat, and standing alone on the battlefield amidst the carnage, struck the mountain three times but the blade – undamaged – merely pierced the rock, opening a gap 80m high and 50m wide.

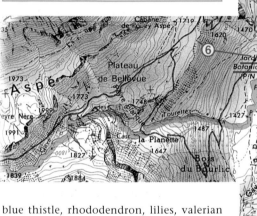

blue thistle, rhododendron, lilies, valerian and asphodel. Certain very rare flowers live only in the Gavarnie massif.

Bears, lynx and ibex are nearly extinct in the Pyrenees, but izards (goat-like antelopes) and marmots are numerous. Among the more curious inhabitants of the mountains are the trumpet-rat – a small, insectivorous, aquatic mammal with an elephant-like proboscis and a long tail – and the midwife toad, which remains a tadpole for 20 years. The central peaks are an important migratory centre, visited by Egyptian and griffon vultures, golden eagles, peregrine falcons, lammergeiers and other birds of prey.

Good places for observing the fauna and flora are the Cirque de Troumouse, a single tier of smooth, white limestone nearly 1,000m tall, and the Cirque d'Estaubé.

RIGHT: the Pas de Roland, south of Cambo-les-Bains, is one of the sites associated with the legendary hero

LEFT: exploring the rugged Parc National des Pyrénées on horseback, against a backdrop of snow-capped mountains

W A L K

length of walk: 10km
time: 1 day
IGN Top 25: sheet 17480T

This walk includes the Botanical Gardens as well as the full splendour of the cirque, with its 422m waterfall. If you prefer not to risk the steep parts of this walk, remain in the valley and go directly to the Hôtellerie du Cirque. Ask at the Maison du Parc about the weather conditions. If the course marked on the map differs from the signposts, follow the latter.

❶ Park on the outskirts of Gavarnie near the route de Boucharo and walk into the centre (Maison du Parc National and the church), then continue through the town and follow the marked path up the valley. At the **Pont Brioule**, take the left fork and cross the Gave de Gavarnie stream.

❷ Cross the bridge and turn right immediately. After about 150m the path forks again. Take the path on the left (Chemin des Espuges) which follows a small stream up the valley towards the forest. As it enters the trees, the path climbs steeply in sharp zigzags. After about 500m the path forks again. Take the path on the right towards a *Colonie de Vacances* (holiday camp).

❸ Go past the holiday camp and into the Bois de Arribama, where the path follows the contour of the hill. When you reach a clearing, continue towards **le Hount-Blanque**. From here the path follows the contours through the forest to a clearing at the base of the rocks.

❹ Go back into the forest, where the path descends to a clearing and passes a reservoir. Follow the path down to l'**Hôtellerie du Cirque**. Follow the path towards the cirque for about 100m, then take the path on the left to go into the cirque.

❺ Crossing several tiny streams, continue to the base of la Grande Cascade. Return to the Hôtellerie du Cirque along the same path.

❻ Back at the Hôtellerie, take the path on the left, through a clearing, then into the forest and another clearing. At a stream, cross the bridge and continue towards a picnic area. Take the path on the left, cross the Gave de Gavarnie over another bridge to the **Jardin Botanique du Parc**. From the gardens, take the path back towards Gavarnie. After about 100m, take the upper path on the left and return to town by the marked path.

Make sure to bring your binoculars for sightings of the majestic peregrine falcon and other birds of prey

MASSIF DU CANIGOU

***T**he Pic du Canigou, boldly presiding over all of Roussillon, is one of the most beautiful mountains in the Pyrenees. As the ultimate sentinel of the range, this massif stands alone before the mountain chain finally plunges into the Mediterranean at the Côte Vermeille.*

Mont Canigou, at a height of 2,784m and visible from great distanes both on land and at sea, was an important landmark for ancient Greek mariners who considered it to be the highest mountain in the world. Although it was exploited for iron ore in ancient and medieval times, the massif is now a protected area.

The valleys of the Tech and Têt rivers allow Mediterranean influences to penetrate deep into the massif. Canigou, drained by a multitude of mountain torrents, has distinct zones of vegetation, depending on their altitude, starting from exotic and Mediterranean species

A fiery tribute

The Pic du Canigou has special significance to the Catalan people of this region bordering Spain. This culminates in the annual Fête des Feux de la St-Jean held on the summer solstice (21 June), when the Catalans climb the mountain to mingle and light fires in commemoration of the saint.

The summit of Canigou, which can be reached on foot, is marked with a cross draped in Catalan red and gold

The elegant façades of shuttered houses in Villefranche-de-Conflent, the medieval city still trapped within its original ramparts

through mountain forests of pine, beech and birch, and finally to high alpine pastures above the treeline.

The pyramidal summit of Mont Canigou retains its snow-cap until late spring, in sharp contrast to the flowering orchards spread around its base. Poets have written of the mountain, myths still surround it and Catalans in both France and Spain venerate it. The mountain personifies the spirit of this southern land.

The Yellow Train

The Yellow Train, in its bright Catalan coat of red and yellow (blood and gold), offers a unique travel experience: Romanesque churches, medieval castles, Vauban fortifications, deep gorges, hot springs, lush forests and high mountain massifs all roll by at an incredible speed of 30kph. This is the highest railway in France, and has specifically designed rolling stock, including an open sightseeing car in summer. Open all year, there are six trains per day linking Villefranche to Latour-de-Carol (2½ hours). A round trip takes a single day.

■ SCALING THE PIC ■

There are several ways to reach the summit of Canigou, but the last section must be tackled on foot. Marked trails leave from all sides of the mountain: Vernet (GR 10) and los Masos near Valmanya (GR 36) are convenient points of departure.

Climbing Mont Canigou takes at least a full day. To avoid the heat, start early in the morning. Jeep services also depart from Prades and Vernet to Cortalets, and from there a round trip to the summit takes only about 3½ hours. From the Pic you are treated to magnificent views of France, Spain and the Mediterranean.

■ VERDANT VALLEYS ■

Surrounded by high massifs, the Conflent is a sunny and well-watered agricultural region in the narrow Têt basin, renowned for apricots, peaches, apples and cherries, as well as various wines and livestock, including horses, cattle and sheep. Villefranche-de-Conflent, caught in a gorge between steep mountain walls, is a fortified medieval city which never expanded beyond its original ramparts.

On the forested slopes of Canigou, Vernet-les-Bains, at a height of 660m, with its special Mediterranean mountain microclimate, is a famous thermal spa (open all year) known since ancient times.

Eus is a small fortified village on a terraced *solana* (southern slope). From the ruined walls of the fortifications round its quaint 18th-century church there is a splendid view of Canigou towering over peach orchards and vineyards on the slopes below.

■ DRY MEDITERRANEAN FOOTHILLS ■

The Aspres, dissected by deep dry gorges, form a crescent of rocky hills between the Têt and Tech basins. Covered by heat-loving *garrigue* plants, including fig, cactus, agave, pomegranate, olive, arbutus, cork oak, thyme, rosemary and lavender, this wild and sparsely populated region also abounds in game and wild flowers.

Small vineyards and orchards of peaches and cherries surround villages perched on sunny southern slopes. Romanesque churches as well as medieval secular architecture can be found in almost every tiny community. The Augustinian priory at Serrabone, dark and unprepossessing from the outside, has particularly fine Romanesque capitals.

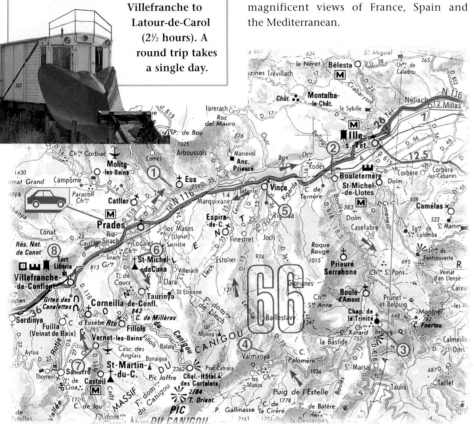

T O U R

length of tour: 125km
time: 1 day
IGN Top 250: sheet 114

This drive from Prades falls into two sections, which could be spread over two days. The first part takes in a traditional Catalan church, passing through olive groves and orchards, and following narrow gorges to a church with a 12th-century Byzantine painting. The high points of the second part are an inaccessible abbey, a beautiful Romanesque church and a small fortified town. If you decide to take two days, spend the night in Prades.

1 From Prades, take the D 35 towards Eus, passing through orchards to cross the River Têt. At **Eus**, park near the foot of the village and climb the narrow cobbled streets to the church. Afterwards, continue on the D 35 towards Marquixanes, through more orchards and olive groves.

2 Recross the River Têt and turn left on to the N 116 towards Vinça. Pass the lake, cross the railway and turn right at the first roundabout towards **Bouleternère**

where you can visit the church and the 13th-century fortifications.

3 From the village, follow the D 618 along the narrow Gorges de Boulès, where the winter torrent almost dries up in summer. After 7.5km, turn right on to the D 84 to reach **Prieuré Serrabone** (priory). Return to the D 618 and turn right towards Boule-d'Amont, where there is a Romanesque church. Continue to the Col Fourtou and turn right on to the D 618 towards Amélie-les-Bains-Palalda. Carry on to the **Chapelle de la Trinité**. This small Romanesque chapel has a magnificent door and a 12th-century Byzantine crucifixion scene.

4 Stay on the D 618 to the Col Xatard, then turn right on to the D 13 towards Valmanya. Drive past la Bastide to the Col de Palomère and then continue to **Valmanya**. You can take the GR 36 to Canigou from los Masos, 2km further up the side valley.

5 From Valmanya follow the D 13 to Baillestavy, through a narrow gorge, then orchards down to **Vinça**. Visit the medieval town, the 13th-century ramparts, and the Romanesque chapel. From Vinça, take the N 116 back to Prades via the signs to *centre ville*.

6 Cross Prades and take the D 27 to **l'Abbaye St-Michel-de-Cuxa**.

7 Continue on the D 27 towards Taurinya, pass the Col de Millères and Fillols and continue to **Vernet-les-Bains**. Go down through the village to the main road. At the *gendarmerie* turn left towards Casteil. From the far end of the village, a path leads to l'Abbaye St-Martin-du-Canigou. The path is steep but a jeep-taxi is available.

8 Return to Vernet-les-Bains, then continue on to Corneilla-de-Conflent. The 12th-century Romanesque basilica is a masterpiece. Continue past the Grottes de Canalettes to **Villefranche-de-Conflent** to visit the medieval town and fortifications. Then take the N 116 and return to Prades.

Reaching the summit of Mont Canigou

Pyrénées
Collioure

*T*he Côte Vermeille (Vermilion Coast), which encompasses Collioure, is a marriage of mountain and sea. This rocky coast of Roussillon, with its famous vineyards and fish-rich waters, offers a succession of ancient maritime cities and royal fortresses. Uncompromisingly Mediterranean, it is a rough land with a rich heart.

With its pastel houses, orange roofs, flower-filled balconies, amber beaches, blue skies and ever-present azure sea, Collioure is a colourful Catalan village blessed by both land and sea. An important Roman town, later raided by the Arabs, Collioure saw its golden age in the 14th century: the medieval city was then the main commercial port of Roussillon and its navy reigned over the entire Mediterranean. Visitors to the town can still see the colourful fleet of vividly painted Catalan barques.

Built on a rocky spur, the Château Royal separates the naturally protected bay into two small, fortified ports. Vauban refortified the castle and razed the upper town in order to build Fort Miradou.

The fortified baroque church of Notre-Dame-des-Anges, standing almost in the sea, was built to replace a former structure. Its strangely domed bell-tower was in fact a former lighthouse. Behind the church is the old Moorish district with its small, low houses and narrow, winding, cobbled streets.

■ WORKING COLLIOURE ■

Collioure is renowned for its preserved anchovies. Although the fishing boats (*lamparas* – lamp boats) are now based at Port-Vendres, the salting workshops are still in Collioure. Once landed, the fish are headed, gutted and salted according to traditional methods, and between May and August a slow fermentation occurs. When 'ripe' the fish are washed, boned, and blotted dry. Salted anchovies, an important ingredient in Catalan cuisine, are sold at the workshops in every size from small jars to large buckets.

LEFT AND BELOW: the Château Royal guards the harbour at Collioure, which is today busy with pleasure craft

■ ARTISTIC COLLIOURE ■

Numerous artists have succumbed to Collioure's charms, and the village is still a favourite place among artists and craftsmen. For Matisse, there was no bluer sky in France than at Collioure. He and Derain arrived in 1905 and other Fauvists soon followed. Later Picasso and Foujita also frequented the area. Several reproductions of Matisse's and Derain's works are displayed along a route called the Chemin du Fauvism near the sites where they were originally painted.

■ THE CÔTE VERMEILLE ■

Despite stretching just 25km, the Côte Vermeille has been important since ancient times. Celtic settlements of Collioure, Port-Vendres and Banyuls were reoccupied by the Greeks, who brought olives and vines to the region, then by the Romans.

ABOVE: the rich light of the Mediterranean continues to attract artists to Collioure

TOUR

length of tour: 105km
time: 1 day
IGN Top 250: sheet 114

This drive begins at Collioure along the Côte Vermeille, which makes an interesting excursion in itself if time is limited. The first part of the route takes winding roads through vineyards and cork oaks, via the major towns on the coast. The second part sweeps inland, taking in old towns with fascinating churches, then returns to the coast and a nature reserve. It is best to choose a clear day and to make an early start to catch the sunrise over the Mediterranean. The roads are steep and narrow.

❶ Leave Collioure and head towards Perpignan. At a roundabout, take the D 86 towards Madeloc and continue along the track up into the vineyards. At the first crossroads take the lower road to the **chapelle de Notre-Dame-de-Consolation** which contains numerous votive offerings on a maritime theme. Return to the D 86 and turn left towards **Madeloc**. There are several splendid viewpoints amongst the cork oaks. At the Col de Mollo, turn right on to the D 86 towards **Banyuls-sur-Mer**. The road climbs uphill between tidy vineyards and then past abandoned barracks. At the next crossroads, take the road on the right, past several abandoned military buildings to a small fortification. Either park here and walk (the remaining section is steep and narrow) or continue to the parking area higher up. The tower offers an exceptional panorama.

❷ Return to the D 86, and turn right to visit **Banyuls-sur-Mer**. The road winds downhill through cork oaks, then vines. At the roundabout, go to the town centre and park near the port. Now take the N 114 towards Port-Vendres, following the coast through vineyards.

❸ At the crossroads just before Port-Vendres, turn right towards Port de Commerce. At the roundabout turn right on to a small road. After 100m the road forks: the lane on the left goes to the *marine*, the one on the right to **Cap Béar**. Return to the roundabout and follow signs for the *centre ville*. Park near the fishing port, where a fishing auction takes place each afternoon. Leave the port on the N 114 towards Collioure to visit the church, castle and port.

Alternative route via the Bas-Rousisillon

❹ Leave Collioure on the N 114 towards Perpignan. At Exit 11, take the D 618 to St-André, whose Romanesque church has a splendid carved lintel. Continue to **St-Genis-des-Fontaines** and visit the cloisters.

❺ In the village, turn right on to the D 2 towards Brouilla. Cross the River Tech, turn right onto the D 40 to Brouilla, and continue to the old town of **Elne** to visit the cathedral and cloisters.

❻ Take the D 40 towards St-Cyprien, then the D 22 towards **St-Cyprien-Plage**. Turn right on to the D 81 towards Argelès-sur-Mer, past the Natural Reserve, through Argelès-Plage and back to Collioure.

The elaborate interior of the church of Notre-Dame-des-Anges

The Côte Vermeille is the southernmost and warmest region of mainland France, with mild winters, temperate summers and nearly 300 days of sun per year. Between mountain and sea, its steep slopes of terraced vineyards produce the grapes for the famous Banyuls wine, prepared using methods introduced by the Knights Templars. Its deep, fishing waters are backed by protected coves and small, bustling harbours.

BANYULS-SUR-MER

Banyuls-sur-Mer, sheltered from the northern winds, is home to numerous exotic plant species as well as a marine research station and a nature reserve. The resort was the birthplace of renowned sculptor Aristide Maillol (1861–1944), whose work *The Thinker* marks his grave. The busy harbour of Port-Vendres is the most active fishing port (anchovies, tuna, sardines) in Roussillon. There is a lively fish market every afternoon.

THE ALBÈRES

The rocky coast of the Albères is formed by the last spurs of the Pyrenees as they plunge abruptly into the Mediterranean. Capped by rugged crags overlooking the sea far below, steep slopes covered by dry thorn *garrigue* and cork oak give way to neat vineyards hugging the slopes as they stretch to the sea. Littered with watchtowers and other fortifications, the Albères offer many splendid views of the Pyrenees, Roussillon and the Côte Vermeille.

The panorama from the Tour Madeloc (652m), a medieval watchtower overlooking the coast, is most impressive.

Bas-Roussillon

The Bas-Roussillon plain, an alluvial area of intensive agriculture (apricot and peach orchards, vineyards and market-gardens), offers some very fine examples of Romanesque architecture: Elne, St-André and St-Génis are especially interesting.

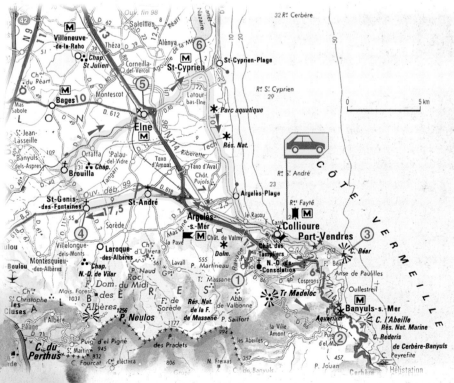

CHÂTEAU DE PEYREPERTUSE

Splendidly (and precariously) poised on a high crest of jagged limestone are the ruins of the largest and finest medieval fortress in the Corbières. Silhouetted on its spur of rock, this imposing stronghold seems to grow from the massive mountain wall itself. But the ruins are now all but lost, completely buried in dense vegetation.

A Cathar stronghold

The Château de Quéribus (right), perched on a rocky peak 728m above the Roussillon plain, was the last stronghold of Cathar resistance. In the 13th century it became a royal fortress guarding the then border of France and Aragon. The polygonal keep, with its elegant, Gothic, vaulted chamber, affords exquisite views of Roussillon, the Pyrenees, the Corbières and the Mediterranean. The massifs of Canigou and of Carlit are particularly noticeable.

Peyrepertuse, the 'pierced rock', has been an important stronghold since prehistory. First a formidable feudal fortress and then an impregnable royal citadel, it remains a bold tribute to a troubled past. The 796m summit, consisting of a long and narrow triangular spur, dominates the Corbières to the north and the Fenouillèdes lowlands to the south.

■ WHICH CASTLE? ■

The actual fortifications consist of two completely distinct, yet complementary castles surrounded by a common rampart, which encloses an area of 300m by 60m.

The lower eastern castle, the Château Bas, was the original feudal fort. Built on a slender rocky ridge, the Château Bas consists of a strong feudal keep, an adjoining fortified chapel and an inner court. The ramparts, hugging the narrow spur, are massive on the north side but consist of just a parapet above the precipice on the south.

The higher western castle, the Château St-George, overlooks the Château Bas. Separated by a craggy platform, the upper fort, 60m higher, has never been accessible by horses or even by mules. An impressive winding stairway hewn from solid rock and descending over the northern edge of the spur was the only means

LEFT: looking westwards over the dramatically sited Chateau de Peyrepertuse
INSET: Cucugnan village

of access to the royal fortress. The eerie, windswept parapet walk still seems to be keeping its watchful vigil. From near the keep there is a splendid view of the Château de Quéribus to the southeast, the Verdouble, the Pyrenees and the Mediterranean.

■ THE CORBIÈRES AND THE FENOUILLÈDES ■

The Corbières form an imposing southern crest of hard limestone cut by deep gorges and crowned by lofty feudal fortresses. These arid, rocky mountains, scorched by the southern summer sun and battered by violent winter winds, are a land of contrast: after heavy rain, usually sluggish streams may rise into terrifying torrents.

The gateway to Catalonia and Spain, the Fenouillèdes comprise a complex region of forests and wild scrub, alternating with orderly vineyards. Autumn is a particularly fine time to visit: it is not too hot and the vineyards and heathland explode with colour.

■ THE CORBIÈRES CASTLES ■

High above the plains, the austere fortresses of the Corbières are masterpieces of medieval military architecture. These so-called Cathar castles (Arques, Villerouge-Termenès, Padern, Aguilar, Peyrepertuse, Puilaurens, Quéribus, Termes) were in fact former feudal fortifications, later occupied by Cathar troops.

The latter five – the 'five sons of Carcassonne' – were later transformed into royal garrisons as advanced outposts in Carcassonne's line of defence against Aragon, then Spain. After the Treaty of the Pyrenees (1659), however. these strongholds lost all strategic value as Roussillon was annexed by France and the border moved south to its present position.

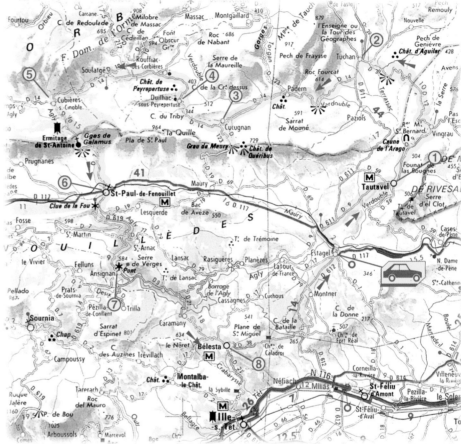

T O U R

length of tour: 110km
time: 1 day
IGN Top 250: sheet 114

This drive, starting from the town of Estagel, includes high-perched Cathar castles, thorn scrub, vineyards, a Roman aqueduct and a spectacular gorge. The castles can be dangerous in high winds, and hot in summer, so take water supplies and a hat to protect from the sun.

❶ Leave Estagel on the D 117 towards Maury. Cross the River Agly and turn right onto the D 611 towards Tautavel. The road crosses the railway and passes between vineyards. At the next crossroads take the D 9 to **Tautavel** and visit the Prehistory Museum.

❷ From Tautavel take the D 9 to Vingrau. Turn left in the centre of the village and take the D 12 towards Tuchan. The road climbs through vineyards, then scrubby heathland. The road number changes to the D 39 as it enters the Aude *département*. At a *table d'orientation*, there is a good view of the Corbières and the **Château d'Aguilar**.

❸ From Tuchan, take the D 611 towards Padern. At the roundabout, take the D 14 to Padern, then **Cucugnan**. Just after the village, turn left on to the D 123 to **Quéribus** and its castle.

❹ Return to Cucugnan and turn left on to the D 14 towards **Duilhac-sous-Peyrepertuse**. Just before the village, turn left towards the castle. Return to the D 14 and turn left towards Rouffiac-des-Corbières.

❺ Continue to Soulatgé and the tiny village of **Cubières-sur-Cinoble**.

❻ Just after Cubières, turn left on to the D 10 towards the Gorges de Galamus (restricted access, no caravans). Drive through the narrow and spectacular gorge to **St-Paul-de-Fenouillet**. At St-Paul, take the D 619 through the Clue de la Fou to Ansignan. The road fol-lows the River Agly through vineyards and scrubland. Just before the village is a remarkable two-tiered Roman aqueduct crossing the valley.

❼ In **Ansignan**, turn left just after the Arbre de la Liberté towards Caramany. Cross the River Desix and turn left on to the D 9. Cross the lake and follow the left bank.

❽ At the crossroads, turn right on to the D 21 towards Caramany. Cross the lake again, drive into the village and continue on towards **Bélesta**. Visit the Neolithic Museum and the pre-Romanesque church. In Bélesta, turn left sharply in front of the winery and take the D 38 to Col de la Bataille. At the col, turn right, then left towards the Ermitage de Força Réal, from where there is a spectacular panorama. Return to the col and take the D 612 back to Estagel.

MONTSÉGUR

*T*he Pog or Rocher (rock) de Montségur, a massive limestone peak towering several hundred metres above the surrounding valleys, overlooks and dominates its wild, mountainous setting. Perched boldly on a rocky summit, this robust medieval fortress endured one of the most famous sieges of the Middle Ages.

Rebuilt in 1204 on the site of a former feudal fortress, this Cathar stronghold was garrisoned with about a hundred knights, squires and sergeants. Montségur held out against the central powers of France for 40 years but, after its Cathar garrison had massacred the Inquisition Officers in Avignonet in 1242, its fate was sealed: an army nearly 10,000 strong arrived to besiege it.

■ THE SIEGE ■

Several months later, after scaling a sheer cliff during a long winter night, mountain troops reached the peak. They then assembled a *trebuchet* (catapult) and opened a quarry on the summit to provide stone shot. Doomed, the Cathar command sued for peace, and a truce was negotiated. The population of simple believers was banished from the *pog*, while 200 of the elite (bishop, deacons and 'perfects') who refused to recant their faith were burnt at the stake.

During the siege, treasure was supposedly smuggled out of the castle, giving rise to rumours and romantic legends involving hidden treasures, solar temples and the Holy Grail. The fall of Montségur in 1244 symbolically marked the end of the Albigensian Crusade and the submission of Languedoc to the French Crown.

■ A LOFTY FORTRESS, A LORDLY ABODE ■

As vassals of the King of France, the Lévis took Montségur and rebuilt the stronghold as both a fortress and elegant abode. Many details of the structure are very similar to the late 13th-century royal castles of the Corbières.

Constructed to follow the contours of the mountain, the 70m-long pentagonal edifice consisted of a small, rectangular keep measuring 20m by 9m and a high, crenellated rampart. Windowless and with only two small doors on the north and south, the battlements were to maintain the defence of the fortress. Originally, there was a huge, wooden

The startlingly white limestone peak rises above the greens and golds of the wooded slopes below

Looking down on the village of Montségur

The aerial view, left, shows the wild and rugged setting of this fortress on the edge of the Pyrenees

Perched on a high ridge, the 13th century-fortress, above, replaced the besieged Cathar stronghold

platform inside which probably supported a catapult. The central interior court, paved with solid rock, contained various buildings leaning against the ramparts.

■ THE VILLAGE ■

The village of Montségur (950m) nestles at the foot of the *pog* near the Gorges de Carroulet. The surrounding Lavelanet region is mountainous, with forests and pastures. Montségur is a starting point for excursions to the Pic St-Barthélemy, the Plateau de Sault, the Gorges de la Frau and the Fontaine de Fontestorbes.

The Cathars

Catharism, judged by the Roman Catholic Church as a hereticism from the East, spread rapidly in Western Europe during the 12th to 13th centuries. It became particularly radical (and political) in southern France, and was a popular religion, attracting a dissatisfied and growing proto-bourgeoisie (lower clergy, poor knights, artisans and merchants). From its religious roots, Catharism degenerated into a political struggle for the control of the Languedoc. Ironically, the only surviving legacy of the Cathars was the Inquisition.

WALK

length of walk: 8km
time: 3 hours
IGN Top 25: sheet 22470T

This walk takes in the peak of this dramatic, though peaceful, hill – with its tragic history. It follows a route that gives impressive views of the *pog* and its surrounding village. The view is magnificent at sunrise. The path round the *pog* is not particularly difficult and is shaded for a good part of the way. But take care if the weather is windy.

1 Park at the base of the village of Montségur, then walk into the centre and visit the small archaeological museum. Continue towards the cemetery and take the small lane that climbs on the far side of the main road. The lane sweeps around and returns to the main road, near a second parking area at the foot of the *pog*. The castle path, on the right near a small clump of trees, winds up the hill to the base of the fortress. The remains of a Cathar village are on the far side, at the foot of the keep. Return to the base of the *pog*.

2 Near the clump of trees, a marked path (the red and white GR 7, not the red and yellow path) leads down a small valley through the forest, taking in several sharp turns and a dry stream bed, to a makeshift stile. The path formerly continued around the hill and is still rather well-used. Cross the stile and continue through the forest to a small spring, the **Fontaine de Miegesole**. Continue down the slope over a low narrow ridge. A wider path joins the GR 7 on the left. Up to this point, the castle has been almost continually visible through the trees on the right; it now disappears from view as you cross to the far side of the ridge and continue on the marked path. At an open pasture, several paths meet. After another makeshift stile, the GR 7 continues along a former tree-lined lane across the pasture towards a ruined building. Do not cross the stile to follow the GR 7 but turn right and take the cattle path, with the red and white markings, for about 100m. The castle is once again in view on the right.

3 The cattle path winds down from the crest of the hill, then flattens out. As the path opens up, several lanes meet. Take the lane which follows the electric poles uphill towards **Serre-Longue**. Refreshments are available at the auberge.

4 Take the paved lane back towards Montségur. The lane makes a sharp bend, then descends towards the main D 9 road. At the intersection, continue uphill through the **Lasset gorge** and return to the parking area in Montségur.

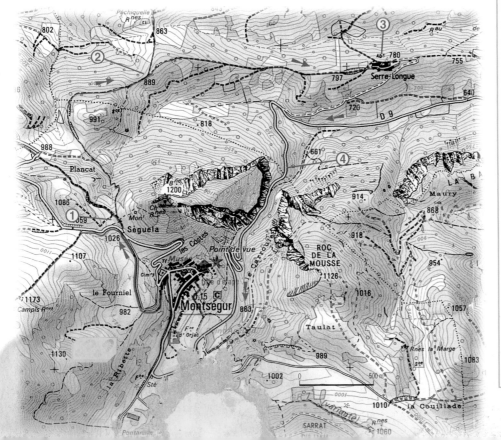

The simple but evocative monument to the Cathars in Montségur

CARCASSONNE

Carcassonne is really two towns. The Cité, solidly set into a precipitous and isolated hill, is the largest medieval fortress in Europe. The Bourg, bustling on the left bank, is a former royal stronghold nestling between the Aude and the Canal du Midi.

Commanding links between the Atlantic and the Mediterranean, Carcassonne has always been of strategic importance: Celts, Romans, Vandals, Visigoths, Arabs and Franks all battled for ownership. The Cité later bore the brunt of the Albigensian Crusade before falling to the French Crown. As the royal headquarters for the Languedoc, the fortress underwent considerable modification.

■ CITÉ: MEDIEVAL FORTRESS ■

The Cité, an extraordinary assemblage of fortifications, is unique. Without any near rivals, this medieval town appears to be frozen in time, yet is still inhabited by a working population.

The double ramparts, nearly 3km long overall, contain over 50 towers. Many were independently defendable, while others were deliberately left unprotected from the rear. With only two small entrances, the *lices* (the enclosed area between the inner and outer ramparts) became a death-trap to any would-be attackers.

Two elaborately defended gates, the Porte Narbonnaise and the Porte d'Aude, were the only means of access to the Cité. The Porte Narbonnaise, the principal and eastern gate, is a small fortress in itself with a double drawbridge.

BELOW: the Porte d'Aude is one of two gates in the outer ramparts which give access to the the medieval fortress of the Cité
LEFT AND ABOVE: musicians form part of a display in the Château Comtal

The near demise of the fortress

After the annexation of Roussillon to France (1659), Carcassonne lost all strategic importance as the border moved south to the Pyrenees and the Cité fell into disrepair. Demolition actually began in the early 19th century, with the western tower near the Porte d'Aude dismantled in 1821. The fortress was saved from doom, however, by Mérimée (the author of *Carmen*), Cros-Mayrevieille (a local archaeologist) and Viollet-le-Duc (the architect). Restoration of St-Nazaire began in 1844 and work on the ramparts continued up to the mid-20th century.

The Porte d'Aude, the western gate, was formerly protected by a large tower which allowed access to the River Aude.

Adjoining the inner ramparts near the Porte d'Aude, the Château Comtal was a third line of defence, completely independent from the town. Having been taken over by the French Crown, the original feudal castle was transformed into a strong citadel, complete with the latest military innovations of the times, including an enormous moat and a large semi-circular tower.

Detail from the superb 14th-century Tree of Jesse stained-glass window in the basilica of St-Nazaire

This elaborate wayside cross in the keep of Château Comtal is surrounded by 12th-century frescoes

The 11th- to 14th-century Basilique St-Nazaire, built on the site of a former Carolingian cathedral, comprises a mixture of styles: the nave is Romanesque but the transept and apse were Gothicised. The windows, in a pure 'Ile-de-France' style similar to Notre Dame de Paris, are considered to be the most interesting in the Midi. During restoration, Viollet-le-Duc crenellated the bell tower, mistakenly believing it to have been part of the original Visogoth ramparts.

■ THE BOURG: A ROYAL STRONGHOLD ■

Built to the traditional chessboard pattern, the Bourg (or Ville Basse) was founded in 1260 by St-Louis to replace the earlier civilian town that had been razed to the ground. The Bourg quickly outgrew the Cité in size and importance, and in turn the 17th-century Canal du Midi, followed by the 19th-century railway, secured the Bourg's status as the commercial centre of the Aude.

A wealthy town, prospering first from textiles, then from wine, the Bourg contains several fine monuments: the churches of St-Vincent and St-Michel (both 13th-century Languedocian Gothic); Pont-Vieux (14th century); Notre-Dame-de-la-Santé (15th century); Montmorency House (16th century) and the Fontaine de Neptune (18th century) are among the most notable.

The Black Prince

An impregnable fortress, the royal Cité was more than a match for the Black Prince when he raided Carcassonne in 1355. Edward of Woodstock – Earl of Chester, Duke of Cornwall and Prince of Wales – was content with merely pillaging and burning the lower civilian town. The Bourg was immediately rebuilt with stone ramparts. After the French Revolution, the ramparts were dismantled, the moat filled in and the new boulevards planted with trees.

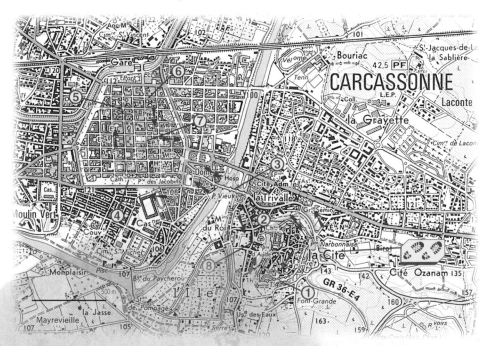

W A L K

length of walk: 8km
time: 1 day
IGN Top 25: 2345E

This walk takes in the distinct areas of old Carcassonne, the Cité and the Bourg. The whole walk, which includes a crossing of the River Aude, is a journey through the city's history. Good views of the Cité are from near the Cimetière St-Michel (to the south of the Bourg), the Plateau de Grazailles (behind the railway station) or l'École d'Agriculture Charlemagne.

❶ Park near the Porte Narbonnaise and go into the Cité by the Pont-Levis. At the Porte Narbonnaise, which houses an information centre, turn immediately right towards the 13th-century **Tour du Trésau** and enter what is now a regional wine promotion centre. The ceiling is splendid. Go back towards the Porte Narbonnaise and turn right towards the centre of the Cité. Follow rue Cros-Mayrevielle towards **Château Comtal**, then through the tower into the 12th-century castle. Leave the castle and turn right. Follow rue St-Louis to the **Basilique St-Nazaire**. From the church take rue Dame-Carcasse which runs alongside the church to place St-Nazaire. On the right, in a garden behind the basilica, is the **Grand Théâtre**. Go though the tower out onto the Lices Hautes.

❷ Turn right and follow the ramparts to Porte d'Aude. Continue around the back of Château Comtal and into the Lices Basses, which overlooks the Ville Basse. Enter the Cité by Porte de Rodez opposite the **Tour Notre-Dame**. Follow rue Notre-Dame to rue du Grand Puits and turn right towards the square and well. Then turn left on rue Viollet-le-Duc, past the tower and cross rue Cros-Mayrevielle towards place Marcou. At the far end of place Marcou, turn left back to Porte Narbonnaise.

❸ Leave the Cité and take rue Trivalle past several fine buildings, including the Renaissance Maison de Montmorency, to the **Pont-Vieux**.

❹ Go past the Bastion Montmorency, through the Portail des Jacobins and turn left into rue Voltaire towards **Cathedrale St-Michel**.

❺ Follow rue du Dr Albert Tomey to the Maison du Sénéchal, the Halle aux Grains and **St-Vincent**.

❻ Turn right into rue du 4 Septembre, then left into rue Clémençeau to the **Chapelle des Carmes**.

❼ Return along rue Clémençeau and continue to **place Carnot**.

❽ Return to the Pont-Vieux and cross the river, then turn right up rue Barbacane towards **St-Gimer**. Enter the Cité by the Porte d'Aude and take either the Lices Hautes or the Lices Basses back to the Porte Narbonnaise and the parking area.

PYRÉNÉES

LANGUEDOC

CANAL DU MIDI

Coming down from the Minervois, you first catch sight of the Canal du Midi after turning west on the Béziers road. A wall of plane trees winds through a landscape of orchards and vineyards, creating a stately, bucolic vision, rather like an 18th-century landscape.

Shady trees flank the locks of the Canal du Midi at Castel Naudary

The canal is in some ways like an aristocratic garden, dappled with sun and shade, silent except for the murmuring leaves and twittering birds, and unruffled by human chaos. It is also a marvel of civil engineering and one of the Ancien Régime's greatest public works. The idea of connecting the Atlantic and Mediterranean coasts of France via a navigable waterway, thereby avoiding a long and hazardous sea passage around Spain, goes back to Roman times, but it was not until the 17th century that the science of canal-building was sufficiently advanced to make such an immense undertaking possible. Even then it might well have remained a dream had it not been for one man who pos-

sessed the talents of a financier, an engineer, a general and a visionary – along with the fortune of an extremely wealthy provincial gentleman.

■ RIQUET'S OBSESSION ■

Pierre-Paul Riquet, whose statue stands on the main boulevard of his native Béziers, was Languedoc's *fermier général*. Under the pre-Revolutionary fiscal system, he paid the province's taxes out of his own pocket and reimbursed himself by collecting from his fellows. The inspiration to dig a canal to the navigable, Atlantic-bound Garonne at Toulouse seems to have come to him in his fifties. By 1666 he had persuaded Louis XIV's

finance minister, Colbert, to approve his project and to grant him and his heirs sole ownership of the future canal in perpetuity. It was, in effect, the last of the royal fiefs and one of the first great capitalist undertakings.

The canal took 15 years to build. Riquet sank his fortune into it, and solved every financial, human and technical problem that

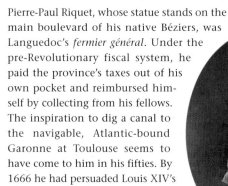

Pierre-Paul Riquet, left, supervised the construction of the Canal du Midi, which passes through Béziers, his birthplace, by means of an aqueduct, below. A statue in the town commemorates his achievements

arose. There were many, beginning with the question of where to find the water to fill the canal – it was eventually brought down from the Montagne Noire at Naurouze, the highest point on the canal at 192m above sea level. He had just finished digging the tunnel at Malpas when word arrived that Louis XIV, alarmed at the staggering cost of the project, had ordered a halt to construction. But Riquet managed to get the order rescinded and carried on. In 1681 he died, heavily in debt. The canal reached the sea a month later.

■ A TRIUMPH ■

In the end Riquet was vindicated. The canal was a triumph, transforming the economy of both Languedoc and Roussillon. Fortunes were made as barges laden with barrels of wine went up to Toulouse and returned with wheat. But what is most remarkable is that the canal, with its 57 locks, its aqueducts and bridges, quays and towpaths, is still in use. More than three centuries after its construction, it teaches a vital lesson: great public works essential to a nation's economy need not destroy the environment.

■ THE OPPIDUM D'ENSÉRUNE ■

The *oppidum* (Roman for a fortified hilltop town) is ancient. Its earliest settlers arrived in the 6th century BC and, judging from shards of pottery found on the site, traded with

---

Drains built to last

Northwest of Colombiers (best seen from the *oppidum*) the fields form a circle about a kilometre wide, divided into thin wedges. A work of art? An irrigation project? It is in fact a drainage system in what used to be a swamp. From the centre of the circle a ditch runs south, traversing the Pas de Malpas 20m under the canal tunnel and a further 10m under the 1858 railway tunnel beneath the canal. It was dug in 1270!

Spain and Greece. Two cisterns and the foundations of early dwellings can be seen along the southern rim of the hill – small stone rectangles, hardly bigger than a closet, each with its buried earthenware jar for storing grain.

Destroyed by Hannibal in the 3rd century BC, the town was rebuilt and prospered under the Romans – as can be seen from the remains of far more elaborate houses built along a terrace on the north side. But the building of the *Via Domitiana*, the great military road to Spain (a section of which survives 2km southwest, just off the road from Poilhés to Nissan-lez-Ensérunne), was its downfall. The road made the surrounding plain safe, and as a result villages sprang up below and the hill-dwellers moved down and settled closer to their fields and orchards.

WALK

length of walk: 6km
time: 2 hours
IGN Top 25: sheet 2545ET

This is an easy walk, cool and pleasant along the canal but hot work on the road up to the oppidum – especially if you are have small children. But it's worth it, as the view from the hill is superb.

❶ The walk starts at the village of **Colombiers**, west of Béziers, on the N 9. Park on the north side of the canal and head due west on foot along the towpath. Continue in the green shade of the stately plane trees on either side of the canal until, about 500m beyond the last houses of the village, the path slopes up slightly, then forks. Take the left-hand path down the tunnel of **le Malpas** (which could be translated 'dire straits'). The more adventurous can try the walkway in the tunnel.

❷ Return to the fork, turn left, uphill, and carry on until you reach the road above the tunnel. Keep straight on, winding up the slope between cypress and olive trees, towards the **Oppidum d'Ensérune**. At the car park, turn left on the footpath leading through the iron gate.

❸ Return to the Malpas junction, cross to the other side of the canal and turn left onto the small road to back to Colombiers. Enter the town along the tree-lined rue de l'Oppidum. At the church, turn left onto rue des Douches, then down to the pretty, humped-back bridge over the canal.

The canal, once busy with commercial barge traffic, passes through peaceful villages such as Quarante

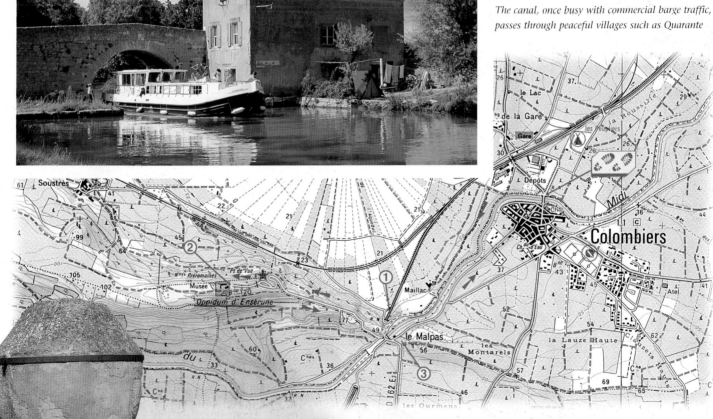

MONTPELLIER-LE-VIEUX

The last thing you would expect to find on one of the Grand Causses is a garden, but Montpellier-le-Vieux is just that: a garden designed by a Zen-Buddhist monk with a passion for Surrealism.

As you travel up the road crossing the Causse Noir from the Dourbie valley to the Jonte and Tarn gorges, you reach a dense forest of young pines covering a series of gentle rises. Turning left onto the road signposted Montpellier-le-Vieux and Millau, you might think that you have left behind the dry wilderness and from now on the landscape will be less wild. Even though you may spot several bizarrely-silhouetted rocks on the horizon to your left, the abiding impression is that you have strayed, by some strange geographical trick, into pleasant Alpine foothills. Then the wood ends. A sign points left, you pass a shady roadside café and,

a few hundred metres further on, you reach a car park on the edge of another wood. A short walk brings you to a ticket booth and, after you have paid your fee and gone a little further down the road, you suddenly find yourself on the perimeter of what appears to be a ruined city invaded by trees.

■ A WORLD APART ■

There is in fact nothing artificial about Montpellier-le-Vieux. The drovers – who are said to have named it – may never have seen anything larger than a small town, but they had certainly heard of the bewildering maze of avenues and alleyways in the Languedoc's capital, and perhaps of dangers lurking there as well, and they decided that this chaotic jumble of natural ruins, once a lair of wolves, was in its way a metropolis too – albeit devastated.

The curious thing is that no one knew of Montpellier-le-Vieux until it was 'discovered' in 1883, apart from the drovers who may have sheltered in the caves of Montpellier-le-Vieux on their way from the lower Languedoc to the high pastures of the Aubrac. Two years later the founder of modern speleology, Edouard-Alfred Martel, charted its warren of gullies, tumbled *cirques* and weirdly eroded towers and keeps.

An eerie experience

The best time to visit Montpellier-le-Vieux is in the late afternoon on a clear day, when the sun, beginning its descent above the Dourbie gorge, casts the rocks into jagged relief and brings out the sweet smells of the vegetation. A strange thing happens as you wander through its maze: your eyes, sharpened by the strangeness of the place and the fantastic shapes of the rocks, begin to pick out details – the squiggle of a root, the ochre tones of a rock in the sun, the deepening green shadow at the foot of a twisting pine. The experience is strangely evocative.

RIGHT: *strange rock formations of Montpellier-le-Vieux; above, this wild area is the habitat of the rare lammergeier, or bearded vulture*

▪ CREATION ▪

The seemingly capricious geological process that shaped the chaos of Montpellier-le-Vieux is very similar to that which carved out the Grottes de l'Aven Armand and the Jonte and Tarn gorges: live water gnawing away at limestone. The rock here is dolomitic, which means that it contains both calcite and magnesite. Calcite, which is more soluble than magnesite, dissolves faster and breaks down into relatively fertile calcareous clay. Hence the strange, rounded shapes of the rocks and the plant life: pines and holm oaks, boxwood, junipers, holly and arbutus.

▪ ERMITAGE ST-MICHEL ▪

Like Tibet, early Christian Europe had its share of solitary hermits who withdrew to almost inaccessible spots in order to spend years of prayer and meditation close to the sky. The ruins of the Ermitage St-Michel, a pre-Romanesque hermitage, stand on the northern rim of the Causse Noire, on a rocky spur jutting out high above one of the nar-

A series of well-marked paths make the rock formations of the Dourbie valley readily accessible

rowest bends of the River Jonte. To reach it, drive about 9km east from Montpellier-le-Vieux on the D 29, turn left just before the turning to the ruined church of St-Jean-de-Balmes onto a forest track marked by a Club Alpin Français plaque. Continue in a northerly direction for 2.5km to the car park by the toadstool-shaped rock called le Champignon Préhistorique.

The walk to the hermitage and back takes an hour, along a well-marked path to a col, from which you can climb, via metal rungs, to the ruins. From the top you can look straight down to the canyon floor 300m below. There is a magnificent view of the escarpment of the Causse Méjean above le Truel, where the Pyrenees vultures, which have been reintroduced to these parts, make their nests. You may even glimpse one of these rare birds of prey, with a wing span of up to 3m, wheeling high above the canyon.

A graceful arch spans the river in the Dourbie valley

W A L K

length of walk: 2km
time: 45 minutes
IGN Top 25: sheet 2540E

A number of well-marked trails loop through Montpellier-le-Vieux, and if you stick to them it is impossible to get lost. The shortest is the blue trail which leads, via a short flight of stairs, directly to the rock known as the Belvédère. Non-walkers and families with small children can take the little train that leaves just west of the car park. It takes you to the Belvédère, the caves and the woods just below the Porte de Mycènes.

❶ Follow the blue trail as far as the **Belvédère**, from the top of which is a magnificent view of the Dourbie valley.

❷ After descending from the lookout point, cross the bridge over the ravine and turn right onto the path than runs parallel to the paved road, but slightly above it. After passing several caves (and, if the weather is hot, enjoying their cool shade), turn north below the rock known as **Porte de Mycènes**.

❸ The path narrows as you climb steeply towards the rocky ridge of the **Rempart**, from where you look down over the maze of Montpellier-le-Vieux and the ravines to the south, west and east.

❹ After a further 200m, you reach **le Douminal**, the biggest of Montpellier-le-Vieux's monumental rocks. Climb the steep stairs that lead to its top for another spectacular view. Return by descending the ravine at the foot of le Douminal until you rejoin the blue trail, then turn right, back to the car park.

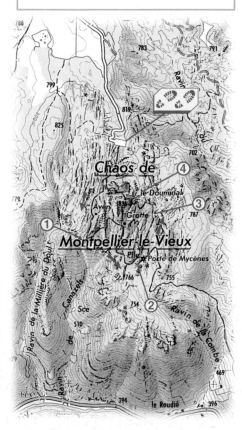

CAUSSE DU LARZAC

*A*pproaching from the olive trees of the Midi to the summit of the great Pas de l'Escalette, the landscape changes suddenly, as if you've strayed into a stony desert. There are no trees or houses, the land neither rises nor falls, and even the sky, which seems higher here, stands back, as if recoiling from the desolation below.

ABOVE: *visitors explore the sunny village centre of la Couvertoirade and below, the view over the roof tops from the medieval ramparts looking east*

The Larzac is actually a much less empty than at first it appears. It is the largest and most southerly of the great *causses* that extend south of the central plateau of France to the Languedoc. The *causses* are limestone plateaux with rivers that burrow deep in canyons and underground waterways, leaving the pastures above permanently parched. The get their name from the Provençal word for lime – *cau*. The winter here is long and bitter, the summer mercilessly hot, so the vegetation is hardy, made up of grass as tough as wire and prickly scrub. Only creatures that can make do on the meanest of diets thrive here.

■ TIMELESS TRANQUILLITY ■

The Larzac has hardly been touched by the events that have shaken the rest of Europe since the Middle Ages. Its walled villages are virtually intact: la Couvertoirade to the south (where the only building in ruins is the Templars' Castle), Ste-Eulalie-du-Cernon with its charming Provençal square and, to the west, the small, silent and perfectly preserved fortress of St-Jean-d'Alcas.

Walled villages of Larzac

In the early 12th century, the Knights Templars were granted large territories on the Larzac, where they built fortresses, guarded the route from the north of France to the Languedoc and Spain, and raised sheep and battle chargers for the Crusades. They prospered and provided protection for the Caussenards, who built villages in the shelter of their strongholds. It was only some two centuries later, during the turmoil of the Hundred Years War, long after the order of the Templars had been dissolved and their castles and lands had been handed over to their rival military order, the Hospitaller Knights of St John, that the villages were fortified.

T O U R

length of tour: 120km
time: half to one day
IGN Top 250: sheet 114

This suggested loop offers many sights to enjoy along the way, so allow yourself plenty of time, as you will doubtless decide to linger in Roquefort. The Templar towns are also well worth visiting.

❶ Start at la Pezade, the first village of the Aveyron *département*, north of Pas de l'Escalette. Turn left onto the D 7 which runs west along a rise commanding some fine views of the southern Larzac. After a while the road twists down steeply to **Cornus**, at the foot of the Larzac's southern escarpment.

❷ Stay on the D 7, following the River Sorgues and its pleasant green valley, to **St-Félix-de-Sorgues**.

❸ Turn right onto the D 516 towards **St-Jean-et-St-Paul**, the Templars' westernmost stronghold on the Larzac. The village was fortified by the same builder who walled Ste-Eulalie-de-Cernon and la Couvertoirade. Leave St-Jean-et-St-Paul and follow the D 93 and D 516 to **Roquefort-sur-Soulzon**. Bear left after 2km on the D 293 through **St-Jean-d'Alcapiès**.

❹ At the main road (D 992) turn right, then right again at Lauras, onto the D 23. Follow the D 23 east from Roquefort, through Tournemire and Viala-Pas-de-Jaux. At the crossroads with the D 77, turn left to **Ste-Eulalie-de-Cernon**, the main Templars' town on the Larzac and well worth visiting.

❺ Return to the crossroads, turn left onto the D 277 to **la Cavalerie**, to enjoy the view of the Cernon valley from the cliff road. At la Cavalerie, cross the N 9 and continue eastwards on the D 999, past extensive army training grounds, straight through the driest section of the Larzac, then down a spectacular section of road to the valley of the River Dourbie.

❻ At Nant, turn right onto the D 55 to the walled village of **la Couvertoirade**. Return to la Pezade, the start of the drive, via the village of le Caylar.

▪ WHITE GOLD OF THE CAUSSES ▪

There are thousands of sheep on the Larzac and its neighbouring *causses*, outnumbering the humans by a long way. They have occupied these lands continuously since before Roman times, and have contributed to their transformation into desert (trees do not grow where sheep graze), while at the same time keeping them alive.

There are not many farms on the *causses*, but when you do come across one, generally on the edge of a *sotch* – a dip in the land where rye grows in the red clay earth – it is huge. In times past, the farmhouses were built above sheepcotes, so that during the lambing season the farmer was never more than a few metres away from the ewes giving birth. Now the flocks winter in great hangars which are virtually factories for the production of the 'white gold' of the *causses*: ewes' milk, the essential ingredient – with a pinch of *Penicillium roqueforti* – of Roquefort, the 'queen of cheeses'. This famous cheese is aged in cellars and caves in the eponymous village. Roquefort is a delicacy, but also big business as it is the economic hub of an area covering several thousand square kilometres.

Of course it is unfair to reduce the *causses* to a cheese, however delicious. If the growth of Roquefort production (now running to about 20,000 tonnes annually) is a kind of economic miracle, and one that has kept the Caussenards on their ancestral lands, the real miracle here is the spare, timeless beauty of the landscape.

▪ ROQUEFORT ▪

If you do not mind crowds and outright commercialism of the 'Roque 'n' Roll' sandwich bar variety, Roquefort is a convenient place for lunch. The town nestles at the foot of a cliff high above the River Soulzon and is one of only a few places offering a bird's-eye view of the Larzac (climb to the viewpoint at the Rocher St-Pierre above the Société car park).

It is not so much for the vista (or the cheese) as for the caves that anyone visits Roquefort. The town is built on a huge chunk of collapsed limestone, fissured and broken into dozens of separate blocks. The passageways between these blocks are ventilated by thousands of cracks in the rock and keep an even, moist temperature of 8°C – ideal conditions for ageing the 2.5kg wheels of cheese packed together on long oak racks.

Roquefort-sur-Soulzon, lies on wooded slopes in the shelter of towering limestone cliffs, and the town's famous cheese is matured on long oak racks within cellars and caves, below

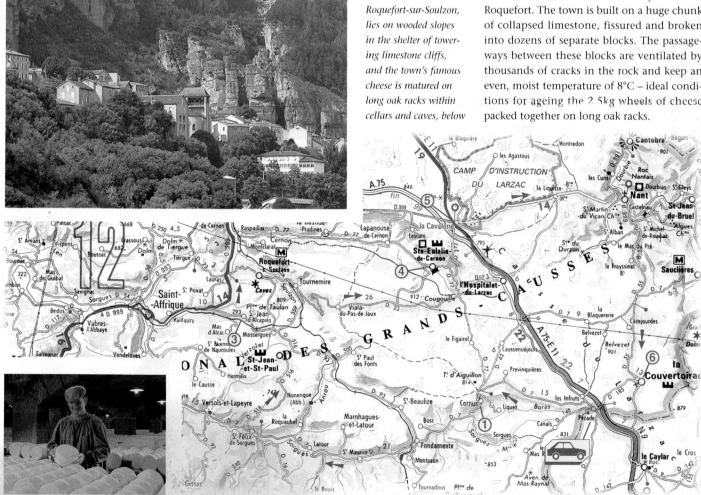

LANGUEDOC

GORGES DU TARN

*T*he canyon of the River Tarn, like those of the Jonte to the south and the Dourbie to the east, is inseparable from the high, limestone plateaux through which it cuts so dramatically.

The terrain in this area is a maze of varying landscapes. The *causses* are desert-like, horizontal, windswept plateaux with few colours, while the gorges are precipitous and sheltered, their shapes and hues infinitely varied. The underlying rock is made up of soluble limestone mingled with a more resistant magnesium carbonate, and the torrents that rush down from the mountains of the Cévennes, through the faults and fissures of this sedimentary deposit, erode it at different rates and in different ways. This results in *cirques* (corries or amphitheatres), hollowed cliffs, caves, and strangely shaped pinnacles.

On their lower levels, the gorges can be as green and life-sustaining as their grey and russet cornices, towering as high as 500m, are forbidding and arid.

BELOW: the rugged limestone landscape of the Gorges de la Jonte is typical of the region
INSET: the picturesque village of Ste-Enimie slopes steeply down to the River Tarn

The chaste Ste-Enimie

Ste-Enimie, a beautiful Merovingian princess, was stricken with leprosy as a miraculous, though drastic, way of discouraging a host of suitors and preserving her chastity. By an even greater miracle, she was then cured when bathing in a pool formed by water gushing from the site of the present Fontaine de Burle on the slope above the village. The hermitage where she is said to have spent the rest of her life in prayer can be reached by driving 2.5km up the D 986 and walking down to the little chapel below (enquire at the presbytery in town for the key).

■ HIDDEN VILLAGES ■

Where side valleys meet the canyon, tracks lead down from the *causses*. Villages, often dominated by a castle and most possessing an old, stone, hump-backed bridge, perch on terraces above or below the ancient road that runs alongside the torrent. Nearly every village has a Romanesque church and a maze of narrow, cobbled streets between flinty, stone-roofed houses. There are never more than a few hundred inhabitants to a village –

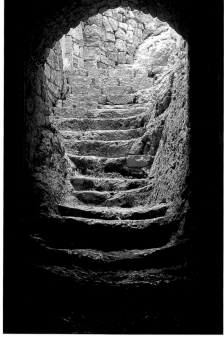

often considerably fewer – whereas the sheep that graze on the *causses*, in flocks owned by some of these few villagers, can easily number many thousands.

▪ STE-ENIMIE ▪

The upper, medieval part of Ste-Enimie contains several very old houses; one of them, the Vieux Logis, has been furnished to show how the villagers lived before progress caught up with them. The 12th-century church boasts a fine, Gothic statue of the Virgin Mary and a mark, visible on the wall by the font, left by the waters of the Tarn during the famous flood of 29 September 1900. The modern part of the village stands closer to the river. The early inhabitants knew better than to build that far down.

The monastery above the village, the foundations of which date back to AD 536, is associated with the legend of Ste-Enimie. Its remains have been rebuilt and now house a school, but the Romanesque chapter room has been preserved in its original state and is open to visitors.

Take care when exploring the narrow passages and flights of steps (left) of medieval Ste-Enimie, as the stones are well-worn with age

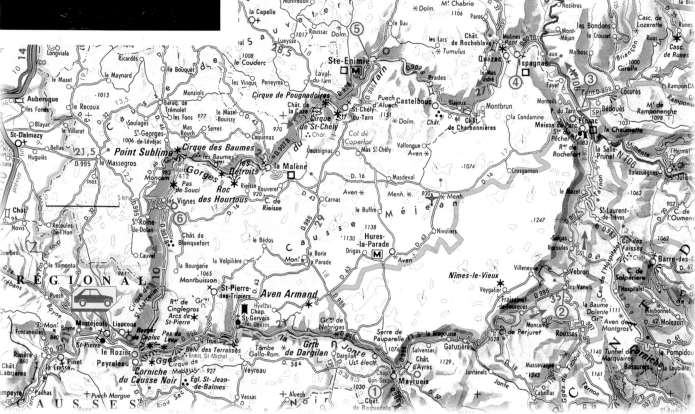

TOUR

length of tour: 150km
time: 1 day
IGN Top 250: sheet 111

Apart from kayaking or trekking one of the dozens of well-marked trails along the escarpments or the river, the most convenient way of visiting the gorges is by circling the Causse Méjean by car.

❶ Start at **le Rozier**, at the junction of the rivers Tarn and Jonte (21km northeast of Millau), heading due east on the D 996. The tourist office is on the left as you leave town. The lower reaches of the Gorges de la Jonte are impressive and you can get a good view of them from the Terraces du Truel. Just before you reach le Maynial, the road forks. Keep right if you want to continue along the gorge. Alternatively, from the D 996, turn left onto the D 63 for a steep drive up to the Causse Méjean (see also pages 150–1) along the Ravin des Bastides, as far as La Parade, then right onto the D 98b and back down to the Jonte at **Meyrueis**. (This adds 20km to the itinerary, but the drive on the bare plateau and the view as you descend towards Meyrueis makes it well worth it.)

❷ At Meyrueis, turn left and resume your drive on the D 996. The valley of the Jonte gets wider, greener and more alpine as you climb up towards the Col du Peyronnet. When you reach the top of this pass, just over 1,000m high, the landscape changes dramatically. Far to the east the Cévennes mountains form the horizon, and on your left the tawny cliffs of the Méjean will remind you of all the cowboy and Indian films you have ever seen. As you descend, the houses are the typical stone dwellings of the Cévennes, built with alternating bands of round grey and flat ochre stones. At **les Vanels**, turn left onto the D 907 and follow the Tarnon, which winds through fields and orchards as far as Florac where it joins the Tarn.

❸ At the entrance to **Florac**, cross the bridge, then turn left on to the N 106.

❹ Roughly 3km after Pont du Tarn, turn left again on to the D 907b towards **Ispagnac**, where you enter the deep gorge looping back, to the north and west of the Causse Méjean, to le Rozier.

❺ From here on there are many places you will want to visit: the 12th-century church at Ispagnac, the Gothic bridge at Quézac, the views of the village of Montbrun, further on, the ruined castle of **Castelbouc** on the slope across the river, and the 13th-century castle of Prades. Continuing along the main road (D 907b) are the villages of **Ste-Enimie**, St-Chély, Pougnadoires, the 15th-century Château de la Caze, and the viewpoint above the rapids at Pas de Souci.

❻ At **les Vignes**, you may want to climb the seven hairpin bends of the D 995 to St-Georges-de-Lévéjac and appreciate the breathtaking view from the Point Sublime. Then rejoin the D 907b and head south, past the ruined stronghold of Blanquefort and the great rock of Cinglegros, back to le Rozier.

ABBAYE DE CONQUES

*P*artway up the slope of an ancient cirque at the junction of two gorges, in a deserted corner of the old province of Rouergue, stands one of the supreme examples of Romanesque architecture – the abbey church of Ste-Foy at Conques.

For those who are accustomed to the more ornate cathedrals north of the Loire, Conques may seem at first glance somewhat austere, if not indeed stark. Its tall, narrow façade, flanked by twin square towers, makes only the most minor of concessions – a plain round moulding here, a slender, unadorned column there – to the universal craving for ornamentation. This is religious art at its most understated.

The abbey church of Ste-Foy at Conques attracted countless pilgrims from the 11th to the 13th centuries

As you enter the church, you see a nave disproportionately tall, bare and simple – yet what power it has, and how it soars!

■ SIMPLE GRANDEUR ■

The quiet beauty of Conques unfurls itself slowly. For example, the stained-glass windows – designed by Pierre Soulages and recently installed in the church's lofty bays – may at first seem dull and lifeless. Then as you gaze at the simplicity of the shattered black ripples on an opaque white background, you begin to see them come to life under the shifting light.

ABOVE: Lush hills surround Conques

Similarly, the variegated walls subtly combine greenish schists with blocks of sandstone ranging through every tone from honey gold to deepest orange. If you visit the abbey church early in the day, you'll want to come back later to see how the light and the colours intensify at sunset; if your first sight of it is in the afternoon, you'll want to spend the night in the lovely, unspoiled village and wander around the church in the morning.

■ THEFT OF A SAINT ■

The history of Conques goes back to the 8th century when, according to the *Book of Miracles of Ste-Foy*, compiled shortly after the year 1000, a hermit called Deodatus ('Godgiven') withdrew to the wilderness by the River Dourdou. He was soon joined by others of similar resolve, and together they formed a struggling community that would doubtless have disappeared after a few decades had it not been for a daring and enterprising young monk. Having gained admission to a rival monastery, the friar made off with the bones of Ste-Foy, a 12-year-old girl who had been martyred several centuries earlier in Agen and was revered throughout Aquitaine. Armed with this precious relic and the patronage of the emperor Charlemagne, Conques prospered.

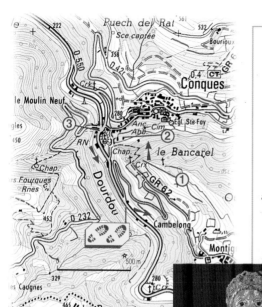

Saving graces

The decline of the pilgrimages marked the end of Conques' glory. However, thanks to the devotion of the townspeople and to its position well away from main roads and big cities, the abbey survived the Hundred Years War, the Wars of Religion and the French Revolution. Every time its fabulous treasure whetted a plunderer's appetite, the local inhabitants stashed it away in hiding places in the surrounding woods. Its jewel-studded processional crosses and reliquaries – including those of Ste-Foy herself – are displayed in the museum behind the arcade, which is all that remains of the cloisters.

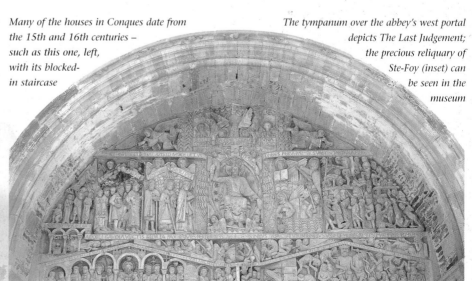

Under the abbot, Bégon III, who headed the monastery from 1087 to 1107, the cloisters were built and the abbey church rose to a height hitherto seen only in the great churches of St-Sernin in Toulouse and St Iago de Compostella. For like them, Conques had become a major shrine in the circuit of holy places visited by the millions of pilgrims who streamed through southern Europe in the 12th and 13th centuries.

▪ THE TYMPANUM OF THE LAST JUDGEMENT ▪

In the southern Romanesque tradition, the monumental, stone carving above the church portal – a masterpiece of 12th-century sculpture – combines high purpose with low comedy. Its message is stern, commit one of the seven deadly sins and you are in for a rough time in the hereafter, and was driven home with a forcefulness plain enough to be understood by the throngs of pilgrims, many of whom were illiterate and spoke many different languages and dialects. There is no mistaking the majesty of Christ enthroned in the centre, his right hand raised to bless the righteous, his left palm down to consign sinners to eternal fire.

Immediately below his feet are the scales of the Last Judgement, tipped towards virtue despite the efforts of the leering demon who is pressing his thumb down on one of the trays. The arcade in the triangle on the far left, between the bottom and the middle sec-

W A L K

length of walk: 3.5km
time: half a day
IGN Top 25: sheet 2338E

Like all pilgrimage towns, Conques is best approached on foot. This walk follows part of the route once trodden by pilgrims to the abbey. Spare some time to discover its attractive setting as well as the interior.

❶ Coming from the south, on the D 901 from Rodez, turn right (about 500m before the Conques bridge), onto a steeply climbing road signposted Montignac. At the third hairpin bend, bear left. Park by the stone cross of **Bancarel**. The abbey and the village of Conques lie directly across the gorge. The view is best seen in the golden light of late afternoon.

❷ Follow the path to the right of the cross, winding down through a chestnut wood. The brook running along the bottom of the valley is called the **Ouche**. After crossing the **footbridge**, turn right onto the path towards the abbey. This brings you to a paved lane that leads to the square in front of the church.

❸ After visiting the abbey and the village, leave by the pilgrimage route along **rue Charlemagne**. Shortly after the **Du Barry gate**, take the left road down towards the Romanesque bridge over the River Dourdou. *Do not cross the bridge.* Turn left onto the D 901 and continue south until you reach the Montignac turning. A 15-minute climb will bring you back to your car.

tions, represents the abbey church itself, with Ste-Foy prostrating herself before the hand of God.

The circular objects hanging from the arches are shackles. Ste-Foy was the patron saint of prisoners, and those who were set free after praying to her would make a pilgrimage to Conques and hang up their chains in the church in thanksgiving. Tradition has it that the handsome choir grille in the church was forged from prisoners' manacles.

Many of the houses in Conques date from the 15th and 16th centuries – such as this one, left, with its blocked-in staircase

The tympanum over the abbey's west portal depicts The Last Judgement; the precious reliquary of Ste-Foy (inset) can be seen in the museum

L'AUBRAC

There are no peaks on the Aubrac, no tortuous escarpments such as you find along the causses to the south – only granite boulders, lakes and lean high pastures as far as the eye can see.

ABOVE: the seasonal migration of the herds of cattle from the lowland meadows to the high summer pastures is still celebrated in the village of Aubrac

Here the winds blow harshly and there is no shelter, except in the lee of the boulders left from the last glaciation. Yet even in winter the highlands of the Aubrac, over 1,200m high, have an almost dreamy gentleness. This is the least French of French landscapes, instead resembling parts of Scotland and thus at its best in autumn and spring, when the snow melts and the wild daffodils flower.

Cheese and knives

Ironically, many of today's visitors come to Aubrac not to recover from the effects of over-indulgence, but to feast on a local specialty, *l'aligot*, a dish of mashed potatoes with large amounts of fresh cheese, cream, butter and crushed garlic. It makes a delicious meal but is best followed by an energetic walk. Near by is the town of Laguiole, famous for its beautiful trademark knives. Made by local craftsmen, the ivory- or horn-handled knives make excellent souvenirs of the area.

◾ OVER THE YEARS ◾

This was once a thick forest covered the whole plateau, but the monks began burning it and cutting it down, and local landowners, who found more profit in pastures than in woods, quickly followed suit. By the time of the French Revolution, the Aubrac had become a vast grazing land for herds of cows and sheep, brought up to its meadows in huge droves from as far away as the plains of the Languedoc.

As late as 1928, it housed over 300 *burons* – summer farms where the drovers slept overnight and made the cheese for which the region is still famous. By the 1870s the old ways were dying out, killed off by industrialisation. During the 20th century, the Aubrac has lost three-quarters of its population, mostly to big cities, and is now one of France's least-populated areas.

◾ AUBRAC VILLAGE ◾

The village of Aubrac owes its existence to the pilgrims who tramped the oldest and most dangerous of the routes to Santiago de Compostella. In the early 12th century, when throngs of men and women poured across Europe to worship at the shrine of the apostle

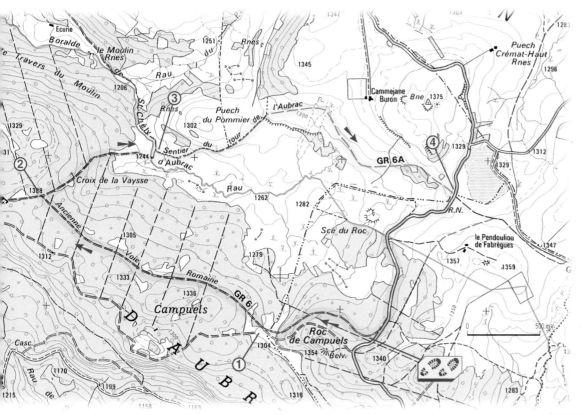

Gascon and English looters. A fine view of these rather severe-looking remains can be had from the *draille* (cattle trail) leading east from the village.

In around 1900, the village of Aubrac enjoyed a kind of renaissance as it became a health resort for city-dwellers who came for a cure of mountain air and whey, which was reputed to be effective for liver and kidney ailments. The town's hotels date from this period, as does the sanatorium (now turned into a holiday centre), sadly impossible to miss on arriving in Aubrac from the road to Nasbinals.

BELOW: the village of Aubrac, one of many on the pilgrimage route to Santiago de Compostella

James, the Aubrac was covered by a forest 'so horrible and terrifying', in the words of one traveller – it was infested with wolves and bandits – that the Count of Flanders established a hospice deep in its heart to offer shelter.

BELOW: L'Aubrac, now a tranquil area of high pastures criss-crossed by drystone walls, was once covered by a dense forest

■ AUBRAC AND CATTLE ■

Aubrac is still an important cattle-droving centre, celebrating the centuries-old tradition of moving cattle annually from the lowlands to high mountain pastures in the last week of May. Towards the end of the 17th century the hospice, built in the 12th century by the Count of Flanders, fell into disuse – except for the occasional shepherd camping in its ruins. All that remains is the austere Romanesque church, built around 1220, and the Tour des Anglais, erected in the following century to defend Aubrac from marauding bands of

W A L K

length of walk: 8km
time: half a day
IGN Top 25: sheet 25380

This walk gives a good impression of the nature of l'Aubrac. It is not difficult, but waterproof hiking shoes are recommended, as the meadows can be soggy in wet weather. For a shorter walk (about 2km), start out as below, but at the first clearing turn right onto the Roman road and return to the D 219, then right again to the picnic area.

❶ The starting point is at the **Roc de Campuels** picnic area to the right of the road 600m after it enters the Forêt Domaniale d'Aubrac. Take in the view from the top of the rise, said to have been a lookout point for robbers who preyed on isolated pilgrims bound for the hospice of Aubrac. Then return to the car park and take the right-hand trail northwest through a wood of stunted beech trees. A short walk brings you to the **ancienne voie Romaine** (old Roman road) that crossed l'Aubrac from east to west. Cross the meadow, past a granite milestone, to the woods on the opposite side. The rough Roman paving stones are clearly visible.

❷ Follow the Roman road for 2km until you come to the GR 6 hiking trail as it runs past a small wooden shack. Turn right and follow the red and white markers of the GR 6 straight downhill, ignoring the two trails leading back into the woods to the right. After a further 500m you pass a wooden cross on your left. As you emerge from the woods you can see the village of Aubrac in the distance.

❸ Continue for about 100m beyond the wooden bridge over the brook at the bottom of the meadow, then leave the trail to Aubrac. Turn right on to the GR 6A and keep to the brook side, following the dry stone wall skirting the hill (**Puech du Pommier**) for about 800m. When you are still about 50m from the wood at the end of the wall, turn right and head directly east, across the meadow, until you see a stone farmhouse and barn on the ridge above the D 219. The GR markers are difficult to spot here, but the road is clearly visible.

❹ Turn right onto the D 219 to return to the picnic area of Roc de Campuels about 2km down the road.

GROTTES DE L'AVEN ARMAND

Looking out over the Causse Méjean a few kilometres south of the grey village of la Parade – taking in as austere a landscape as any in France – you would never suspect that an enchanted forest lay beneath your feet.

No one had the slightest idea that les Grottes de l'Aven Armand were there before the end of the 19th century when Louis Armand, a locksmith from le Rozier, ventured down the shaft of one of the plateau's countless *avens* (the local term for pot-holes) and returned, wildly excited, declaring, 'I've stumbled on a supreme hole, surely one of the best...'

For years, Armand had been exploring the *causses* and the gorges around them, along with Edouard-Alfred Martel – a Paris solicitor with a passion for caves – whom the French regard as the father of speleology. Martel had already made several spectacular finds, notable among them the Grotte de Dargilan and the underground course of the Bramabiau, both discovered in 1888. Two days after Armand's discovery, he climbed down into the new pot-hole and set eyes on the most remarkable collection of stalagmites and stalactites he had ever seen.

■ AN UNDERGROUND WOOD ■

Some of the excitement that Armand and Martel felt can still be experienced by visitors today, despite the milling crowds, the tunnel that has been bored down to the cave, the catwalks and railed stairs. These distractions are all easily forgotten once you reach the end of the tunnel and look down on the magnifi-

cent array of stalagmites rising from the floor of an underground cavern quite large enough for a Gothic cathedral. They are elegant and delicate, but are mostly reminiscent of trees,

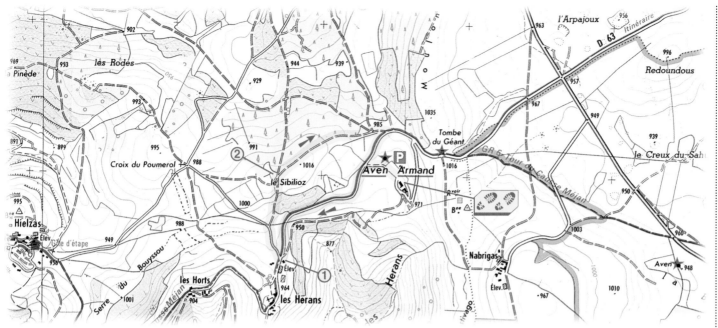

The 'virgin forest' of stalactites and stalagmites inside the Armand caves (below and left) is the result of thousands of years of water action

W A L K

length of walk: 2km
time: 1 hour
IGN Top 25: sheet 26400T

There is no better way to warm up after visiting the cave than to go for a hike. The more intrepid can go to Hielzas on foot along the GR 6, overlooking the Jonte gorge, then back on the D 63 to Aven Armand by way of the stone cross at Poumerol and les Hérans (about 8km altogether). But the following shorter walk may be preferable on a very hot day.

❶ Start at the north end of the Aven Armand car park and follow the trail that leads gently uphill to the left of the fenced-in pot-hole down which Louis Armand ventured in 1898. After 150m turn left onto the D 63. Continue along this road until you are approaching the sheep farm on the outskirts of the village of les Herans.

❷ Turn sharp right on the road signposted Hielzas. (To visit the farmhouse village, turn left then right on to the GR 6.) When you come to the bend 150m uphill, carry straight on up a grassy track lined with wild boxwood shrubs. At the top of the rise, before the track enters the wood, bear right and follow the sheep fence. The low pine trees here offer a pleasant spot to picnic under a little welcome shade. When you reach the glen at the bottom of the hill, turn right onto the first dirt track, which leads back to the D 69. Turn right, and then, after 150m, turn left and go back to the car park below.

with their strange calcite 'foliage' brought into exquisite relief by the skilful lighting arrangements in the cave.

▪ STALAGMITES AND STALACTITES ▪

The peculiarity of the Méjean and the other great limestone *causses* is that their surfaces cannot hold water. The rain seeps straight down through joints in the bedrock and the fissures through which it trickles are widened and eventually form great caverns. The drops of water hit the floor, depositing the tiny amounts of calcite they have collected on their journey through the rock. These deposits grow at the rate of about 1cm every century, forming stalactites hanging from the cave roof and stalagmites rising from the cave floor. If left undisturbed, a stalactite and the stalagmite below it will eventually fuse to form a slender column. It is a common process, but every cave has its own unique conditions, and Aven Armand is a delightful example.

The cave is open from mid-March to early November and can be visited by special arrangement during the rest of the year. The tour takes about 45 minutes and as the temperature underground is 10°C, it is best to dress warmly.

▪ LOCAL FARMHOUSES ▪

Hielzas, once a typically Caussard village, deserves a visit. Although now rather spoiled by the construction of several modern houses, it still has at least one superb farmhouse, which has been lovingly restored and converted into a museum showing how the inhabitants of these parched highlands have lived for centuries.

The hamlet of la Retournade, which lies about 3.5km north of Hielzas, just off the road to la Parade, has a dozen farmhouses and is utterly unspoiled. Several of the farms have been well restored and all are now private summer residences. None can be visited, but a stroll around la Retournade will give you a feel of this parched, high-plateau country where the inhabitants nail large, dry thistles to their doors – a symbol perhaps of their determination to cling to a soil that holds no life-sustaining water.

MONT AIGOUAL

A *s the eagle flies, it is just a short distance from the causses to the slopes of Mont Aigoual, yet the contrast between the two landscapes could not be greater.*

Mont Aigoual gets its name (*aigoual* or *aqualis* means 'watery') not only because the River Hérault and three of the River Tarn's main sources – the Tarnon, the Jonte and the Dourbie – spring from its slopes, but also because the mountain gets plenty of rain from both sides, being situated at a meteorological crossroads between Mediterranean winds and low-pressure fronts sweeping in from the Atlantic.

Inevitably, the summit is often shrouded in cloud, but when the sky clears, the view is stunning. On an exceptionally fine day you can make out both the Alps and the Pyrenees from the 1,565m peak. Even on a hazy summer afternoon visibility extends to the Cévennes in the east, the mountains of the Cantal to the north, the *causses* to the west and the plains of the Languedoc to the south. Standing on the weather station terrace, it is easy to imagine how it feels to soar like an

BELOW: there are spectacular views from Mont Aigoual and, right, the gushing waters of l'Abîme de Bramabiau emerge from the rock face

eagle or one of the rare reintroduced Pyrenees vultures which nest on the cliffs high above the Jonte gorge.

■ AN ECOLOGICAL SHOWCASE ■

The massif of the Aigoual, like that of Mont Lozère, with which it has been united to form France's largest nature reserve – the Parc National des Cévennes – is an ecological showcase and an impressive example of how to restore a severely damaged environment. Only a century ago, large tracts of both mountains were almost bare, their forests destroyed by fires, many of them started by charcoal-burners and farmers making a living from pasturing sheep and cows. Stripped of trees, their slopes were losing topsoil and ground vegetation due to the frequent torrential rains.

One man singlehandedly reversed this trend. After showing that sediment in the harbour of Bordeaux had been washed down from Aigoual, Georges Fabre, a high-ranking forestry official, won government backing to

reforest the massif. In 1875, despite heated opposition from local farmers, he began planting the thousands of hectares of beech forest which now cover the northern and eastern flanks of the mountain as far down as the village of Meyrueis. His work has been continued, notably since 1973 when the evergreen forests on the southern and western slopes were planted.

The Parc National des Cévennes, which includes most of Mont Aigoual, is a particularly interesting conservation project, aiming to preserve – and in places to re-establish – a natural balance between geology, animal, plant and bird life, farming, tourism and even meteorology (the summit's weather station, built in 1887, is still in operation). In 1985, UNESCO recognised it as a 'biosphere' conservation area.

Information about the park can be obtained at two castles: the 17th-century

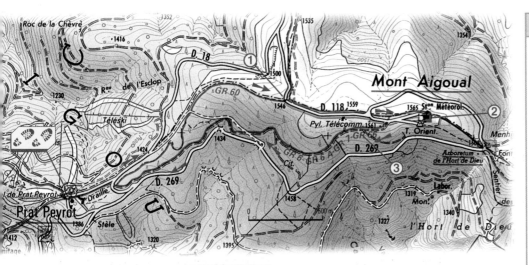

length of walk: 7km
time: 2½ hours
IGN Top 25: sheet 2640E

You can enjoy the summit view from the comfort of your car, but there is much more satisfaction in discovering the landscape on foot. The map shows the shorter of two routes that take you to the prehistoric megalith at Font de Trépaloup. Both start from the car park at the junction of the D 118 and D 269 at Prat Peyrot.

❶ From the car park climb through the woods along the GR 60, actually an old drovers' trail, until it meets the D 118. This can be steep in places.

❷ Continue on the road as far as the **station météorologique** (weather station), then descend steeply to the *col* 500m east. The menhir at **Font de Trépaloup** is a watershed between the Atllantic and the Mediterranean. Look north down the valley and you can make out the headwaters fo the River Tarnon. Face shouth to discover a torrrent in the ravine below. Further down it rushes into the Hérault, which takes its waters through the garrigues to the Languedoc plains and the flat coast west of Montpellier.

❸ Return to the summit and turn left, just after the weather station car park, on to the GR 6 (also indicated as the GR 7 and the GR 66), which leads back to Prat Peyrot. For the other, slightly longer, route on a surfaced road, from the car park follow the D 269 uphill in a loop around the weather station, then turn right on the D 118. Go downhill for 1km, then turn left on the D 18 back to the car park.

Château de Florac and the Château de Roquedols, 2km south of Meyrueis on the D 986. The latter, dating from the 15th and 16th centuries, is well worth visiting: the gold of its walls seem to shimmer against the surrounding dark green forest.

▪ L'ABÎME DE BRAMABIAU ▪

About 1km before you reach the village of Camprieu on the D 986 from Meyrueis, you can glimpse on your right a river gushing from the base of a cliff. Its name sounds like something out of a Gothic novel – l'Abîme de Bramabiau (the Abyss of Bramabiau).

The cavern through which the river thunders can be visited (summer only) by following a guide along a series of railed ledges overhanging the river and leading deep into the ground. It is all perfectly safe, but nerve-wracking if you are with small children. The guide will tell you that you are walking in a future Gorge du Tarn – although on a much smaller scale.

The roaring of the waters of l'Abîme de Bramabiau clearly reminded people long ago of the lowing of oxen (*brâme-biaou* in patois). It is a mysterious site and, depending on the weather and season, it is either eerie or magical. It seems to have been a place of pilgrimage for nature-worshippers and curiosity-seekers since prehistoric times. To reach it you walk down a ravine to a point just below the mouth of the river, from where you look up at a cascade issuing from an immense cleft in the rock face.

ABOVE: beehives in the Cévennes National Park

Naming the mystery

The mystery of fthe origins of the waters of l'Abîme de Bramabiau was explained in 1888, when Edouard-Alfred Martel, the co-discoverer of the Grottes de l'Aven Armand (see page 170), succeeded in following the course of the river underground to its entrance, some 700m to the southwest, thereby establishing that the charmingly named Bonheur (Happiness) and the booming Bramabiau were one and the same watercourse.

*L*ES BAMBOUS D'ANDUZE

*T*ucked away in a region known for its lovely forests, sparkling blue lakes and wild, lonely mountains is the Bambouseraie de Prafrance, a curious tropical bamboo grove planted in the mid-19th century by Eugène Mazel, a wealthy spice merchant.

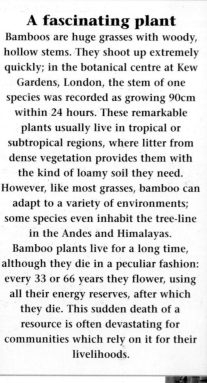

It was in the 1850s that Eugène Mazel began to establish his fabulous collection of bamboo, gathering species from all over the world. He built greenhouses and employed a small army of gardeners to care for them. However, bamboos need water, and the cost of diverting the River Gardon to the garden was too much, resulting in the bank repossessing the land. Mazel died bankrupt.

For some years, the bank tried to return the bamboo groves to farmland, but was unsuccessful. Then, in 1902, the grove was bought by the Nègre family, who decided to save it for future generations. Since Mazel's time, it has been extended considerably and is now a botanic park of extraordinary variety and interest.

■ GREEN, YELLOW AND BLACK ■

Even people not particularly interested in bamboo will be impressed by the gardens at Prafrance. It is an excellent opportunity for the uninitiated to learn that bamboo forests are not all pale yellow canes, but come in a vast array of shades and colours ranging from

A fascinating plant

Bamboos are huge grasses with woody, hollow stems. They shoot up extremely quickly; in the botanical centre at Kew Gardens, London, the stem of one species was recorded as growing 90cm within 24 hours. These remarkable plants usually live in tropical or subtropical regions, where litter from dense vegetation provides them with the kind of loamy soil they need. However, like most grasses, bamboo can adapt to a variety of environments; some species even inhabit the tree-line in the Andes and Himalayas.

Bamboo plants live for a long time, although they die in a peculiar fashion: every 33 or 66 years they flower, using all their energy reserves, after which they die. This sudden death of a resource is often devastating for communities which rely on it for their livelihoods.

RIGHT: the flourishing gardens at Prafrance depend on water diverted from the river
LEFT: the colours of the bamboo stems are remarkably varied

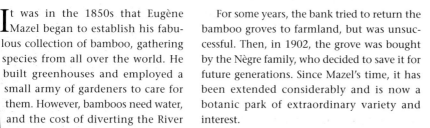

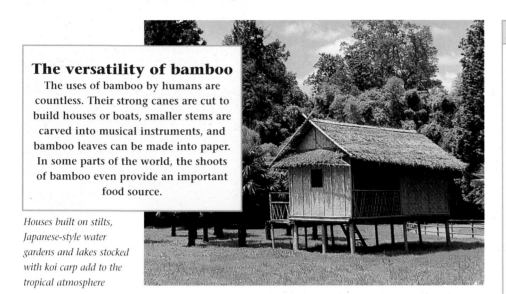

The versatility of bamboo

The uses of bamboo by humans are countless. Their strong canes are cut to build houses or boats, smaller stems are carved into musical instruments, and bamboo leaves can be made into paper. In some parts of the world, the shoots of bamboo even provide an important food source.

Houses built on stilts, Japanese-style water gardens and lakes stocked with koi carp add to the tropical atmosphere

length of walk: 1½km
time: 2 hours

The Bambouseraie is actually in the village of Générargues, about 3km to the north of Anduze, near where the River Gardon comes rushing down from the Cévennes. The untamed countryside around these mountains has always been popular with visitors, some of them, like Robert Louis Stevenson, great literary figures who set down their own impressions of the area for posterity. The walk is through the Bambouseraie, following suggested routes shown on a colourful illustrated map available from the centre.

❶ Park in one of the car parks signposted from the road and cross the footbridge into the entry complex. The hiss of water as it is channelled from the river to feed the bamboo groves provides a pleasant welcome to the garden.

❷ Walk under the railway bridge (a steam train, established in 1906, operates between St-Jean du Gard and Anduze in the summer) and along the gracefully arching bamboo and sequoias that form the garden's main avenue. A path to the left leads to the Asian village – houses on stilts in a sunny forest clearing.

❸ Return to the main avenue, and turn left towards the park's farm headquarters, a handsome house painted in the terracotta shade typical of this part of France. Here, a path runs along the northern boundary of the park, where a walkway to the left leads through plantations of magnolias and rhododendrons, as well as past the black bamboo much used in furniture making.

❹ The path eventually turns south, near the banks of the River Gardon. Here, dark green bamboo grows in abundance, mixed with species of pale yellow, and hemmed in by fences made, not surprisingly, of bamboo.

❺ Cross the stream and continue until the path swings north along the palm tree alley, backed by a dense growth of bamboo on both sides. Here is the *Magnolia grandiflora*, reputedly one of the largest of its kind in Europe, and more of the brilliant green *Phyllostachys bambusoides*.

❻ Turn right at the farm, and then left (marked *Sortie*) towards the water gardens. Paths wind past gurgling brooks and peaceful ponds, some stocked with bright goldfish and lotus flowers. Greenhouses boast some of the rarer species of bamboo.

❼ At the far end of the greenhouses is a statue of Eugène Mazel. The path then leads to some impressive nurseries, where plants are for sale. Follow the exit signs to the entry complex.

creamy white though all hues of yellow to a deep amber, and from apple green to a verdant emerald. Some are even black.

It is easy to imagine yourself in some wild jungle as you wander through the bamboo groves. They even sound alien as the breeze rustles through their papery leaves, conjuring up images of tropical islands and giant pandas. Late in the evening, when the crowds have gone, stand for a few moments among the dense green avenues and listen to the silence of the mountains and the distant gurgle of the River Gardon as it flows towards the sea.

▪ SEQUOIAS VERSUS BAMBOO ▪

Many visitors will be completely unprepared for the impenetrability of the bamboo grove, where many stems (culms) have grown to a height of 28m. But even these monstrous plants are dwarfed by the sequoias imported from California. These mighty trees, which can grow to a height of 112m, are the tallest living things on Earth. At about 50m, the specimens at Prafrance have some way to go before they reach these proportions.

▪ HOUSES AND GARDENS ▪

Among the park's other attractions are a delicate, Japanese-style water garden, complete with giant koi carp, and houses built on stilts, like those seen along the rivers of South-East Asia. They are so convincing that a number of French film-makers have taken advantage of this tropical landscape on their doorstep, and scenes from such movies as *The Wages of Fear*, starring Yves Montand, were shot here rather than overseas.

LEFT: detailed maps highlighting routes and the major trees are available from the site

PONT DU GARD

*T*ier upon tier of graceful rounded arches span the lazy River Gard in a feat of engineering all the more remarkable because it is 2,000 years old. The aqueduct is built from great blocks of dressed stone, some weighing six tonnes, and none held in place by mortar.

Crossing the bridge

The aqueduct can be crossed in several ways. Most people choose to stroll along the lower tier, where there is a wide, paved road. For the more adventurous, the upper tier is accessible, and you can either walk along the top of the conduit or inside it. Little can be seen from the inside of the conduit (unless you are tall), however, and it is blocked in places by chalky deposits. The top of the conduit is narrow, some tiles have been removed to illuminate the channel beneath, there are no guard rails, and it is often buffeted by winds.

During the 2nd century BC, when the Romans decided southern France would make a pleasing addition to their expanding empire, they did more than just fight the odd battle to secure their new lands. Instead they colonised them and imposed their own culture on the local people, replacing winding tracks with straight roads and bringing a higher standard of living. This included improving water supplies; the great aqueduct at Pont du Gard was one of several schemes for providing towns and villages with a constant supply of clean water.

■ DISTANCE NO OBJECT ■

In 19 BC the Romans selected a little spring near Uzès as the best source of water for the developing town of Nîmes. Although Uzès is some distance from Nîmes, this presented no significant problem to the skilful Roman engineers. Within a few years a 50km pipeline had been constructed

The village of St-Laurent-des-Arbes, with its castle and Romanesque church, is situated in typical Provençal farmland

between the spring and Nîmes, an impressive stone conduit that was capable of providing a constant supply of good-quality water for the whole town.

The biggest obstacle to the project was the unpredictable River Gard, but the engineers simply designed a vast bridge which measured 49m high and 275m long. The Pont du Gard has three tiers of arches with the covered water conduit on the top level.

Visitors will notice several stones projecting from the surface: these were designed as scaffolding supports, deliberately left in place so that the bridge could be repaired more easily when necessary.

■ SURVIVING TIME ■

The Pont du Gard is a striking sight, built of neatly cut stones in pale gold. With its arches still intact, and spanning a tree-lined river, it is regarded as one of the best examples of surviving Roman architecture in Europe. But it has not always been

T O U R

length of tour: 80km
time: 1 day
IGN Top 250: sheet 115

This drive, on paved roads, takes in the attractive countryside surrounding Pont du Gard, a region where *garrigue* and forest scenery give way to some of the best vineyards in Provence. The bridge itself can only be crossed on foot. Start in Bagnols-sur-Cèze, which has a modern art museum (founded in 1854, then rebuilt after it was accidentally burned to the ground by firemen).

❶ From Bagnols travel south on the N 580, passing great flat-topped limestone plateaus, then turn right on to the D 26. This is wine-growing country. The first village is **St-Laurent-des-Arbes**, which once belonged to the bishops of Avignon. It has a Romanesque church and an impressive castle that dominates the town from its rocky outcrop. (Watch for unexpected speed bumps.)

❷ Continue to **Lirac**, famous for its full-bodied reds and fruity whites, and then on to **Tavel**. Medieval kings enthused over Tavel wines, and replanting in the 1930s has secured its strong, pale rosés a place among France's best *appellations*. Wine to take home can be bought from any of several *caves*.

❸ Take the D 4 west towards **Valliguières**, passing through the Forêt de Tavel and the Forêt de Malmont, where vineyards give way to orchards and woods. The D 4 meets the N 86 near Valliguières' château.

❹ Turn south on to the N 86, then west on to the D 981, and take the road signposted to **Pont du Gard**. Park in either the north or south car park. Some of the best views of the aqueduct are from the footpaths along the riverbanks, so follow one of the marked trails before crossing the bridge.

❺ On leaving Pont du Gard, take the D 981, through gentle hills cloaked in vineyards and orchards, to the attractive town of **Uzès**. There you will find an 18th-century church, a medieval ducal palace, a Romanesque Tour Fenestrelle and an elegant town hall. Jean Racine lived here with an uncle who wanted him to take holy orders. As the D 982 leaves Uzès, there is a stunning view towards misty mountains. Much of this road is shielded from the sun by parallel rows of trees, through which you can glimpse the chateau at St-Siffret on the right.

❻ Turn left on to the N 86, past **la Capelle-et-Masmolène**, a fast road that speeds through typical Provençal farmland; here people tend the vines that form the centre of industry in the area, and pale limestone cliffs gleam in the distance. The N 86 leads back to Bagnols-sur-Cèze.

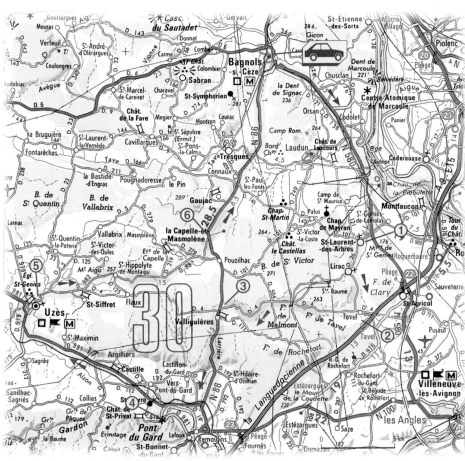

in such good repair: whenever Nîmes was besieged, the water supply was invariably attacked, and so the aqueduct constantly needed renovating.

After about the 4th century AD it was not maintained at all, and by the 9th century the accumulation of limescale had blocked it completely. Gradually it fell into disuse. Local people took the fine stone for their homes, and the Romans' once handsome bridge became a sorry sight.

It was not until the 19th century that it found a champion in Emperor Napoleon III, who ordered the bridge to be restored, resulting in an influx of visitors anxious to see this wonder of the ancient world.

Plans in the 1990s to build a theme park around it were mercifully thwarted – thanks to public objections – and its arches remain free of 20th-century encumbrances. The Romans clearly intended their aqueduct to last, although even their imaginative engineers could surely not have envisaged that it would survive for almost two millennia.

The three-tiered aqueduct (left) spanning the River Gard was built by the Romans to help carry water from its source, the spring near the town of Uzès (right) to Nîmes, where it was needed for domestic use and for the city's many fountains and public baths

Scrub and stones

The land around the aqueduct is dry and chalky, and noted for a type of vegetation called *garrigue*. This is essentially thorny scrub, which seldom grows taller than 50cm. *Garrigue* plants include aromatic herbs such as basil, thyme, marjoram, rosemary (right), lavender and sage, and hardy, tenacious species such as thistles, box, holm oak and gorse. However, it is not all tough green bushes and bare stone: in the spring, tulips, irises, cistus and orchids bloom in an explosion of colour.

FONTAINE DE VAUCLUSE

In a basin of grey, stone cliffs in northern Provence lies a deep emerald pool. After heavy rain, water from the pool spills out along a tree-lined valley in a tumble of froth and foam, briefly making Fontaine de Vaucluse one of the most powerful resurgent springs in the world.

In the middle of the 14th century, the Italian poet and philosopher Petrarch sat beside the silent Fontaine de Vaucluse, shaded by towering rocks and fig trees, and wrote verses of extraordinary beauty and profundity.

Centuries later in the 1990s, owing to the million visitors each year, this small pool of green water is seldom peaceful; and a thriving tourist industry has developed in the nearby village of Vaucluse.

Despite the crowds and the gauntlet of souvenir shops and boutiques, it is still possible to see why Petrarch chose this place to spend 16 years of his life. During the spring, when water levels are raised by melting snow, the River Sorgue roars out of the rocky basin and thunders its way down the valley. In the summer, when water levels are low, the river is reduced to a bubbling trickle, meandering gently around boulders and making tiny waterfalls.

Limestone landscapes are full of springs, swallow-holes and hidden water systems, and the Plateau de Vaucluse is no exception. Water from rain or snow seeps through the porous rock to form underground rivers which can flow great distances before re-emerging. The spring at Fontaine de Vaucluse is a typical example, and the water that bursts

The lovesick poet

Francesco Petrarca (Petrarch, 1304–74) was born in Italy, but moved to Avignon as a child. In 1327 he fell in love with a married woman who was to have a profound influence on his life. In his poetry she is referred to as Laura. Petrarch fled from Avignon and settled for a lonely life of contemplation in Fontaine de Vaucluse. Laura died during the Black Death (1340s), but Petrarch never forgot her and never married. A museum, said to stand on the site of his home, has exhibits of his life and work.

The spring at Fontaine de Vaucluse is joined by secondary springs before it reaches the lake in the centre of the village

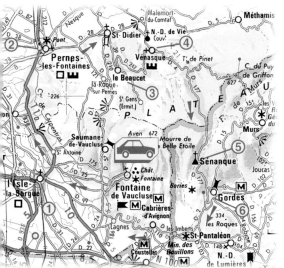

the source of the River Sorgue has intrigued people for centuries, the first recorded dive was not until the 1870s, when an intrepid adventurer descended some 23m before admitting defeat.

In 1983, a purpose-built submersible reached 250m and, in 1985, a device with remote-controlled cameras achieved a depth of 315m. However, despite the bravery of divers and advanced technology, the source of the Sorgue still remains a mystery.

■ SNAKES AND SAINTS ■

People have always been fascinated by the spring, and many legends and myths surround it. One is that Véran, who was bishop of nearby Cavaillon in the 6th century, killed a monstrous snake (*Coulobre*) here, proving that the site was protected by God. Véran was canonised and his tomb is in the pretty 12th-century church near the river.

from the rocks in a mighty green trail of foam has probably travelled many kilometres from its original source.

The hollow that surrounds the spring, the *vallis clausa* (enclosed valley), gave Vaucluse its name. Sheer grey cliffs rise about 200m on three sides of the pool; the fourth side is open, which allows the river to flow through it.

■ SPELEOLOGY AND SOURCES ■

The exact depth of the chasm below the spring is still not known, despite valiant efforts by speleologists and scientists to uncover the secrets of the labyrinth of tunnels and caverns that riddle the area. But although

TOP: houses seem to cling to the terraces in the hillside village of Gordes

ABOVE: the source of the River Sorgue

The River Sorgue

The River Sorgue has always played a vital role in the area's economy, and over the years has provided power for at least 70 watermills downstream. These mills have allowed the growth of industries such as flour production, paper-making, leather tanning, and textile manufacture (chiefly wools and silk). Some of them have been preserved in l'Isle-sur-la-Sorgue.

T O U R

length of tour: 65km
time: 1 day
IGN Top 250: sheet 115

The only way to reach the Fontaine de Vaucluse is to walk the 40 or so minutes from Vaucluse. The route is lined with souvenir stalls, and it is good to escape the crowds into the peace of the surrounding countryside. The driving tour takes in a number of delightful Provençal hill villages, some with ancient churches, and others with unexpectedly large castles.

❶ Park in Vaucluse and walk to place de la Colonne, the shady village square with its statue of Petrarch. On the way to the spring is the history museum (1990), and a museum dedicated to the French Resistance. Follow the woodland path to the spring (you may be disappointed by its output in summer).

❷ Walk back to the car park and start the drive by heading for **l'Isle-sur-la-Sorgue**, a town with canals and watermills, noted for its antiques sales. Take the D 938 north to **Pernes-les-Fontaines**, a delightful town ringed by leafy boulevards and boasting almost 40 fountains, many dating from the 18th century. Notre-Dame-du-Grâces and medieval Notre-Dame-de-Nazareth are also worth seeing, while the Tour Ferrande offers some of the oldest frescoes in France, dating from the 1270s.

❸ Leave Pernes following signs for St-Didier, and then **le Beaucet**, which has cave houses, a ruined castle and a pilgrimage site dedicated to rain-maker St Gens. The car park has a moving monument to French Resistance fighters, erected in 1995.

❹ Take the D 247 to **Vénasque**, a cliff-top village that was once the seat of bishops. The baptistry was founded in the 6th century and rebuilt in the 1100s. Both le Beaucet and Vénasque are typical Provençal hill settlements of outstanding beauty.

❺ The D 4 twists through a sea of vines until it meets the D 177, where it enters the Forêt de Murs and then plunges through a steep and mysterious gorge, with towering limestone walls on either side. At the other end is **l'Abbaye Sénanque**, a Cistercian monastery founded in 1148 and now famous for its lavender. At dusk, all that can be heard is the hollow clank of bells as sheep are rounded up for the night.

❻ After Sénanque is the startling hill village of **Gordes** – a cluster of houses dominated by a Renaissance palace of honey-coloured stone. The village has a museum dedicated to artist Victor de Vasarély. Leave Gordes on the D 2 and follow signs to **le Village des Bories**. *Bories* are stone huts with vaulted ceilings, first built in megalithic times, although the style was still in use in the 1800s. The Gordes *bories* form a rural museum. The D 2 ends with signs to Fontaine de Vaucluse pointing in opposite directions. Take the **tourist route**, which is prettier, to complete the circuit.

ℒES BAUX-DE-PROVENCE

***T**he village and ruined citadel of les Baux cling to a rocky spur high above the surrounding countryside. This formidable fortress – stronghold of the medieval lords of Baux – was famous for its 13th-century troubadours, who sang about love and chivalry.*

People have lived on les Baux's barren mass of rock since Neolithic times. The most lasting impression was made by the powerful lords of Baux: their ruined castle still clutches at the edge of precipitous cliffs that drop away on all sides. In the evening, the setting sun turns its craggy walls to gold.

The complex site has two parts: the lower town or village, and the upper town or citadel. The citadel squats on the top of the massif, which is about 600m long, 200m wide and 245m high, while the village has grown up on the lower slopes. Most of the early medieval buildings are in the citadel, while the village boasts elegant churches and handsome little mansions.

■ TROUBLESOME BAUX ■

The first evidence of settlement left by the lords of Baux dates from about 950; by the 1100s these proud warrior-princes were among the strongest barons in the south of France. One of them, Raymond de Turenne, terrorised the countryside in the 1390s, fiendishly forcing his prisoners to jump off the castle walls if they were unable to raise their ransoms. So outrageous was his behaviour that the pope, the Lord of Provence

Steps lead up to the ruined citadel, which was partly carved out of the solid rock above the village

and even the king of France joined ranks against him.

After Turenne's defeat, les Baux passed to the French Crown, but was dismantled in the 1480s because it had become a centre for insurrection. Eventually the ruin passed into the hands of one Anne de Montmorency, who promptly restored it to its former glory.

Les Baux became a centre for Protestantism in the 16th century, but was partly destroyed by Cardinal Richelieu in the 1630s when he became tired of the troublemakers it housed. He declined to finance the demolition himself, however, and forced the inhabitants to pay instead. The fortress was then given to the Grimaldi family, who

Bauxite

In the 1820s, rich deposits of an unusual red, clay-like mineral were discovered in les Baux – it was named bauxite. In the late 1880s, scientists realised that bauxite could be used economically to produce aluminium – then a rare and expensive element – and it quickly became a valuable commodity. Mining operations in the les Baux area were successful for some years, until France started importing most of its bauxite from Guinea.

The narrow streets of les-Baux-de-Provence throng with visitors during the summer months

were dispossessed in 1791, after which time it gradually fell into disrepair. Restoration and excavation has been in progress since the 1940s, although the project is not expected to be completed until 2010.

▪ A HAUNTING RUIN ▪

Baux is famous for many things – the internationally renowned restaurant founded by the doyen of chefs, Raymond Thulier; its links with culture, beginning with its reputation as a Court of Love in the 1200s and continuing to the 20th century; and for its association with the figurative painter Yves Brayer (1907–90).

But perhaps its most famous asset is the glorious sunset across the rocky white walls. As evening draws in, the sun throws an amber veil across the medieval ruins and the huddle of buildings below.

Les Baux vineyards

Vines thrive here, partly because of the warm climate and partly because of the favourable clay and gravel soil. The Greeks first cultivated grapes here, and the resulting wine has always had an excellent reputation.

The local wines are mainly reds and rosés; the area is officially designated as 'Coteaux d'Aix-en-Provence – les Baux'. There is a signposted wine route that provides a good introduction to viticulture in this region.

length of walk: 1.5km
time: 2 hours
IGN Top 25: sheet 30420

Les Baux can only be visited on foot. It is host to some 1.5 million tourists each year, so the best time to see it is out of season, when the peace and isolation of this extraordinary hill village can be truly appreciated. If you do find yourself there in the summer, go early before the coaches arrive. The terrain is uneven, with some steep slopes.

❶ Approach the village through the Porte Mage, where cobbled streets wind upwards past stone houses and stepped alleys to the 16th-century Hôtel des Porcelets, now housing the Musée Yves Brayer. Also en route is the Église St-Vincent, in which lie the long-dead lords of les Baux. Walk to the charming, 16th-century **Hôtel de Manville**, now an art museum and town hall.

❷ Follow the narrow rue de Trencat to les Baux's history museum, housed in the 14th-century Hôtel de la Tour de Brau. You must pay to go further, since this is the only way into the citadel. The first stop is the **Chapelle St-Blaise**, restored and containing an exhibition on olives. The artist Yves Brayer is buried in the cemetery opposite.

❸ Continue along the cliff edge, where parts of the medieval fortress have been eroded by wind and time. To the left is the shell of a 16th-century hospital, while the mill ahead played an important role in the economy of les Baux. Past the mill is the **Monument Charloun-Rieu**, from where there is one of the most glorious views in France, looking out across neat rows of vines to blue grey mountains shimmering in the distance.

❹ Walk back towards the village to see the most impressive parts of the ruins: the craggy **Tour Sarrasine** and the vaulted **Chapelle Castrale**.

❺ The *donjon* (keep) steps are uneven and potentially dangerous, but it is possible to clamber up and see how the medieval engineers used the mountain itself to form some of the castle walls. From the top of the keep you will see why the barons chose this site for their fortress; it is clear that any attack on the citadel would have been almost unsustainable. Walk past the full-size wooden siege machines to the exit.

This medieval trebuchet is one of the impressive seige weapons on display in les Baux

PALAIS DES PAPES

A vignon's mighty, yet elegant Palais des Papes, created by 14th-century popes, is one of the most impressive buildings in France. The frescoes and contemporary accounts of life in the papal court suggest an interior as sumptuous as the exterior is formidable.

The area around Avignon was first settled by Neolithic people, although it only began to prosper when the Greeks founded a port here some time after the 6th century BC. After Gallic and Roman occupation there followed a period of obscurity until a city state was founded in the 1100s. This was razed to the ground in the 1220s because it had supported a heretical sect called the Albigensians (or Cathars).

▪ PAPAL DISPENSATION ▪

It was in the 14th century, however, that Avignon became famous, when, in an unprecedented move that left the Christian world stunned, the pope decided to abandon Rome and head north.

By the early 1300s, life in Rome had become all but impossible for anyone elected as pope. The *curia* (papal court) was rife with political intrigues, and the pope was constantly dragged into disputes. When Frenchman Bertrand de Got was elected Pope Clement V in 1305, he decided to take his *curia* to southern France and solemnly entered Avignon in 1309. He died in 1314, but another six French popes ensured that for almost 70 years the town was a centre for culture and enlightenment. The university flourished and the palace thronged with scholars, artists and pilgrims. Sadly, the magnificence of the court also attracted less desirable visitors, and the popes were obliged to fortify the whole town and employ an army of mercenaries to protect it.

> ### Festival d'Art Dramatique
> Avignon's vibrant annual festival of dramatic art was founded in 1947 by Jean Vilar, and has become an important date in the calendar of major events in this region of festivals. From the beginning of July to the beginning of August, the courtyard of the Palais des Papes and many other venues around the city host a huge variety of performances from the world of dance, music and theatre, attracting artists from all over the world.

The magnificent Palais des Papes in Avignon housed the papal court in the 14th century

PALAIS DES PAPES ▶
◀ PETIT PALAIS-MUSEE

■ HOME AND FORTRESS ■

The French popes wanted a building that would be appropriately magnificent enough to house them and their glittering court, but they also wanted a structure that was strong enough to withstand attacks from their many enemies. The result was the Palais des Papes, one of the finest palace-fortresses in the world, a formidable edifice with battlements, turrets, pinnacles, arrow slits and intimidating gateways.

■ OLD OR NEW? ■

The palace is on two floors, and is really two separate buildings ranged around three open spaces (the main courtyard, Benedict XII's cloister and Benedict XII's garden). The Old Palace was built mainly by Benedict XII (1335–42), while the New Palace was created under Clement VI (1342–52).

When the popes moved back to Rome, most of the glorious treasures and paintings either went with them or disappeared over time, as the palace was used variously as a prison, a military garrison and an administrative centre. However, few people wandering through the great

Sur le Pont d'Avignon

The Pont St-Bénezet (above), subject of the famous song, *Sur le Pont d'Avignon*, stands below the Palais des Papes, and consists of only four remaining arches, ending abruptly halfway across the River Rhône. Originally it had 22 arches and was about 900m long. Legend has it that, in 1177, an angel ordered a shepherd called Bénezet to build a bridge. Volunteers formed a 'bridge brotherhood' and the structure was completed within eight years. It was rebuilt in the 1230s, restored in the 15th century, then reduced to its present state when the Rhône flooded in the 17th century.

halls and chambers will fail to be impressed by the princely grandeur of this noble building; if you can grab a few quiet moments, you may be able to imagine the wealth of gold and silver that once turned the cold, bare rooms into sumptuous chambers and halls.

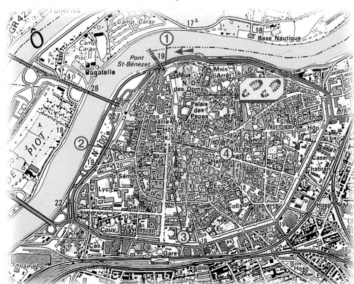

ABOVE LEFT: *the huge arched interior of the Palais des Papes*

RIGHT: *elaborate carved panels on the door of Église St-Pierre*

length of walk: 3km
time: half a day
IGN Top 250: sheet 102

Although it is possible to drive to many of Avignon's attractions, you will be able to see and appreciate far more if you walk. This short walk takes in some of the most famous sites, but also includes a few of Avignon's less publicised attractions – including cobbled streets and secret gardens.

❶ From the place du Palais, walk to the 12th-century **Notre-Dame-des-Doms**, the gardens of which offer superb views of Pont St-Bénezet. (From April to September, the bridge can be reached from the park; the rest of the year, follow the signs down narrow streets and worn steps to the river.) This is the **Quartier de la Balance**, renowned in the 19th century as a gypsy area. Visit the **Pont St-Bénezet** and its chapel.

❷ After leaving the bridge, turn right and carry on until you reach rue du Rempart-du-Rhône and the remains of the papal fortifications. Walk in their shadow until you reach place Crillon, with its shady trees and pretty paved square, then turn right to the **Musée Calvet** (the main museum) and Musée Requien (geology and science).

❸ At the end of rue Joseph Vernet, turn left into rue de la Republique, the city's main thoroughfare. This provides a startling contrast to the peaceful lane near the city walls, with its bustling atmosphere and chic shops. Continue to **Musée Lapidaire**, located in a former Jesuit college. Along rue Prévot is the pretty place St-Didier which has a lovely Provençal-style church and the powerful tower of the Livrée de Ceccano.

❹ Retrace your steps to rue de la Republique, then turn right and continue until you reach **place de l'Horloge**, a large, shady square with a medieval clock-tower and plenty of street cafés. It is worth stopping at one of these to watch the town teem with life in the bright Provençal sun while you eat excellent French pastries. Take the pedestrianised rue des Marchands to the **Église St-Pierre**, with its Renaissance carvings, and then cross place St-Pierre to follow signs to the **Palais des Papes**. The route weaves through narrow alleys and to a tiny garden filled with olive trees behind the palace. From here, steps wind up to place du Palais.

Detail from the Hôtel des Monnaies in Avignon

AIGUES-MORTES

Standing on the lonely, windswept salt marshes of the Rhône Delta is the atmospheric medieval city of Aigues-Mortes. Pale, tower-studded walls rise majestically from the stark landscape – a sight not easily forgotten, especially when strands of light mist seethe and twist around it.

In the 1240s, the saintly King Louis IX owned no Mediterranean port of his own, so he decided to build one. For its location he chose a desolate scrap of land near the sea that belonged to the monks of Psalmody. The monks willingly sold him the area he wanted, and he immediately ordered his architects to design him a handsome, fortified port.

Work first began on the Tour de Constance; this was followed by the construction of the town walls, forming a rectangle enclosing an area roughly 300m by 550m. Additional protection was provided by a series of defensive towers built at regular intervals along the walls.

■ A GOLDEN AGE ■

Sensing that few people would willingly exile themselves to the isolated wetlands of southern France – not for nothing is the town called Aigues-Mortes (dead waters) – Louis offered tempting tax exemptions to prospective residents. In those days, Aigues-Mortes was linked to the sea by a wide channel, and ships laden with goods from the Mediterranean countries could moor there. With merchant barges flooding the town with exotic goods, and crowds flocking to it to take advantage of Louis' generous tax deals, Aigues-Mortes began to flourish.

The impressive fortifications of Aigues-Mortes were built by Louis IX in the 13th century on wasteland bought from a monastery

INSET: the powerful sight of the Tour de Constance, the first and largest of Aigues-Mortes' towers

WALK

length of walk: 2km
time: 2 hours
IGN Top 25: sheet 28430T

The only way to really appreciate Aigues-Mortes is on foot – the medieval architects naturally did not have cars in mind when they designed the narrow streets and slender gateways. Gaze up at the powerful ramparts and the stalwart towers, and you will begin to understand the full extent of the builders' achievements, using only pulleys, wooden scaffolds and labouring peasants.

❶ The circuit begins at **Porte de la Gardette**, a menacing tower sporting arrow slits and an uncomfortable selection of machiolations from which defenders could drop hot oil or pitch and rocks on attackers. Cross the cobbled place Anatole-France to the ticket office at the **Tour de Constance**. Steps lead to the top, which offers views of the city's grid-like layout and the marshes beyond. (It is possible to stroll along the walkways on the walls from the Tour de Constance, but the tour described here keeps to the foot of the walls to allow detours.)

❷ Leaving the Tour de Constance, walk parallel to the Chenal Maritime to the sinister-looking **Tour des Bourguignons**.

❸ Continue past Porte de l'Organeau (an *organeau* was an iron ring to which ships were fastened), Porte des Moulins (the mill gate), Poterne des Galions (where galleys moored), the ceremonial entrance at Porte de la Marine, Porte de l'Arsenal and **Tour de la Poudrière** (where gunpowder was kept).

❹ Still in the shadow of the walls, pass Porte de la Reine and turn left down rue Paul-Bert to the 17th-century **Chapelle des Pénitents Gris**. Now neglected, it stands

at the head of a paved square with a new post office.

❺ Walk back to the wall and pass the Tour de Villeneuve and Tour de la Mèche (the wick tower) to **Porte de St Antoine**, a twin-towered keep pierced by a narrow entrance passageway. Turn left into boulevard Gambetta, and right down rue de la Republique to the **Chapelle des Pénitents Blancs**, the baroque church of a brotherhood established in the town in the 1620s.

❻ Continue along rue de la Republique, which boasts potted trees and multicoloured window shutters, and turn left towards place St Louis, the town centre, with its bronze statue of Louis and the Gothic church of **Notre-Dame-des-Sablons**. Walk along grand rue Jean-Jaurès, back to Porte de la Gardette and the start of the walk.

▪ DECLINE ▪

Although the channel began to silt up in the 14th century, the town remained a strategically important stronghold, and in 1418 it was seized by an invading Burgundian army. The soldiers were subsequently massacred and their bodies thrown into a tower still known as the Tour des Bourguignons. Salt was poured over them to prevent them from rotting until labourers could be hired to dig a grave.

By the 18th century Aigues-Mortes was well and truly in decline, with only a fraction of its former population left.

▪ IMAGES OF THE PAST ▪

Walking along the Chenal Maritime in the shadow of walls that have remained unchanged for centuries, it is easy to imagine the noisy chaos of a busy medieval port. On quiet summer evenings, when the crowds have gone and the town is swathed in fog winding in from the marshes, it is almost possible to hear the voices of the prosperous merchants and ambitious crusaders who once ruled here.

Modern Aigues-Mortes offers its visitors a more hospitable greeting than a volley of arrows from its ramparts or a demand for a toll to enter its gates. The walls and towers are open to the public, and its narrow streets have excellent restaurants and shops. The town also stands in an important wine-growing area, and there is little to match sitting in the pleasant main square enjoying a glass of full-bodied Provençal wine.

Saint Louis

In 1244 a Turkish army destroyed Jerusalem. At the time he heard the news King Louis IX of France was ill, so he made a pact with God: if his life were spared, he would lead a crusade to rescue the Holy Land from its unholy invaders. He survived, massed his troops in Aigues-Mortes and set off in 1248.

The campaign was not easy, but Louis managed to rule Palestine for four years. When he returned to France, the kingdom in the east immediately began to fragment, so Louis left once again from Aigues-Mortes to lead another crusade. He never saw the Holy City, but died in Tunis.

The Tour de Constance

The biggest of Aigues-Mortes' towers is the mighty Tour de Constance. Built in the 1240s, it is a round keep separated from the rest of the town by a water-filled moat.

Virtually windowless, this formidable structure was later used as a secure prison, and the 14th century saw monks of the Order of the Knights Templar incarcerated, while in the 17th century the tower was filled with Huguenots. In the 18th century various Protestant women, including the courageous Marie Durand, were held for as long as 38 years before they were finally released.

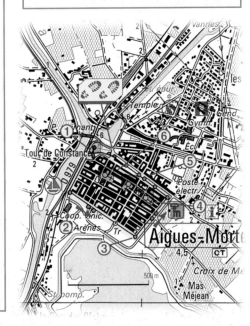

LA CAMARGUE

Simply the name – La Camargue – summons up images of snow-white horses galloping through silvery expanses of water, elegant pink flamingos stabbing the shallows for brine shrimps, and silent, mysterious marshes swathed in mist.

La Camargue is an area of 1,466sq km of alluvial plain, lying on the pancake-flat, boggy land between the two arms of the mighty River Rhône. It can be divided into three distinct geographical areas. The land to the north of the delta is drained and cultivated and is an important region for growing crops. Further south, the salt marshes are a patchwork of salt pans, shallow brackish lakes and small islands with clumps of trees and reeds. Finally, near the sea is a huge expanse of ponds and sand dunes.

A gypsy pilgrimage

For two days each May gypsies from all over the world flock to Saintes-Maries-de-la-Mer for the festivals of Marie Jacobe, sister of the Virgin Mary, and Marie Salome, mother of the apostles James and John. Amid colourful scenes, the gypsies make offerings to their patron Sara, whose bones are thought to be in the crypt of the town's church, which also features her statue.

▪ CARE AND CONTROL ▪

Thanks to the French government, this lovely area of coastal wetland has been preserved in its natural state. It was designated a national reserve in the 1970s and is famous for its flora. Tourism

The desolate, marshy area of the Rhône delta supports a rich and varied wildlife including pink flamingos and herds of the famous white horses

Saintes-Maries-de-la-Mer

In about AD 40, Mary Magdalene and other friends of Jesus were placed on a ship without sails or oars and abandoned to the ocean. Favourable winds brought them to La Camargue, where they built an oratory. Mary Magdalene travelled to Ste-Baume, but some of the others stayed and were eventually buried in the oratory.

The oratory became an important pilgrim site and was replaced by a grander church in the 9th century. In 1130 this was in turn replaced by one of the finest fortified churches in the country – a magnificent piece of architecture that is still standing.

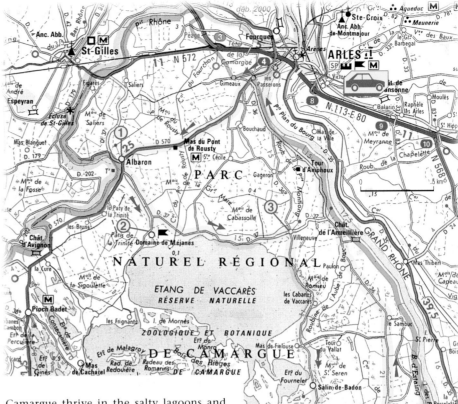

and agriculture are strictly controlled, and the water balance is carefully regulated. Salt-loving plants thrive here, forming dense mats of colour in the spring and summer.

▪ LAND AND SEA ▪

For thousands of years the sea has had an uneasy relationship with the land in this area. During the 13th century, the nearby city of Aigues-Mortes was an important port, but over time the sea receded more and more, and the channels that once teemed with ships became silted up, which has resulted in the fortified town now standing 6km inland. In other places, continental subsidence has caused the sea to invade the land, so that buildings once considered safely distanced from Mediterranean storms are now protected by giant sea walls.

But while humans might struggle to keep the sea in what they consider to be its rightful place, many animals and plants in La

Camargue thrive in the salty lagoons and marshes that are half-ocean, half-land. Perhaps the most remarkable of these is the brine shrimp, a crustacean just over 15mm long. This curious little animal has evolved in such a way that it can live in virtually fresh or very salty water with equal ease, and so is able to survive both floods and droughts.

▪ THE IMPORTANCE OF SALT ▪

The vast, sea-soaked tract of land between the Petit Rhône and Salin-de-Giraud has been mined for salt for millennia. The land is artificially flooded with a shallow layer of sea water, which then evaporates in the heat. As it does so, the solution left behind becomes increasingly salty and is pumped into crystallising pans. Far from damaging the environment, the salt industry is important to La Camargue's ecology. Because the same areas are flooded each year, they provide stable breeding grounds for birds.

▪ A HAVEN FOR BIRDS ▪

La Carmargue is famous for its dazzling white horses and unique, sturdy black bulls, but this wilderness is also home to countless birds. These include rarities such as the collared pratincole as well as a myriad ducks, waders and geese. The wide, shallow lagoons provide excellent feeding grounds for swans, avocets and egrets, while the freshwater reed beds are used as nesting sites by bitterns, herons and warblers. Surveys have also recorded 24,000 pink flamingos here, a truly spectacular sight.

T O U R

length of tour: 160km
time: 1 day
IGN Top 250: sheet 115

La Camargue is huge, and comparatively few roads penetrate its marshy secrets. Therefore it is well worth taking a boat trip from a town such as Saintes-Maries-de-la-Mer. That way you will pass herds of grazing Camargue bulls, watched over by their cowboy *gardians*, and far more birds than can be seen from the roads. As with many driving tours of La Camargue, this begins in Arles, famous for its Roman remains, photography and as the haunt of painter Vincent van Gogh.

❶ Head west from Arles and cross the Grand Rhône. Take the D 570 signposted to Saintes-Maries-de-la-Mer to **Albaron**, once a powerful stronghold, however, today the town is better known for fighting off the sea with its pumping stations than repelling human invaders.

❷ Next take the D 37 to **Méjanes**, a lakeside village with a small electric railway, a bull ring and horse-drawn carriages. From here follow the D 37 as it runs past the Etang de Vaccarès, the largest of La Camargue's lagoons. Stop the car at any of the lay-bys and the distinctive smell of marsh will immediately become apparent – a combination of salt, rotting vegetation, and warm plants.

❸ At **Villeneuve**, turn towards la Capelière, the reserve's headquarters. There is an excellent visitor centre with marked nature trails – but it is poorly signposted, so be ready to stop. The 1.5km path around the centre has information boards describing the ecology of the plants and animals of the area.

❹ Continue south past Salin-de-Badon, noted for its birds, to **Salin-de-Giraud**, best known of the salt-producing towns. The tree-lined avenues are dominated by the Solway refinery, where glittering piles of white salt can be glimpsed through the railings. Now take the D 36 north again as it slices through the marshy land to the west of the sluggish Grand Rhône. Eventually it joins the D 570, which leads back to Arles.

MONTAGNE STE-VICTOIRE

Paul Cézanne's most famous painting of Montagne Ste-Victoire (there are many) shows it as a blue-grey pyramid rising above ochre clay and scrubby green olive trees. It is an imposing sight which captures perfectly the delicate colours and dramatic terrain that characterise France's sunny south.

Paul Cézanne

Cézanne was born in Aix-en-Provence on 19 January 1839. A distant, lonely man, he loved the hills around his native city and Montagne Ste-Victoire in particular. It appears in many of his paintings. After an unsuccessful foray into the world of law, Cézanne concentrated on art. He was introduced to Impressionism by the author Émile Zola, and soon his work was dominated by the powerful colours that reflected his observations about light and nature. In 1874, his work was harshly criticised, and he retired to Aix for a life of seclusion. He remained there until his death in 1906.

Montagne Ste-Victoire is a limestone ridge extending for about 16km to the east of Aix-en-Provence. It may not be the highest mountain in Provence (its tallest peak, Pic des Mouches, rises to 1,010m), nor is it the most difficult to scale, but it is one of the most impressive.

In 102 BC opposing forces faced each other under the shadow of the mighty limestone mass of the mountain near the recently founded town of Aquae Sextiae (Aix-en-Provence). One was the well-organised military machine of the Roman army under a ruthless general called Marius; the other was a rabble of ill-equipped but fierce Teuton fighters from the Baltic coast. Legend has it that 100,000 Teuton warriors were killed in the ensuing battle; after the fighting had petered out, the women and children in the baggage train killed themselves rather than surrender to the Romans. It is said that this ancient, craggy mountain was named after Marius's victory over the Barbarian hordes, and was the vantage point from where he watched the massacre.

BELOW: the impressive limestone ridge of Montagne Ste-Victoire is one of the many locations in the Provençal countryside which Cézanne captured in his paintings (inset)

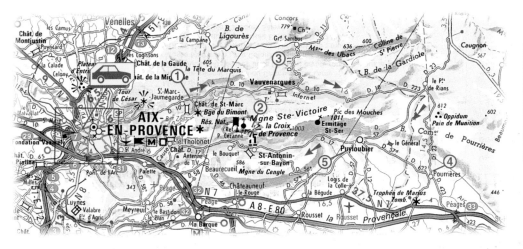

■ MYTHS AND LEGENDS ■

The forbidding way in which Montagne Ste-Victoire looms over the surrounding countryside has ensured that tales and myths about it are many. One story is that Marius, after watching his troops slaughter the Teutons, took 300 captured chieftains and threw them off the mountain to their deaths.

The sinister Gouffre du Garagaï (Garagaï Chasm) also has its share of legends: one maintains that there is an enchanted lake at its base, surrounded by magic grass; another suggests that it is the entrance to hell, guarded by evil spirits.

Another story with a little more credibility is that in the 1600s, the citizens of Aix-en-Provence offered a criminal his freedom if he would agree to be lowered to the bottom to see what was really there. Unfortunately, he was strangled by the ropes used to haul him back up again, and so never told the curious citizens what they wished to know.

■ AN ARTIST'S PALETTE ■

Of all the painters who have been inspired by the Montagne Ste-Victoire, perhaps the one who captured it best was Cézanne. The peak appears in at least 60 of his canvases, but he never portrayed it the same way twice. It is easy to see why: as the shadows and sunlight move across its craggy features, the rock changes colour, ranging from pale blue at noon in summer to a glorious amber during an autumn sunset.

Montagne Ste-Victoire is also associated with Spanish painter Pablo Picasso, who owned the pretty château at Vauvenargues. He is buried in the garden of the castle, overlooking the Infernet valley with the mountain as a backdrop.

La Croix de Provence

The most famous peak on the Montagne Ste-Victoire ridge is la Croix de Provence (above), which stands at the western end. It is 945m above sea level, and is named after the series of crosses erected on the site. The only way to reach the summit is on foot; wear sturdy shoes and take a bottle of water for the journey. Once reached, you can stand on a terrace and admire a view that stretches seemingly endlessly across the Massif de la Ste-Baume, the Provençal Alps, the Vitrolles and the Chaîne de l'Étoile.

This drive is a circuit of Montagne Ste-Victoire, with panoramas across fields of red soil crossed by neat strips of olive trees and vines. However, the places with the best views are inaccessible by car, so a walk of about 3 hours (6km) to Croix de Provence along the long-distance footpath GR 9 is included. The path is slippery and steep, rising 350m in 3km, but anyone taking the time to hike to Croix de Provence will not regret the effort.

❶ Start in the handsome city of **Aix-en-Provence**, the old capital of the region, which boasts a cathedral, elegant squares and 18th-century buildings. Take the D 10 towards **Barrage du Bimont**, an impressive structure that forms a small lake by damming the River Infernet. The area has been turned into a pleasant park. Leave the car and stroll through leafy woods to a second dam, built by the writer Émile Zola's father.

❷ Back on the D 10, the landscape opens out to reveal massive limestone ridges. Park near les Cabassols farm (poorly signposted, but near the bus stop) and walk through the pine trees up the Venturiers path (GR 9) towards **la Croix de Provence**. Visit the priory, then continue to the summit, from where distant mountain ranges stand blue and purple in hazy waves on the skyline. Further to the east lies the **Gouffre du Garagaï**.

❸ Returning again to the D 10, drive east to **Vauvenargues**, a pretty village with narrow streets and tall houses. Picasso's 17th-century château stands on a rocky plug nearby, protected by iron gates and often some unfriendly dogs – their yaps, howls and whines echo eerily through the valley. Stay on the D 10 as it winds along the Infernet gorges, speeding through thickly wooded slopes. A fabulous view of the river is on offer at **Col des Portes**, a rocky pass at 631m.

❹ Turning south, head for the D 23 where, set in woodland, is the village of **Pourrières**, supposedly named after the rotting corpses of the Teutons that were massed here after their defeat. This is an area noted for its wines – Coteaux d'Aix-en-Provence – which have a reputation for excellence.

❺ Take the D 623 and then the D 57d to **Puyloubier**, an attractive place surrounded by vineyards. Follow the road as it winds along the southern slope of the mountain on its way west. It snakes between the Montagne Ste-Victoire and the Montagne du Cengle, before becoming the D 17 and returning to Aix-en-Provence.

GORGES DU VERDON

T he River Verdon gains speed as it travels from the Alps and races through a narrow chasm of limestone cliffs to form the deepest and longest gorge in France. Footpaths meander along the base of this spectacular chasm and hardy trees cling to its precipitous sides.

Viewing the gorge

The best-known hiking route is the Sentier Martel, snaking between Rougon and Mayreste in the valley. The hike takes at least two days and is best made with an experienced guide or in a group. There are also easier walks., including the winding path from Point Sublime, a stony route that zig-zags sharply downwards through the trees. There are viewing platforms all along the roads but, some are little more than narrow ledges where the rock face tumbles away below, and are not for those who suffer from vertigo!

In the early 1900s Edouard-Alfred Martel, a famous French speleologist, successfully travelled the entire length of the Gorges du Verdon and proudly announced his achievement to his country. Nobody was particularly interested. The local people knew the canyon as an evil place inhabited by the spirits of the damned. Furthermore, it was dangerous, almost inaccessible and – worst of all – useless for agriculture.

■ SALVATION ■

In the 1950s, the French government considered building a dam and flooding the entire area, but fortunately the project was abandoned. By the end of the 20th century the Verdon Gorge – no longer regarded as a useless piece of real estate – was appreciated as a thing of spectacular beauty and wildness – to be protected and cherished. It is certainly popular with 'big wall' climbers, who come from all over the world to test their skill and nerve on its smooth faces.

■ A THRILLING CHASM ■

The River Verdon is fed by melting snows at the southwestern end of the Alps, gathering momentum as it tumbles south. The main gorge is roughly 19km long, with cliffs soaring up from the river to about 700m. In places, the walls are only 198m apart; to hikers walk-

The River Verdon, carving its way through the limestone plateau of Haute-Provence, has created one of the natural wonders of Europe

T O U R

length of tour: 100km
time: 1 day
IGN Top 250: sheet 115

Driving along the roads clinging to the walls of the gorge is an excellent way to explore the unusual and startling countryside around the River Verdon. Take note, however, that the roads are narrow and winding and in places there is only just enough space for two vehicles to pass. If you have a few moments to spare, it is worth walking a little way down one of the footpaths to enjoy the true grandeur of this magnificent valley.

❶ Just south of te pretty town of **Moustiers-Ste-Marie** take the D 957 past towering orange and grey cliffs and little olive groves towards the area of forest that marks

the edge of the gorge. Turn left on the D 19, then join the D 71, which is the famed **Corniche Sublime**, one of the most spectacular roads in France. It was hewn from the rock in the 1940s, winding in a series of heart-stopping bends along the southern rim of the gorge. Among the many magnificent viewpoints are the **Cirque de Vaumale** and the **Falaises des Cavaliers**.

❷ More breathtaking views can be glimpsed between the **Tunnels du Fayet**, after which the River Artuby meets the River Verdon near a spot called **Balcons de la Mescla** (*mescla* means 'mixing' and refers to the confluence of the waters).

❸ The D 71 then winds away from the canyon, so take the D 90 towards **Trigance**, and then the D 955 north. The D 955 meets the D 952, which winds westwards along the northern rim of the gorge. The best-known spot in the area is the viewing platform at **Point Sublime** (a 10-minute walk from the car park). Many people will

recognise this famous panorama, where massive cliffs plunge down towards the river 180m below.

❹ After Point Sublime, take the **Route des Crêtes** (D 23), perhaps the most spectacular part of the tour. This offers viewpoints such as the **Belvédère de l'Escalès**, a railed semicircle where the rock face drops sheer away and the river is a tiny, roaring band of green far below. These clean walls are popular with climbers, who appear as minuscule figures against the massive cliff faces.

❺ Eventually, the road winds north to rejoin the D 952. **La Palud-sur-Verdon** is a small village that sells climbing equipment and offers camping facilities.

❻ Back on the D 952, it is worth stopping at **Col d'Ayens**, 1,032m above the gorge, and at the viewpoint at **Belvédère de Galetas**. After 6km of gentler countryside, you will arrive back in Moustiers-Ste-Marie at the start of the drive.

ing beside the turbulent water, the sky is nothing but a narrow slit of blue far above.

The volume of the River Verdon is controlled by the French electricity board, which uses this fast-flowing channel to produce hydro-electric power. The river, surrounded by the steep slopes of the gorge, is also popular with canoeists. Visitors who brave dripping tunnels and precarious rope crossings to walk the Sentier Martel – the footpath that runs along the valley bottom – need to beware of sudden rises in the water level as sluices and dams are opened upstream.

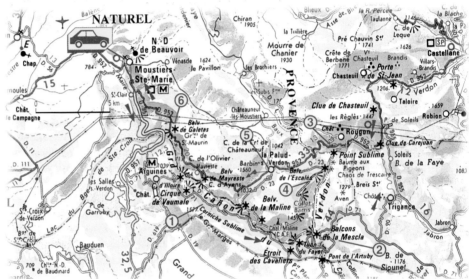

■ MYSTERY AND DANGER ■

There are many stories of demons and spirits reputedly inhabiting the Gorges du Verdon: visitors need walk only a little way from the road along one of the footpaths to see why. It is a vast, forbidding place where the distant roar of the river vies for attention with the eerie hiss of the wind in the trees.

Scrubby vegetation clings to the valley sides where it can, though in places the rock face is so sheer that nothing grows. Those intrepid enough to clamber to the foot of the valley will find a frothy, green river running hard and swift on its way to the azure Lac de Ste-Croix. Standing on the river's gravelly shores and looking up at the stark grey cliffs looming above, it is easy to understand why this evocative place has so often been the subject of stories of hauntings and mystery.

Moustiers-Ste-Marie

This attractive town is best known for its pretty faïences. They first became popular in the reign of Louis XIV and were still being produced in the 1870s. Today, potters haunt the town by the hundred, selling their wares from shops or in the streets, taking advantage of the high-quality clay found in the area. The Musée de la Faïence is a must for anyone interested in pottery. Moustiers-Ste-Marie's other distinction is a chain suspended between two cliffs with a star in the middle. Folklore says that a local knight was imprisoned by Saracens and vowed to hang a silver medal over Moustiers if he ever returned.

MONT VENTOUX

This white-capped Provence mountain, dominating the Rhône valley, rises in a vast, blue-grey mass above gently rolling vineyards and red-roofed villages. The view from the summit is awe-inspiring, covering the hazy Provençal plain, a living map of roads, olive groves, villages and fields.

Whether its upper reaches are swathed in cloud or standing stark and pale against a brilliant blue sky, Mont Ventoux is impressive, marking Provence's northern boundary. In winter it is dusted with snow, while in summer its 1,909m limestone cap always glistens white, giving the impression that it is perpetually ice covered.

▪ CONQUESTS AND TEST DRIVES ▪

Mont Ventoux is claimed by some to be the home of mountain climbing, after the Italian poet Francesco Petrarca (Petrarch) scaled its rocky sides in the 14th century, simply because it was there. But Petrarch was not the first to venture on to Ventoux's unwelcoming slopes. Archaeologists have discovered hundreds of small terracotta trumpets left there by the Celts, perhaps as votive offerings to the wind gods that these ancient people believed lived there.

In the early 20th century, the mountain was used to test drive cars, and many international records were broken on its uneven lower slopes. Sometimes it is even included in the Tour de France bicycle race, and is a route to daunt even the fittest of cyclists: it is not unknown for them to collapse and even die in the effort. For most travellers, however, the ascent involves no more than a pleasant drive up a well-maintained road, through forest, then low, tough bushes and finally across the white shingle of the summit itself.

Winding roads sweep up the lush slopes towards the summit of Mont Ventoux

The summit

Mont Ventoux's summit (above) is very different from how it would have been when Petrarch scrambled onto it so long ago. Not only does a tarmac road snake across it, bringing visitors by the thousand, but there is also an observatory which monitors the mountain's weather.

The views on a clear day are superb. To the south, a ribbon of sea glitters beyond the misty smudge of Marseille, while the Pyrenees are a flash of white to the south west. The view is best at dawn or dusk, since a haze tends to settle over the countryside in the middle of the day, even when the weather is clear.

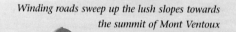

Excavations have uncovered extensive Roman remains in Vaison-la-Romaine

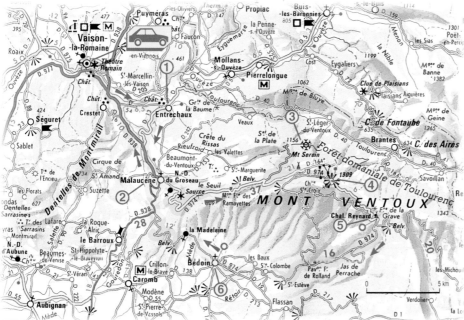

Home of the winds

Mont Ventoux (literally 'windy mountain') is aptly named. At Col de Tempêtes (Pass of the Storms) winds have been recorded at 250kph, and when these are accompanied by driving snow or stinging needles of rain, conditions on the summit can be unpleasant, if not dangerous. Temperatures regularly drop to –27°C at the observatory in winter, when the upper slopes are often thick with snow. This makes the area popular with skiers, although the roads to the top are often closed between December and April.

◾ A BALD MOUNTAIN ◾

It was the Romans who first began the deforestation of this mighty mountain, and its trees have been used as a source of good-quality timber for hundreds of years. During the 16th century the wood was used by the shipyards of Toulon, so that by the 19th century the slopes were almost completely denuded and a programme of replanting had to be initiated. Now the lower slopes, rich in beech, oak, larch, pine and cedar, present a pleasing sight – particularly in the autumn – as the road meanders through them in its ascent to the summit.

Although frequently drenched by rain and smothered in snow, the peak is almost completely devoid of vegetation. A few hardy polar species – such as the Spitsbergen saxifrage – grow in sheltered spots, but for the most part the summit is coated with hard, dry, white limestone rubble. On a clear day – as the sun is setting across a green and yellow patchwork of vineyards far below – there is little that can compare with the views from the top of France's breeziest mountain.

T O U R

length of tour: 76km
time: 1 day
IGN Top 250: sheet 115

There are two alternative plans for exploring Ventoux: an ascent from the east starts in Sault, while an ascent from the north starts from Vaison-la-Romaine. A north ascent is generally considered to be more pleasant in summer, however, because there is often a welcome breeze – an important consideration when temperatures soar. The roads are steep and narrow, with sharp bends. This tour starts in Vaison-la-Romaine, a town with important Roman remains and a spectacularly sited castle.

1 From Vaison-la-Romaine take the D 938 south, then the D 54 to **Entrechaux**. This village was a stronghold of the bishops of Vaison and it had a formidable castle (now in ruins) to protect it. It is on the **Route des Vins**.

2 Back on the D 938, continue to **Malaucène**, a pretty village with shady streets. Take the D 974, Ventoux's own road, which winds up to the summit and down the other side. Near Malaucène the road travels through outstandingly beautiful countryside, where the dark green of coniferous forest contrasts vividly with jagged limestone peaks.

3 The road begins to wind almost immediately, and for a while it appears as though it will end at the limestone cliffs that loom ahead. Then it veers to the right and snakes up through hardy trees that eke meagre nourishment from the soil. Before the summit is the turning for the winter resort village of **Mont Serein**. It is littered with chalets, and the skiing is good. Back on the D 974, the patchy vegetation grows even more sparsely as the road climbs higher.

4 The summit of **Mont Ventoux** is a stony hump scattered with telecommunications and meteorological gadgets. The views are incredible, but when the mistral is blowing it is no place to linger.

5 Leaving the summit continue east along the D 974, descending gradually over bare rocks, then past tough little bushes and finally reaching the forest again. At **le Chalet-Reynard**, you can visit the local shops before following the D 974 south and then west. Between 1900 and 1973 this part of the road was a racing circuit; the bend at St-Estève was notorious – perhaps because the view from here across to the jagged Dentelles de Montmirail is certainly wonderful enough to be distracting.

6 The hillside village of **Bédoin** has an elegant church while, further west, the viewpoint at **Belvédère du Party** allows visitors to gaze across the ochre roofs of Crillon-le-Brave and back up to the mountain itself. Turn right onto the D 938 and return to Vaison-la-Romaine.

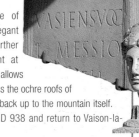

VALLÉE DES MERVEILLES

A horrified 15th-century traveller stumbling into the Vallée des Merveilles recorded what he saw: 'an infernal place with figures of the devil and thousands of demons scratched on the rocks.' He had found some of the 100,000 different images carved into the smooth glacial boulders by ancient peoples.

Passes and tunnels

Even the merest glance at a map of this mountainous region will show that many of the roads forge paths bravely upwards, only to peter out into nothing. Routes between Italy and France in this area are few and far between. The best-known route is Col de Tende, a tortuous track linking Provence with Piedmont. This precarious pass is used less often now that a tunnel has been provided, although it is a mixed blessing: the journey is quicker, but an ever-increasing number of lorries roar through the once-peaceful slate-roofed town of Tende.

The Vallée des Merveilles is in the eastern part of the Parc National du Mercantour, in the Alpes-Maritimes region of the Provençal Alps. With the adjoining Parco Naturale dell'Argentera in Italy, it houses a vital preserve of Alpine and Mediterranean flora and fauna. At least 25 of its plant species are found nowhere else in the world, and at least half of all France's flower species are represented. With some of the loveliest scenery in France, it is aptly named the 'Valley of Marvels'.

It forms an imposing valley dominated by the formidable Mont Bégo (2,872m) to the east, and Mont des Merveilles (2,718m) and Mont du Grand Capelet (2,933m) to the west. At the lower end of the valley, raspberries and blueberries grow in the woodlands, while higher up wild flowers carpet the shores of Lac Long in spring.

■ ART OF A LOST AGE ■

The evocative rock drawings were not properly studied until the 1890s, when naturalist Clarence Bicknell excavated and catalogued them. He showed how the diagrams of hunting weapons, daggers, animals and mysterious

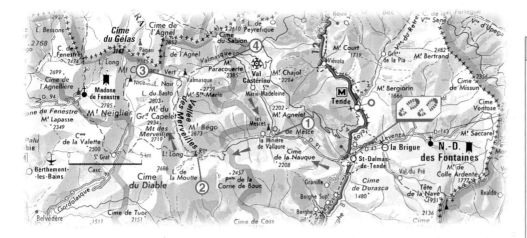

symbols provide a unique insight into the Ligurian culture. No one knows why these intriguing images were carved here, although one theory is that Mount Bégo (sometimes called the Magic Mountain) was a sacred site, and the images were etched into the rocks as votive offerings by prehistoric pilgrims.

FAR LEFT: hikers survey the Vallée des Merveilles

Fauna and flora

The Parc National du Mercantour is home to a number of animals who have adapted to the harsh conditions. Mammals include the powerful ibex and agile chamois.
Birds of prey are also well represented and eagles, lammergeiers, falcons, kestrels and buzzards have thrived since the area was declared a national park in 1979.
The symbol of the park is a type of saxifrage that lives only here, although more than 2,000 different plant species have been documented, including lilies, orchids, gentians (right) and even edelweiss; in spring the valleys explode with colour as tulips, pansies, geraniums, violets and anemones bloom.

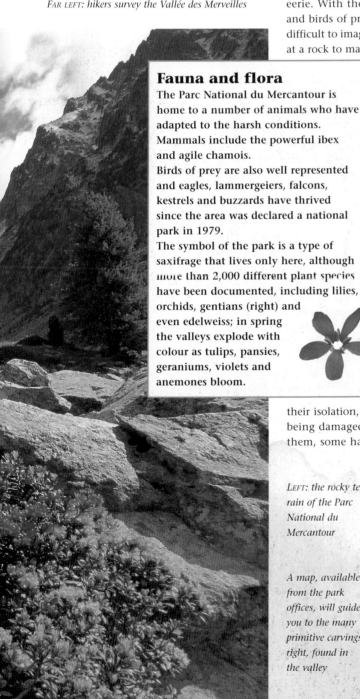

LEFT: the rocky terrain of the Parc National du Mercantour

A map, available from the park offices, will guide you to the many primitive carvings, right, found in the valley

■ MOVING AND MYTHICAL ■

Despite their huge number, it is easy to miss these ancient carvings, especially in the winter, when many are covered with snow. It is thought that the oldest of them date from about 1800 BC, with others added under the Romans. They are primitive, moving and eerie. With the wind buffeting around you and birds of prey soaring overhead, it is not difficult to imagine a fur-clad hunter kneeling at a rock to mark out the shape of one of the animals he stalked.

The carvings gave rise to many stories during the medieval era. The valley was thought to be haunted by evil spirits, a belief echoed in surrounding place names such as Cime du Diable (Devil's Summit) and Valmasque (Sorcerer's Valley).

■ DEFACED ■

But not everyone has been sufficiently awed to leave the carvings alone, and souvenir hunters and graffiti vandals have added their own signatures to the ancient monuments. Despite their isolation, so many of the carvings were being damaged that, in an effort to protect them, some have been closed to the public.

W A L K

length of walk: 30km
time: 1 day
IGN Top 250: sheet 115

The only way to reach the Vallée des Merveilles is on foot – not only are there no real roads, but cars are generally banned from this section of the park because it is a 'protected zone'. You need to allow at least a day for this walk, which is more properly described as a hike, and start early in the morning. It is possible to book a night's shelter at one of the *refuges* – Valmasque, Lac Long or Lac de Mesce. There are also hotels at the winter sports' resort of Castérino, although not all are open year round.

Warning: walkers should be wary of sudden storms. It is advisable to plan any hike with the park offices and to take their map with you. Be aware that it is sometimes not possible to complete trails in winter.

❶ The gateway to the **Vallée des Merveilles** is the little village of St-Dalmas-de-Tende. Drive up the D91 towards Lac de Mesce, passing through peaceful woods with the rocky heights of Cime de la Nauque to the left. The D 91 ends at the lake, petering out into a spacious car park. The first of the *refuges* is here.

❷ Follow the GR (*Grandes Randonnées*) footpath towards **Lac Long**. At first, the walking is pleasant and easy, winding through wooded slopes, but then the path begins to rise quite steeply. Pines surround Lac Long's chilly shores and in spring the area is a mass of colour as wild flowers bloom. However, all around is the stony mass of mountains, with Mont Bégo looming to the north. This is the southern end of the Vallée des Merveilles. The valley can be sinister in dull light, with rocks glistening a threatening dark grey. Climb until you reach **Mont des Merveilles**, at which point you can start to look for the carvings. As there are few obvious landmarks to describe their location, at this point you will appreciate the maps collected from the park offices.

❸ The footpath continues past a string of lakes through the heart of the valley towards **Valmasque**. Although difficult to find, the engravings are littered all along the path, some of them close and others towards the slopes of the mountains. There is a *refuge* at **Valmasque** near Lac Vert, a lovely place where Mont Ste-Marie looks down from its imposing height of 2,738m. Here the path turns northeast for the homeward run.

❹ After **Mont Peracouerte** further on, turn right and head south to Castérino. There are taxis which cover the last few kilometres to the car park at **Lac de Mesce**.

ℱORÊT DE LA STE-BAUME

*T*ucked away to the north of the sunny Mediterranean coast and its lively villages lies a dark, ancient and mysterious forest. Its silent, brooding atmosphere warned away early settlers in the area, and by medieval times it was a sacred place where ancient trunks seldom felt the bite of an axe.

The Forêt de la Ste-Baume is part of a large area of limestone crags known as the Massif de la Ste-Baume. The highest point of this rocky plateau is at the Signal de la Ste-Baume beacon (1,147m).

While the southern slopes are barren and arid, comprising the white ridges that so characterise this part of France, the northern slopes are covered with rich forest vegetation. Separating them is a jagged crest about 12km long, the eastern part of which is popular with mountain climbers.

The forest occupies about 100ha of mountainous terrain, in places covering rocky peaks as high as 1,000m. Remarkably, towering beech, oak, pine, lime, maple and sycamore trees form a light canopy, like an umbrella of leaves, over a secondary layer containing a thick growth of yew, holly and ivy.

RIGHT: the chapel on the summit of Col de St-Pilon overlooks the ancient Forêt de la Ste-Baume, below

This kind of vegetation is more typical of northern France than the sunny Mediterranean climate of Provence. The forest has developed in this way because the steep ridge that dominates its southern side casts a deep shadow, creating a cool, humid micro-climate. These are just the conditions in which the

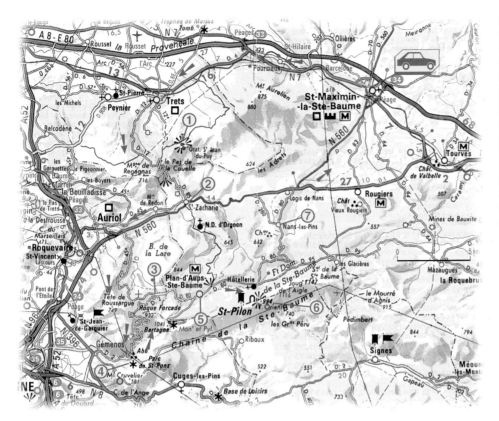

ABOVE LEFT: Mary Magdalene is believed to have spent her last years in this cave on the massif

temperate species that make up the Forêt de la Ste-Baume thrive. Away from the shade of the ridge, the vegetation reverts to the more usual Mediterranean species.

■ AS OLD AS THE HILLS ■

Gloomy, impenetrable in parts and curiously unwelcoming, the Forêt de la Ste-Baume has an undeniably primeval air about it, and the feeling of timelessness is not entirely in the imagination: the forest is believed to date back to the Ice Age. It is thought that it was already considered sacred when the Gauls inhabited the area, and its reputation as the haunt of spirits meant that it escaped the fate of many European woodlands.

In more modern times, the forest relies on the protection of the law rather than superstition, and the whole area is carefully monitored and managed.

■ SAINTS AND RELICS ■

Forêt de la Ste-Baume offers visitors more than just the chance to wander in a unique ecosystem; it has been a place of pilgrimage at least since the 12th century. According to local lore, the dissolute Mary Magdalene, reformed when she became a disciple of Jesus, came to Provence and retired to a cave, where she spent her remaining 33 years in prayerful solitude. Just before her death she left the cave and met one of her fellow pilgrims, so that she c   d receive final communion. A mon-ume   t St Pi   mark   he spot where this   taken place.

Mary's cave has become a sacred place (*baume* comes from a Provençal word meaning 'grotto'), with a little chapel dedicated to her. In medieval times it was one of the most important pilgrimage sites in Europe, and kings and popes scrambled up the steep inclines to pray here. Inside, the cave is dimly lit and atmospheric, while outside it is easy to see why cherubs brought Mary here seven times a day: it was close enough to heaven for her to hear the angels sing.

Basilica Ste-Marie-Madeleine

In the 13th century, Charles of Anjou set out to 'recover' the bodies of four saints (Mary Magdalene, Maximin, Sidonius and Marcel) which had been hidden from Arab raiders. Naturally, the authenticity of the bones he found was questioned – especially as Mary's body was already on display in Burgundy. Pope Boniface VIII, however, keen to curry favour with Charles, declared them true relics and work began on a shrine in which to house them – the basilica at St-Maximin-la-Ste-Baume.

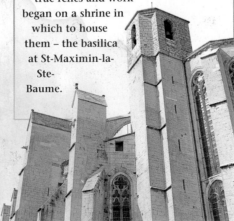

TOUR

length of tour: 100km
time: 1 day
IGN Top 250: sheet 115

Although probably the best way to see the Forêt de la Ste-Baume is by car, Mary Magdalene's cave can only be reached on foot, a trip of about 2 hours. This drive takes roads that wind through some of the loveliest parts of the forest and past vineyards, while the walk allows you to escape from the traffic to appreciate the silence of the woods that surround the grotto.

❶ Start in St-Maximin-la-Ste-Baume, with its handsome Gothic church, and drive along the N 7 and D 6 past fields of vines towards Trets. Then take the D 12 south until you reach the sign to the Oratoire de St-Jean-du-Puy. The oratory is a 15-minute walk, and offers magnificent views.

❷ Back in the car, continue south, passing the 500m Pas de la Couelle and the red-roofed village of St-Zacharie, where you turn right on the N 560.

❸ After 5km, take the D 45a south through attractive hilly woodlands to la Coutronne.

❹ At la Coutronne, take the D 2 to make the 24km round trip to Parc de St-Pons past the 728m viewpoint at Col de l'Espigoulier. Park near the bridge at Parc de St-Pons and stroll along the stream to the romantic ruins of a 13th-century Cistercian abbey.

❺ Back at la Coutronne, take the D 80 towards Plan-d'Aups-Ste-Baume and carry on until you reach a *hôtellerie* (guesthouse) on the right-hand side of the road. Park and walk up the path that winds past moss-covered rocks and through forest. At the Oratory crossroads, turn right to the stone-cut steps that lead to the Terrace. The cave is at the far end, a cool, damp place with a statue of Mary Magdalene and an altar.

❻ If you are feeling energetic, you may wish to continue to the St-Pilon summit (994m), where Mary Magdalene is said to have listened to the music of heaven. Return to the Oratory crossroads and take the right-hand fork along the Chemin des Rois. Continue until you reach the D 80, then turn left and walk back to the car.

❼ Follow the D 80 as it winds north towards Nans-les-Pins, still surrounded by forest, until it meets the N 560. There are several wine-growing businesses along this road which welcome visitors. Continue back to St-Maximin-la-Ste-Baume.

LEFT: the Gothic church in St-Maximin-la-Ste-Baume displays the sarcophagi of four saints, including that of Mary Magdalene, above

197

MASSIF DES MAURES

Covering the Massif des Maures, a deeply fissured rocky plateau, west of the glittery seaside town of St-Tropez, is a huge, dark, silent forest where streams cascade down steep cliffs, and trees grow in a dense tangle. Near the coast, however, are little coves with golden sands and lively villages.

Few areas in Europe are truly inaccessible to humans – but large tracts of the Massif des Maures come close. In places the woods are so thick with chestnut, pine, cork and oak trees that even the most adventurous and determined of hikers cannot penetrate far. Gazing from one of the viewpoints at the seemingly endless series of valleys and hills stretching away into the distance, it is difficult not to feel in awe of the Massif's sheer size. The forest is several hundred years old and makes the glamour and fuss of the Côte d'Azur resorts seem oddly insignificant.

■ HILLS AND VALES ■

The Massif des Maures, a plateau of granite, slate, mica and gneiss, is about 60km long and 30km wide. Although the area feels mountainous, with its tortuous winding roads and steep paths, the highest point is less than 800m. The Massif can be considered as two parts: the Corniche des Maures, a spectacular coast road winding past tiny bays and pretty villages, and the Massif proper, a thickly wooded sea of hills and vales dotted with the occasional village.

Cavalaire-sur-Mer on the Corniche des Maures

Cork and chestnuts

The forest has always provided its sparse population with a living. The residents of la Garde-Freinet learned in medieval times that cork is essential to the wine industry, and thus cork-making became a major occupation in the area until the 19th century.

In the very heart of the Massif is Collobrières, where the faint smell of chestnuts is always in the air. It is most famous for its ice-cream, although the town produces a range of other, equally mouth-watering foods made from chestnuts, including purée, jam, chocolate and nougat.

▪ THE CORNICHE TOWNS ▪

The Corniche is full of life, with many attractive settlements. Some, such as Cavalaire-sur-Mer, a charming town dominated by a ruined castle, have ancient origins. Others, like the popular Venetian-style resort of Port Grimaud, are more recent, serving the holiday-makers who flock to this part of France to enjoy the hot climate, long, sandy beaches and warm sea.

▪ DARK AND UNCANNY ▪

The Massif proper lies to the north, away from the cheerful bustle of the coast. It is sometimes said that *Maures* is a derivation of 'Moors', the name for the dark-skinned invaders from the south who ravaged the area after the 10th century, but the true origin of the name is the Provençal word *maure* (or *moure*) meaning 'dark' or perhaps 'uncanny'.

Chartreuse de la Verne

A winding road leads from Collobrières to the 12th-century monastery at Chartreuse de la Verne, perhaps one of the loveliest medieval buildings in Provence. It was founded in about 1170 for the Carthusians, although it has had a turbulent history since the monks first started to build their little city in the woods. Originally the complex was vast, with a church, cloisters, guest hall and other buildings. It was badly burned during the French Revolution, and the 19th-century novelist Guy de Maupassant wrote that the ruins were more melancholy than anywhere else in the world. Restoration started in the 1980s.

Drivers making their way along one of the winding tracks in the uncertain light of dusk will understand why the description is so apt: it is the kind of forest which features in age-old folk tales about wolves, bears and wicked witches!

Few roads pass through it, although there are some footpaths that allow visitors to reach parts of the forest that are otherwise inaccessible. The best known of these is the GR (Grande Randonnée) 9, which winds west from Port Grimaud to Notre-Dame des Anges, a pilgrimage site on the crest of a hill reaching 771m.

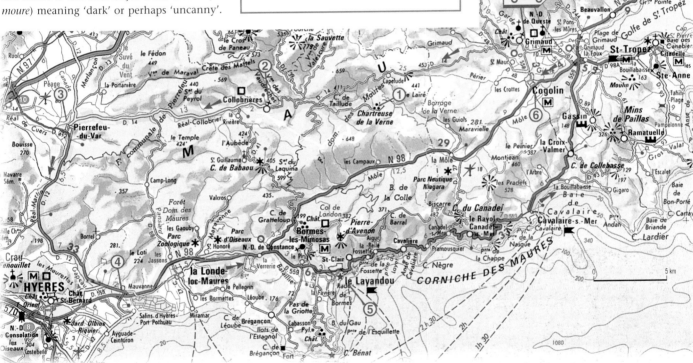

TOUR

length of tour: 116km
time: 1 day
IGN Top 250: sheet 115

This route first takes you inland to explore some of the peaceful hills and valleys around Collobrières and Grimaud, before heading along the lovely coastal Corniche des Maures. In many places, the roads wind and twist so much that it is impossible to travel quickly. However, you will find your efforts well worthwhile, given the scenery and spectacular views that can be enjoyed along the way.

1 The route starts at the old Templar stronghold of **Grimaud**, where the House of the Templars is one of a few structures left by this secretive Order of dier monks to have survived in Provence. Then take the D 14 west. This offers one of the most splendid drives in Provence, zig-zagging through endless expanses of green as it ventures further into the forest. There is little in the way of human habitation here, although there are several marked viewpoints where you can stop and enjoy a few moments of peace. On the left, after 20km, is the turn to the medieval monastery of **Chartreuse de la Verne**, a rewarding detour to romantic ruins which were once a thriving Carthusian community.

2 Back on the D 14, you will come to **Collobrières**, with its chestnut factory and snake-like patterns in the pavements.

3 After another 15km you will reach **Pierrefeu-du-Var**, where the D 14 meets the larger D 12 that speeds south towards the coast.

4 Follow the D 12, which merges into the N 98, where orange-tiled roofs poke through the green trees, providing cheerful, colourful scenery. There is something about these lively, pretty coastal towns that seems essentially Provençal, and it is worth making detours to explore a few. Most have restaurants which allow you to sample the local cuisine in traditional surroundings.

5 At la Verrerie, take the D 559 to **le Lavandou** to begin a meandering 30km coastal journey through the **Corniche des Maures**. The road skirts pretty bays, where fishing villages hug tree-clad hillsides and gleaming white yachts tug against their moorings. The road sometimes climbs quite high, giving you a bird's-eye view of intimate little coves.

6 Follow the D 559 north across the neck of the peninsula to the junction with the N98, and turn left towards **Cogolin**, which is famous for its craft factories. Then take the D558 north towards Grimaud and the start of the drive.

ÎLE DE PORQUEROLLES

A *hazy blue-green smear in a silver sea is all many people ever see of the Île de Porquerolles, despite the fact that it is only a 20-minute boat journey from Giens. Inland Porquerolles offers vineyards, while its beaches provide gold sand fringed by lush woodland.*

The Îles d'Hyères are a chain of three islands – Porquerolles, Port-Cros and Levant – lying to the south of the Corniche des Maures. They are sometimes called the Îles d'Or (Golden Islands), perhaps because of their glittering yellow rocks, although a more fanciful explanation is that the name comes from the treasure hoarded by ancient pirates. The largest island is Porquerolles, about 7km long and 2.5km wide; from the mainland it appears green and hilly.

Fort Ste-Agathe, above right, overlooks the harbour at Porquerolles, below

A colonial outpost

Porquerolles' main village, also called Porquerolles, owes many of its buildings to Napoleon's veterans, who were given the island as a paradise in which to retire after years of fighting for the empire. As a result, parts of the island have a distinctly colonial air, and it does not take much imagination to summon up a scene of war-scarred old men smoking their pipes in shady place des Armes, or exchanging stories of their younger days in the cafés and bars.

Île de Port-Cros and Île du Levant

The other two islands in the Îles d'Hyères are equally lovely. Port-Cros is a nature reserve; a series of footpaths leads visitors on strenuous walks through valleys and up hills. It is noted for its rich vegetation, and the best time to visit is spring, when the island bursts into colour as the trees blossom. Most of Île du Levant is owned by the military. The island's chief claim to fame is the naturist village that was established in the 1930s. Hot and humid, the island is home to a wide variety of plant life, with giant eucalyptus trees vying for attention with vivid nasturtiums and geraniums.

■ A PIRATES' PARADISE ■

Reclining on one of Île de Porquerolles' glorious beaches, or walking through its scented vegetation, it is difficult to imagine that this peaceful, sunny place has seen more than its fair share of violence. Originally, the Îles d'Hyères belonged to the monastery of St-Honorat, but in medieval times pirates discovered that they were excellent bases for launching raids on the mainland. Powerless to resist, the monks abandoned the islands to the raiders after a particularly vicious encounter in 1160, when the entire population was taken prisoner.

The pirates ruled supreme for centuries, and eventually the French authorities decided that there were already so many thieves on Porquerolles that it should be used as an official penal colony. Within a short time criminals began to arrive in droves. The plan backfired when the disgruntled convicts took to piracy themselves and began attacking French ships.

In the 19th century, the islands were used as a reformatory for juveniles, and then as a hospital for veterans of various wars. A foul-smelling sulphur factory, military tests and unchecked fires all but destroyed the islands, and it was not until the 20th century that laws were passed to protect them.

■ VINEYARDS AND VEGETATION ■

Some areas of Porquerolles are covered in vegetation so lush that they are sometimes used by film-makers seeking a tropical backdrop. In other places the vegetation is dry and scrubby, dominated by hardy shrubs such as gorse. Vineyards cover 200ha of the island, producing wine designated as AOC Côte des Îles.

One of the most memorable aspects of a visit to Porquerolles is the heady scent of the vegetation. The fragrance changes with the seasons. In the spring the island explodes into an immense aromatic bouquet, while in the winter months the sharp tang of pine is often mixed with the sweeter aroma of herbs crushed underfoot by walkers.

■ CONSERVATION ■

In 1990 the French government declared Porquerolles a national botanical conservation area, ensuring the protection of some 2,000 species of plant, including wild and rare flowers, trees bearing ancient varieties of fruit and a diverse range of herbs and grasses.

W A L K

length of walk: 16km
time: 1 day
IGN Top 250: sheet 115

The only way to explore Île de Porquerolles is on foot or by bicycle. Porquerolles village offers bicycles for hire in the summer, and the relaxed pace of a leisurely ride past vineyards and through shady woodlands suits the atmosphere of this peaceful little island very well. The island gets very hot in summer, so make sure you take plenty of water for your journey.

❶ Park at la Tour Fondue in the charming village of **Giens**, and take the ferry to the island. The ferry docks in a **pretty harbour** on the north coast of the island. It is worth visiting **Fort Ste-Agathe**, the castle that dominates the harbour. It is built of creamy white stone that can be dazzling in the bright summer sun. There has been a fortress on this site at least since 1200, although most of what survives today was built later. Most bicycle-hire shops are located in place des Armes, the village's central square, where you can pause and savour the colonial atmosphere.

❷ Take the road that leads north east towards **Plage Notre-Dame**, winding through woods and passing sand-lined coves. If you are feeling energetic you can turn left to the Fort de la Repentance, and then on up to **le Sémaphore**. At 142m, this old semaphore station offers an excellent view of the island, and on clear days you can see **Île de Port-Cros**. Plage Notre-Dame is an excellent place for a refreshing swim. If you have time for a detour, continue up the road to **Cap des Mèdes**, the northernmost tip of the island, from where the mainland can be seen shimmering across a vivid blue sea.

❸ Leaving Plage Notre-Dame, take the path towards **Mont des Salins**. This eventually reaches the south coast, where a footpath meanders through woodlands restocked with native plants and across barren heathlands. Strong currents, fierce waves and sharp rocks make swimming dangerous on the south coast.

❹ At the lighthouse at **Cap d'Arme** the cliffs plunge into a sea that seethes and heaves some 96m below. Take the road north, past more of the fragrant shrubs that make any trip to Porquerolles so memorable, to arrive back at the village.

LEFT: the clear blue-green waters around Île de Porquerolles, which can be reached by ferry from nearby ports; this peaceful island, above, is ideal for exploring on foot or by bicycle

CAP CORSE

Cap Corse is 'an island on an island' – a slender spine of dark green mountains surrounded by deep blue seas. Towering cliffs and quiet coves constrast with small fishing ports and secluded vineyards, feudal ruins and Romanesque churches, all amidst groves of chestnuts and umbrella pines.

Cap Corse, the Sacred Promontory of the ancient Romans, is a mountainous peninsula with a central ridge over 1,000m high. It is 40km long and, at 15km wide, fairly narrow. But despite its apparently small area, this rugged region features two contrasting coastlines. The rocky Mediterranean coast, dominated by the high central ridge, plunges directly into the sea, and its villages and watchtowers are perched on jagged cliffs high above the water. The Tyrrhenian coast, with its gentle hills, is lower and less fragmented. Open to the sea, its longer and wider valleys are criss-crossed with fields and meadows.

PEOPLE AND TRADE

The position of Cap Corse has made it a cross-roads for traders and commerce – but also a prime target for conquest. Its numerous invaders include the Carthaginians, Romans, Lombards, Moors, Aragonese, Genoese... yet it has retained its own distinct character, blended with typical Corsican insularity.

The flow of traders – and trade – has made Cap Corse the only region of Corsica to have developed a maritime tradition. While the rest of the island has resolutely turned its back on the sea and remained secluded in its mountain strongholds, the *cap-corsins* became skilful sailors and merchants, frequenting Italian, French and African ports. Wine, oil, wood, cork, coal, and fish (lobster, tuna, anchovies) were exchanged for cloth, building materials and wheat. The imported grain was ground into flour in the windmills that abounded on this windy cape.

THE SEA AND INLAND

The sea has brought not only prosperity but also danger, which meant that the churches and dispersed hamlets of the cape were often built on steep, rocky slopes set far back from the sea,

Torri

In response to increasing raids by Barbary pirates, the Genoese created a series of *torri* or watchtowers (below) to keep an eye on the vulnerable coasts of Corsica. Financed by the inhabitants, the towers served both to warn and protect the local populations, and were also an excellent means of communication. The approach of enemy ships could be signalled by fire at night or by smoke during the day. The whole of Corsica – from Bastia to Bonifacio – could be warned in less than an hour. In Cap Corse alone, there were 32 *torri*. Miomo, Erbalunga and the Tour de l'Osse are among the best examples.

to avoid invasion. The numerous *torri* (watchtowers) still along the coast bear witness to an ever-present menace from the sea.

Due to the mountainous landscape, each settlement nestles in a small river valley running from the central ridge to the sea. Each

The ancient village of Nonza, with its Genoese watchtower, is set on the rugged west coast of Cap Corse

Houses line the busy harbour at Port de Centuri, on the west coast of the Cap

has its own *marine* (port) as well as a region on higher ground.

Most of the roads along the valleys are dead ends. However, intrepid visitors can make detours up the side valleys, among the high meadows and woods, to find hamlets on the eastern side of the peninsula; their churches often contain unexpected treasures.

▪ CORNUCOPIA OF WINES ▪

Cap Corse has long been recognised as a producer of some of the best wines in Corsica, exporting wine to Italy during the Middle Ages, and Cap Corse muscat was much appreciated on papal tables during the Renaissance. For such a small area, there is great variety: *vin cuit*, Malaga type, Madeira-type white wine, muscat, as well as many good red, white and rosé table wines. Luri, Pino, Macinaggio and Rogliano are small wine-producing regions. Nicrosi, an exceptional white from the tip of Cap Corse, is in very limited supply. The muscats from Patrimonio are excellent.

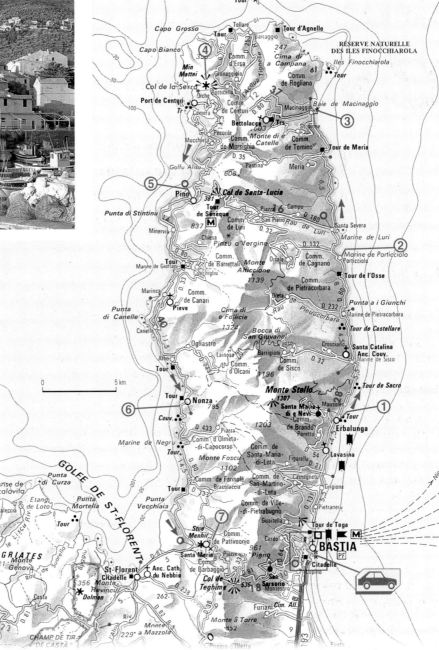

T O U R

length of tour: 160km
time: 2 days
IGN Top 250: sheet 116

Starting from the Port of Bastia, this extensive and somewhat demanding drive takes in most of the coastal areas of Cap Corse and includes some diversions inland. The busy *marines* (ports) of the villages are particularly interesting, as is the remarkable system of signal watchtowers. Look out for the traditional tiled roofs, made of *teghje* (schist slabs), still to be seen in Port-de-Centuri.

❶ Leave **Bastia** on the D____ heading towards Pietrabugno and drive to Ste-L____. Continue ____ **Miomo** and vis__ the towe__. Then _____ the D 80 _____ ch. D__ _____ue to t__ _____ake the D 32; a small _____ St-Martin and St-Michel, an__

11th-century church with a *teghine* roof. The Santa Catalina Convent (12th-century) is 2km north of the marina on the D 80.

❷ From the Marine de Sisco, take the D 80 to the Marine de Pietracorbara, where you can visit the tower. Continue to the Tour de l'Osse, an excellent *torre*, and then to the village of Porticciolo, with its pleasant port and beach.

❸ Continue on to Santa Severa, then on to the Tour de Meria and Macinaggio. From **Macinaggio** there are several pleasant walks. The Sentier des Douaniers follows the coast to Port-de-Centuri (a full day). A former pilgrims' path cuts across the *maquis* to the Chapelle Santa-Maria and a *torre* (2½ hour round trip).

❹ Leave Macinaggio on the D 80, across the tip of the peninsula. At the Chapelle Santa Anna turn left onto the D 53 towards **Bettolacce**. The village, with its fine view over the sea, has an interesting tower and church. From Bettolacce take the D 53 towards Centuri. Turn left on to the D 80 and continue to **Min Mattei** (the belvédère du Moulin Matte), which offers an excellent panorama. Contin__ to Camera, then turn right on to the D 35

towards **Port-de-Centuri**, which has a charming port and several restaurants. Leave Port-de-Centuri and take the D 35 towards Morsiglia.

❺ Turn right on to the D 80 towards **Pino**, then take the D 80 for a one-hour round trip to the Col de Santa-Lucia and the Tour de Sénèque

❻ Once back at Pino, take the D 180 to Marinca, then continue along the coast to the clifftop village of **Nonza**, with its remarkable *torre*.

❼ From Nonza, continue on the D 180 to **Cardeto** and visit the prehistoric carved *menhir*. Turn left on to the D 81 to Santa Maria – the commune of **Patrimonio** is famous for its wines.

Continue on the D 81 to Col du Teghime, heading left towards Bastia, then take the D 338 to **Serra di Pigno** to enjoy the excellent view. Return to the D 81 and turn right to return to Bastia and the start of the drive.

BONIFACIO

onifacio, poised 60m above the Mediterranean on white limestone cliffs, is the best-sheltered port in Corsica. Its imposing citadel and fortified town tower above the active port. Lying in a vast, bare region, Bonifacio is distinct from the rest of Corsica in its customs and its geography.

Situated about 3km west of Cape Pertusato, Bonifacio has given its name to the narrow, treacherous straits that separate Corsica from Sardinia and controls many of the strategic routes in the western Mediterranean.

The low, arid and empty plateau supports scattered orchards, vines and olives, which are protected by small walls. *Baracconi* (drystone huts) are dotted among the cork oak and scrubland.

Many Bonifacians are trilingual, speaking French, Corsican and Bonifacian (an Italian dialect), and although Corsica is somewhat infamous for its vendettas, they are not common in Bonifacio.

▪ A TUMULTUOUS PAST ▪

According to legend, the rock promontory of Bonifacio was inhabited by the Lestrygon giants who devoured Ulysses' fleet. However, although prehistoric remains – both Greek and Roman – have been found on the promontory, Bonifacio was

Corsican coral

According to ancient mythology, when Perseus beheaded Medusa her blood ran into the sea and set into coral. Mediterranean red coral once decorated Celtic helmets and weapons, and was held in high esteem by the Romans. Amongst red varieties, Bonifacian 'beef blood' is considered the best. Its density and deep colour are due to the strong marine currents washing the coral beds, which are 'fished' only once every ten years, by a maximum of five boats.

This limestone staircase forms an escape route to the sea

traditionally founded by the Tuscan count Bonfice II, as a defence against pirates, in about AD 828.

Tuscan rule ended in 1195, when Genoa seized the town by stealth. The indigenous population were expelled and replaced by colonists, who built a new town to a geometric plan.

The blue-green waters off Bonifacio are magnificently clear

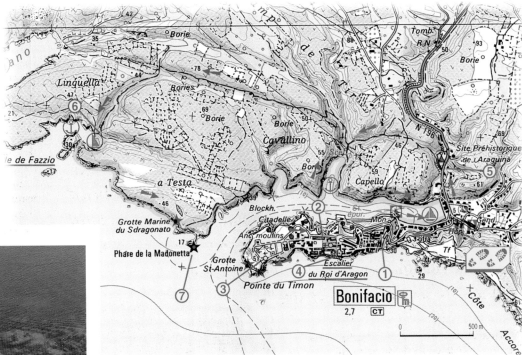

The new Bonifacio was granted numerous privileges and designated a semi-independent republic, coining its own money and having a local senate. Once one of the most renowned fortresses of the Mediterranean, Bonifacio lost much of its status after the Treaty of Versailles (1768) when it became a French garrison town. After Algeria gained its independence from France, the town became the headquarters of the Foreign Legion.

◼ THE OLD GENOESE TOWN ◼

The massive citadel, occupying the western end of the promontory, is set back from the cliffs, but the old town sits precariously on the precipice. Enclosed within the ramparts, the old town consists of narrow, shady streets with high houses, built as individual fortresses and once accessible only by means of retractable ladders. Each house had its own courtyard, oven, cistern, olive press, cellar, granary and sometimes a

---

Bandit country

During the 19th century, Sardinian bandits sought refuge across the straits in Bonifacio, returning to Sardinia to replenish their coffers when they ran low. In the same fashion, Corsican bandits based themselves in Sardinia, returning periodically to Corsica to thieve.

---

stable. The flying buttresses over the streets are gutters for collecting precious rainwater.

A flight of 187 steps (the Escalier du Roi d'Aragon) hewn from the limestone cliff connects the town to the sea. Although no doubt used as an escape route if the port were blocked, the stairway was traditionally carved overnight by Aragonese invaders in an attempt to capture the city.

◼ AN ACTIVE PORT ◼

The port in Bonifacio, built on an inlet 1,500m long and only 100m wide, offers exceptionally safe anchorage for vessels, and hosts commercial, ferry, fishing and tourist activities. Boat excursions to the local sea caves are an excellent way to see Bonifacio in all its towering splendour.

W A L K

length of walk: 10km
time: 1 day
IGN Top 25: sheet 142550T

This two-part walk starts with a stroll around the town, followed by a ramble along the coast. In the town, you can walk along a street where two emperors have stayed, as well as visit some early churches, a marine cemetery, a museum and windmills. The coast walk takes ... eaches, a sea cave and a lighthouse, as well ... pressive views of the citadel.

The ... n walk

❶ ... near the ... ke the ... ved ... m ... Porte d ... d'Arm ...

❷ From pla ...

Charles Quint once lodged in number 22, and number 31 housed Napoleon. Take the third street on the left, to visit the 13th-century Eglise Ste-Marie-Majeure. After visiting the church, take rue Archivolto to the Maison du Podestat, also 13th-century. Walk on to place Montepagano and take rue St-Dominique to the 13th-century Oratoire Ste-Croix and **église St-Dominique**.

❸ From here, continue to the western end of the promontory to visit the 14th-century **église St-François**, the marine cemetery, the Musée d'Arts et Traditions Populaires (housed in a former convent), the Pointe du Timon, several windmills and fortifications. Return to place Montepagano.

❹ From place Montepagano, take rue Simon-Varsi to the limestone steps of **Escalier du Roi d'Aragon** which lead down to the sea. Return to place Montepagano by rue des Pachas and take rue Doria to place Manichella and place du Marché, 65m above the sea, with a breathtaking vista. Take ruelle de la Madonnetta back to place d'Armes, then return to the port.

The coast walk

❺ From the port, leave the town and head north along the N 196 towards the **Site Préhistorique de l'Araguina**. At the campsite, turn left and follow the path towards the plage d'Arinella. Continue for about 750m towards a small bay with a beach (plage de la Catena) opposite the citadel of Bonifacio. Just above the beach, the path forks. Take the path on the right that leads away from the sea.

❻ Continue westwards about 1500m. The path makes a sharp turn to the left and heads towards the Anse de Fazzio. (The other path continues to the plage de Paraguano.) About 200m further on, the path reaches the plage de Fazzio, opposite a small island.

❼ The path continues around the eastern side of the bay. Follow the coast towards the lighthouse (**Phare de la Madonetta**). At the Grotte Marine du Sdragonato sea cave, the path leaves the shoreline for about 100m, then rejoins it in a small bay. Follow the marked path and continue around two small bays (plage de l'Arinella and plage de la Catena) back to the port.

ACKNOWLEDGEMENTS

The Automobile Association wishes to thank the following photographers and libraries for their assistance in the preparation of this book.

AKG, LONDON 38a; J ALLAN CASH PHOTOLIBRARY 41, 42a, 45, 115, 135b, 159b; AVEN ARMAND 170, 171; BAMBOUSERAIE DE PRAFRANCE 174a, 174b, 174c, 175a, 175b, 175c; BRIDGEMAN ART LIBRARY, LONDON 36a Waterlily Pond: Pink Harmony, 1900 (oil on canvas) by Claude Monet (1840–1926) Musée d'Orsay/Lauros-Giraudon/ © ADAGP, Paris and DACS, London 1999, 188b Montagne Sainte Victoire, c.1887 (oil on canvas) by Paul Cezanne (1839–1906) Courtauld Gallery; MICHAEL BUSSELLE'S PHOTOLIBRARY 30b, 42/3, 92a, 104b, 105, 107, 127, 130, 135c, 154b; JEAN-LOUP CHARMET 147a; BRUCE COLEMAN COLLECTION 31, 39a, 103b, 132c, 139c, 147c; CORBIS 16b (Yann Arthus-Bertrand), 140b (Tom Bean), 152a (Nik Wheeler); ROGER DAY 17b, 38b, 152c; DIAF 6a (Pratt-Pries), 13a (Pratt-Pries), 18b (H Gyssels), 22a (Alain le Bot), 26b (Pratt-Pries), 38c (G Gsell), 40a (Pratt-Pries), 40c (H Gyssels), 44a (R Mazin), 47c (F Daniel), 50a (Guillot), 50b (G Gsell), 52a (D Thierry), 58/9 (R Mazin), 64a (Ouzounoff), 64b (Pratt-Pries), 66a (R Mazin), 66c (D Thierry), 67b (R Mazin), 68a (Guittot), 68b (R Mazin), 74b (R Mazin), 80 (E Planchard), 82a (G Gsell), 82b (P Somelet), 85 (P Somelet), 86b (J-Ch. Gerard), 90b (M Grenet), 90/1 (G Gsell), 95a (H Gyssels), 96/7 (J Sierpinski), 101a (C Moirenc), 101b (J-Ch. Gerard), 106b (J-D Sudres), 109b (J-D Sudres), 110a (J-D Sudres), 110b (G Gsell), 111b (J-D Sudres), 112 (R Mazin), 122 (H Gyssels), 123a (B Regent), 123b (H Gyssels), 124a (E Planchard), 124b (E Planchard), 129 (A Fevrier), 135a (P Somelet), 136a (P Somelet), 138a (P Somelet), 139a (P Somelet), 144a (J-D Sudres), 146 (J-D Sudres), 148b (Pratt-Pries), 149b (J-P Garcin), 150b (B Morandi), 150/1 (F Daniel), 151 (B Morandi), 155a (J Sierpinski), 155b (J Sierpinski), 155c (Pratt-Pries), 156 a/b (D Thierry), 157a (D Thierry), 157b (D Thierry), 158a (G Simone), 158c (G Simone), 159a (J-P Garcin), 163a (J Gerard), 166b (A Even), 168b (Pratt-Pries), 172/3 (D Faure), 176b (J-P Garcin), 188/9 (C Moirenc), 189 (J-Ch. Gerard), 195b (J-Ch. Gerard), 196b (D Faure), 196c (F Daniel), 198a (J-Ch. Gerard), 200a (C Moirenc), 200b (C Moirenc), 201a (D Thierry), 201b (C Moirenc), 202a (Y Travert), 202b (P Somelet), 203 (J-Ch. Gerard), 204b (J-Ch. Gerard), 205a (C Moirenc); MARY EVANS PICTURE LIBRARY 19a, 178a, 197b; EXPLORER 6c (Thouvenin), 14a (S Cordier), 14c (S Cordier), 140a (T Tetrel), 153 (F Jourdan); FRENCH PICTURE LIBRARY 91a; GIRAUDON 117b, 158b, 167a; ROBERT HARDING PICTURE LIBRARY 34c, 75a, 94a, 97, 106c, 133, 186c, 192b; IMAGE BANK 32a; INTERNATIONAL PHOTO-BANK 111a, 111c, 136b; JOHN MILLER 36b, 46, 48b, 78b, 98b, 125, 179a; ROGER MOSS 152b; EDMUND NÄGELE F. R . P. S front and back cover; NATURE PHOTOGRAPHERS LTD 42b (D Osborn), 160a (R Tidman), 177b (P R Sterry); PARC ASTERIX 65; PICTURES COLOUR LIBRARY 14b, 15, 26/7, 48a, 68c, 108, 109a, 138b; SCOPE 7b (B Galeron), 18a (J-L Barde), 19c (J-L Barde), 22b (P Blondel), 51 (J Guillard), 51b (B Galeron), 52b (M Guillard), 53b (J Marthelot), 55a (N Pasquel), 55b (N Pasquel), 95b (J Guillard), 112/3 (J-L Barde), 113b (J-L Barde), 114a (M Guillard), 114c (M Guillard), 116b (J-L Barde), 117a (B Galeron), 119a (B Galeron), 126a (Balzer), 126b (Balzer), 128/9 (J-L Barde), 137a (L Juvigny), 141 (J-L Barde), 143a (J-L Barde), 145a (J-L Barde), 145b (J-L Barde), 150a (N Hautemaniere), 156c (P Desclos), 160b (G Simon), 161a (J-L Barde), 163b (J-L Barde), 168a (J-L Barde), 169 (J-L Barde), 172b (J-L Barde), 176a (J Guillard), 177a (J Guillard), 186a (N Pasquel), 186b (N Hautemaniere), 194 (D Gorgeon), 194/5 (D Gorgeon), 195a (D Gorgeon), 198b (J Guillard), 199 (J Guillard), 204a (VMF/Galeron); SPECTRUM COLOUR LIBRARY 8, 28b, 33a, 40b, 47b, 49, 69c, 78a, 79a, 128, 144b, 166a; THE STOCKMARKET PHOTO AGENCY, INC. 52c; TONY STONE IMAGES 44b, 47a, 56/7; WORLD PICTURES LTD 12b, 44c, 72, 74a, 113a, 132b, 139b

The remaining photographs are held in the Association's own photo library (AA Photo Library):
PAT AITHIE 114b; ADRIAN BAKER 9b, 13b, 17a, 24c, 183b, 190a, 190b, 190/1, 196a; PETE BENNETT 149a; STEVE DAY 24a, 24b, 24/5, 25a, 25b; JERRY EDMANSON 70a, 75b, 76b, 116a; PHILIP ENTICK-NAP 57a, 62a, 63a; PAUL KENWARD 10c, 10d, 21a, 21b, 70c, 118a, 118b, 118c, 119b, 120, 131a, 131b, 137b, 137c, 142a, 142b, 143b; MALTINGS PARTNERSHIP 62/3 Louvre illustration, 67a Versailles Palace illustration; ROB MOORE 29b, 30a, 32b, 33b, 70b, 71, 73, 76a, 76c, 77a, 77b, 164b, 165, 102a, 102b, 103a, 121, 148a, 154a, 162a, 162b, 167b, 167c, 181b, 187, 205b; ROGER MOSS 34b, 35, 53a, 81a; DAVID NOBLE 54, 64c, 66b, 69a, 69b; TONY OLIVER 39b, 43a, 43b, 161b, 164a, 172a, 173, 192a; BERTRAND RIEGER 62c; KEV REYNOLDS 147b; CHRIS ROSE 106a Bonelli's eagle illustration; CLIVE SAWYER 26a, 27, 28a, 37; MICHAEL SHORT 79b, 81b, 83, 84b, 86a, 87a, 87b, 87c, 88a, 88b, 89a, 89b, 91, 92b, 92c, 93a, 93b; BARRIE SMITH 84a, 94b, 132a, 191; TONY SOUTER 57b; RICK STRANGE 6b, 7a, 9a, 9c, 10a, 11, 16a, 23a, 23b, 99, 100a, 100b, 176c, 178b, 179b, 179c, 180/1, 181a, 182a, 182b, 183a, 183c, 184/5, 184, 185, 188a, 193a, 193b, 197a; JAMES A TIMS 56, 58, 59a, 59b, 60, 61a, 61b, 61c, 62b, 63b; ROY VICTOR 10b, 12a, 19b, 20, 20/1; JOHN WHITE 96.

All other illustrations by Michael Ogden.